W9-CBS-315

3 1668 01943 1599

Gift ce
NOF

#297

To Lynn Oates
With best regards to a fellow
Texas Republican at our national
convention —
John Knaggs
Houston, Texas
Aug. 19, 1992

324.09764 KNAGGS
KNAGGS, JOHN R.
Two-party Texas.

JAN 2/ 1995

TWO-PARTY
TEXAS

The John Tower Era
1961–1984

JOHN R. KNAGGS

EAKIN PRESS ★ Austin, Texas

Library of Congress Cataloging-in-Publication Data

Knaggs, John R., 1934–
    Two-party Texas.

    Bibliography: p.
    Includes index.
    1. Texas — Politics and government — 1951- 2. Tower, John. 3. Political parties — Texas —
History — 20th century. I. Title.
F391.2.K62   1985   324'.09764   85-16110
ISBN 0-89015-529-1

FIRST EDITION

Copyright © 1986
By John R. Knaggs

Published in the United States of America
By Eakin Press, P.O. Box 23066, Austin, Texas 78735

ALL RIGHTS RESERVED. No part of this book may be reproduced in any form
without written permission from the publisher, except for brief passages included
in a review appearing in a newspaper or magazine.

ISBN 0-89015-529-1

This book is dedicated to the memory of my father,
A. U. (Dutch) Knaggs of Cotulla, Texas,
who died long ago.
Though he never used any tools of modern campaigning,
he was a successful politician for many years —
because above all, he understood people.

Whether in America or any place else, lopsided political control is a deadly threat to a free people. Two vigorously contending political parties are our great weapon against unwisdom on high, abuse of the public trust, and even tyranny whether of the benevolent or police state variety.

— Dwight D. Eisenhower
1960

. . . I was, as many are, discontented with the one party political stagnation in our state. I think that every state should have a two-party system, and I have been working toward that end.

— John G. Tower
1961

Contents

Tower with the author, preparing for a news conference at Bryan, late in the 1966 campaign.

— Photo by Jim Culberson

Conferring with the author at the Reagan–Bush state headquarters in Austin, during the 1984 campaign.

— Photo by Charles Pantaze

Preface

In the fall of 1984, I informed then-Senator John Tower that I was writing this book and asked him some questions about his life and tenure in office. However, this is not an authorized biography, nor is it truly a biography. It's the story of modern two-party development in Texas in which Tower played the leading role, and it's a story containing warts along with the glory.

The conclusions drawn about elections, political trends, and other aspects of the era are mine, or those of sources credited in the narrative. I purposely steered away from consulting politicians extensively because they've long since had their say.

If a potential reader is looking for an unbiased, nonpartisan account of this period, read no farther. This is written from the perspective of one who was in Republican command posts and trenches during most of the era, 1961–1984.

It's also written in the lexicon of the political arena with words such as "targetted" and "winnable" that won't be found in dictionaries, but are in common usage by those vitally interested in political campaigns.

For those friends and former colleagues in campaigns who might wonder why I'm not even listed as having been present, I made the decision to remove myself completely from the narrative. When I started the book, I wrote two chapters with myself as a participant and found that I was getting in the way. Therefore, I chose to remove myself so I could write as an observer only — and I believe the book is better for that decision having been made.

In recreating meaningful events of this period, I tried to be accurate by pursuing extensive research and balanced in interpreting various aspects and nuances. Above all, it was my goal to write a candid and colorful account of this pivotal era in the political history of Texas.

JOHN R. KNAGGS

Austin, Texas
December 5, 1985

Books by John R. Knaggs

Two-Party Texas
The Bugles Are Silent

TWO-PARTY

* *

TEXAS

The John Tower Era
1961–1984

Tower, second from right to President Nixon, during a top level White House conference on Southeast Asia.

— White House Photo

CHAPTER ONE

Scoring the Big Breakthrough

If a political Richter Scale had existed on May 27, 1961, it could not have registered the magnitude of the sudden, fierce earthquake that shook the entire State of Texas.

Nor could it have measured the massive aftershock that rumbled across every other state of the old Confederacy.

A Republican had been elected to the United States Senate.

Two-party politics had burst upon the Texas political scene.

The once Democratic Solid South, shaken somewhat by the revolt for Dwight Eisenhower in the 1950s, had been cracked wide open.

Texas Republicans, who hadn't even held a primary election in 1960, suddenly found themselves with a coveted prize, catapulting them into prominence as a competitive force.

No longer would many thousands of independent-thinking conservatives across Texas arbitrarily vote Democratic other than for President. They could now believe their votes might be effective for qualified Republican candidates at other levels of government.

The unlikely hero of this pivotal drama was John Goodwin Tower, a diminutive son and grandson of Methodist ministers, who had been a government professor at Midwestern University, a small school in the heavily Democratic community of Wichita Falls, in Northwest Texas.

A native Texan, Tower was born in Houston on September 29, 1925, the son of Dr. and Mrs. Joe Z. Tower. He grew up in a number of East Texas communities where his father was preaching, and he graduated from Beaumont High School. As the son of an outstanding preacher, Tower's

1

ears had been tuned to the ring of words and phrases, of reasonable conclusions drawn from sound premises.

Tower was far from the generally held "country club" perception of Texas Republicans. He, his wife, and three daughters lived in a middle class neighborhood from which they had pursued a modest lifestyle. And, at thirty-five, he was the youngest member of the Senate when he was elected, hardly in the musty mold of graying Republican senators from the Midwest and East who had worked their way through various elected positions before attaining such lofty status.

Being young for a major challenge was nothing new to Tower. At seventeen, he had enlisted in the Navy shortly after the outbreak of World War II, and saw combat on a gunboat in the Western Pacific. Following the war he came home to earn a bachelor's degree in political science from Southwestern University, a small Methodist school in Georgetown, virtually under the long shadows of the nearby University of Texas at Austin where many a successful political career had its genesis. After graduation, Tower's ability to communicate was enhanced by his work as a disc jockey on Radio Station KTAE in Taylor, near Georgetown. "Tex Tower" learned to condense thoughts on a subject to a precise number of seconds, a valuable knack to be used later when answering questions from broadcast news media or recording thirty second political commercials for radio and television. Most new candidates struggle with their delivery for concise answers or sound awkward when rushing through scripts for commercials, but Tower had learned early on how to give the answer or follow the script with ease, precision and near-perfect modulation. Pursuing his education, Tower earned a master's degree, also in political science, from Southern Methodist University in Dallas, and subsequently studied at the London School of Economics.

What Tower learned in London about economics may be a matter of conjecture, but how the Tory attire, composure and politics affected him were obvious after he returned. He was perhaps even more of a staunch young conservative, now with a "political uniform" to match, a penchant for British suits with vest and suspenders, starched collar and thin ties. His political personality was perceived to be in keeping with the attire — throughout his career, Tower would be branded as "cool and aloof."

Thus, as a major statewide political figure, Tower was paradoxical from the beginning.

Tower had considerable party credentials from activity in the 1950s, including his role as a 1952 delegate in support of Senator Robert Taft of Ohio, the staunch conservative who contested Eisenhower for the presidential nomination, causing a bitter intraparty battle over the seating of the Texas delegation at the national convention. Eisenhower's forces prevailed and their candidate's victory in the general election helped heal the wounds.

At first glance in 1960, most political observers wrote him off. Too young, too short, cool and aloof, dressed almost foreign to the Texas scene, never held an elected office of any kind, and representing a small minority party. Hardly the stuff of which to compare with stalwarts such as Lyndon Johnson or Allan Shivers.

Add to all that the fact that Tower had been soundly defeated in a race for a House seat in the Texas Legislature. Further, he brought no personal wealth into his statewide campaign, a rarity for a newcomer in an age rapidly awakening to the importance of paid media, particularly the expensive but powerful vehicle of television advertising. But there were crucial subjective factors in Tower's favor. He possessed an extraordinary retentive mind that he used to great advantage by discussing complex issues on an extemporaneous basis which he much preferred to the regimen of prepared speech texts. Further, he employed a special command and appreciation of the English language, sounding as though he were a walking thesaurus, an accomplished speaker with a resonant voice who would calmly evoke the desired response by deftly choosing the appropriate words and phrases, never relying upon the political clichés and jargon of the times. Tower knew his issues. He knew what he wanted to say and how to say it.

The road to Tower's special election victory of 1961 began in 1960 when the State GOP Convention chose him to run against LBJ. Thad Hutcheson had carried the party banner in the special U.S. Senate election of 1957, but he did not choose to run again.

Tower's educational and broadcast experience — plus some amateur acting in Wichita Falls — were significant in preparing him for the enormous challenge of articulating his conservative philosophy, carrying the Republican banner across the vast Texas landscape. Tower was able to generate a spirited campaign against Johnson in 1960, capitalizing on LBJ's controversial dual candidacy for the vice-presidency and reelection to the Senate, plus an anti-liberal climate which almost carried the state for Richard Nixon. Tower's campaign was underfinanced throughout, and there certainly was no two-party system in Texas in 1960, but there was also no unified Democratic Party. A serious liberal-conservative division had existed for decades, highlighted by such as in 1952 when then-Governor Allan Shivers led conservative Democrats, or "Shivercrats" as they were often known, behind Republican Eisenhower for President over the Tidelands issue. Eisenhower sided with the Texas position of owning offshore mineral rights, a condition for the Republic of Texas becoming a state in 1846, rather than conceding those rights to the federal government.

This was a highly emotional issue since proceeds from offshore production were dedicated to public schools. Shivers's position ultimately prevailed, solidifying a special place in Texas history for him. The state's liberal Democrats supported their party's nominee, Adlai Stevenson, in 1952. They were bitter enemies of Shivers, whose gubernatorial terms were challenged fiercely but unsuccessfully by Ralph Yarborough, the undisputed political leader of populist-liberal forces in Texas during most of the 1950s and 1960s.

In 1960, Shivers was chairman of the Democrats for Nixon Committee in Texas, further heresy to party loyalty insofar as liberals were concerned. Though he was an ex-governor without public office, Shivers maintained a large following among conservative Democrats and independents. His support almost — but not quite — put Nixon across the line in Texas in 1960, an election in which Texas Republicans alleged that widespread vote fraud had occurred, as was charged in Illinois. Some of those "Shivercrats" eventually gave up the idea of maintaining any semblance of allegiance to the Democratic Party and changed to the GOP with fanfare, encouraging others to come along. Such actions were called "resignation rallies," and were formally begun in February 1961, when Travis County GOP Chairman Marion Findlay accepted the "resignations" of some prominent conservative Democrats in Austin.

The victory of the Kennedy – Johnson ticket and Johnson's Senate victory in 1960 made Tower viable in 1961 since Johnson had to resign the Senate seat in order to assume the vice-presidency. That turn of events created the need for a special election in 1961.

Johnson was the powerful Senate majority leader in 1959 when John F. Kennedy had launched his presidential bid. Johnson would eventually challenge Kennedy for the nomination, but he would be up for reelection to the Senate in 1960, and didn't want to risk giving up the Senate seat should his Presidential plans not materialize. Never one to miss out on using his political power, Johnson pressured the Texas Legislature to provide for an earlier primary, permitting him to run for reelection to the Senate and seek the Presidency simultaneously. Thus, LBJ sought *both* offices, ultimately settling for vice-president. His supporters went along with his shrewd manipulation, but thousands of Texans who otherwise would have voted for him, protested by voting for Tower. They perceived Johnson's maneuverings as nothing more than a selfish, high-handed power play.

Tower's forty-one percent (926,653 votes) against Johnson wasn't enough to crowd the powerful Democrat but it was adequate to establish Tower as a viable future contender with a secure though small political base among the state's Republicans.

Reviewing Tower's 1960 race, it was obvious the GOP strength was most evident in the state's two largest cities, Houston and Dallas. The party's state headquarters was located in booming Houston, where the venerable leader, National Committeeman Jack Porter, resided along with State Chairman Thad Hutcheson. In the ceaseless quest for political dollars, a group of fund-raisers, including Al Fay, mixed and mingled with independent oil operators, developers, and other entrepreneurs, along with business and professional people.

Hutcheson had made a creditable race for United States Senate in a special 1957 election, but he divided conservative votes with Martin Dies, Sr., permitting Ralph Yarborough, the outspoken liberal leader of the 1950s and beyond, to win without a majority of the vote. Fearing an upset by a Republican or liberal Democrat, the conservative Democrats had rammed a bill through the Legislature while the Senate election was in progress. The bill required a runoff between the top vote-getters in a special election if no candidate received a majority in the first round of voting. But they were unable to muster the two-thirds vote necessary in both houses for the bill to take immediate effect. Yarborough slipped by, ahead of the effective date of the bill. That bill had become law long before Tower's race in 1961, assuring the conservative Democrats of what they believed to be protection from such as the major upset achieved by Yarborough in 1957.

In Dallas, Congressman Bruce Alger had been elected in 1954, serving the entire county which comprised the most populous congressional district in the nation in those days before "one-man — one-vote" was a gleam in the eye of a Federal judge. In fact, Alger's district, following the 1960 Census, was an incredible 128.5 percent above the state average of 416,508.

The Dallas GOP was fast becoming known as one of the best organized in the United States with leadership from Peter O'Donnell, Jr., the county party chairman. O'Donnell's organizational genius was credited in large measure for the leading big-city majority received by Nixon in the 1960 presidential race. That tremendous 1960 push for Nixon in Dallas produced an impressive card file of 15,000 people who could be counted upon to assist GOP campaigns, and a major breakthrough was achieved with the election of Republican Frank Crowley as a county commissioner.

Alger's unabashed conservatism kept him in hot water among his Texas colleagues in Congress, all of whom were Democrats. But Alger was treated in a generally favorable manner by the politically potent *Dallas Morning News*.

Though *The Morning News* maintained a staunch conservative editorial posture, it favored conservative Democrats over Republicans if there were anything approaching parity in qualifications and/or winnability. But the conservative editorials, and the fact that *The Morning News* was not adverse to taking on LBJ now and then, helped maintain a climate for increasing Republican political influence. Dallas was, indeed, the conservative capital of Texas.

Other population centers in Texas had little Republican tradition or organization. San Antonio once had a GOP congressman, Harry Wurzbach, but his tenure was but a distant memory to veteran Bexar County politicians in 1961. In the Texas Panhandle, Republican Ben Guill of Pampa had won a congressional seat with a plurality in 1950. This was a special election under the old rules, without a runoff, but he was defeated in the subsequent general election a few months later. A decade hence the strong winds of conservatism were whipping up in the Panhandle along with the persistent blue northers. A general distrust of power concentrated in Washington, intensified by a perceived new tilt toward socialism with JFK's New Frontier, were enough to assure a highly conservative climate on the North Plains in 1961. Parts of West Texas, particularly the Permian Basin and Lubbock, were certainly conservative and might swing toward a Republican candidate for United States Senate, but the longstanding tradition of West Texas, exemplified by its courthouses, its members of Congress and the Legislature, was conservative Democrat. Part of the Hill Country, with its heavily German stock, traditionally voted Republican in presidential races, and could be considered potentially favorable to Tower.

Looking at the vast landscape of Texas, Tower and his advisors knew he must maximize his vote in those few favorable areas because more than 200 rural counties would vote for a Democratic candidate, liberal or conservative, rather than for a Republican.

They knew that Democratic bias and loyalties in rural Texas were particularly strong. They knew also that courthouses, which *are* the party machinery in rural Texas, would not activate nearly as well in a special election in which their power was not threatened directly nor was there even a party affiliation on the ballot. Preparing for the special election campaign, Tower had some favorable circumstances — he was fresh off the trail and knew where to hunt, and there was a changed political climate with the fact of JFK's New Frontier, highly suspect in conservative Texas. Perhaps more importantly, Tower had established himself as a viable candidate.

Texas Republicans were spoiling for another campaign. Many of the leaders had been lukewarm toward Nixon for the nomination in 1960, favoring Senator Barry Goldwater of Arizona, who had campaigned effectively for Tower in 1960. The GOP leaders were out to prove Goldwater conservatism held the key to the future. In addition to the philosophical aspect, a victory by Tower would be of strategic significance nationally. The Eastern Republican kingmakers' dominance in nominating presidential candidates to their liking could better be challenged by Goldwater in 1964, with tangible new support from the Southwest.

Tower's 1961 campaign had some new faces, including Tad Smith, a dynamic young El Paso attorney and ardent Goldwater supporter who took over as state party chairman, replacing Hutcheson. Also, Tower obtained the services of U.A. Hyde, a veteran Shivercrat political operative and writer. To deride Tower's adversaries, Hyde brought a unique knack for producing piercing one-liners to enliven Tower's public utterances, and biting news releases for the Capitol Press Room in Austin, where their contents were distributed statewide.

Goldwater conservatism, keyed by rugged individualism, was taking hold in early 1961. Young conservative Texans, eager to learn, related to the novels of Ayn Rand, particularly *The Fountainhead*, and the *National Review* magazine whose editor, William F. Buckley, Jr., had gathered a stable of strong conservative writers to complement his incisive writing. Politically, they related to Goldwater and in turn, to Tower.

This younger element of conservatives had broken with their parents' conservative Democrat politics. They believed a clean break was needed with a strong Republican Party controlled, beyond a shadow of a doubt, by conservatives. To them, it was a cause. They were highly motivated, ready to work. The Texas GOP had a well-disciplined cadre of woman volunteers in its areas of strength. Those women, plus the youth, would provide Tower with solid organizational support for his 1961 campaign.

On the Democratic side, Johnson's resignation from his Senate seat prompted Governor Price Daniel, Sr., to appoint William Blakley, a wealthy conservative Democrat from Dallas, to serve in the interim until the special election could be held. Thus, Blakley received an advantage over the field, starting out as an incumbent, even though he had no previous electoral success, having lost to Yarborough his only other time out in the 1958 U.S. Senate Democratic Primary in which Yarborough was first up for reelection.

Shivers was believed to be preparing to run in the special election, a move that Tower thought would preclude his chances of winning. But Blakley decided to run, Shivers did not, and Tower saw a unique opportunity to divide and conquer.

Because it was a special election, incumbent officeholders were not required to resign their positions in order to run. In the paradoxical nature of Texas politics, that provision would prove to have major impact, perhaps pivotal, in favor of Tower.

The election was scheduled for April 4, 1961. It would attract "six serious" candidates, including three elected officeholders. A total of seventy-one names would appear on the ballot for the first round, thanks to a meager filing fee of fifty dollars. The other sixty-five candidates, enjoying their brief day in the sun, would help the serious six divide the electoral pie into very thin slices.

A touch of glamor was added to the campaign by the daughter of one of the sixty-five "other candidates," Mrs. Bing Crosby, the former Kathy Grandstaff who was a beauty queen in her days at The University of Texas, before becoming a Hollywood actress. She made a brief tour in behalf of her father, Delbert Grandstaff of West Columbia, which included posing in longshoremen's dungarees in Houston.

Included in the serious six were elected officeholders State Senator Henry B. Gonzalez of San Antonio, Attorney General Will Wilson, and Congressman Jim Wright of Fort Worth.

Wright styled himself as a "progressive moderate," one who could attract a broad base of support, perhaps the ideal Democrat to square off ultimately against Tower in a runoff. But Wright was dogged by Wilson, who had a statewide following, and who was also perceived as a middle-of-the-roader.

Gonzalez, the only candidate to support fully the New Frontier, had hoped to be the lightning rod for liberals. He had made a statewide race, losing the gubernatorial primary in 1958. He knew there was a small, but viable liberal base across the state, the type of base needed to score in a special election. To his dismay, he would divide that support with fellow liberal San Antonian Maury Maverick, Jr., a former state legislator who traced his family's political history to Samuel Maverick, a signer of the Texas Declaration of Independence from Mexico in 1836.

Blakley was the fifth Democrat among the serious six candidates. Though he had no customary political base at the outset, he quickly received substantial support from key conservative elements, politicians, and such influential major newspapers as *The Dallas Morning News*.

In the spring of 1961, the New Frontier helped further polarize Texas politics. "You're either for or against the Kennedys," was often heard around the capital city, "and anybody out in the middle of the road will get run over."

Of particular concern to conservatives was an item in the Democratic National Platform of 1960, calling for the repeal of Section 14-b of the Taft-Hartley Act, the enabling legislation under which Texas had enacted its right-to-work law in 1947. The right-to-work-law provides that a person cannot be required to join a labor union in order to get or hold a job.

The Texas business/industrial community holds the law in highest esteem because it prevents compulsory unionism as practiced in most eastern and midwestern states.

Organized labor considers the law highly discriminatory because it permits so-called freeloaders, employees who receive union benefits without joining or paying dues. To independent conservatives, the right-to-work principle is a matter of individual freedom and their sentiments were strongly for retention of Section 14-b.

There were no Republicans in the Texas Legislature during the spring of 1961, but conservative Democrats were indeed concerned about what might happen in Washington regarding right-to-work. They knew that LBJ as vice-president had lost his hold on the Senate, and there was considerable distrust building against him because "he had sold out to the Kennedys" when he accepted second place on the ticket.

Repeal of Section 14-b would be a matter for Congress to decide, but conservatives in the Legislature stewed about the prospect, even though at this time, that prospect was not imminent. The mere fact that repeal of right-to-work had been placed in the 1960 national party platform had upset them and caused many of them to wonder how long they could profess party loyalty when confronted by such heresy to the business/industrial community from which they drew their political support.

Conservative state representatives were further agitated by the fact that liberal-moderate forces in the Texas House had wrested control from them. James Turman's slim victory over Wade Spilman for speaker keyed a stormy legislative session in 1961.

All those fragmenting factors meant that deep divisions among the Democratic candidates for the United States Senate were inevitable. Wilson and Wright were indeed in the middle of the road without a fervent base of supporters. And there wasn't enough in the middle to divide.

Liberals knew they had a fair chance of putting one of their own in a runoff, but only if they united behind one candidate, as they had done with Yarborough in 1957. The fact that Gonzalez and Maverick were adamant on running caused a serious split, preventing either from making the runoff. Though Gonzalez was denied his bid for higher office in the Senate race, he would go on to win a special election later in 1961, for the congressional seat in Bexar County. He defeated John Goode, a Republican attorney in San Antonio, who made a spirited race, losing by about 7,000 votes out of almost 100,000 cast.

On April 4, Tower led the field with 325,000 votes, or 31.5 percent. Blakley was second with 18.3 percent, followed by Wright with 16.4, Wilson 11.8, Maverick 10.2, and Gonzalez 9.3 percent. The balance was scattered among the other sixty-five candidates.

Thanks to the special election ground rules, the crazy quilt pattern of the Texas Democratic Party had come unravelled. For the runoff, the state's Democrats had to choose between the most conservative candidates, both staunch opponents of their party's national administration.

Though Tower led as expected, it was obvious that a united Democratic Party would wipe him out in a runoff. But the natives were restless, particularly the feisty liberals who considered their runoff choices as between "Tweedledum and Tweedledee."

On balmy spring afternoons shortly after the first election, liberals gathered to ponder their situation under the tall trees of Scholz Beer Garten, their quaint old unofficial headquarters in Austin, virtually in the shadows of the state capitol. Over pitchers of cold draft beer, they discussed a steaming dilemma with three major facets:

(1) Bite the bullet and vote for Tower to promote the two-party system.

(2) Refuse to vote for either.

(3) Wait for signals that Blakley might moderate.

In this fluid situation, Tower's chances of victory were enhanced considerably by crucial positions set forth by two key liberal elements, *The Texas Observer* and United States Senator Ralph Yarborough.

Ronnie Dugger and Willie Morris were the intellectual drivers of *The Observer*, whose strong stable of writers helped it maintain considerable clout among the state's liberal intellectuals and political activists. Though it had a modest circulation of a few thousand, it was considered to be the most influential liberal journal in Texas.

Dugger, the longtime previous editor, and Morris, the editor and general manager, reasoned that liberals would be much better off with a victory by Tower, whose election would finally establish something of a two-party system in Texas. Politically astute liberals had long recognized that their hopes of taking control of the Democratic Party machinery were contingent upon conservative Democrats switching to the Republican Party. And the Republican Party, to that time, had not been a viable alternative. Therefore, early in the runoff campaign, *The Observer* temporized, denying Blakley a boost he badly needed.

Yarborough, the unquestioned political leader of liberal-labor forces in Texas, likewise chose to temporize with an ambivalent statement, sidestepping the party loyalty question. "There wasn't a party primary and there weren't any party conventions," Yarborough contended. "As I saw it, the two were in competition as to who could denounce the Democratic administration the hardest."

Thus, Yarborough sent a clear signal to his supporters that he wasn't going to promote Blakley. Soon after that signal went out, some young liberal activists, notably Chuck Caldwell and Dave Shapiro, took it upon themselves to make the runoff a cause for two-party politics. They were among the few liberals who had studied the dynamics of what a two-party system would mean for the future. Drive the conservatives into the GOP and the liberals would control the Democratic Party, sounded so simple. But there were many problems inherent in liberal Democrats pursuing support for conservative Republicans. The late Hawkins Menefee of Houston, who served in the Legislature as a liberal Democrat, wrote his master's thesis at The University of Texas on what he termed were "the two-party Democrats." He traced initial steps to 1954, when Alger defeated a conservative Democrat, Wallace Savage, for the Dallas congressional seat. Roy Evans, then president of the United Automobile Workers local in Dallas, led the anti-Savage drive for which he drew criticism from within his labor ranks. Evans would later become secretary-treasurer of the Texas AFL – CIO, still holding to his belief that working for a two-party system was preferable to liberals than being co-opted constantly by the ruling conservative Democrats.

According to Menefee, Caldwell had written a letter to Tower, outlining what he believed might be accomplished and establishing a loose liaison between the unlikely political bedfellows. As Caldwell and Shapiro stirred about as best they could for Tower — or more often , against Blakley — they found substantial help from Mrs. R. D. Randolph of Houston, former Democratic National Committeewoman and benefactor of liberal causes, including *The Texas Observer*. She signed a potent anti-Blakley letter sent statewide, although she stated she couldn't vote for Tower. In part, her letter said, "I will do one of two things on May 27: either write in the name of a good Democrat, or go fishing. I can't vote for a Republican and I can't vote for a Dixiecrat." Meetings were arranged with prominent liberal leaders in Harris County, including Bob Hall and Chris Dixie, who, according to Menefee, was instrumental in blocking an endorsement for Blakley by a liberal group known as Harris County Democrats, prompting *The Houston Chronicle* to speculate that a "large number of liberals are expected to stay home on election day or even to vote for Republican John Tower." Yarborough hadn't sanctioned the work of Caldwell and Shapiro and upon being informed of their activity, summoned them to Washington. But the groundwork had been laid, and they pursued their program by telephone and mail, convinced that a Tower victory would change forever the course of Texas politics.

To those who could follow it, they outlined the statistical analysis of how high Republican primary voter turnout would eventually enhance liberal Democrat opportunities to be nominated. To those who required a more down-home approach, they made it clear that, "Tower will be easier to beat next time." In top liberal-labor leadership circles, word spread that Yarborough would control patronage easily with Tower as his colleague, whereas Blakley would present serious problems. To the untrained ear that didn't sound so important, but to those loyal liberals maneuvering for fat federal plums, including judgeships, it was a strong message indeed. These melded into the overriding factor, a general frustration from long-standing conservative Democrat domination of their party, causing a substantial number among the liberal-labor forces to defect to Tower or to sit it out.

As important runoff decisions were made, LBJ, Governor Daniel, former Governor Shivers and various conservative political elements rallied to Blakley's banner, as did most of the state's newspapers. Of the 500 newspapers in Texas, counting dailies and weeklies, only fourteen supported Tower and none of those were in the four most populous cities except for the ailing *Houston Press* which was barely hanging on, trying to compete with the *Houston Post* and *Houston Chronicle*. Gonzalez endorsed Blakley, opening late doors to the Mexican-American community, but most of the state's liberal leaders were quietly supporting Tower behind the scenes, or as Maverick stated he would do, planning to boycott the runoff by "going fishing." *Going fishing* became buzz words for those liberals who couldn't stomach voting for Tower, but who were convinced a vote for Blakley was even worse. Tower's opponent was dubbed "Dollar Bill" Blakley by liberals in order to point up Blakley's wealth, and create an image contrast between Blakley the millionaire, and Tower, fresh from the classroom. Other differences perceived between the candidates as individuals were brought forth. Tower was viewed as articulate, intelligent, and reasonable. Blakley was viewed as a Southern reactionary who was insensitive to racial problems at a time when civil rights advocacy was coming forward, particularly in such journals as *The Texas Observer*.

Tower, who often said he had been influenced by Thomas Jefferson at an early age, also related his political philosophy to Edmund Burke when he stated, "I believe change and progress can be best accommodated within the framework of existing institutions." Blakley seemed unable to articulate his position from such a cogent statement of principle.

On April 17, about six weeks prior to the runoff election, the abortive Bay of Pigs invasion of Cuba occurred. This startling development helped Tower, who had taken the hard Goldwater line on foreign policy, including a strong stand against Castro's Communist regime. The failure of the venture was portrayed by Tower as another example of weakness in Kennedy foreign policy. Blakley didn't defend Kennedy, but he was abruptly put on the defensive, having been trying to benefit from his party affiliation and then suddenly having the Cuban fiasco become dominant in the public mind.

Though Tower had strategic factors, nuances and just plain luck going his way, his 1961 campaign didn't come off without serious problems. There was a constant shortage of money, requiring corners to be cut in advertising, campaign materials and traveling. Paid staff was minimal, the campaign relying instead on hundreds of volunteers at various head-quarters to carry out most of the work.

The unpredictable spring weather often took its toll, causing delays and postponements of appearances with all the attendant emotional and logistical problems entailed. During one particularly harrowing thunder-storm, Tower's cool pilot, Pierce Langford, also of Wichita Falls, was forced to land the small private plane carrying the aspiring candidate on a farm road near the tiny Central Texas community of Ammannsville in Fayette County. Tower reportedly took the near-disaster in stride and was soon playing dominos at an old gathering place of the locals who were known to enjoy a few bottles of Shiner Beer during casual contests.

Late in the runoff campaign, Hyde produced for wide distribution a high-impact three-color brochure (bright red, canary yellow and light blue) with twelve pictures, including the traditional large "mug shot" on the front panel, and pictures portraying Tower with his attractive wife, Lou, and their three young daughters. None of the pictures revealed Tower's short physical stature about which he often joked, introducing himself, "My name is Tower, but I don't." The multi-panel foldout brochure con-tained four panels of solid copy on issues. This brochure appeared in the transition era when television was not yet dominant in the communication mix of political campaigns, an era in which issues were perhaps more important than images. The brochure also contained a bold headline on the front panel below Tower's picture, FIRST CHOICE OF TEXANS FOR UNITED STATES SENATE! capitalizing on Tower's first-round finish at the top. Portrayed as a "courageous conservative," Tower took forthright stands on seventeen issues with strong rhetoric that left no doubt as to where he stood. On states rights, the brochure stated that "John Tower is for legislation which protects your Constitutional rights and the rights of your State against the enslaving spread of Federal power." In the biograph-ical section, the copy read in part, "John Tower became a dedicated con-servative when he saw firsthand the trickery of many extreme liberals to plant the alien socialist ideas on college campuses." Shunning the no-tion that such official campaign items as brochures should be all "posi-tive," Tower attacked Blakley with a dab of boldfaced copy boxed in red borders. This pointed out Blakley was absent on forty percent of record votes during his first interim appointment, and missed ninety-five per-

01943 1599 FORT WORTH PUBLIC LIBRARY

cent on record "Yea and Nay" votes between January 3 and April 14, 1961. Tower's 1961 campaign brochure was a far cry from what has evolved in the 1980s with most political brochures containing large carefully posed pictures dominating brief, cliché-filled cutlines and copy tracts that speak blandly to widely held concerns but rarely take stands on specific controversial issues.

Pushing forward with another medium to dramatize the absenteeism issue, Hyde designed a hard-hitting full page newspaper ad that appeared in some of the state's largest dailies on election eve. It featured a stark picture of an empty chair isolated in white space in the top one third of the page with a bold headline TEXANS CAN'T AFFORD AN EMPTY SEAT IN THE UNITED STATES SENATE! A detailed summary of Blakley's absentee record from the *Congressional Record* was printed alongside some vintage hard-nosed rhetoric by Hyde designed to raise the blood pressure of conservative Texans. It read in part,

> Texas's liberal senator, Ralph Yarborough, has been present and voting on each record vote, i.e., 100%. This gives Texas liberals full representation. Texas conservatives are badly shortchanged due to absenteeism ... Unlike his opponent, John Tower has not supported and will not support the radical New Frontier or any other ultra-liberal administration. John Tower owes no allegiance to any entrenched political machine. John Tower will not be beholden to any party or clique. He asks your support on his merits ... not on the basis of blind 'party loyalty.' If you want a full-time, working senator dedicated only to the preservation of Constitutional principles and basic American ideals ... go to the polls and vote for John Tower tomorrow!

As the race had moved toward climax, *The Texas Observer* formally endorsed Tower with a long argument keying on the need for a two-party system. That move, plus the fact that Yarborough had, in effect, neutralized the party loyalty issue, left Blakley virtually head-up with Tower as individual conservative candidates.

Among liberal leaders, the bottom line was to consider "the best interests of the indigenous liberal movement of Texas." Most of them had made their decisions to support Tower, and they could live with it; for the rank and file, it wasn't an easy pill to swallow. In a highly charged atmosphere in which liberal − conservative political philosophy was being debated sharply on the national scene, Texas liberals were confronted by the challenge of voting for a philosophical archenemy, a Goldwater conservative adamantly opposed to their beloved JFK and his New Frontier. Yet, it was a challenge many of them would meet in the interests of their future in state politics.

How many liberals voted for Tower will never be known, nor will it be known how many "went fishing." But in reviewing Tower's razor thin 10,343-vote margin out of 886,091 cast, it must be concluded that the liberal element was pivotal in electing the first Republican United States senator to represent Texas during the twentieth century.

CHAPTER TWO

High Momentum. . .Then,
Tragedy in Dallas

About 300 jubilant Texas Republicans accompanied Tower for the swearing-in ceremony which LBJ himself performed in Washington. Caught up in the fanfare of the moment, Everett Dirksen of Illinois, the eloquent Republican Senate Leader and never one to pass an opportunity to invoke historical perspectives, proclaimed that Tower's victory was "not unlike the election of Lincoln in 1860." On the other hand, crusty former President Harry Truman contended Tower's election was "just a case of one Republican beating another Republican. There was no difference between the two candidates. The so-called Democrat ... ran just like a Republican and got just what was coming to him." On the lighter side, Senator Robert Kerr of Oklahoma, a conservative Democrat not unmindful of the unique addition to his exclusive club, cracked that "Texas's new senator is neither lanky, an oilman, nor a Democrat. He's sort of a new economy model compact that runs on regular Goldwater."

In Texas reaction varied widely, with a positive note sounded by a *Corpus Christi Caller* editorial stating in part,

> The election of Tower could be the beginning of a true two-party system in Texas, if Republicans and Democrats of like persuasion do not sit on their hands ... If it marks the true beginning of a two-party system in Texas, then the cause of good government will be strengthened immeasurably.

An editorial in the *Fort Worth Star-Telegram* pointed to the "supreme irony" of the election being LBJ's maneuver to run for the Senate and vice-presidency simultaneously. "Had this not been done, the successor to Johnson's Senate seat would have been nominated in last year's Democratic primary and would undoubtedly have ridden with the party to victory" in November.

Most Texas daily newspapers shared the sour grapes expressed by the *Star-Telegram*. They were accustomed to operating as opinion molders within the conservative Democratic tradition of Texas, and Tower, like Yarborough, was not in their mold nor would he be for years to come.

LBJ declined comment on the outcome but Governor Price Daniel, Sr., pointed to specific factors. "The hard-working Republican forces, the stay at home voters, and some defecting liberal Democrats deserve the credit or blame ..."

The Texas Observer noted that post-election reports revealed that extensive anti-Tower material was distributed late in the campaign, pointing out that "extreme liberals" planned to vote "for the Republican." As best they could, Blakley's forces had tried to make it a party versus party contest late in the game, but with the small, well-informed turnout of voters, the strategy failed.

Flushed with victory, a group of young conservatives at UT-Austin, who had done volunteer work for Tower's campaign, urged Shivers to change parties. In a letter to the former governor they contended that,

> John Tower's signal victory is the product of a vast political upheaval ... We urge you to consider candidacy for the United States Senate [against Ralph Yarborough] as a Republican ... The history of party-switching by well-known political figures is limited, but Wendell Willkie [1940 GOP Presidential nominee] probably would have become President had not the darkening clouds of World War II cautioned against changing the guard.

Such high flown rhetoric abounded in those days, but Shivers didn't respond — nor would he ever change parties — although he would support Republican candidates from time to time.

Ronnie Dugger would describe what was happening as a three-party system composed of liberal Democrats, Republicans and the ruling conservative Democrats.

With Texas Republican fortunes suddenly on the upswing, one of the first major changes engineered by Tad Smith was to move the party's state headquarters from Houston to Austin. Some feathers were ruffled over the move, fueling a longstanding feud between Houston Republicans and their counterparts in Dallas who favored the move to Austin and who considered themselves more attuned to winning elections, having secured their congressional seat at that time. However, Al Fay of Houston, who succeeded Jack Porter, also of Houston, as national committeeman seemed pleased with the logical idea of moving the headquarters to the state capital, the focal point of the Texas political arena.

Thus, the State Republican Executive Committee (SREC), voted to move the headquarters from Houston to Austin where it was located on the third floor of the Littlefield Building in downtown Austin, at Sixth Street and Congress Avenue. Jim Leonard, a good old boy West Texan originally from Pecos, became the executive director of a modest operation.

Leonard, a one-time GOP candidate for state senator in West Texas, and campaign travel aide to Tower in 1961, had the tedious task of stregthening the Republican organization throughout Texas while aiming for the 1962 elections. He also had a keen appreciation for the importance of the Capitol Press Room in Austin, where he often came with a news release, or appeared on a casual basis to make sure the correspondents were aware of the party's presence and activities.

To the politically astute, one of the most valid reasons for moving the headquarters to Austin was the Capitol Press Room, nerve center for the state's political news. Located on the second floor of the Capitol between the governor's office and the House of Representatives, it was staffed by correspondents who covered politics and government year-round, who knew the major and minor players plus all the undercurrents and nuances. It contained full-time bureaus for both wire services, Associated Press (AP), and United Press International (UPI), plus bureaus for most of the major daily newspapers. In addition, a special bureau, Long News Service, served many medium-sized dailies, provided an insiders' newsletter dealing with trends and developments, and distributed reports on activities of state government agencies.

If one could succeed in getting news on the wire services alone, that guaranteed, if not usage, its circulation to virtually all dailies and commercial television and radio stations throughout the state. For those trying to impact the Texas political arena, at least modest success in the Capitol Press Room was mandatory.

Many political writers and leaders of the conservative Democrat faction downgraded Tower's victory as "a fluke," but the fact that he was in, and what it meant, constituted a major force they couldn't deny. Following Tower's election, O'Donnell spent two months in Washington helping organize the senator's staff and office operation, so that Tower could spend as much time as possible elsewhere in a visible role. It wasn't long before Tower was far from the sedate atmosphere of the Senate, serving his constituents in a crisis. Shortly after Hurricane Carla devastated parts of the Texas Gulf Coast in September 1961, Tower was on the scene. Local officials were indeed surprised to see Tower sloshing into their communities, wearing rubber boots, offering to provide whatever guidance and assistance he might. "Government, especially the federal government, is usually a cold, impersonal thing," Tower told Jimmy Banks of *The Dallas Morning News*, on the scene. "It helps people when it becomes a close, personal thing in time of need." Banks noted that Tower was virtually inaccessable to news media during his time on the coast, working until after midnight without even pausing to eat, then starting again early the following day and working until about 9:30 P.M. "Only time will tell," Banks concluded his article, "but, in the long run, his actions may prove again an often-ignored political theory: shunning political expediency to do your job, frequently turns out to be the wisest political course of all." Such coverage of Tower as the new senator made Republicans even more proud of him. He would serve them as a lightning rod for almost six years, a rallying point around whom could be built a competing political party in Texas.

Tower's victory and afterglow of popularity soon keyed some political results in 1961, with the election of two Republicans to the Texas House late in the year by special election – Ken Kohler of Amarillo, and George Korkmas of Alvin. They served in the third called session but neither was around after the 1962 election.

Tower had made the quantum jump in 1961. Smith, Leonard, and others decided another quantum jump should be planned for 1962 — the governor's race, challenging the very bedrock of the once sacred one-party system of Texas. They believed a primary election statewide would attract conservative candidates with broad-based appeal. And they were right.

In casting about for a candidate, Tower decided there was merit in recruiting a conservative Democrat who had already established name identification by having run a statewide race, and Tower was instrumental in recruiting Jack Cox, forty, a former state representative from Breckenridge, who had lost the Democratic gubernatorial nomination in 1960 to the incumbent, Price Daniel, Sr. Cox had made a creditable showing, contending the state's deteriorating financial condition was such that it must adopt a major new revenue source, a general sales tax. Daniel withstood the challenge by Cox and fought the sales tax for months in 1961, until the Legislature finally forced him to accept it. A staunch conservative, Cox was an outspoken, personable West Texan with a populist appeal. He was welcomed into the Texas GOP in order to make his second gubernatorial race. Even though Cox had widespread support, he drew a primary opponent, Roy Whittenburg, an Amarillo publisher – rancher.

For some grass roots Republicans, preparing for the 1962 primary election was not such a pleasant assignment, particularly in less populous counties where the longstanding Democratic tradition was not receptive toward such upstart moves.

Many counties had never had a GOP primary, and some local Democratic officials could be anywhere from indifferent to uncooperative to intimidating to hostile. Shirley Ratisseau (then Dimmick) of Rockport, the Aransas County chairman and pioneer woman GOP county chairman in Texas, said there was no "available" public facility for her task. She and her family had lost their home in Hurricane Carla, and were dependent upon Democrats to share voting facilities. And after being turned down and turned away many times, this fervent believer in the two-party system awoke one morning to find five dead rattlesnakes and a sign hanging on her fence. The sign read, NO TWO- PARTY. Undaunted, she proceeded to hold that county's first GOP primary under an oak tree, while her children served lemonade to the few who came to vote.

In the spring of 1962, on the Democratic side, conservatives were uneasy about the primary and uncertain about the general election in the wake of Tower's victory. The nucleus of their vast political and governmental power, the governor's office, appeared to be insecure. For the first time, scenarios were being floated in Austin whereby a Republican would evince and for the first time in several years, scenarios were floating about a liberal taking over. Many in the conservative Democrat faction were committed to stay behind incumbent Price Daniel, the embattled six-year veteran, if he sought reelection, which he eventually did. Others looked longingly for a "fresh face," and spoke of John Connally, the handsome LBJ protegé who could enter the race without any Austin-based political scars from jostling with the Legislature.

Attorney General Will Wilson, who had skewered Congressman Jim Wright's Senate campaign in 1961, was another strong contender in the Democratic scheme of things. He was not averse to running a tough campaign, keying on the incumbent's vulnerabilities.

Liberals, licking their wounds from what "might have been" in the 1961 Senate race, were attuned to the need of unifying behind one candidate. They settled upon Don Yarborough, a dynamic young Houston attorney who was no relation to Senator Yarborough but whose name was a natural for the base constituency he set out to solidify.

In addition to Connally, Daniel, and Wilson, two other conservative candidates entered the 1962 Democratic gubernatorial primary, retired

General Edwin A. Walker of Dallas, and Marshall Formby of Plainview. Yarborough was the sixth candidate, the only liberal, much as Tower had been the only Republican among the "serious six" in 1961. Pursuing a similar strategy, Yarborough secured his liberal base while each of the conservative candidates sought enough ground in their turf to make the runoff. Yarborough's plan was successful in that he made the runoff against Connally, who led him by more than 100,000 votes. Daniel's support was eroded by the sales tax he had fought and the multi-candidate field, causing him to finish third, about 70,000 votes behind Yarborough.

For the runoff, the stakes were extremely high in a showdown between fundamentally different philosophical positions.

Many observers assumed that Connally would not be hard pressed to win the runoff because supporters of the other candidates would not accept an avowed liberal and would rally to Connally's banner. Such was not to be the case.

Connally tried to rapidly achieve unity among the moderate to conservative forces, but the spring fireworks had been divisive, and some 340,000 people who voted in the first primary would not return in the runoff in June when vacations were also a factor affecting voter turnout.

Further, in 1962 the dynamics of two-party politics suddenly came into play in the gubernatorial race, almost to a pivotal point. In the GOP primary Cox sailed past Whittenburg 99,170 to 16,136. The fact that more than 115,000 motivated conservatives voted in the Republican Primary meant that Connally was denied that potential vote for his runoff campaign.

Longtime liberals felt their hearts beating rapidly at the prospect of electing the first governor of their liking since Jimmy Allred in the 1930s. Liberal-labor political forces knew they would be outspent by the high-octane financing of the Connally Campaign, but they were well-organized and highly motivated by Don Yarborough, who campaigned tirelessly across the state. They counted on lower voter turnout among conservatives and their ability to make sure their voters made it to the polls.

It was a tough, bitter contest right down to the wire, with Connally pulling out a slim victory by 565,174 to 538,924, a margin of only 26,250.

From not conducting a primary in 1960 to attracting that total vote of 115,306 in 1962 was considered to be a substantial step forward for the Texas GOP. In historical perspective, ten years later, during Nixon's zenith of popularity as President and in the aftermath of the Sharpstown stock fraud scandal that rocked Texas Democrats, a six-candidate field for the Republican gubernatorial nomination drew a total vote of only

114,007. The swirling winds of a new conservatism were indeed blowing strongly across Texas during 1962.

When Connally and Cox squared off after the primaries, they were well-honed for combat.

Connally was the odds-on favorite. Handsome and articulate and with an attractive wife, Nellie, at his side, he was a formidable campaigner as an individual. His support was massive in the power equation of Texas politics in that era. He counted on almost total financial support from the state's business-industrial community that was active in political campaigns, plus most of the state's vast network of Democratic political leaders and officeholders. In addition, an almost solid lineup of newspapers would rally to his banner. At that juncture, Connally was the consummate candidate for the conservative Democrat establishment.

Cox had no such powerful forces behind him, but he did have a modest statewide organization from his previous race in 1960, a following of independent-minded conservatives and Shivercrats that melded fairly well with Republicans. Independent oil operators, wealthy conservatives and the regular Republican contributors comprised the financial base for his campaign.

Above all, Cox was a tough challenger who knew how to punch and counterpunch. Articulate and energetic, he also had an attractive wife, Joyce, at his side. Cox had the considerable benefit of Peter O'Donnell providing campaign leadership during part of the 1962 showdown with Connally. The ubiquitous Dallas County GOP chairman would be elected state party chairman that year en route to developing the reputation as the state's top Republican operative. Wealthy and urbane, O'Donnell managed his investments business in such a manner as to provide him adequate time to pursue political activity, which he did vigorously. In his formal picture used for publicity purposes, O'Donnell resembled Basil Rathbone, the British motion picture actor who popularized Sherlock Holmes, the unflappable fictional super sleuth character created by Sir Arthur Conan Doyle. In addition to appearance, O'Donnell could indeed be compared to Holmes, pursuing difficult objectives with a brilliant, incisive mind and a laconic manner of expressing himself, although he had a wry sense of humor which he employed from time to time when needling the opposition. O'Donnell would draw criticism from some Republicans, mostly behind the scenes because of his considerable clout, for allegedly being aloof or arbitrary or preoccupied with national politics. But those GOP leaders who understood the rapidly developing urbanization of Texas politics in the early 1960s knew O'Donnell possessed a rare ability to assess a strategic situation accurately and be able to bring to bear the necessary resources, financial and organizational, to maximize the opportunity of success for the candidates he supported.

As was the case with Tower in 1961, an invisible bond existed between Cox and some liberal activists who were bitterly disappointed over losing such a spirited contest for the Democratic gubernatorial nomination. To them, Connally's loyalty was to the powerful Texas business-industrial complex, not to the National Democratic Party. Since their champion had received forty-nine percent of the runoff vote against Connally, he was obviously viable for another race if Connally didn't clobber Cox by such a large margin as to appear to be unbeatable in the future. Having determined it was in their interests to promote Cox, these liberals set out to undermine Connally as best they could, mostly behind the scenes. They justified their actions on the need for a two-party system for the sake of liberal principles, a similar scenario to the 1961 Tower – Blakley race, but more difficult for them to implement because it was a partisan general election campaign.

Well-groomed and amiable in his public appearances, Connally was tough and resourceful behind the scenes. He had managed LBJ's campaigns and understood fully the demands and dynamics of the process. While he usually appeared as if he'd just stepped from an important corporate board meeting, he mixed and mingled well at the grass roots level. He was adroit in making speeches that were notable not so much for what he said, but for the manner in which he delivered them. With a stroke of oratory, he could evoke that deep sense of pride most Texans feel about their state.

Cox was up to the challenge, also evoking strong emotions. In selling his candidacy, he was an evangelist for the conservative cause about which he had written a book entitled, *And the Pursuit of Happiness*. To him, principles were more important than programs, and he deplored the liberal direction advocated by the New Frontier.

Cox's position, spelled out in his book, placed him right alongside Goldwater and Tower as a champion of individual freedom, the free enterprise system unfettered by government controls, and a strong national defense to deter Communist aggression. His book was not remarkable for original thought, but it elicited positive responses from several prominent Texans, including Abner McCall, president of Baylor University and Dick West, chief editorial writer for *The Dallas Morning News*, though West, true to the *News'* tradition of that era of backing conservative Democrats whenever plausible, ultimately supported Connally. The book was welcomed in the ranks of Texas Republicans who were becoming encouraged that Cox might produce a miracle to match that performed by Tower.

While Connally was trying to establish his ideas for specific programs, keying on education, Cox was hammering away at Connally with the cutting edge of his campaign, capsuled in the theme line, "Independent of Washington Control." Cox attacked across the spectrum of public concerns, not merely those classified as state issues. In the bitter aftermath of the Bay of Pigs fiasco and the growing dislike of the New Frontier social programs, the strategy of tying Connally, the former Secretary of Navy, back to Washington and LBJ, proved to be strong medicine for Texas conservatives.

Time and again, Cox would elaborate on his *Independent of Washington Control* theme with some issue or another tied to Vice-President Lyndon B. Johnson, then end with a tag line such as "Now, remember, LBJ stands for 'Lyndon's Boy, John.' " Those sardonic thrusts were usually orchestrated by U.A. Hyde, the Shivercrat operative fresh from Tower's 1961 campaign. Using such language as excerpts from speeches by Cox, Hyde had a penchant for tailoring short, biting news releases for the Capitol Press Room that usually earned two or three paragraph wire service stories, ideal for television and radio newscasts around the state.

Cox and Hyde would train their fire as much on LBJ as they would on his protegé Connally, knowing Johnson's vast power would inevitably be brought to bear against them, but also knowing there were certain vulnerabilities in LBJ's public image. Perhaps the most damaging aspect of LBJ's past, that which was most indelibly etched in the political memories of Texans, was the fiercely contested 1948 Democratic Primary runoff for the U.S. Senate nomination in which then-Congressman Lyndon Johnson edged out former Governor Coke Stevenson by only eighty-seven votes out of the almost one million cast.

At the time — in 1948 — the Democratic nomination was tantamount to election, and both candidates had campaigned long and hard for victory. Stevenson had led Johnson by about 70,000 votes in the first primary and seemed to be able to regenerate most of his original support pattern, but in South Texas, LBJ was coming on strong, thanks to the machine county bosses who were lined up behind him and girding for maximum voter turnout. In deep South Texas where Duval, Jim Wells, and nearby counties had been machine-oriented for decades, outcomes of local elections were never in doubt, which was widely known. But just how much sudden, manipulative leverage could be brought to bear in a statewide race was not dramatized until that election.

Stevenson was reported to be leading by 115 votes five days after the runoff, but LBJ's supporters weren't finished counting. George Parr, "the Duke of Duval," was the most powerful boss in South Texas, and his hand has long been suspected to have called the shot that turned the election. Precinct 13 in Jim Wells County reported a "correction" that added 202 votes for LBJ, changing the outcome to his favor by eighty-seven votes.

Stevenson's forces made a fast investigation, as best they could in such a highly-charged hostile atmosphere. They found some of those additional voters' names were matched only with names in the nearby cemetery, or were people who had been in Mexico at the time they were supposed to have voted. Legal challenges were launched and pursued vigorously, but strangely, Supreme Court Justice Hugo Black silenced the most promising challenge in Judge Whitfield Davidson's federal court in Dallas. Though election to a federal office was at stake, the contest was ruled to be a party matter to be decided by the State Democratic Executive Committee (SDEC), where Johnson would win on a close vote.

In the vast brush country southwest of Corpus Christi, George Parr would reign without sustaining any legal problems from "Box 13," as the vote-fraud scandal came to be known. It spawned the nickname of "Landslide Lyndon," repeated bitterly by Stevenson's supporters for years, and Connally was in the thick of LBJ's campaign during the Box 13 episode, a fact Republicans would bring out in the future when Connally became a candidate. Though there were no legal ramifications for LBJ to contend with after he was sworn in, he and Connally sustained a few political scars.

In addition to possessing an ability to bear down on emotional issues, Cox also knew how to campaign at the grass roots, particularly in rural areas where he would often roll up his sleeves and pluck a guitar before making a colorful, folksy speech. Leonard and Hyde were imaginative in promoting Cox. Their first major contrived thrust against Connally was an "expedition" to Duval County where Cox was to speak in San Diego on July 28, to dramatize the LBJ – Connally ties to George Parr. This would also rekindle publicity generated the previous May, when Duval County Republican Chairman Clarence Schroeder had been jailed on a contempt of court charge due to a flap over delivering GOP primary results to District Judge C. Woodrow Laughlin, one of Parr's cronies. Serious though that situation may have been, the newspapers generally treated the "GOP expedition" in a humorous vein, such as the front-page headline that appeared in the *Corpus Christi Caller-Times*,

COUNTDOWN FOR DUVAL'S R-DAY TENSE

Other journals keyed on an invitation issued by Marion Findlay of Austin, the feisty Republican chairman of Travis County. Findlay mailed letters to 1,300 potential Cox supporters, inviting them to ride to San Diego on a chartered bus to hear Cox. With the touch of a Texas history buff, Findlay wrote that,

Not since Old Ben Milam issued his stirring call in 1835 to take San Antonio de Bexar from General Cós has such a challenge been offered to Texans who are willing to stand up for freedom ... The Duke of Duval [George Parr] and his Crown Prince [Nephew Archer Parr] have guaranteed 'safe conduct' to all Republicans entering Duval County on July 28 (naturally the amnesty expires at midnight). Not since Fannin tried to reach the Alamo has a more hazardous expedition been planned ... To immortalize you – if worse comes to worst – Dawson Duncan of *The Dallas Morning News* will accompany our convoy as War Correspondent. He guarantees your name will be spelled right in the casualty lists.

Among special attractions, Findlay cited, "See what life is like behind the Mesquite Curtain ... See the home of Landslide Lyndon's eighty-seven votes ... See the only county where 93.25 percent of the votes went to Lyndon's boy John. [Connally] ... See Texas's first concentration camp — the San Diego calaboose."

For their guests, Duval County Republicans printed passports, which declared:

> *The undersigned, having braved the wilderness and all the King's men, is now entitled to enter the Sovereign County of Duval through any of the gaping holes in the Mesquite Curtain.*

All the needling didn't draw the Parrs into battle — George, the Duke, was not to be seen, but nephew Archer, the county judge, issued a biting but humorous proclamation to the Republicans, declaring,

> Saturday, July 28, 1962, has been officially designated Republican Day in the Free State of Duval. The Mesquite Curtain will be lifted on that day and blanket passports granted to all Republicans so that they may enter and hear that one-time Democrat, Jack Cox, espouse the cause of his adopted minority political party.

More digs were taken at Cox and the Republicans in the long proclamation but Parr made a welcoming appearance at the rally which went off without incident. In his speech Cox alluded to Archer Parr's "attempts at humor," but contended, "I do not consider it a humorous occasion." Cox proceeded to remind the crowd of several hundred that serious crimes, in addition to vote fraud, had occurred because of the political machine in that area, the epitome of one-party, bloc voting power. The Parrs had wisely chosen not to create any new issues for Cox and the "Republican

Expedition," but Cox nonetheless reaped a tremendous amount of publicity from the event.

During 1962, Tower returned often to Texas from Washington to campaign for various GOP candidates. He was learning the ropes in the exclusive club he'd joined and obviously enjoyed his work tremendously. When relaxing, he liked to tell stories about his famous colleagues, sometimes prefacing the story with, "Now, don't use his name publicly, of course," for such quotes as the one he attributed to a veteran Republican senator who once remarked, reflecting upon his philosophy of campaigning, that: "You know, I just never met a man I hated so much that I didn't want him to vote for me." And a corollary, "Never take anyone's vote for granted." Tower liked to repeat the admonition from a veteran senator about sounding off hurriedly, "You can't be held accountable for something you didn't say." The young senator had adopted a "worst case" methodology of studying variables in a difficult political situation. "Start with a worst case theory of what might go wrong," he would say, "before looking at some tempting benefits." He had started an annual tradition of hosting a Texas Independence Day party at which he would recite dramatically the famous letter by the beleaguered Alamo commander, William Barret Travis.

While Tower had been instrumental in recruiting Cox for the race, he found the strategy against Connally precluded his open involvement to a great extent. With Cox running as "Independent of Washington Control" and against "Lyndon's Boy John," too much Tower out front for Cox would have created a "John's Boy Jack" issue with which Cox and Hyde were not anxious to contend.

Neither Cox nor Connally were averse to making slashing personal attacks against one another. The State AFL – CIO convention that summer afforded an opportunity for them to appear, with Cox going first. According to *The Texas Observer*, their speeches kept the delegates on the edges of their chairs. Cox charged that Connally, thanks to "his long career as a behind-the-scenes political accessory" had developed a special knack for smearing the opposition. Cox said that in 1960, Connally had "hauled out a smear gimmick against Jack Kennedy" with the "false charge" that he "suffered an incurable disease and was being kept alive by massive doses of medicine. This year in May, recognizing that he was fast losing ground to Don Yarborough, out came the smear gimmick again. 'Reds!' he said. A month ago," Cox continued, "he took up the still wet smear brush he had used on you [Yarborough backers] and took a swipe at me...And so it is, that everyone who doesn't knuckle under to him is marked for smearing and labelling with one tag or another."

Upon arriving at the platform, Connally opened fire. "You've just witnessed an extremist in action. In his so-called speech he used the word 'truth.' It intrigued me, because I don't think he could spell it or recognize it if he met it in the street." Cox, he charged, was resorting to "unadulterated abuse and vile slander all over Texas." Connally said it would be "ridiculous" for working men and women to align with the Republican Party. "I do not believe there are very many present who think the party of Richard Nixon, Barry Goldwater, and Jack Cox has very much in common with them...There are those who shed their party affiliation as quickly as you shuck your coat under a hot Texas sun. You've seen one of them this morning...One thing is for sure. When the time comes for the showdown, I am not and never will be a turncoat."

Another major thrust that summer was a big birthday celebration — political rally for Cox, turning forty-one — in his hometown of Breckenridge, a small community about fifty miles northeast of Abilene. An old fashioned calliope belting out *The Eyes of Texas* led a parade with three bands, and other attractions kept the event lively throughout. Howard Lee, a wealthy independent oilman from Houston, brought his beautiful wife, Hollywood actress Gene Tierney, who added a touch of glamor to the festivities.

After about 3,000 supporters enjoyed a big barbecue at a city park, Cox stepped before them in sweltering ninety-eight-degree heat to give a strong, yet measured speech. From three terms as state legislator and six years on the Texas Commission on Higher Education, he had a sound working knowledge of state government and took positive stands on economic growth, election law reform, development of tourism and other issues. But the cheering crowd wanted most to hear him unload on LBJ and Connally, which he did with fervor and flair: "... I say to you, my friends, that we face the most ruthless and powerful political combine in all Texas history. The desperate drive to steamroller my opponent into the governor's chair at Austin, in order to protect the interests and future ambitions of his 'friend' in Washington, is an amazing and awesome spectacle!"

Closing on a high note, Cox implored the crowd: "More than anything else, we need to free our state from the stagnation of one-party, one-man rule. A fresh new political climate in Texas will mark the beginning of a whole new era in the lives of every Texan.

"New vigor, new optimism, new outlook, new opportunities will lead us all to a brighter tomorrow and will make possible new pinnacles of prosperity and progress."

Cox was well received that August afternoon in West Texas, creating the desired impression among political writers that his was indeed a strong, upbeat campaign, capable of challenging the polished and powerful Connally.

Cox and Connally would maintain frantic campaign schedules, crisscrossing the state by plane, train, bus, and auto. But 1962 statewide campaigning in Texas wasn't limited to the governor's race. Kellis Dibrell, a San Antonio attorney and former FBI agent who investigated the Box 13 vote fraud that had propelled LBJ into the Senate in 1948, was a candidate for the GOP nomination for lieutenant governor. He was the favorite of many party leaders, including Tower, but was upset by Bill Hayes, a furniture sales executive from Temple. Hayes lost the general election to Preston Smith, a state senator and conservative Democrat from Lubbock, who would subsequently become governor.

Des Barry, a popular Republican trucking company owner from Houston, ran for the Congress-at-large seat, losing a hot contest to conservative Democrat Joe Pool of Dallas. Pool had dodged a West Texas whirlwind in the primary. El Paso County Judge Woodrow Wilson (Woody) Bean, a colorful gadfly who claimed to be related to the legendary Judge Roy Bean (Law West of the Pecos), had generated a strong campaign and was considered the favorite. But midway in the spring, it was reported that Bean hadn't filed an income tax return for the previous five years, and he soon faced law *east* of the Pecos, in a federal courtroom in Austin. Bean pleaded guilty, receiving a slap on the wrist, but the adverse publicity caused his campaign to collapse.

In congressional district races, GOP incumbent Bruce Alger of Dallas's Fifth was conducting another well-organized campaign as was Ed Foreman of Odessa, who was challenging incumbent Democrat J.T. (Slick) Rutherford, also of Odessa, in the Sixteenth.

Republicans contested more legislative and local races. The heavy emphasis was in Dallas, where each of six aspiring candidates for the Texas House tried to cover the entire county. In those days, the ground rules were made by the conservative Democrats who wanted legislative elections conducted on a countywide basis. Since they controlled most of the political campaign dollars needed for expensive advertising to achieve name identification, the at-large system meant virtual total control for them — no Republicans and no liberal Democrats were likely to win.

Change, however, was in the air. Dallas was a Republican hotbed with its outspoken incumbent congressman around whom to rally, bolstered by the ever-expanding organizational programs devised by Peter O'Donnell permeating throughout GOP-oriented precincts of the county. Women were taking larger responsibilities as volunteer leaders. Rita Bass (later to become First Lady Rita Clements), Bobbie Biggart, Mary Ann Collins, Gwen Pharo, et al, were making certain that the various cam-

paigns and party headquarters operations were staffed properly, that programs were implemented on target, yielding maximum results at the polls.
In a showdown based upon organizational muscle, O'Donnell's troops would
prevail.

As the general election neared, Connally and Cox intensified their
communications efforts. In an era in which political oratory was still appreciated, they not only ran the short TV commercials used so widely in
the 1980s, but also appeared in longer segments. They set forth their
positions time and again, hammering home the themes they believed would
persuade an elusive group of undecided voters.

In image comparisons presented on television, the handsome, wavy-
haired Connally had an advantage over his balding opponent, but both
were articulate, diligent, and persuasive.

During the stretch run, *The Houston Chronicle* conducted a statewide
survey based upon interviews with political activists around the state.
The *Chronicle* poll was unscientific, but it had proved to be accurate in
the past. When it reported the race projected out as fifty-three – forty-seven
percent for Connally, those with vested interests in the outcome took
notice. Cox was in a competitive position and his supporters took heart,
redoubling their efforts. Connally's supporters, representing the powerful
ruling tradition of the state, took deadly aim at their objective, fearing
some late break or surge might tip the election to Cox.

Had it been a race to be decided on a straight-up partisan basis,
Democrat versus Republican, Connally would have won hands down, and
absent the "Lyndon's Boy John" issue, Connally would also have won
easily. But Cox, like a tenacious bulldog, had a firm hold on Connally's
Achilles' heel and wouldn't let go. LBJ was Connally's cross to bear because he had "sold out the South by joining with the Kennedys," and
the Kennedys embodied so much of what the Texas conservative uprising
was all about, "Too much federal power, too many federal controls, Eastern liberals ..."

The all-out campaign mounted by Cox had generated tremendous
momentum, but the Cuban Missile Crisis occurred in October, creating
somewhat of a political distortion, a sudden "rally around the President"
syndrome which slowed down and blunted some of that GOP momentum. Republicans would complain for years that they were "Cubanized"
out of winning the race. As it turned out, the *Chronicle* poll was close
to the actual outcome with Connally winning by a margin of fifty-four
to forty-six percent. Though disappointed in defeat, Cox was not crestfallen, pointing to a vote pattern that strengthened the Republican base
across Texas that Tower had established the previous year. It was a strong
sign for the future.

In particular Cox carried Dallas County handily, plus Alger was reelected by 20,000 votes and their campaigns helped carry all six GOP legislative candidates into office. They were Maurice Ball, Ike Harris, Horace Houston, Buddy MacAtee, Dick Morgan, and Henry Stollenwerck.

For the first time, Republicans had managed to pierce the barrier of electing their candidates to the Texas House of Representatives under the at-large system in metropolitan counties.

Carrying Midland by a wide margin, Cox helped elect Bill Davis, an engineer and longtime Republican activist, as a state representative there. In the West Texas Sixteenth Congressional District, Ed Foreman of Odessa scored a major breakthrough, thanks in large measure to the adroit management of his campaign by R. F. (Rudy) Juedeman, also of Odessa, and former Republican state chairman of Montana.

In another congressional race, Republican attorney Bill Steger of Tyler, a World War II fighter pilot and GOP candidate against then-Governor Price Daniel, Sr., in 1960, made a strong challenge for the East Texas district held by Democrat Lindley Beckworth of Gladewater, losing by only 2,000 votes out of almost 52,000 cast.

In comparing the defeat of Cox to the victory by Tower, it was easy to discern that Cox had been up against a much more effective campaigner in Connally than Tower had faced in Blakley. Plus, it was a general election and the voter turnout, particularly among predominately Democratic minority voters, was much higher, providing a substantial edge for Connally. That total voter turnout was 1,569,183 compared with only 886,091 who had voted in the Tower – Blakley runoff the previous year.

In the strategic sense, Tower and Cox had generated a solid base of support in conservative Anglo areas of the state, establishing a Republican voting pattern in urban Texas, but neither had gained substantial support among blacks or the awakening Mexican-American voting population.

O'Donnell had been elected as the new state chairman in September of 1962, succeeding Tad Smith, but he didn't take over until after the election. He brought with him Marvin Collins as executive director and they set out to expand the state headquarters staff and organizational programs during 1963. A onetime aide to Alger, Collins had been executive director of the Dallas GOP and was well-schooled in the O'Donnell methodology of planning and executing organizational programs with precise goals, deadlines and reports. It would be a tight ship.

Staff additions were made carefully by Collins. His headquarters operation contained divisions for organization, public relations, fund-raising, and research, plus staff support was provided for the Texas Federation of Republican Women and Young Republicans. An ambitious field program was launched with eight representatives traveling the state, assisting local leaders with building their organizations and raising funds to support them. The party newspaper, *The Republican Bandwagon*, made no pretense about its posture with a subhead below the masthead proclaiming it to be, "The Conservative Voice of Texas." Its circulation was constantly expanded as names were added by the various activists, volunteers and staff people. As activity increased, so did the flow of news releases to the Capitol Press Room where correspondents were more receptive, having seen the results of the campaigns waged by Tower and Cox.

In addition to his new role as Republican state chairman, O'Donnell became national chairman of the Draft Goldwater Committee, the unauthorized ad hoc group that was beating the drums for the Arizona senator to seek the presidential nomination in 1964. In this vanguard movement, O'Donnell was the skilled organizer, locating people around the nation who were in a position to promote the Goldwater cause with potential delegates or funds. Launched in April of 1963, the committee had F. Clifton White of New York, a veteran political consultant, as its director. The search for delegate potential was foremost, but the organized activity itself had a strong impact in Republican ranks. Particularly was this true in Texas, where Tower was such a prominent spokesman for Goldwater and his philosophy. O'Donnell, Tower, and their allies dreamed of a fundamental change in the Republican Party through a Goldwater Presidency that would break forever the Eastern Seaboard domination. Assuming Goldwater would eventually run, his most likely opponent in a showdown for the nomination would be New York Governor Nelson Rockefeller, viewed scornfully by Texas Republicans as the "leader of the Eastern establishment liberals." These perceptions of Goldwater and Rockefeller by Texans, permitted O'Donnell, the newly-elected state chairman, to function effectively on the national scene without hurting his home base. As activity intensified, the virtually unanimous support for Goldwater in Texas enabled O'Donnell, through his dual role, to have an even stronger hand in the ranks of the state's Republicans.

In addition to the pivotal intraparty aspect of a Goldwater – Rockefeller contest, Texas Republicans were spoiling for a battle between JFK and his liberal, Eastern-oriented New Frontier versus Goldwater, the conservative champion of the Sunbelt and the West where his best-selling books, *The Conscience of a Conservative*, and *Why Not Victory?* had taken grass roots volunteers by storm. To them, the pragmatic Nixon remained respected, but anything less than Goldwater and his unabashed conservatism had become unacceptable.

It was difficult to discern whether some of O'Donnell's moves were aimed at strengthening the state party for future elections in Texas or simply to enhance Goldwater's standing. In 1963, it became evident that Goldwater's support was not only solid at the grass roots in Texas, but throughout money circles not tied to the state's establishment Democratic power structure. It was easier for O'Donnell to build a stronger party around Goldwater's impending candidacy than to sell abstract conservative principles. Thus, the destinies of the Texas GOP and Goldwater became tightly intertwined.

Talk of Texas Republicans becoming better organized in 1963 was converted into reality with three special elections for seats in the Texas House of Representatives. Republicans Hughes Brown and Jack Sampsell won seats in Dallas County, and Chuck Scoggins of Corpus Christi won in Nueces County, where Republicans weren't supposed to win.

Those victories brought to ten the number of Republicans in the 150-member Texas House. This was hardly any threat to the power structure in terms of numbers, but the relative ease with which they had won concerned Democrats considerably. These candidates were winning without huge expenditures for paid media. They were winning on lots of shoe leather and handshakes, supported by skillful, dedicated volunteer organizations that located their favorable voters and turned them out on election day.

These candidates were "independent of Austin control," that is, independent of the business-industrial power structure whose lobbyists and political operatives were accustomed to arranging the financing of expensive campaigns for conservative Democrats. The fact that these Republicans were winning on their turf was not to their liking. But grass roots Texas conservatives, who had either officially joined the GOP or had started voting Republican when viable GOP candidates were available, had become weary of the siren songs of "We must maintain Texas influence in Washington through the Democratic Party," and "A Republican just can't be effective in Austin." Time and again, they'd seen conservative Democrats co-opted in Washington and Austin, voting against the sentiment of their constituents because of arm-twisting from the leaders of their party, now headed at the top by the liberal Kennedy.

Another major GOP development in 1963 was the announcement of his candidacy for the United States Senate nomination for 1964 by George Bush of Houston. Bush, thirty-nine, ambled into the Capitol Press Room in Austin on September 11, with his campaign press secretary, Jack Mohler, a former writer for *The Houston Chronicle*. Though Bush had never run for public office previously, he presented himself in confident manner with an open, refreshing personality. His party credentials

were in order. He was the son of GOP Senator Prescott Bush of Con-
necticut, plus, he had held campaign leadership positions in Texas for
Eisenhower's two campaigns and had served as party chairman for Midland, and Harris Counties, while pursuing his oil well business ventures.
With little fanfare, he made his formal announcement and answered questions, stating preference for Goldwater in the forthcoming Presidential
nomination sweepstakes. He said the principle issue between him and
incumbent Ralph Yarborough would be their philosophies of government.
"Yarborough is diametrically opposed to almost everything I stand for.
He is a 'federal interventionist.' He wants the federal government to do
everything."

George Bush had impressive individual credentials as well. It had
taken him only three years to become a Phi Beta Kappa graduate of Yale
where he was a baseball star. A carrier pilot in World War II, trained
at Corpus Christi Naval Air Station, he was awarded the Distinguished
Flying Cross and three air medals, having been shot down in combat
near the Bonin Islands. Bush said the time in Corpus Christi convinced
him he wanted to return to Texas to live, which he did in 1948, following
his graduation from Yale. A family man with five children, he was a
successful businessman who had apparently groomed himself for the task
he was undertaking. That early autumn day in Austin he made a strong,
favorable impression on many of the state's veteran political writers who
sensed a spirit of dedication to public service and determination to get
there that would carry him far. But when Bush and Mohler departed,
one of the veteran writers shook his head, saying something like, "Great
potential, but two crosses to bear — running as a Republican and not
a native Texan." As the likeable Bush and his charming wife, Barbara,
became known to Republicans and others interested in his candidacy,
mostly in urban Texas, his place of birth was not an issue. In fact, a
line developed in his defense, "Bush is a Texan by choice, not by chance."
What effect his place of birth might have in vast rural Texas in a general
election was an uncertain factor.

Handsome, articulate and enthusiastic, Bush was immediately judged
to be a serious contender and presumed to have behind-the-scenes backing
of the powerful O'Donnell, who, as party chairman, would be neutral
during a contested primary.

Contests for the GOP and Democratic nominations for United States
Senate were anticipated because incumbent Ralph Yarborough was in deep
trouble. He had been feuding bitterly with Governor Connally, who was
rumored to be encouraging a strong conservative challenge for Yarborough,
either from popular Congressman Joe Kilgore of the Rio Grande Valley,
or former Congressman Lloyd Bentsen, a Houston millionaire.

In mid-November of 1963, Texas Republicans looked with longing at the political arena, state and national. They were taking dead aim on the U.S. Senate, believing it likely that Bush could become the state's second Republican U.S. Senator, a lofty goal thought to be utterly unattainable a few years previous. Don Yarborough was pawing the ground again, pulling liberals together for another run at the governor's office. Cox had not made his plans known, but key political observers were predicting that another Yarborough – Connally primary fight could split Texas Democrats even worse than in 1962, paving the way for the first Republican governor since Reconstruction.

For the national scene, Texas Republicans were fervently behind Goldwater, convinced he would wrest party control from the Eastern kingmakers and win the presidency, all for the conservative cause that Goldwater had nurtured so well. Favorable signs abounded, including a flattering color picture of Senator Goldwater and his horse Sunny on the cover of *Life* magazine's November issue with a bold headline, GOLDWATER, THE ARIZONAN RIDES EAST. The article detailed how Barry Goldwater would campaign in New Hampshire, in an early test of strength with Nelson Rockefeller.

Those were heady days for Texas Republicans. Days of challenge, of commitment and confidence. Days of hard work, with daily rewards in the certain knowledge that their party was more disciplined, better organized, and more effective in support of its candidates and their campaigns. They were fighting for the conservative cause, a basic change of direction for their nation and a more independent brand of conservatism for their state. Their momentum was strong and growing stronger every day.

On the morning of November 22, 1963, a new statewide poll was released by *The Houston Chronicle* in an early edition. The poll showed that if the election were held then between Goldwater and JFK, Goldwater would carry Texas by about 50,000 votes, and it reported LBJ's popularity in Texas was at an all-time low, except in South Texas. Since the *Chronicle* poll had been so close to the actual result of the 1962 gubernatorial election, its results in 1963 were considered to be as accurate as one could find. Not long after the *Chronicle* edition with the poll was distributed in Austin, the news of the shooting of JFK and Connally was transmitted from Dallas, causing the *Chronicle* to drop the poll story from subsequent editions.

No assassin's bullets struck any Texas Republicans, but the tragic turn of events shattered the momentum of their movement. That conclusion was driven home hard less than a month after the assassination. Then the Democratic candidate in a special congressional election swamped the

Republican by more than a two to one margin in a race that had foretold a much different outcome. It started out as an opportunity for another Tower-like miracle in the early fall of 1963, when then-Congressman Homer Thornberry of Austin vacated the old LBJ Central Texas Tenth district to accept a judgeship. LBJ would handpick his longtime associate J. J. (Jake) Pickle for the post, and pass the word, but the three-party alchemy that had evolved in 1961 for Tower, and continued somewhat for Cox in 1962, reappeared with the recalcitrant liberals refusing to accept LBJ's decision. They rallied behind Jack Ritter, Jr., of Austin, a former state legislator, and the Republicans supported Jim Dobbs, a thirty-nine-year-old evangelist and radio commentator who had lost to Thornberry in the 1962 general election.

On the surface Pickle's powerful establishment Democratic support appeared to be overwhelming, but on November 9, because of the divisive liberal Democratic thrust, Pickle barely finished first with only 14,386 votes out of 41,115 cast and he faced a stiff runoff challenge from Dobbs who ran a strong second. Dobbs finished first in Travis County, whose county seat of Austin made it by far the most populous among the ten counties in the diverse district that meandered from the Hill Country on the West to near Houston on the East.

Austin was LBJ's backyard where he owned the only television station and received consistent support from *The Austin American-Statesman*, the only daily newspaper. LBJ's power in the business, political and governmental communities of Austin was indeed pervasive.

But Travis County Republicans were a sturdy lot, of necessity, and theirs was a strong organization led by Marion Findlay, John Kingsbery, Frank Montgomery and such dedicated workers as Frank Bomar, who specialized in distribution of signs and other campaign material. They were spoiling for such a showdown with LBJ and so were the liberals. No sooner had Ritter been counted out as a close third than some of his top operatives, including Chuck Caldwell and Dave Shapiro who had helped Tower in 1961, were on the phone to Findlay, talking strategy to upset Pickle. Pressure mounted rapidly, including interest from national news media since LBJ's prestige was on the line. One writer from a national magazine told Findlay that a Dobbs victory would land him on the cover because it would be a tremendous setback to the New Frontier. Despite LBJ and all his power, a Republican-liberal Democrat tandem could carry Travis County for Dobbs, an outstanding speaker with a religious background, who had also run first in three rural counties — key ingredients to conjure up a winning formula, and Ritter did his part.

On the night prior to the assassination, he was on television, remarking that he would vote in the runoff for a Democrat "if I can find one on the ballot." That was a clear signal to his supporters similar to that which Ralph Yarborough had sent in the spring of 1961 regarding the Tower – Blakley runoff. In the world of *What if?* — that election will always be one to ponder, but the Republican-liberal Democrat alliance collapsed in the immediate aftermath of the assassination. Pickle won the runoff handily, riding almost total Democratic unity behind LBJ, the new President, who now carried the banner of the fallen martyr.

CHAPTER THREE

A Defeat in Depth

Dallas, the citadel of conservatism in Texas, had acquired a right-wing image as well, partly due to the emergence of the controversial John Birch Society, a militant ad hoc anti-Communist organization. It was relatively new and secretive, but was believed to be strong in Dallas. Its positions became highly visible when the founder, Robert Welch, a candy manufacturer from Massachusetts, would publicly castigate prominent Americans, even Dwight Eisenhower, for allegedly helping the Communist cause.

Prior to the assassination of President Kennedy, a few ugly incidents implicating Republicans and the right-wing atmosphere in Dallas had occurred, including hecklers jostling Vice-President Johnson in the lobby of a downtown hotel; and Adlai Stevenson, then United States ambassador to the United Nations, was hit by a poster brandished by an anti-United Nations picket. Though no serious physical injuries had been sustained, the public image of Dallas was tarnished by the widely publicized incidents.

When the news broke that Kennedy and Connally had been shot, some network news reporters and commentators immediately pointed to those incidents as almost conclusive evidence that the shootings were the product of a right-wing conspiracy. As most Americans hung on every word from television sets and radios, this assumption was pursued through the short, chaotic period of time until Lee Harvey Oswald's arrest and affinity toward the Soviet Union and Fidel Castro were reported. But rather than change the intrinsic motivation of the assassin from right to left, the strong liberal element in the national news media merely changed the motivation to a "climate of hate" in Dallas, which had allegedly inspired Oswald's deed.

The cumulative effect was devastating. It created a pervasive sense of guilt in Dallas that would ultimately impact upon elections in a dramatic manner. Thousands of moderate-conservatives had not condoned the disrespectful acts toward LBJ and Stevenson, but they had held to their political convictions until the terrible moment when the traumatic assassination occurred in their proud city. Dallas was branded around the nation and the world as having created a "climate of hate." It was too much for them, and those out front for the conservative movement, Goldwater and Alger, would pay the price.

Tower said the accused assassin was "a man who had changed from a normal American into an advocate of the diabolical concepts of Marxism ... There are those in our society who are quick to blame all Texans, to blame the people of Dallas, in fact, to blame everyone in the nation including themselves ... So much has been simply an exercise in self recrimination." But some elements in the news media, along with many adroit politicians, kept up a drumfire of rhetoric. Such was the vindictive mood created on the Eastern Seaboard, that it transcended politics. It was spotlighted by the New York Touchdown Club which voted Navy the 1963 national collegiate football champion after the unbeaten Texas Longhorns, ranked Number One by the wire services, bombed the Middies and Roger Staubach, 28 – 6, in the season-ending Cotton Bowl Classic in Dallas on January 1, 1964.

As the surrealistic shock of the assassination melded into painful reality, the dominant figure of Lyndon B. Johnson moved onto center stage. Granted the enormous power he had coveted for so many years, and suddenly free from the constraints of the vice-presidency, he moved rapidly to consolidate greater power throughout the United States.

In a nation reeling from emotional trauma, Johnson's presidential power grew almost beyond comprehension. He had calmly picked up the torch from the fallen martyr, and he knew, better that any politician in the nation's capital, how to consolidate the support being offered to him from leaders of various political, economic, ethnic, and social elements. Style mattered far more than substance during this period — the American people wanted to know there were stable hands guiding the ship of state, that an orderly transition was being carried out.

During his long political career in Washington, LBJ had often been accused of trying to be "all things to all people," and in this unique atmosphere, his brand of consensus politics would soon generate an awesome political power structure that many Texas conservatives, and even some prominent liberals, would come to consider as being monolithic and dangerously powerful.

In the aftermath of the assassination, a cloud of gloom spread over the Goldwater camp. A Kennedy – Goldwater scenario had promised all the elements of a fascinating political battle, including a marked image contrast between the polished, Harvard-educated President and the forthright, jut-jawed Senator from the West. There were clear differences in political ideology, style and substance, yet both men were handsome and articulate, persuasive in stating their positions. And both, who had been friends and fellow photography buffs while serving together in the Senate, appeared to be relishing the idea of squaring off for the Presidency.

All that vanished. As Goldwater and his advisors assessed a race against Lyndon Johnson, the scenario was blurred, uncertain. LBJ, they feared, could maneuver in the emotionally charged atmosphere to undermine Goldwater's potential long before the partisan campaign would be under way. Goldwater's top operatives were convinced their candidate's base of support would remain loyal, but the potential among those voters classified as moderate-conservatives and ticket-splitters had suddenly been removed from their reach. If there weren't sufficient time or motivation to recreate that potential, Goldwater's campaign was already doomed almost a year before the election.

Such considerations were difficult indeed and there was quiet talk in high conservative circles about the desirability of Goldwater pulling out of the race. The thinking was that neither Goldwater nor Rockefeller could effectively challenge LBJ in 1964, therefore let Rockefeller take the beating. Otherwise, they reasoned, if Goldwater took a shellacking, the news media would discredit the conservative movement since the Republican Party had never nominated an outspoken conservative in modern American history. Had that been the only major consideration, such logic might have prevailed, in which case the conservative movement would have avoided the pounding it would ultimately sustain. But the matter of party control, the shift from the Eastern Seaboard to the Sunbelt, was paramount in the heads and hearts of many Goldwater strategists. They understood their chances of winning the Presidency had been virtually doomed by the assassination, but nominating Goldwater would end the reign of Rockefeller, et al in the Republican Party and that was a coveted, long-standing goal. Thus, Goldwater stayed in the race and girded for a series of bitter primary battles with Rockefeller.

Pamphlets and paperback books abounded in those days, and Phyllis Schlafly, then president of the Illinois Federation of Republican Women and a delegate to the forthcoming GOP national convention, penned a 1964 paperback entitled *A Choice Not An Echo*. The book was a stinging attack on Eastern kingmakers whom she alleged had dictated, behind the scenes, the GOP candidate for President over the past decades. She became something of a cult figure among Goldwater Republicans for advocating that the grass roots finally assert itself by nominating Goldwater whom she described as a candidate who combined the integrity of Robert Taft with the glamour of Dwight Eisenhower.

Such strong messages as those from Schlafly's book were motivational fodder for grass roots Texas Republicans. But they didn't need any convincing about Goldwater. State Representative Dick Morgan of Dallas, the Texas Goldwater chairman, found his most important duties were to keep them informed and supplied with campaign materials. In addition to all the usual political paraphernalia, gimmicks flowed forth promoting Goldwater, incuding, thanks to his name, a canned soft drink bearing his name, sold by volunteers to raise campaign funds, and "Coldwater for Goldwater," ice water dispensed by volunteers at booths set up for county fairs, rodeos, and the like.

As LBJ settled into the Presidency, the power equation of Texas politics was altered dramatically. The proud Connally had been canonized politically as governor of Texas by the high drama surrounding the serious wound he had sustained and his recovery, but when he was operative again in the political arena, he found that his ability to control certain major moves in the Texas Democratic Party had been curtailed drastically.

His old political mentor, LBJ, wanted a united Democratic Party throughout the nation and particularly in his home state. Therefore, LBJ was adamantly opposed to the feud between Connally and Senator Yarborough and was willing to take whatever measures were necessary to prevent serious opposition to Yarborough in the primary. Connally apparently pursued his support of Kilgore to the point of causing a showdown near the filing deadline for candidates.

Indicative of the moment was an article by Capitol Bureau Chief Bo Byers of *The Houston Chronicle*, and which appeared in its editions of February 4, 1964:

> People who follow Texas politics closely witnessed an amazing demonstration of power politics the past four days.
> The winner — and none but the naive would think otherwise — was President Lyndon B. Johnson ...

There were other important, politically potent people who shared Connally's view. People like former governor Allan Shivers, who would like nothing better than to see Ralph Yarborough defeated, as Shivers himself defeated him in the 1952 and 1954 gubernatorial races.

There were powerful lobbyists who favored Kilgore. Many newspaper editors and publishers wanted either Kilgore or Shivers to run.

Kilgore listened to all.

He also listened to Washington.

Mr. Johnson won.

Ralph Yarborough won.

Kilgore, Shivers and Connally lost.

Later, there was an article by veteran capitol correspondent Jimmy Banks of *The Dallas Morning News* which appeared February 5:

> Conservative Texas Democrats seethed Tuesday over a White House operation which persuaded Representative Joe Kilgore not to enter the United States Senate race.
>
> Some political insiders predict privately that President Johnson's labor-inspired move, aimed at assuring U.S. Senator Ralph W. Yarborough's reelection, would backfire and perhaps put a second Texas Republican in the Senate.
>
> Johnson's move undoubtedly strained almost to the breaking point his longtime friendship with Connally, who resented strongly the Washington interference in Texas political affairs.
>
> Connally's feeling reached the point over the weekend, as Kilgore weighed his decision here, that the governor seriously considered either running for the Senate himself or even retiring from politics.
>
> Although both Connally and Kilgore refused to discuss it, *The News* learned from reliable sources that Johnson sent word to Kilgore that he would fight him if he ran against Yarborough, and that he could 'assure' his defeat.
>
> A close associate of Johnson's even went so far as to tell Kilgore that the President could 'cut off' his campaign financing and could also 'handle' the Texas newspapers, persuading them to oppose him.

Several other capitol correspondents opined that Texas Republicans were gleeful over the divisive flap that made front page news across the state. But O'Donnell and Fay were not gleeful in their public statements. They took the hard line against LBJ, taking him to task with stinging statements that received widespread coverage. Playing to Texans' pride and independence, Fay blasted "strongarm tactics" from Washington.

O'Donnell charged that,

> LBJ's latest power play has:

Attempted to completely control Texas politics from Washington.

Attempted to cram Ralph Yarborough down the throats of Democrat voters by forcing Lloyd Bentsen and Joe Kilgore out of the U.S. Senate race, denying Democrats a meaningful choice.

Served the interests of the most liberal elements of the national Democratic Party who placed Joe Kilgore on a purge list last April. What the liberals in Kilgore's district couldn't do, Johnson did for them.

... Despite their personal dislike for one another, Johnson and Yarborough have now formed a cynical alliance of convenience which undercuts Texas conservatives.

Republicans also reminded Texans that when Johnson was trying to keep the Federal government from investigating the Box 13 vote fraud in 1948, by which he first won his Senate seat, LBJ had been quoted thusly: "Under no circumstances should the Federal government be permitted to intervene in a state election."

Jon Ford, longtime capitol correspondent for the *San Antonio Express-News*, pointed out that O'Donnell and Fay were using LBJ's power play as an open invitation to conservative Democrats to move over into the GOP. Some would surely come, but for the most part, those in leadership positions licked their wounds, remained loyal to Connally, and waited for better days. In the final analysis, LBJ, "The Great Manipulator," had arranged matters to his liking and was willing to take the heat. He certainly pleased the AFL – CIO, saving Yarborough from a dangerous primary situation because Bentsen and Kilgore were both known as adroit politicians who could have exploited Yarborough's weaknesses. Should Yarborough have survived such a primary challenge, it would have been very divisive and the Republican nominee's chances to win in November would have been greatly enhanced. But the political arena always contains a few big *What ifs,* and the fact was, LBJ had been able to defuse what he considered to be a major problem.

Rockefeller's primary campaigns were tough and telling. He portrayed himself as the savior of traditional moderation, protecting the Republican Party from a virulent new strain of "extremism." This searing theme was developed to discredit the candidate supported by those "extremists" who created the "climate of hate" in Dallas and their colleagues elsewhere around the country. This category included the John Birch Society and other right-wing elements that, although nowhere near in control of the Republican Party, were portrayed as part of a sinister movement poised to dominate the GOP.

Couched in cleverly-crafted rhetoric that was designed to elicit the darkest connotations without spelling them out, this theme was the most divisive that one could imagine for the Republican Party at that time. In a relatively calm political year, such tortured logic would probably have fallen on its face, but in the highly emotional aftermath of the assassination, it was effective rhetoric, nurtured by many of the national news media people who had created the theme initially.

Goldwater started out campaigning on his favorite positive themes, those of providing a society where the individual can develop his or her potential with the minimum of interference from government, and the need for the United States to develop a stronger posture and national defense to deter Communist aggression. But Goldwater, hounded by Rockefeller and the news media, often found himself on the defensive, somehow trying to convey the fact that most of his supporters were extreme only in love of country and were not part of any secret organization or sinister movement.

Goldwater must have known his chances of becoming President were slim indeed, but he was a tough competitor who took the abrasive abuse thrown upon him and kept on campaigning hard for the nomination. The race was predicted to be close, with Rockefeller granted the East and parts of the Midwest, while Goldwater was conceded the Sunbelt, some of the Midwest and most of the West. The question mark and probable pivotal state would be California, where an eighty-six – delegate winner-take-all primary would be held on June 2.

On the Texas scene, Tower and O'Donnell found the State Republican Executive Committee (SREC) receptive to a presidential preference poll, not binding on delegate selection but to be held as part of the regular May primary. There was no question Goldwater would win handily, but this was an innovative ploy to provide publicity and a boost for Goldwater about a month prior to the California primary. Rockefeller's political operatives had sniffed the Texas winds in the spring and found them highly unfavorable to their candidate. Though stuck on the Texas GOP poll ballot, Rockefeller conceded Texas to Goldwater, who took seventy-five percent of some 145,000 votes cast with Rockefeller, dividing twenty-five percent of the also-ran vote. Regardless of the poll, Goldwater was assured of all fifty-six Texas delegates to the Republican National Convention. He went on to win the California primary, causing Rockefeller's campaign to collapse. This virtually assured Goldwater the nomination, but Rockefeller had deepened Goldwater's wounds and would continue that process at the ensuing GOP convention in San Francisco.

From an early start when he had announced, until near the filing deadline for candidates in February 1964, George Bush had been the odds-on favorite to win the GOP nomination for United States Senator. Near the deadline, Jack Cox surprised most Texas Republicans by announcing for the Senate, shunning another crack at the governor's office he had sought the previous two elections. The decision by Cox left the GOP without a "known" gubernatorial candidate, but Jack Crichton (pronounced Creighton) of Dallas, an independent oilman with no political credentials, stepped forward to make the race.

Bush and Cox were joined in the GOP primary race by Dr. Milton Davis and Robert Morris, both staunch conservatives from, and known in, Dallas, with little support among the rank-and-file elsewhere. Since all four candidates were solidly for Goldwater, there were no strong ideological issues. It settled down to a Bush or Cox choice based largely upon which was perceived as more likely to win against Ralph Yarborough in the fall. Cox did attack Bush a few times, trying to capitalize on Bush's Eastern heritage as perhaps hiding some liberal leanings "Behind the Bushes." But Bush had developed rapidly as a strong candidate, attracting broad support among the grass roots to complement the establishment Republican support he had secured before entering the race.

Bush was the leader in the first primary, with forty-four percent to thirty-two percent for Cox who forced him into a June runoff which Bush won handily. Cox, whose 1962 campaign against Connally had been effective and unifying for Republicans, found the timing of his 1964 candidacy to have been clearly off the mark. Whatever chance he may have had was lost in the fall of 1963, because Bush solidified so much support before Cox entered the race. The defeat for the United States Senate nomination ended the political career of Jack Cox.

In the Democratic Primary, LBJ's persuasion tactics had protected Ralph Yarborough from challengers with political credentials, but Gordon McLendon, a Dallas radio station executive, decided to make the race. Unknown in the political arena, McLendon had something of a following from days as "The Old Scotchman" as he billed himself when recreating major league baseball games on radio, carried by the Liberty Broadcasting System years prior to his political debut.

Billie Sol Estes, the onetime West Texas tycoon, had sustained the collapse of his financial empire, which had been built largely upon fraudulent transactions with the federal government. In the wake was a long trail of implications and unanswered questions, one of which was whether Yarborough accepted $50,000 in cash from him, as reported in *The Dallas Morning News*. Yarborough denied it vigorously, but McLendon jumped

on the issue and gave the senator some uneasy moments before late-break-
ing news just before the primary tended to absolve Yarborough, although
conflicting evidence would appear later. Yarborough had been tarnished
somewhat by the upstart McLendon, but he won the primary by a decisive margin as LBJ had desired.

Don Yarborough, who had run such a close race against Connally
in 1962, couldn't resist the temptation of another try for the governorship. But all the chemistry and alchemy of 1962 were gone with the
swirling political winds of 1964 relating to Connally's post-assassination
perception by Texas voters and LBJ's penchant for a unified party. To
that purpose LBJ engineered a "no-endorsement" of Yarborough from
organized labor which distressed many of the longtime liberals who held
to their convictions in spite of LBJ's manipulations. Connally went on
to swamp Yarborough by more than 650,000 votes, a bitter result for
those liberals who had fought so hard in the trenches during the previous Connally – Yarborough contest which they had lost by such a small
margin. They found in May, as would Texas Republicans in November,
that the major changes brought about on November 22, 1963, were irreversible in 1964, and they feared, perhaps far beyond.

Tower was chairman and O'Donnell vice-chairman of the Texas delegation to the Republican National Convention. As spokesman for the
delegation, Tower's words were often taken as representing the entire South
since he had campaigned so effectively for Goldwater in that GOP-emerg-
ing region of the nation. O'Donnell, the organizational genius, was assisted by Marvin Collins, the skilled executive director of the state party
and Dick Morgan, state Goldwater chairman. They made sure the needs
of the Texas delegation were attended to at all times and that coordination with the Southern delegations would always be at peak efficiency.
For the July convention in San Francisco, the Texas delegation was housed
at the Jack Tar Hotel, symbolic in that it was new and located away
from the traditional downtown hotels, such as the Fairmont, the Mark
Hopkins, and the St. Francis.

The Jack Tar also served as nerve center for the eleven-delegation
political consortium representing states of the old Confederacy, with most
of their delegates pledged to Goldwater. With GOP unity for Goldwater
throughout the South, O'Donnell and Alabama State Chairman John
Grenier managed their powerful team with an elaborate communications
system that kept them in constant contact with delegation leaders at various
hotels and at the convention center, the Cow Palace. Two press rooms
were operative in the Jack Tar to accommodate the media from Texas
and the South, plus occasional national media people who dropped by
from time to time.

Long before the ERA movement developed, women were playing a major role in the Texas GOP. Of the fifty-six delegates from Texas, second only to California in number for Goldwater, seventeen were women being rewarded for pioneer work in the precincts and with higher levels of party organization. Among those known for their diligent organizational work were Frances Atkinson of Lufkin, Bette Jo Buhler of Victoria, National Committeewoman Flo Kampmann of San Antonio, former National Committeewoman Barbara Man of Wichita Falls, and State Vice-Chairman Kathryn McDaniel of Borger. The great potential of Anne Armstrong of Armstrong, Texas, was recognized when she was named to perhaps the most important committee of the convention, Resolutions (Platform), along with Tower. Subsequently, she would attain high party positions, including national committeewoman and co-chairman of the Republican National Committee. She would receive a signal honor when President Nixon named her United States Ambassador to the Court of St. James. Beryl Milburn, of Austin, would subsequently attain many prominent party and campaign positions before being named vice-chairman of the Texas Constitutional Revision Commission and ultimately became a member of the Board of Regents of The University of Texas.

In reviewing the 1964 list of delegates and alternate delegates from Texas twenty years later, only a few remained active in politics and/or government throughout those two decades: Tower, Bush, Fred Agnich of Dallas, John Hurd of San Antonio — then from Laredo — and Dr. Walter (Wally) Wilkerson, Jr., of Conroe.

Throughout the Goldwater forces in San Francisco, dedication and organization were evident. It had been a long, uphill struggle at times and these delegates had worked hard for this moment in history when they would change the philosophical orientation of their party, and perhaps the nation. They were in no mood to be dissuaded by the divisive rhetoric of Rockefeller, who would bring his "extremism" issue before the convention. Nor would they be sidetracked by the last-minute quixotic candidacy of Governor William Scranton of Pennsylvania, who had taken up the moderation banner following the demise of Rockefeller's candidacy. The Goldwater delegates knew they had the votes to nominate their candidate and they were anxious to get the job done and return home to campaign.

Of the 279 Southern delegates, Tower – O'Donnell – Grenier – et al, would deliver 271 to Goldwater's first-ballot nomination for President of the United States. All fifty-six delegates cheered loudly as the convention proceeded in Goldwater's favor, often filling the Cow Palace with their resounding whoops of *Viva!* echoed by *Ole!* Their mission was finally being accomplished, but the convention was probably the most divisive in modern Republican history. Unlike previous conventions, including the bitter Taft – Eisenhower struggle of 1952, the wounds appeared to be so deep as to defy healing. Rockefeller refused to endorse the new standard-bearer and his platform. Months before the convention, O'Donnell had sent a memo to Goldwater recommending that he consider Scranton for vice-president. If there were any such thoughts being entertained by Goldwater, they were dissipated by the slashing rhetoric in a Scranton letter to Goldwater during the convention. It read in part, "Goldwaterism has come to stand for nuclear irresponsibility ... Goldwaterism has come to stand for being afraid to forthrightly condemn right-wing extremism ... Goldwaterism has come to stand for a whole crazy quilt collection of absurd and dangerous positions ..."

The division was deep and Goldwater chose to stay with the undiluted nature of his conservative supporters by choosing as his running mate, Congressman William Miller of New York. Miller, as Republican National Chairman, had built ties to party leadership around the nation, but to the American people, he was unknown, an obscure member of the House from upstate New York. In the outreach sense of ticket-balancing often practiced in vice-presidential selection, Goldwater's choice added little appeal to his candidacy. It was a conservative ticket, though, and the convention's majority was prepared to go out and try to sell it.

A huge sigh of relief from Goldwater's supporters following the convention was accompanied by a deep sense of foreboding, upon assessing the aftermath. The moderate-to-liberal wing of the party had departed San Francisco convinced Goldwater and his radical right campaign did not merit its support. If a crushing defeat were impending in November, so much the better, they reasoned, for they would then pick up the pieces and rebuild the party as it had been before this aberration occurred. Further, there was concern among conservatives about the manner in which Goldwater, himself, had assumed control. O'Donnell, Clifton White, and other longstanding leaders of the Goldwater movement had been set aside while the "Arizona Mafia" was installed in campaign and party leadership positions. Some were generally inexperienced in national politics, not having been involved in such positions in the primaries which usually serve as proving grounds for staff and advisors to presidential candidates on their first try. Some were overly-protective of Goldwater, shielding him from badly-needed advice about the problems of transition, relying upon what had worked in a small Western state as opposed to the vast, complex national scene.

Even among those who were most competent, problems arose that might easily have been avoided. Dean Burch of Arizona was named the party's national chairman. He was no relation to the late John Birch, for whom the right-wing organization was named, but the surnames were the same over the air, confusing people who had heard so much from Rockefeller, about the alleged evils of the "Birchers" and "Birch Society." Had a place been found for Burch without such visibility, this additional problem regarding the "extremism issue" could have been averted.

Outside the firm base of Goldwater support, prospects for cracking other potential voting elements were not promising. As the campaign unfolded, Goldwater was saddled with extremism, which he had championed during the convention as,"no vice in the defense of liberty." In addition, he was perceived as a warhawk who would bring American military strength to bear decisively in Southeast Asia, if necessary. In a national news story, hotly disputed by Goldwater, he was portrayed as one who would also use nuclear weapons carelessly while LBJ cooed as a big dove, promising no major involvement in Vietnam. Thus, the image contrast on the war issue became sharply divided — Goldwater, the warmonger, versus LBJ, the man of peace.

On the domestic scene, LBJ had engineered passage of the landmark Civil Rights Act of 1964, a sweeping piece of legislation that granted, among substantive changes, the right of equal access to public accommodations. That struck at the heart of the Jim Crow laws and syndrome of the Deep South, whose leaders, steeped in their devotion to states' rights, denounced it as federal encroachment of the worst order. Goldwater and Tower had voted against the bill. However, in the Southwest — of which, Texas is more a part than the old Confederacy — the bill was fairly well accepted except for East Texas where Old South traditions remained strong. State Representative Ben Jarvis, a conservative Democrat from Tyler, would even announce a change in party affiliation. For LBJ, it was a tremendous boost to his emerging image as a powerful President. In one swift stroke, he had proved that he could pass major legislation that JFK could not, and that he could no longer be tied to the racist Southern past.

The issue orientation of the contest was obviously in LBJ's favor, bolstering the polling results which continually showed the incumbent leading the challenger by wide margins. Outside the conservative movement, the American people were simply not interested in Goldwater's concerns about individual freedom, the free enterprise system or limited government. He contended the Democratic Party had a long-standing proclivity toward tax-spending policies for nonessential programs that would fuel inflation and drive up prices. There was, of course, no inflation problem at that time. LBJ was wheeling and dealing, assuring business that all was well, while delivering — or promising to deliver — legislation to various liberal interest groups whose grateful leaders were fervently passing the word to their members to stay hitched with the Democratic Party. They were joyfully surprised to deal with this powerful leader who was carrying JFK's torch forward with greater authority and effectiveness.

It appeared as though Johnson simply had no major vulnerability, until one aspect of his image began cropping up in polling data compiled for the Goldwater forces — LBJ's long-standing record of wheeling and dealing had caught up with him to some extent. A few members of the national media had delved into his past, posing questions about the manner in which he and his wife had acquired such vast wealth, including a monopoly on the lucrative television market in Austin. Also explored was Johnson's close relationship with Brown and Root, the vast engineering-construction firm with headquarters in Houston. Brown and Root appeared to have benefitted greatly from huge federal contracts since LBJ had entered elective office in Washington. This relationship spawned the line that, "To understand LBJ, you must first get down to the Brown and Root of the matter." Questions were raised about LBJ's relationship with that much-publicized fallen star, Billie Sol Estes, the West Texas tycoon whose labyrinthine, fraudulent West Texas empire had been exposed by Oscar Griffin, reporting for *The Pecos Independent*, for which he won the Pulitzer Prize. Another of LBJ's questionable relationships, that with Bobby Baker, was contemporary. Baker, the secretary of the U. S. Senate, whose wheeling and dealing had indeed landed him into deep legal problems — widely reported in 1964 — was considered to be a protegé of Johnson's. LBJ had made every effort to make that relationship appear to be, and to have been, at arm's length. And, of course, there was the Box 13 scandal to be bandied about again.

In that general subject area, in 1964, Panhandle rancher and writer J. Evetts Haley wrote a scorching attack on LBJ entitled *A Texan Looks at Lyndon*, subtitled *A Study in Illegitimate Power*. An article appeared in the September 26th issue of *The Dallas Morning News* in which Haley stated that a staggering total of 7,350,000 copies of his paperback had been printed.

Some GOP needling of LBJ was done on a humorous basis. The State party GOP newspaper suggested a few cabinet changes:

> Attorney General — George Parr — Infinite knowledge of election procedures.
> Secretary of Agriculture — Billie Sol Estes — Nation's only expert on subsidy-storage matters.

Secretary of Commerce — Bobby Baker — Financial prowess could wipe out the national debt.

Secretary of the Navy — John Connally — If you can't beat 'em, rejoin 'em.

It was also suggested that, "LBJ thinks an extremist is anybody who believes Austin ought have two TV stations."

When LBJ released a financial statement placing his personal fortune at $3.5 million, O'Donnell said he would form an investment committee and pay LBJ $4 million in cash, which would furnish him with a nice profit and relieve him of any conflict-of-interest charges. "We are confident," O'Donnell said, "the television monopoly and other assets could be resold promptly for approximately $14 million ... We intend to apply $10 million profit to Senator Goldwater's presidential campaign as the product of the largest single political fund-raising venture in history."

So much alleged chicanery surrounding LBJ's personal background prompted Goldwater's strategists to make an issue of "morality in government." Their candidate had no such liabilities and they believed an image contrast between the individuals would inure substantially to Goldwater's benefit. Given the post-assassination political climate in which substantive national issues seemed of little importance, perhaps the nature of Goldwater's campaign was destined to turn more negative and personal, but the "morality in government" theme failed. Late in the campaign the disclosure of the arrest of LBJ's longtime friend and aide, Walter Jenkins, (on morals charges), seemed to play into the hands of the Goldwater camp. But major international developments, including the ouster of Soviet Premier Nikita Khrushchev, caused that situation to fade from the front pages.

At the bedrock of Goldwater's problem was the fact that the public wanted to let LBJ carry forth the Kennedy banner and Goldwater's credibility as a presidential candidate had been undermined, his image tarnished badly by Rockefeller. LBJ's campaign took full advantage of this by using an emotional TV commercial showing a little girl picking daisies shortly before a nuclear explosion. To a great number of American ticket-splitting voters, Goldwater was perceived as a political extremist, a right-wing warmonger, a dangerous personality at a time when they wanted a calm, steady hand at the wheel.

Tad Smith, the former GOP state chairman, had been named state chairman for the Goldwater Campaign which he headquartered in the Littlefield Building near the Republican State Headquarters. His top operatives included Tom Gilliland working on the organizational programs, and Mack Braley as press secretary. Smith's group worked closely with the State GOP in order to implement various programs of the campaign, the most important of which was the door-to-door canvass. This program was carried out by volunteers who knocked on doors in generally favorable precincts to determine the voting sentiment in each household. Respondents were separated into three groups, favorable for Goldwater, unfavorable, and undecided. Those in the first and third categories were recontacted by mail and phone before the election while those opposed were not recontacted on the theory that trying to convert them would be a diminishing return. Smith, prematurely balding, was a dynamic individual who believed leaders should fight in the trenches as well as from the command posts, so he would canvass at night door-to-door in Austin. What he found was always discouraging — the trend for LBJ was strong and steady.

A gloomy atmosphere pervaded the stretch run of Goldwater's campaign which appeared to be dead in the water until along came a political paradox of the first order. It was a thirty-minute speech delivered on television October 27, 1964, providing a litany of conservative principles and concerns set forth by a Hollywood actor who was never of a superstar status and was considered by many as one whose time had passed, an individual citizen with no real political credentials, no public office nor title. But Ronald Reagan stated the positions in a concise, forthright manner, more convincingly than conservatives had heard since the early days of Goldwater's ascendency. Reagan framed the campaign succinctly by looking viewers squarely in the eye and stating, "You and I are told increasingly that we have to choose between a left or right, but I would like to suggest that there is no such thing as a left or right. There is only an up or down — up to man's age-old dream — the ultimate in individual freedom consistent with law and order — or down to the ant heap of totalitarianism ..." That struck a gut appeal, rekindling enthusiasm among the tired volunteers who had worked so hard but had seen or heard so little that was encouraging. Suddenly orders and money poured into the Littlefield Building from Republicans who wanted copies of the speech and who would pay to have videotapes run on television in their local areas. Reagan had provided a refreshing moment late in a dreary campaign, establishing himself indelibly as a future factor. To Smith, O'Donnell, and some others, however, the handwriting was on the wall — nothing changed the polling results which were consistently discouraging.

As Barry Goldwater's campaign appeared to be foundering, George Bush's was gaining momentum. Jim Leonard, who had been the executive director for the state GOP, was campaign manager for Bush, pulling together a strong coalition of Republicans and conservative Democrats, who simply could not bear to support their longtime archenemy, Ralph Yarborough. Though not being a native Texan may have been somewhat of a liability in parts of rural Texas, Bush was catching on throughout urban Texas with his upbeat personality and ability to present himself as an articulate candidate of conservative conviction. Bush was selling himself, and his political views and he was attracting adequate campaign financing to challenge Yarborough in a forthright manner. Bush's television commercials were effective and his campaign ran impressive full-page endorsement ads in most of the major newspapers, several of which endorsed his candidacy. In fact, Bush was endorsed by four metropolitan dailies, including the hometown *Houston Chronicle*, and thirty-six other newspapers around the state.

Yarborough began feeling the pressure from Bush, and his campaign went on the attack, keying on the emotional anti-Goldwater syndrome with such things as a full-page newspaper ad containing a huge headline, VOTE AGAINST EXTREMISM! In addition to charges about nuclear policy, the copy contended that "George Bush's expensive advertising campaign conceals one crucial point: his alliance with the extremist Goldwater–Tower–John Birch wing of the Republican party!" At the bottom of the ad was the call to "Vote For Sane Government ... Vote for Lyndon Johnson and Ralph Yarborough ..." Those in the news media and the political arena who had come to know him scoffed at the idea of George Bush being branded as extremist, but in the unique atmosphere that existed then, the attacks probably helped Yarborough check some of the momentum of the Bush campaign.

Nonetheless, in the stretch run of 1964, it was becoming increasingly obvious that Bush, the political newcomer, would run substantially ahead of Texas Republicans' revered favorite at the top of the ticket.

On election night, as the Johnon landslide was being reported, LBJ held a huge victory celebration at the Driskill Hotel next door to the Littlefield Building where the GOP and Goldwater staffers were distressed by the results. They felt beleaguered by the helicopters circling, Secret Service atop nearby buildings, and the persistent noise of revelry on the sidewalks below. LBJ swamped Goldwater in Texas with sixty-three percent of the vote, 1,663,185 to 958,566. Despite George Bush's strong campaign, Yarborough rode out the challenge by a margin of 1,463,958 to 1,134,337, a result wich confirmed the notion that substantial ticket-splitting was becoming a reality in Texas elections. *The Dallas Times-Herald* was among several newspapers that had encouraged ticket-splitting between LBJ and Bush and the results followed with those two candidates carrying Dallas County.

To illustrate the wide variance of voter turnout between a general election in the presidential year and a special election, Bush received more votes in losing the 1964 U.S. Senate election than the combined vote for Tower and Blakley in the United States Senate runoff of 1961.

Bush's showing was impressive, but still it was a defeat. In general, the 1964 election was disastrous for Texas Republicans with almost all their candidates losing, from Goldwater at the top to various local offices and most in between. Though Goldwater lost, his conservative movement had generated in Texas a prodigious amount of political activity by candidates and their campaigns, by party and volunteer organizations, and by those dedicated contributors who provided fuel for the engine.

Within a week after the election, Tad Smith prepared to close his Goldwater office in the Littlefield Building and return home to El Paso. In his final moment as a statewide Republican leader, he paused at the door to bid farewell to a few loyal staffers who had worked diligently night and day, seven days a week, for the cause in which they believed so fervently. "Well, gentlemen," he sighed with a sardonic smile and a twinkle in his eye, "it was the best organized and best financed political disaster in American history."

CHAPTER FOUR

Almost a Farewell to Arms

For Texas Republicans, the postelection battlefield was littered with badly wounded troops, most of whom would be retrieved to fight again but whose leadership ranks had been decimated. Virtually all the gains of the past several years had been wiped out. Defeated was Congressman Alger whose decade of public service had included his highly visible political role of serving as the conservative magnet around whom the Dallas County GOP enjoyed such tremendous growth. Also defeated was the other Texas GOP member of Congress, Ed Foreman of Odessa, whose eventual comeback would be in New Mexico.

Ten of the eleven Republican seats in the Texas House of Representatives were lost, with only Midland — then as now a GOP bastion — voting to send Frank Cahoon to Austin. Of the eight Republican state representatives elected from Dallas in '62–'63, all were defeated in 1964 and only one, Ike Harris, would ever mount a successful comeback. There were no GOP state senators, thus Cahoon was the only Republican in the entire Legislature with 180 Democrats.

All statewide GOP candidates had been defeated with only George Bush polling adequately to maintain viability for a future race. Losses at the local level were severe, with only a handful of Republican officeholders surviving around the state whose 254 courthouses were in Democratic control. One of the few survivors was Harrison County Judge John Furrh of Marshall, who would subsequently pursue a judicial career, and serve with distinction.

Goldwater's conservative movement was roundly denounced in the media as a failure, out of touch with the needs of Americans. These needs, supposedly, were being addressed in the Great Society program whose author, LBJ, had swept most of the nation, losing only Goldwater's Arizona and five states of the Old South.

For Texas Republicans the political climate following the 1964 election was adverse and uncertain. It was also frustrating, exemplified by a biting letter to *The Dallas Morning News* from Dick Morgan, the Dallas County state legislator who had lost his seat while serving as the Texas chairman for Goldwater.

He denounced the newspaper for its "courageous stand of neutrality" in the presidential contest. Morgan contended the Republican Platform "could easily have been mistaken for an editorial from *The Dallas News*," while the Democratic Platform "was a rehash of the liberal 1960 document with a few Johnsonian flourishes of a New Deal flavor thrown in."

Political writers in Texas were quick to point out that Tower, the "fluke of 1961," who had been in the vanguard of the Goldwater movement, would surely have been defeated had he been up for reelection in 1964, and now that he would be up in 1966, he was ripe for plucking by whomever the Democrats might nominate. Early speculation for that role centered around John Connally, Jim Wright, and Attorney General Waggoner Carr, a former Speaker of the Texas House of Representatives.

On a cold, damp November afternoon a few days after the 1964 election, a small group of Texas Republicans gathered quietly for a secret meeting in the old Commodore Perry Hotel in downtown Austin to assess the damage and look to the future. Attending were Tower and O'Donnell with their top aides, National Committeeman Al Fay, and a few others. Tower stunned the gathering by opening the meeting with an offer to stand aside, not seek reelection if the group felt another candidate, presumably Bush, would have a better chance of holding the seat which Tower said was the party's, not his. Filled with remorse, the once exalted knight offered his sword to the somber court.

O'Donnell would have none of that, pointing out the party leadership had been unified behind the Goldwater movement and the grass roots had been there all the way — no excuses or apologies were in order, public or private. Certainly no stepping aside by Tower was in order. He would remain the standard-bearer for Texas Republicans. But postures would have to be changed and thought was given as to how a party recovery might be attained. Most importantly, how might they best enhance Tower's fortunes for a successful reelection campaign.

At this dismal time, divisive charges and countercharges continued to fly between Goldwater supporters and those GOP leaders, mostly on the Eastern Seaboard, who had opposed Goldwater or had been neutral. Al Fay, as national committeeman, expressed his belief that some sense of unity would eventually prevail, with the Republican National Committee (RNC) and congressional leadership to remain in relatively conservative hands, although Goldwater's influence, per se, would be greatly reduced. As the discussion progressed, it became apparent that just as Goldwater's presidential bid and the Texas GOP fortunes were tightly intertwined in 1963 – 1964, the destinies of John Tower and the Texas GOP would march closely together through the two-year election cycle already in progress. Fine-tuning his thoughts, O'Donnell laid out, in laconic terms, concepts for a disciplined strategy of circling the wagons in a tight formation around Tower, whose reelection bid would carry top priority. Every effort would be made to retain all the volunteers and contributors who had come aboard for Goldwater and Bush, melding them into Tower supporters or participants in the party organization which would function almost solely for the benefit of Tower.

If that base could be secured, it would provide a strong building block for Tower's reelection, a goal O'Donnell obviously believed to be vital. Emphasis would be on Tower's campaign to the exclusion of a governor's race or any other for statewide office. No potential candidates for other offices, such as Congress, would be encouraged to run unless the winnability factor was clearly there or some need were seen to file a token candidate, in which case a loyal party person could serve in that unsavory capacity. Therefore, the Texas GOP changed strategy drastically from 1964, when full slates of competitive candidates had been encouraged to run as part of the conservative movement. Tower would be the only individual statewide candidate around whom the Republicans would rally, causing some insiders to wince at the thought of writing off the governor's race two years before the election, and wondering what would be left two years hence, if Tower were defeated.

In essence, the strategy was to reelect Tower with a key element of holding down the Democratic voter turnout by contesting only the most winnable races around the state. In Texas Republican politics of the 1980s, such a strategy would be unthinkable. Candidates come out running in all sorts of unlikely races that are marginally winnable to certain *kamikaze*, causing party leaders simply to grit their teeth. They know resources will be squandered and Democratic turnout increased, perhaps hurting winnable GOP races up and down the ticket. Back in those bleak days following the 1964 election, O'Donnell et al could indeed control, to a great extent, the makeup of the ticket, particularly statewide candidates. There simply weren't that many potential candidates to discourage, and outside of Tower, there was no potential GOP statewide candidate for 1966 with the ability to raise significant campaign funds. Therefore, as a practical matter, a token candidate could be recruited where desirable without causing the other side to respond by mounting a serious campaign.

With those ideas on the table, Tower seemed to perk up. He could envision a campaign emerging that would be disciplined and resourceful, with perhaps its most important element a careful plan to dodge the big bullet of extremely high Democratic voter turnout which in 1964 had dealt such a severe setback to the fledgling GOP in Texas.

Thoughts then turned to the other side. In assessing the potential opposition, it was concluded — perhaps with a dash of wishful thinking — that Connally was an unlikely adversary for Tower, having aimed at the Presidency on top of the executive ladder in government service. It was felt he had neither the desire nor patience for a legislative position. Wright was considered to be quite formidable, having served several terms in Congress and being perceived as a mainstream Democrat. Carr was an enigmatic consideration. He had a strong statewide following which had helped him become the top vote-getter on the Democratic state ticket in 1964, but he was not perceived as being a dynamic campaigner. Further, unlike Wright, he had no experience in Federal government in a rapidly changing political era in which sharper focus on campaigns through television required candidates to know their issues thoroughly and to be prepared to articulate their positions on the spur of the moment. Perhaps most importantly, Carr's political philosophy was strongly conservative, conjuring up the possibility of liberal backlash, a repeat of the decisive factor for Tower in 1961. The adversary considerations were not pursued beyond the surface. Regardless of whomever might evince as the opponent, the task at hand for a year was for Tower to perform his best as an incumbent Senator serving his state, while O'Donnell, Fay, and the party organization would try to revive grass roots Republicans and contributors around Texas whose morale was low indeed.

When the meeting was adjourned, the mood of the participants hadn't swung from dark gloom to shining optimism, but at least some strong threads of strategy had been stitched together for the 1966 election, a showdown already recognized as pivotal in the life of the Republican Party of Texas.

John Tower knew he had to contend with an image problem. He was perceived more as a reactionary than a conservative, yet his own supporters hated the word moderate which they associated with the slashing attacks from Rockefeller and some of the liberal national news media. He had written a book published in 1962, *A Program For Conservatives*, more philosophical and reflective in nature than Goldwater's *Conscience of a Conservative*, which preempted the market. Nonetheless, Tower went back to some of the ideas he had used in the book to describe a conservative, as he sought to redirect public thought on the term.

> The conservative would leave as much to popular control in the area of public decision as possible ... His is an essentially optimistic outlook, reposing great confidence in the ability of people to make major decisions, not only affecting their individual lives and destinies, but the destiny of the social order as well. Liberty, then, becomes the dynamic of human progress in material, social, and spiritual spheres ... The American conservative is then a champion of the capitalistic or market-regulated economy — the economic democracy which complements political democracy ...

Then, trying to find some special label, Tower began referring to himself as a "progressive conservative." That didn't sit well with some of the media who considered those terms contradictory a a and many Republicans associated the word "progressive" with "liberal." Tower soon decided to let his words and deeds produce what he hoped would develop into a favorable public image with the term "forward-looking" being applied now and then by his writers instead of "progressive."

Bob Baskin, chief of *The Dallas Morning News* Washington bureau, perceived a change in Tower's posture in mid-January, after Tower spoke of supporting some positions of LBJ's legislative program.

> He [Tower] knows that if the [1966] election were held today, the odds would be greatly against him if the Democratic nominee has any stature at all ... One of the great lessons on the 1964 election is that Republicans must not allow Democrats to preempt the middle of the road. A moderate approach, at least in tone and attitude, is going to be needed in future contests. The exclusive character of Goldwater conservatism, while admirable for its courage, is not likely to win many elections ... Tower is considered a political realist. The course he follows ... with 1966 looming ever larger, will be interesting to observe.

Still being branded as "cool and aloof," Tower was also under pressure to improve his personal image as a campaigner. The fact of the matter was that Tower was quite at home on the floor of the United States Senate and behind a microphone anywhere, but in a crowd of people he was basically shy, almost the complete opposite of most successful politicians. He would try harder "to work the crowds," but he never overcame that reluctance to wade in and "press the flesh" as LBJ had done in legendary fashion.

As events unfolded in 1965, Tower would essentially take the high road, articulating his positions on various issues, in Washington and in Texas, while O'Donnell took care of the partisan posturing in the state. To capitalize on the strong focus of Washington issues, Tower had developed a skilled staff to contend with trends and developments there. Ken Towery succeeded Ed Munden as administrative assistant. Munden, a rural East Texan, was one of the few original "Tower people" from the 1961 campaign, along with Tom Cole of Amarillo, and Pierce Langford, the Wichita Falls pilot who had finessed the landing on a farm road. Cole and Langford remained on staff with Cole becoming legislative assistant.

Though Ken Towery informed the senator that he had voted for Blakley in 1961, Tower hired him in 1963 from the Capitol Press Corps in Austin, where Towery had served for seven years as a correspondent for *The Austin American-Statesman*. Previously, he had won a Pulitzer Prize for breaking the Veterans Land Scandal in 1954, while writing for *The Cuero Record*. Well respected among his peers, Towery thus brought an element of credibility and strength to Tower's staff when he became press secretary in 1963. When he became chief of staff as administrative assistant (or "AA" as one is known in Washington), he brought to bear overall political guidance and direction for the staff in Washington, D.C., and throughout the Tower Senate and political apparatus in Texas.

Of amiable personality, but firm in political conviction and steadfast in pursuing goals and objectives, the balding Towery possessed an indomitable spirit and inner strength that friends believed were products of deprivation during his long confinement in a Japanese prison camp during most of World War II. He was a veteran of the courageous American stand at Corregidor, in the Philippine Islands, early in the war when United States forces were hopelessly outnumbered.

Though they were worlds apart in personality and the manner in which they conducted their personal lives, Tower and Towery, they of similar names, were destined to work together closely off and on through many years of Senate duty and in the Texas political arena.

When Towery moved up to AA, Jerry Friedheim succeeded him as press secretary. Friedheim, a bright young journalist from Missouri, developed an efficient system for his early acquisition and rapid release of information regarding the award of federal contracts in Texas. Even though the Democrats controlled the White House and both houses of Congress, the brash unflappable Jerry Friedheim, through contacts in the bureaucracy and sheer diligence, kept gathering and breaking such information under

Tower's name. This was to the great dismay of most Texas Democratic members of Congress and Democratic political operatives in the state. They wanted to continue painting Tower as the anti-everything reactionary who had crashed and burned in 1964 with Goldwater, but couldn't be confirmed dead until the 1966 election. Instead, substantially through Friedheim's Gatling gun barrage of timely news releases, 1965 would become a positive, image-building year for Tower, who appeared to be a highly effective senator, taking care of federal projects for Texas. Some of the smaller projects might not warrant more than two or three paragraphs in the newspaper serving the community involved, but each story was another drop on the rock, softening Tower's political image.

In his role as legislative assistant, Tom Cole was not as visible as Towery and Friedheim, but he performed an invaluable service in the complex, tedious legislative process of the United States Senate. As often stated, timing is crucial in politics, whether relating to campaigns or to the legislative process. Cole, a soft-spoken and diligent young attorney, made certain Tower was usually well-briefed for probable courses of action and consequences regarding key legislation.

Tower's Washington office attracted other bright young Texans who kept the heavy flow of work moving. These included Richard (Rick) Parker and Sondra Walters, both attorneys from Houston.

These high level staffers were top talent, hard-nosed advisors who would not hesitate to confront Tower head-on when they believed him to be headed in the wrong direction. In give-and-take strategy sessions, when Towery or Friedheim would challenge him, the senator might flash a brief frown of disdain before smiling with the rejoinder, "Well, no one can say that I surround myself with yes-men."

A big break came Tower's way early in 1965, when the young senator was named to the Armed Services Committee, probably the best assignment he could have landed. The extent of military/defense activity in Texas was staggering. Texas was host to 250,000 military and civilian personnel associated with national defense, with $1.2 billion worth of defense wages paid annually.

In his new capacity, Tower set out to learn the military/defense policies and programs of the United States from the highest strategic concepts to the needs of the enlisted ranks where he had served in World War II. He maintained that status through the Reserves as the only enlisted man in the Senate. Tower and Yarborough were on opposite ends of the political philosophy spectrum but they shared a deep concern for American troops. Both introduced a Vietnam GI Bill that would provide educational and loan benefits similar to those provided veterans of World War

II, and the Korean Conflict. Needless to say, such moves were well received throughout the ranks of active military personnel and veterans in civilian life. Tower would become "their man in Washington."

While Tower poured over the endless details of American military and defense programs, he hadn't lost his admiration for Great Britain, nor his flair for the dramatic with high-flown rhetoric about historical perspectives. Shortly after the death of Winston Churchill in early 1965, he was quoted in the *Congressional Record*:

> He [Churchill] was possessed of an infinite and unequaled capacity for leadership. He distinguished himself in so many ways that it staggers the imagination. His eloquence not only inspired us but brought to our ears the soaring majesty of the English language.
>
> If from some eternal domicile the immortals of the past — Richard the Lionhearted, Edward II, Elizabeth I, Wellington, Nelson, Disraeli — could look upon the earthly procession of this era, they would concede that this leader of epic proportion was the greatest Englishman of them all.
>
> His passing marks an epoch in human history.

Churchill's death came as LBJ rode the crest of popularity derived from his landslide victory, which produced staggering Democratic majorities in Congress, 68 to 32 in the Senate, and 295 to 140 in the House of Representatives. However, some conservative Democrats in both chambers could be counted on to vote more on philosophical conviction than party affiliation. Nonetheless, LBJ, with his majorities and with his intimate knowledge of Congress, would move the United States down the path of accelerated domestic spending for various new social welfare programs and rapid escalation of the Vietnam War, with attendant high cost in men and resources. His 1965 State of the Union Message was largely predictable except for an Achilles' heel in his domestic program. Having become heavily indebted politically to organized labor, he called for the AFL – CIO's most coveted legislative goal — repeal of Section 14-b of the Taft – Hartley Act, the section under which Texas enacted its right-to-work law. LBJ's old nemesis, *The Dallas Morning News*, commended the President's position on Southeast Asia, but was sharply critical of his domestic program. From an editorial printed January 6, 1965:

> Many of the proposals are left over from the New Deal, Fair Deal, and New Frontier. They are as disturbing now as they were when first proposed. Massive federal aid to education, medicare under Social Security, price-wage 'guideposts' — these are longer steps toward total federal control and the welfare state.

The Dallas News, which claims credit for having coined the term, "right-to-work," was not at all pleased to contemplate the loss of the law in Texas. The editorial continued,

> The promise of changes in the Taft – Hartley Law, including the section on right-to-work laws, may be political dressing for the unions' benefit. The President said that he hoped to 'reduce conflicts.' If he plans to reduce conflicts by making every American worker join a union before he can get a job, there will be many who wonder if the Great Society is worth the cost.

The *San Antonio Express* came down even harder on LBJ's proposal with an editorial that stated in part,

> ... Repeal of Section 14-b is immoral ... Why is it necessary for the federal government to intrude in this area? ... Labor is attempting to do by law what it cannot do by voluntary action by workers ... Union employees would hold their jobs almost literally at the pleasure of the bosses.

Three times during January, O'Donnell released statements calling on Connally to support retention of the right-to-work provision, which he eventually did, lending further strength to Tower's position. Repeal of Section 14-b would eventually pass the House of Representatives, but in the Senate, outnumbered right-to-work supporters girded for an all-out battle with the filibuster as their chief weapon. Their top leader was the irrepressible Everett Dirksen, the powerful and popular GOP Senate leader from Illinois. Tower signed on early as one of Dirksen's lieutenants, a shrewd strategic move that would ultimately provide him with a key reelection issue. Anyone credited with saving the Texas right-to-work law couldn't be branded as ineffective among conservatives in the state.

Also in early 1965, the national party chairmanship changed hands from Dean Burch to Ray Bliss, the former Ohio Republican state chairman who was known as one of the best political organizers in the nation. Al Fay, the national committeeman, praised Bliss as a "real political craftsman, a pro's pro, and an experienced organizer." National Committeewoman Flo Kampmann of San Antonio said that there was no doubt the party's direction would remain conservative, and O'Donnell pointed out that a few years previously, Rockefeller had once opposed Bliss for the position.

Bliss's initial and crucial contribution was to assure factions and personalities that he would run the organization for the benefit of all Republican candidates, not engaging in intraparty squabbles nor taking public stands on issues. With a divided minority party in shambles, Bliss knew

he must maintain a steady hand in rebuilding from the devastation of
1964. He would prove to be a great asset to the party, avoiding the
potential controversy of intraparty factionalism or the grandstanding of
taking positions on issues. He once remarked in a conversation in his
Washington office, his greatest concern about issues: "The two-party system
is an issue now. It's that basic."

Bliss and his staff were never flashy, but they stuck to the basics
in a manner that would have pleased Darrell Royal — it was the blocking and tackling of politics, or the nuts and bolts as organizers might
prefer to state it. Seminars and workshops were conducted in Washington
and around the nation for candidates, party leaders, political operatives
and staff people. All major facets of campaigns were taught by experienced politicians who drilled home established procedures for mapping
out campaigns, large and small and those in between. Discussed in detail
was what works best for advertising, organizing, raising funds, scheduling of the candidate's time, press relations and all matters relating to
communications. Under Bliss, the Republican Party as a national force
would become much more professional, prepared to win those marginal
races that would be crucial to the party's comeback hopes for 1966.

Operatives for Tower and the State GOP attended such seminars,
learning new techniques. They found many of those attending from other
states to be amusing when they complained of how difficult it was to
conduct a campaign for some reason or another. The Texans believed their
state was the most difficult in the union by far because, as one Texan
would comment, "It's a logistical nightmare." When they planned the
Tower 1966 race they contemplated trying to reach more than 1,000 separate municipalities spread over those great stretches of land, more than
700 miles from the farthest east – west and north – south points, discover-
ing a little known fact — it is closer from El Paso to Los Angeles than
it is from El Paso to Houston. There were 103 daily newspapers, plus
518 weeklies; forty-seven commercial television stations, and 325 radio
stations. Scheduling of the candidate in Texas, who must also maintain
a voting record and attend to other duties in Washington, became a central consideration of the campaign.

At the state level, O'Donnell continued to emphasize a strong headquarters operation in Austin that, rather than retrench after the staggering defeat of 1964, actually expanded its scope of activity and professional
staff. In projecting what would be needed to win in 1966, Collins, the
executive director, and key staff people studied the 1962 election carefully rather than 1964 because that was a presidential year in which voter
turnout was traditionally much higher than in the so-called off years,
such as 1962 and 1966. The 1961 Tower – Blakley race was not consid-

ered a good yardstick either because of the very low voter turnout in that special election. Analysis indicated that a strong moderate to conservative Democrat would be favored against Tower, despite his incumbency, because of the Democrats' long-standing advantage in rural Texas and among the most-populous minorities, blacks (or Negroes as they were often designated) and Mexican-Americans, who were undergoing something of a name identification problem. Some groups were known as "Mexican-American," and others as "Latin-American," still others, "Spanish-speaking." A few Tower supporters, such as Vidal Cantu, from the unique, long amalgamated community of Laredo, would argue that no prefix was needed. Later, the term "Chicano" would emerge, but it wasn't in widespread use in 1966. Political scientists studying the Republican growth in urban areas of the Sunbelt had coined the term "WASP" to designate White Anglo-Saxon Protestant populations in precincts that strongly favored the GOP. Many conservatives living in those designated areas were unhappy with the tag since they were neither Anglo, defined as of English origin, nor Protestant. Nonetheless, the tag was widely used by the news media, but the Tower Campaign simply adopted the short forms of Anglo, Mexican-American (or "M-A"), and black for designating the three major ethnic groups for purposes of planning and executing its programs. It became obvious that even if Tower were able to maximize his potential among urban Anglos, the outcome didn't project well. Though voting traditions are indeed hard to change, it was decided an outreach program must be launched to the M-As in several urban areas of Texas with whom Tower could relate better since his Armed Services Committee assignment. In San Antonio, El Paso and Corpus Christi, their high M-A populations contained many civilians who worked in white and blue collar jobs on military installations. Their concerns might be more focused on adequate funding for those installations, or in smaller communities, keeping the installations open, rather than on some of LBJ's welfare schemes or simply following the tradition of voting straight Democratic against Republicans.

It was decided that an open door policy would be pursued toward blacks, but their strong ties to the Democratic Party couldn't be changed substantially in the short run. Cracking that Democratic voting tradition among M-As would be a tall order indeed. Collins hired Celso Moreno of Corpus Christi to head up the program, officially under the auspices of the Republican Party of Texas, but geared almost totally to enhance Tower's reelection. Moreno was a tireless operative with an upbeat personality, but he was also a realist who spoke candidly of the basic challenge. "Most Mexican-Americans in Texas are born Catholic and Democrat. They tend to stay that way." To gain credibility, Moreno first had to convince M-A leadership that Tower and his political party were sincere in making this outreach effort, that it would continue beyond 1966, win or lose. In the Byzantine world of M-A politics in Texas, Moreno found that for the time being he had some maneuvering room by virtue of the unrest caused by Connally's ascendency and canonization as governor. Most moderate to liberal M-A leaders didn't relate well to Connally, whom they considered to be elitist and insensitive to their needs. They knew the chances of defeating Connally were nil, but they could quietly undermine whomever Connally's ruling faction of the Democratic Party might nominate against Tower. "Quietly" was underscored in most cases because supporting a Republican was anathema to so many of the rank and file M-As in the major established organizations, such as the Mexican-American Chamber of Commerce, the League of United Latin American Citizens (LULAC) and the American G.I. Forum, which was founded after World War II, by Dr. Hector Garcia of Corpus Christi.

Through Moreno's work, Tower soon learned that many local M-A leaders considered his Republican Party label a problem, but not a barrier. They were weary of the conservative Democrat politician coming to their meetings to shake a few hands at the head table, deliver a patronizing speech, and then move on his way. They wanted recognition as individuals and understanding of their problems as an ethnic group which they felt had largely been ignored by the Texas Democratic Party dominated by Connally, Carr, et al, not by the liberal Democrats who were so much more simpatico. It seemed incongruous for Tower, the conservative Republican in the British outfit, to mix and mingle with barrio leaders from South Texas, but in the uncertain political chemistry leading toward the 1966 election, this was a beachhead on a Democratic island that had to be secured.

In addition to the anti-Connally sentiment, there was a small but growing number of politically aware M-As who had digested the two-party arguments set forth by *The Observer* and other liberal sources. They believed that the M-A vote was generally taken for granted by the Democratic Party and that two-party competition would be healthy for their cause in the long haul.

An aggressive statewide organization, the Political Association of Spanish-Speaking Organizations (PASO), had developed from remnants of the "Viva Kennedy" clubs that had sprung up to support JFK's 1960 campaign. PASO had generated a great deal of publicity because of its forthright political activism, much more pronounced than that of any other major M-A organizations.

In PASO, Moreno found substantial maneuvering room. He worked out an arrangement for its state chairman, Albert Fuentes, Jr., of San Antonio, to address the SREC in the spring of 1965. This move raised eyebrows throughout Austin where astute political operatives understood a new and perhaps significant signal was being sent by Fuentes, who relished his role. Interest was high among Republican leaders, some of whom considered Fuentes to be far too liberal to be congenial with the GOP. Others were simply curious as to what he might say — or imply.

Fuentes was a short, articulate man in middle age but in high gear in the political arena. Crafty and gutsy, he came before the SREC with a careful speech avoiding current PASO issues, which would have been divisive to discuss at the moment. Instead, he sought common ground, scoring with a theme that M-As should use more independent judgement in making their political decisions. "Look over the candidates, the parties, the platforms, the situation at hand. Don't be taken for granted." Then, Fuentes made one of those poignant points that only an accomplished speaker could make — that M-As had been discriminated against unjustly because of Anglo resentment from the Texas Revolution against Mexico. He traced his ancestry to Antonio Fuentes of San Antonio, a friend of Jim Bowie's and one of several ethnic Mexicans who fought to the death on the Texas side at the Battle of the Alamo. Invoking the Alamo in that context was highly effective, and Fuentes departed the podium to a standing ovation. It had been a risky venture, but the first major thrust of Moreno's program was a profound success.

Throughout most of South Texas, where entrenched courthouse machines tightly rule government and the political process, Fuentes's move meant little, but in urban areas where military/defense dependence was strong, plus areas in which M-As were amalgamating into mainstream Anglo society, his signal had substantial impact.

Tower was encouraged. He instructed his staff to give Moreno at least equal consideration for scheduling his time when he would be appearing in areas in which Moreno might arrange a productive appearance. Tower played to open audiences well. An ardent Texas history buff, he, too, used the theme of Federalist history of Texas M-As, who fought at the Alamo, were delegates to the Declaration of Independence, and fought in the decisive Battle of San Jacinto.

Moreno would often arrange closed sessions for local M-A leaders to talk candidly with Tower. Some of these meetings created tense moments when PASO-type firebrands would grill Tower about positions the senator was unwilling to take, but on balance, they were productive because the leaders came to perceive Tower as an honest politician, who would stand his ground.

Moreno found that many M-A leaders, who wouldn't or couldn't endorse Tower openly, nonetheless didn't object to having their picture taken with the senator. Photography bills mounted at the GOP state headquarters because Moreno found this to be a most effective tool. When a leader had his picture made with Tower, it might find its way into the local newspapers. Or, at least prints would be distributed to other leaders, creating a new air of acceptability toward Tower, whose incumbency was now coming to bear in the M-A community.

So much of the liaison work done by Moreno to Mexican-American political elements was in the category of political backlash, courting leaders who believed their people had been taken for granted by the ruling conservative Democrats. They might help Tower in 1966 in order to punish the culprits and vent their frustrations, but they'd be back home for liberal Democrat candidates in the future. On the positive long-term side, some young businessmen had made strong commitments to the Republican Party and were taking active roles. They included Rudy Garza of Corpus Christi, who would join Tower on the 1966 GOP statewide slate as candidate for comptroller; A. F. (Tony) Rodriguez of San Antonio, who would eventually land on the White House staff; Hilary Sandoval, Jr., of El Paso, who would head the Small Business Administration and Brownie Trevino of Dallas, who would maintain influence in the party for many years. Others, such as Bocho Garcia in South Texas, would help Tower again in future campaigns before seeking elective office on a non-partisan basis, becoming mayor of Bishop.

In the spring of 1965, the Legislature undertook congressional redistricting, prompted by a Federal court. With their overwhelming advantage, the conservative Democrats sought to protect their incumbents while minimizing GOP opportunities. Their foremost effort, known as "Plan A," was an abominable gerrymander which completely ignored the principle of community of interest. It fragmented Dallas and Tarrant Counties into a meandering district running all the way to Houston. It divided the Permian Basin counties of Midland and Ector, running Ector some 300 miles southeast to San Antonio.

In response to such chicanery, Bill Cassin, the cagey GOP attorney from Houston who argued and won the original suit and appeal, headed a special task force which supervised the tedious task of redrawing the lines into an equitable plan, using the desirable standards of equal population, compactness, and community of interest. The plan was presented as House Bill 734 by Representative Frank Cahoon, the lone GOP member. "The Republican Plan," as it came to be known, received favorable treatment by the news media, including front page coverage by *The Houston Chronicle* and *The Fort Worth Star-Telegram*. Soon after the plan was presented, *The San Antonio Light* ran an in-depth study of the Republican Plan as opposed to Plan A, under a heading "Strong Support" for the Republican plan which "satisfies so many objections which have been voiced about others submitted to the 59th Legislature that it might find strong support, at least in the House." Such was wishful thinking. In the redistricting process, partisanship and protecting incumbents supercede all other considerations. Nonetheless, the GOP plan served a valuable purpose in demonstrating to the news media and the voting public of Texas that the Republicans, unlike the ruling Democrats, could devise an equitable plan that managed to divide the state's great diversity into relatively compact districts that recognized economic communities of interest.

In addition to Cassin, the Republican Redistricting Committee included Houston attorney Sidney Buchanan who served on the legal staff with Cassin on the suit; Midland County Judge Barbara Culver, State GOP Committeeman Jim Garvey of Fort Worth, former State Representative Dick Morgan of Dallas, and Bexar County GOP Chairman Frates Seeligson, a former member of the Legislature.

Morgan described Plan A as a "gerrymander drawn up in a private room marked 'establishment Democrats only.' In those closed-door sessions, they concocted a reapportionment plan which is an atrocity — a plan so blatant a gerrymander that I am amazed at their audacity in presenting it for legislative consideration."

Such heated rhetoric made the issue also of value to the party as a rallying point for the troops who saw the ruling Democratic faction as oppressive, worth opposing with all they could muster in the next election.

Cahoon took his role in stride, knowing his chances of passage were nil, but he noted that a plan by moderate Democratic Representative Skeet Richardson of Fort Worth was similar to his regarding the Metroplex and much more equitable in general than Plan A.

Cahoon's plan generated fireworks when he presented it on the floor of the House. It received sharp criticism from some Democrats, with Representative Gene Hendryx of Alpine leading the attack. Hendryx charged that "the Republicans have chosen to walk the pathways of political sin and as far as I'm concerned, they can follow in the footsteps of their glorious leaders, tricky Dick Nixon and Barry Goldwater, and go to political hell in style ... They apparently drew up this plan by the light of the moon when they circled the wagons ... "He termed the bill a "sham" designed by a "highly vocal small minority to gerrymander the vast majority of the people of Texas."

With hoots, jeers and taunts ringing in his ears, Cahoon inquired of Speaker Ben Barnes, "Does the Alpine representative know that he called 47.9 percent of his constituents stupid?"

State Representative Howard Green of Fort Worth, a lifelong Democrat, rose on personal privilege to defend Cahoon. "Let him who is without political sin, cast the first speech," he intoned. "All my life I have resented those instances when an entrenched political order would jump on a lonely underdog. It does no honor to our party, especially when we have such overwhelming control of the Legislature, to accuse our sole opponent here of political sin. We are not entirely without it ourselves ... Frank Cahoon belongs to the Republican Party and he is a gentleman." Upon conclusion, Green drew long, loud applause and a handshake from "Lonesome Frank," who wasn't accustomed to receiving open support from Democrats.

Cahoon had taken a lot of flak from some of the Democrats but he kept his composure and his stinger out for opportunities to retaliate. One of those came along when he found out by chance that Speaker heir apparent Gus Mutscher was enjoying a long weekend in the Bahamas as the guest of a prominent lobbyist. Since this was occurring during a legislative session, Cahoon tipped the GOP state headquarters from where the information was relayed, unattributed to Cahoon, to *The Houston Post* state capitol Bureau. *The Post* broke the story on its front page the following day, much to the consternation of an embarrassed Mutscher, who tried in vain to determine who had blown the whistle on him.

By late June of 1965, Tower's posturing and incessant activity in Washington and Texas were beginning to produce results. A column appeared on the editorial page of *The Austin American-Statesman* by David Hearne, a state capitol correspondent who analyzed the forthcoming Senate race with a warning for complacent potential Democratic challengers who considered Tower an easy target.

> The diminutive senator has been running hard since election returns came in last November. His campaign has been stepped up in recent months with numerous appearances in the Lone Star state. He has appeared at every sort of function from official meetings to AFL – CIO conferences.
> The flood of handouts [press releases] from Tower's office in Washington in past days almost inundated newsmens' desks.

Hearne pointed to Tower's incumbency and such stands as retention of Section 14-b, with which Connally and the Texas Legislature agreed heartily, and to the conclusion that Tower "is a stronger campaigner than some think."

> ... Tower's mellifluous voice is familiar to Texans in his radio reports to the homefolk. He has the special knack of speaking without apparent notes in his increasing public appearances, and an easy, reasoning way of handling the public issues and nagging reporters' questions.
>
> In short, Tower is much more than an apparition. Democrats may find he is more wolf than woof.

Tower was also the beneficiary of the renewed fractious feud between Connally and Ralph Yarborough that LBJ had capped for the 1964 election. On a number of matters in addition to Section 14-b, Connally and Tower were in agreement. Because of the feud, Connally and his key aides sometimes found it more efficient to work with Tower's office on various matters involving the governor and the Senate. Ned Curran of *The Austin American-Statesman* wrote from Washington in late September, devoting a whole column to the "Tower – Connally union" which he described as a "marriage of convenience ..." After reviewing a great deal of cooperation between the two, he wrote, "In sum, the state's Republican senator appears to be much more compatible with the Democratic administration in Austin than the Democratic senator, or the Democratic President in some instances."

By year's end, Connally and Ralph Yarborough were firing those hot charges at one another again. Yarborough contended that the Connally-dominated SDEC had supported his Republican opponent, George Bush, in 1964. To which Connally responded, "That is a wild and irresponsible statement, obviously untrue ... In fact, the Democratic Party was so strong that we even carried Yarborough back into office in a hotly contested race."

Part of Tower's unspoken "moderating" process was to distance himself from such controversial right-wing groups as the John Birch Society, which had been a prime target of Rockefeller, Scranton, et al during 1964. In the fall of 1965, Tower was quoted as saying he believed the Birch Society was a liability to the conservative cause. That stirred some hard feelings among strong grass roots conservatives who weren't members of the Birch Society but believed it had been used as a whipping boy to discredit conservatives, particularly Goldwater. In any event, the posturing by Tower continued to be effective as he weaved his way through various challenges.

Throughout the 1965 Washington scene, Tower became more prominent as a spokesman for the military and its needs in Vietnam. His role as a filibuster leader to retain the Taft – Hartley right-to-work provision was certainly a strong asset as the year neared an end. And, there seemed to be a subjective concern about lopsided one-party control that was developing in Tower's favor — but it was difficult to measure.

As Tower looked toward his reelection campaign, two Republican hopefuls from 1964 were gearing up for congressional races — George Bush in a newly created Houston district and Bob Price, the Pampa rancher, for a rematch against incumbent Walter Rogers for the Panhandle seat. With no viable statewide options available to him and with the need to make a race in order to maintain his momentum from 1964, Bush opted for the congressional race for the open seat with a basically conservative constituency. Price had run a credible race against Rogers in 1964 and he, too, believed momentum could be regenerated.

Fund-raising efforts in 1965 were extensive with Paul DesRochers, the finance director at the state party headquarters, distributing high-impact brochures dealing with Tower's valuable service to the state and the crucial need for the party to retain him as its rallying point in Texas. Several successful fund-raising dinners were held during the year, including one in Houston commemorating Tower's fortieth birthday on September 29, at which Senator George Murphy of California was the featured speaker, and one in Dallas on November 4, which featured Richard Nixon.

Late in 1965, O'Donnell decided it was important to make a tour of the key urban areas of the state to determine grass roots strength and to present the troops with the strategic game plan for reelecting Tower. On a twenty-two city tour, he would lead the delegation which would include Marvin Collins, the party executive director and Jim Leonard, Tower's campaign manager who had managed the campaigns of Cox in 1962 and Bush in 1964. Leonard had an elaborate slide presentation prepared that extolled the virtues of Tower and his incumbency, and his value to Texas and Texans in general, avoiding the conservative movement or the Republican Party. The other speakers explained why and how the emphasis on Tower's race was necessary, how the organizational program would be conducted and what might be expected from the opposition.

In plausible if not inspiring terms, O'Donnell surmised that the Democratic opponent, whomever he might be, would hit Tower as being "negative, ineffective and Republican." Therefore, Tower and his campaign must preempt that as much as possible by portraying a positive, effective role with bipartisan support.

Reaction was mixed, and not particularly encouraging in most areas where the grass roots turnout was moderate to meager. Whatever progress Tower and the party had made during 1965 had not regenerated anything remotely resembling the enthusiasm that had been evident for Goldwater. Morale remained low and there was some sniping that Tower had "moderated" with questions as to why the word "conservative" was no longer used in promoting Tower. But as the gravity of the situation soaked in, ideological considerations yielded somewhat to pragmatic politics. They were confronted with the proposition that, "If we lose John Tower, for whatever reason, there's no more rallying point for the conservative movement in Texas. Period." It was a sobering proposition for those in attendance who had weathered the crushing 1964 defeat, and were trying to get motivated to sally forth once more. Many of their comrades from 1964 had given up after that election. Some of them would never return to a Republican campaign. Others would resurface later on for George Wallace.

Those who signed up in 1965 for Tower's 1966 campaign composed the bedrock.

CHAPTER FIVE

From the Breach Unscathed

Early in 1966, center stage belonged to Congressman Jim Wright of Fort Worth, who appeared to be gearing up for the Senate race. He had made a statewide telecast in mid-December, appealing for support and campaign contributions but stopped short of announcing his candidacy. Though he would receive substantial contributions as a result of the televised speech, he decided against making the race, leaving the Democratic nomination virtually assured to Waggoner Carr, a key figure in the conservative Democratic establishment who had formally announced his candidacy on September 18, 1965. Carr had become restless, not wanting to sit another two years as attorney general. His gubernatorial ambitions were well known in Austin. But to contest Connally would have meant political suicide so he had revised his career plan, shifting toward a campaign for the Senate.

Republican strategists had hoped for a divisive Democratic Primary that would divert attention from Tower until summer, leaving him free to take the high road while serving his constituents in Washington. Wright's withdrawal quashed that hope, but Carr soon found the issue orientation of the race was not shaping up all that well for him. Tower's positions on Vietnam and right-to-work were squarely on target with conservative-minded Texans, many of whom were Democrats who had supported Carr in the past. Further, economists were beginning to express concern about LBJ's "guns and butter" policy of escalating the Vietnam War while enacting many new social welfare programs. Inflation and higher prices were developing, not a happy sign for a Democratic United States Senate candidate whose party controlled the White House and both houses of Congress. Nonetheless, Carr's strategists believed that Democratic partisanship, with its long-standing tradition and appeal throughout the vast network of officeholders and political operatives around the state, would overpower the "fluke" senator from the vastly outnumbered minority party with little political clout beyond his office. Their strategy would work if they could maintain the united Democratic Party that was evident in Texas during 1964.

Tower's candidacy for reelection — which had been taken for granted — was made formally on February 7, in the state capitol. As expected, Tower bore down on incumbency when he stated, "This evening I will return to Washington. As you know, I am a debate leader in the continuing fight to save our state's right-to-work law. In addition, the Armed Services Committee, on which I represent Texas, has a great deal more work to do in seeing that our fighting men receive everything they need in their confrontation with Asiatic communism." And to the matter of effectiveness, "I have worked to establish an influential position among Senators and on important Senate committees, in order that I might better serve the State. I seek reelection in the hope this seniority and this influence can be retained for Texas ..."

In subsequent speeches to supporters around Texas, Tower would repeat, in measured tones, those nonpartisan thrusts. Then he'd bear down on the tremendous challenge of the campaign, always closing in a dramatic fashion with his call to arms, *Once more unto the breach dear friends, once more ...* gleaned from Shakespeare's *King Henry V*.

Al Fay decided to run against Jerry Sadler, the incumbent land commissioner who had become controversial for such things as snubbing reporters and making supposedly public information inaccessible to them. Fay's candidacy, which he stated would not be token, was not considered to be in violation of the "Tower only" statewide strategy since Sadler wouldn't draw any heavy support from Connally and others. T. E. Kennerly, a Houston attorney and lifelong Republican, agreed to "run" for governor, his role actually being to file and stay on the ballot but not attempt to contest Connally. Kellis Dibrell filled a similar role as the GOP candidate for lieutenant governor.

Ronnie Dugger, editor of The Texas Observer, made some motions toward running for the Senate as an independent — a potentially dangerous problem for Carr had he carried it out — but Dugger decided against trying to make such a difficult race. Thus, the Senate race settled down to Tower versus Carr, except for a minor challenge in the Democratic Primary to Carr by Jack Willoughby of Houston. For the first time in memory there was no hot statewide primary contest to liven up things in the spring and the Tower – Carr race would be the only major statewide contest in the fall. Not much action for a political arena that had been host to so many spirited contests over the previous election years. Add to that the fact that both candidates were avowed conservatives and it would appear to be a ho hum affair in prospect. But political activists and writers would be treated to a year filled with intrigue and a sharp division in the state's majority party.

Hungry for some action after that long hangover from 1964, the State GOP headquarters found a way to utilize 1964 canvass results in early 1966 in order to retune organizational procedures. It was a local, nonpartisan election in Austin for a school board seat sought by a prominent GOP leader, Mrs. Bob (Sitty) Wilkes. Because of her well-known party affiliation, she was virtually written off early on by political observers since the Democratic ticket had swamped the Republicans in the previous election and no GOP candidate had ever carried the city. Plus, the news media didn't hesitate to remind voters of her party affiliation, from which she didn't shy away. With the assistance of Carlton Suiter, organization director for the state headquarters, the Wilkes Campaign projected low voter turnout, thus little need for mass media advertising. Canvass cards, derived from the door-to-door effort for Goldwater in 1964, were used to locate favorable voters who would be encouraged by phone and direct mail to turn out on election day. With a low-budget campaign that included limited last-minute advertising, Sitty Wilkes won the election, proving again that under fairly favorable general conditions, the organizational procedures would still pay off on election day.

Major strategic decisions were made early in 1966 as to how best Tower could meet the challenge. A "soft sell" was adopted to promote such basic themes as these: "it's advantageous for Texas to have a senator from each party; Tower, with his key committee assignments, had already acquired valuable seniority for Texas; and that Tower, the individual, is effective, responsible, and votes the way most Texans would want him to vote." The Rives – Dyke Advertising Agency of Houston, was assigned the task to get this message to the public, with Bob Heller as account executive, along with Jim Culberson, an excellent still photographer – graphics designer. A thirty-minute television documentary was produced about Vietnam and sponsored by an ad hoc committee. Weaving Tower into the program in a news, rather than campaign format, made the film particularly effective in the spring when no formal campaign was underway. A rotogravure, or newspaper supplement, was produced that portrayed Tower in a pictorially strong manner through twelve pages, with strong color pictures on the front and back. On the front, Tower appeared walking from the capitol in Washington with a large caption reading "The presence of Senator John Tower in Washington gives Texas the distinct advantage of having its voice heard in the highest leadership councils of both parties" with TOWER, WASHINGTON, and TEXAS in large red capital letters and the other copy in smaller black upper and lower case letters. This was the only way the Tower Campaign would use his party affiliation in a positive manner, the notion that having Tower, the Republican, helped Texas because he could muster votes on that side of the aisle, cooperating with his Democratic colleague on matters of vital interest to the state. It was a dull, unemotional issue about which voters must make a subjective judgement, but it was a means to elevate Tower from the campaign that was sure to come from Carr, stressing the need for another Democrat "who would be more effective" with the Democratic congressional delegation and, of course, the President. But the supplement was nonpartisan, mostly an image piece that didn't even mention the election. Inside, Tower appeared with such luminaries as former President Eisenhower, President Johnson, and Senator Dirksen. Two pages were devoted to Tower on the scene in Vietnam, and the center spread contained a wide picture of the senator with his wife, Lou, and their three daughters, Jeanne, Penny, and Marian. The family, including Tower's parents, were featured on two other pages, and still two more pages were devoted to Tower in various scenes around Texas, including one picture of Tower on a platform with Governor Connally. This was an image piece, if one were ever produced, and the "roto," as it came to be known in the Tower – State GOP scheme of things, was considered a centerpiece of the early stage of the campaign. About 1.7 million of the rotos were distributed with the smallest possible legal "paid political" disclaimers in Sunday editions during May and June in the twenty-six metro-urban markets of Texas in which some eighty percent of the population resided. Feedback was received from all over the state that many people were pleasantly surprised to see their local newspaper carry such a fine feature section on the senator. In addition, the state headquarters staff took the press kit — which contained a biographical sketch and pictures of Tower plus a summary of his legislative record — added a few more pictures, and more copy, and converted it into a black and white booklet, lending itself to a unique distribution system. Through the work of Nola Smith of Austin, medical and dental auxiliaries were contacted to place the booklet in waiting rooms, where the sturdy stock on which it was printed allowed it to be glanced through many times before being replaced. The newspaper supplement and the booklet were unusual because they didn't mention an election nor ask for a vote. They were strictly "soft sell" image pieces for Tower as an effective senator and they seemed to buoy the spirits of the grass roots Republicans who, beyond urban Texas, dug deep to sponsor the supplement in their local papers and who expanded the booklet distribution in rural areas to any places people gather, such as gas stations, barbershops, beauty salons, and drugstores.

Also in the spring, the state party produced a two-party brochure that proved to be valuable as the year unfolded, and support developed among young students and disenchanted liberal Democrats.

Above a picture of former President Eisenhower with Senator Tower, Ike was quoted:

> *Whether in America or any place else, lopsided political control is a deadly threat to a free people. Two vigorously contending political parties are our great weapon against unwisdom on high, abuse of the public trust and even tyranny, whether of the benevolent or police state variety.*

The copy continued:

> One-party government says one thing at campaign time, but does another or goes to sleep on the job after the election ... You can't take a party to task for its platform and programs unless you have two strong parties competing for the right to serve you. No longer will a candidate and party be able to come before the people without telling them what they have in mind for the present and future. The Texas Republican Party is young, dynamic and growing. The door is open to all who want to build a better Texas through good government provided by the two-party system.

Though a partisan piece, the brochure was presented on an "institutional basis," not asking for a vote nor mentioning an election.

On board again for Tower was U.A. Hyde, serving as consultant and writer, providing guidance for courting independent conservatives and conservative Democrats, or Shivercrats. A bipartisan Tower organization, "Texans For Tower," was formed as the main umbrella committee with Fort Worth attorney Sproesser Wynn as chairman and Dudley Sharp, Sr., a Houston industrialist, as the finance chairman. Jim Leonard, Tower's campaign manager, soon began staffing up and acquired a large headquarters facility on Twelfth Street, a few blocks from the capitol. Jerry Conn, a former AP correspondent in the capitol, joined the staff as campaign press secretary and every effort was made to maximize media exposure for Tower's many trips to Texas. John de la Garza departed *The Houston Chronicle* capitol bureau to join the public relations department of the State GOP as it prepared to play a strong support role for the Tower Campaign. In the spring of 1966, the cooperation and coordination between the Tower Campaign and the State GOP was close indeed — both entities realized their fates were on the line come November 8, and every effort was made to ensure that all resources were used wisely. Weekly meetings were held in Austin every Sunday afternoon, usually in the Ransom Room of the Forty Acres Club near the campus of The University of Texas. During those meetings Tower would hold court as chairman of the board of his campaign, but O'Donnell, speaking for the State GOP, would exert strong influence for whatever course of action he might deem warranted. A few top aides from both entities attended regularly, plus volunteer operatives whenever their assigned lines of endeavor needed to be discussed, and representatives of the advertising agency and other party leaders from time to time. Major and minor decisions were hammered out at these meetings, which usually lasted three or four hours. Important, perhaps crucial, to the well-coordinated conduct of the campaign, these meetings were irritating in the fall months to those involved — including Tower — who wanted to follow the Dallas Cowboys on television. But Sunday afternoon was about the only time they could be pulled together for maximum effectiveness and least disruption to the campaign. Memos were floated constantly between the Tower and State Party people to the point that often memos weren't addressed to individuals, but to ALL CONCERNED, with distribution to the same people in the two camps.

In terms of general policy and direction, there were no deep divisions between Tower and O'Donnell, but a flap developed over Tower's campaign theme line, or slogan. Lest anyone consider that item as seemingly trivial, it's widely held in advertising circles that the theme line is one of the most important elements of a campaign. So much so that if one can't be devised that properly capsules a campaign, then it's probably better not to use one at all. The value of an effective theme line is that it helps drive home, or reinforces the central point that needs to be driven home in a relatively short period of time. An ineffective theme line may cause confusion in the minds of voters who aren't well-versed in issues and aren't likely to become so. Each thought, and each word are put under the magnifying glass of careful minds to make sure there is nothing confusing, or open to interpretation in any manner other than what's desired. In politics, the theme line may be overstated by ad agencies because most are more accustomed to selling products than politicians.

With Bob Heller, that wasn't a problem. He was an old pro with experience dating to Shivers's campaigns, and he knew the range of what needed to be portrayed throughout the campaign insofar as Tower, the individual, was concerned. But nailing down those few thoughts and words, capitalizing on incumbency to the approval of Tower and O'Donnell, would prove to be elusive. It all had started in late 1965, when a theme line suggestion was first floated within ALL CONCERNED, *John Tower works for you where it counts*. That didn't sell, and several other suggestions were tossed around in the winter and spring. On May 3, Leonard reported by memo to ALL CONCERNED, that there seemed to be a consensus developing for, *Reelect Senator John Tower — He has done a good job for Texas*. To which Friedheim responded with a memo on May 9, recognizing slogans as "tough and equally crucial," pointing out that he preferred *Vote Texan, Vote Tower*, or *Senator John Tower — Leadership in Action*. "However," Friedheim continued," if the attached suggestion [from Leonard] is to be used, it definitely should be modified to read, "He *is doing* a good job,' or 'He's good for Texas,' or 'He works for Texas.' These lend immediacy and continuity and help eliminate the made-to-order response, 'Sure, Tower *has done* an okay job, it's just that Carr can do a better job! This 'better job,' is, it seems to me, the second prong of Carr's whole attack: 1. I'm a Democrat, 2. Therefore, I can do better ... We must," Friedheim concluded, "avoid a slogan that plays into his strength and/or can be turned in our face." Friedheim's point about lending immediacy was well taken, and the camps then settled toward, *Reelect Senator John Tower — He's doing a good job for Texas*. However, someone tossed in the idea of elevating Tower's performance to a *great job*, but that was shot down as too much. *Good job* was believable, credible, sellable.

It seemed as though the problem had been solved and all material would contain that unifying theme line, but the ad agency came up with an alternative line, *Keep Tower U.S. Senator* (shortened to simply *Keep Tower* on small signs) with a theme line of *He knows his job and does it well*. Tower liked the alternate material which would appear on billboards and other materials. O'Donnell was strongly for the *Reelect* line, as were others in the state party who thought *Reelect* was a much stronger word for an incumbent then *Keep*, plus *doing a good job* seemed to have more staying power in a voter's mind than the other line: *He knows his job and does it well*, and having *for Texas* in the theme line seemed to be stronger than going without the name of the state. In any event, Tower and O'Donnell were indeed divided over the issue and it was evident in subsequent material distribution. The state party would produce a series of voter group brochures, including those for women, youths, senior citizens, Mexican-Americans, and military; plus a general appeal pro-Tower – anti-Carr brochure — total number in excess of one million pieces — all with the "Reelect" theme line. Also, the canvass brochure, an excellent piece distilled by the ad agency from the roto and used throughout urban Texas in the

GOP – Tower organizational program, contained, at the insistence of O'Donnell, the *Reelect* line. Thus, the *Keep Tower* line was used on the outdoor advertising, including billboards, and the *Reelect* line was used on virtually all printed material.

During the winter and spring of 1966, Moreno pursued his program with major results. On January 22, in Alice, back in George Parr country, some 200 South Texans, including Republicans and prospective Mexican-American converts, turned out for a barbecue to hear speeches by Tower, O'Donnell, and Fuentes, who was still state chairman of PASO. That gathering produced a highly published SREC meeting on March 14, at which Reynaldo Salinas of Benavides acted as a spokesman for more than 100 people in Duval County, who were switching to the GOP. Salinas drew a standing ovation when he announced that, "We are sick and tired of some of the things the Democratic machine has done to us in Duval County. We believe it is time to build a strong two-party system and we want to help our good friend, Senator John Tower." Tower made many appearances among M-As in the spring of 1966, including that of featured speaker before the graduating class of El Paso Technical High School on May 26, an appearance arranged by his longtime friend, Hilary Sandoval. Using his experience as an educator combined with his considerable talent as a speaker, Tower drew several ovations, including a teary-eyed standing ovation upon closing from the proud Mexican-American parents, who were indeed delighted to have a United States senator for that most special occasion.

On the legislative front, Tower was gaining a reputation among M-As for his support of military and defense programs, including better pay for civilians employed on bases. This had a strong appeal at the grass roots and Tower pleased the leadership by introducing a bill in May to increase the size of the Equal Employment Opportunity Commission (EEOC) in order that Mexican-Americans "might get a fair shake."

For the canvass program, O'Donnell and Collins had devised a "Tower Early Bird" plan for taking advantage of the longer daylight evening hours and less competition with football and other school-related activities in the fall. The plan also provided for more time to recontact those households found to be favorable toward Tower — or undecided. It was a hot summer of sweaty brows for the dedicated volunteers, couples, and teams that canvassed for Tower door-to-door, but that early spadework would prove to be invaluable in what would become the final such extensive door-to-door canvass on a statewide basis. Bibb Falk, the crusty former baseball coach at The University of Texas, once remarked in the 1950s that television and air conditioning would spell the doom of minor league baseball. He might have added door-to-door political canvassing.

O'Donnell's organizational theories and practices had been gleaned from organized labor's COPE manual and a political organization handbook published by the Chamber of Commerce. He tailored those as he gathered considerable experience from precinct work to presidential campaigns. His programs were not difficult to understand, but success depended upon skillful recruitment of the right people for the right slots, not always easy when considering the tremendous amount of volunteer work that was entailed.

O'Donnell had a few cryptic axioms he would bandy about to nail down a point. He believed primaries should be conducted in as many precincts as possible. "The more buckets you put out, the more rain you catch." If an established procedure was under unwarranted challenge, "Don't reinvent the wheel." When anyone approached him about planning the initial stage of a campaign, he'd say, "In the beginning, there was money." O'Donnell's axioms about established procedures and campaign financing were obviously foremost in his mind for the Tower Campaign.

In addition to the regular party organizations, Beryl Milburn was named to head "Womanpower For Tower," a strong statewide group that provided valuable campaign support. Her effective program helped her become president of the Texas Federation of Republican Women the following year. There wasn't much that could be done regarding building interest in the GOP primary. With no statewide contests and few at the local level, only 50,000 bothered to vote. The spring of 1966 had been so quiet that almost 100,000 who had voted in the 1964 primary were "no-shows" in 1966. The Democratic side had a similar problem. In mid-May, Bo Byers pointed out in *The Houston Chronicle* that the "pathetically low total vote of 1,228,000 for the Democratic Primary should be a danger signal to Carr ... It could portend a meager turnout in November that would weigh heavily in Tower's favor ..."

Tower and O'Donnell were united in their efforts to offset the propaganda value of adverse polling results being reported by Joe Belden whose periodic "Texas Poll" results were carried by many of the state's major newspapers. Belden's results started hurting in September of 1965, when he reported a hypothetical Carr – Tower race at fifty-seven percent Carr, thirty percent Tower, and thirteen percent undecided. In December of 1965, he found the same matchup as forty-eight percent Carr, thirty-two percent Tower and ten percent undecided. Leonard, who had retained John Kraft of New York for polling George Bush's 1964 campaign, retained Kraft for Tower. In May of 1966, Kraft reported it stood at forty-four percent for Tower, thirty-nine percent for Carr — balance undecided.

That same month, Belden reported it fifty-seven percent Carr, thirty-three percent Tower — balance undecided. Lance Tarrance, who would ultimately set up his own polling firm, was research director for the State GOP and kept close tabs on Belden. Tarrance produced fact sheets for the party, entitled "VIM" sheets (Very Important Material) that delved into various subjects. His VIM sheet on Belden quoted several sources, including former Attorney General Will Wilson, denouncing Belden for what Wilson branded as producing "a standard propaganda device in Texas politics." O'Donnell had pointed to several instances in which Belden's final poll results shortly before an election were nowhere near what the voting actually reflected. Tower released the Kraft results in May, receiving widespread newspaper coverage that was crucial for the morale of his supporters during a period when they had to become mentally conditioned to go out and do the hard canvassing work, while others raised the funds necessary to sustain his race and the party organization. Time and again, O'Donnell would express publicly and privately to Tower supporters that he suspected Belden was more interested in molding opinion than measuring it. And when canvass results started coming in, O'Donnell knew that in the strong conservative base areas across urban Texas, where voter turnout would be highest in the fall, Tower was running consistently ahead of Carr. Tower had conducted an essentially positive campaign through the spring, low-keyed as were his campaign materials. O'Donnell seemed to relish his role as the partisan and needled Carr constantly. He found that referring to Carr's gubernatorial ambitions was a subject the news media seemed to enjoy. At the Dallas County GOP convention, O'Donnell was quoted in a UPI story that Carr would be no more than "a two- year senator whose eyes would be glued to Austin" if he won. "The real reason Waggoner Carr refuses to discuss significant issues is the fact that he does not want to say anything now which might be used against him when he runs for governor in 1968 ... Last year Carr's timetable called for an advance and his long state political career had been aimed for the governor's chair," O'Donnell said. "But he backed away when Governor Connally announced for reelection." O'Donnell also hit Carr hard for his criticism of Tower having gone to Vietnam. Carr had said he found it "strange" that Tower "never thought it important enough to go before he announced for reelection, but has been twice since." In a *Houston Chronicle* article of May 5, O'Donnell said Tower visited South Vietnam as early as 1961 at his own expense. "I'd like to remind Mr. Carr that Senator Tower has stated time and again that Vietnam is no political football ... Carr's inaccurate statement is bad enough, but the implication conveyed is worse — that the Armed Services Commit-

tee of the United States is playing politics with American lives in Vietnam."
Carr's criticism of Tower for going to Vietnam was one of the true strategic
errors of his campaign, pointing out the weakness of a candidate whose
only grounding was in state politics moving into a national – international issue of such sensitivity. Most people, including many in the news
media, believed Tower had not only the right but the responsibility to
go to Vietnam since he was a member of the Armed Services Committee.
Carr also seemed to slip a bit when discussing the 14-b right-to-work
issue when he said he thought "the matter ought to be left to the people
of Texas." No doubt all conservatives would agree to that, but it appeared to be an uninformed statement since the issue was before Congress, and that if he were elected, he might be in the thick of it with
a colleague, Ralph Yarborough, on the other side. But Carr was trapped
on that crucial issue since Tower had taken it for his own. Yet Carr had
to side with Tower. It caused a difficult situation for Carr with Al Barkan,
national director of COPE, Committee on Political Education, the political arm of the AFL – CIO. When Carr told Barkan he would support
organized labor on many issues but not 14-b, Barkan reportedly replied,
"that sounded like telling an oilman you'd be with him on everything
but the depletion allowance." And in Texas, Carr's support of right-to-
work made it easier for labor leaders inclined to help Tower to tell their
brethren concerning the Carr – Tower race, "A pox on both their houses."
At Scholz Beer Garten, liberal activists dusted off the old line from 1961,
that the choice was between "Tweedledum and Tweedledee." Plus, someone coined a new one, "This choice is between arsenic and strychnine."
In the early summer *The Texas Observer* commented,

> It's too early to get excited about Tower vs. Carr. Let those two
> time-tested reactionaries do the best they can to persuade the more
> enlightened voters to their side ... the longer they jockey for the sup-
> port of the liberal folk the better, since all either of them can do is
> move to the left — if either moved any further right he'd fall off the
> cliff."

The Observer had developed a habit of hounding Carr. In May of 1962,
an editorial detailed Carr's record as Speaker of the House, in summation
stating that, "Carr served the gas lobby, the supporters of the general
sales tax, the lobbyists who were watering down the lobby control law,
and the segregationists."

Carr plugged away at his central theme of effectiveness, that Tower
couldn't get much done and he, as a Democrat, could accomplish more
for the state. Playing to the party faithful was probably his best pitch,
but the question of Democratic defection was becoming evident. Tower

seemed to have a great deal moving his way the summer of 1966 until June 26, when disaster struck.

It was a late afternoon news conference in Houston and Tower was weary from several days on the campaign trail sandwiched with his work in Washington. It was also one of those news conferences that lasted too long, when a mistake is more likely to be made. Tower was asked about the plight of farm workers in the Rio Grande Valley who were seeking a minimum wage of $1.25 per hour, a question he'd been asked many times and had answered with a sense of balance and sensitivity. But when the question was pursued, Tower, as quoted in a UPI dispatch, said that, "The question of whether people can live on eighty-five cents an hour is not the point ... The point is, eighty-five cents an hour is better than nothing." Tower elaborated on food prices, the President's plea for housewives not to buy certain allegedly overpriced items, but when the "eighty-five cents an hour is better than nothing" quote winged across the wires, AP having filed a similar story, the pressure was on. Tower's Senate and campaign offices received some antagonistic phone calls, plus calls from friends and supporters who wanted to know what in the world could be done to soften the damage. The liberal-labor leaders who were quietly helping Tower, always in a delicate situation at best, were suddenly slammed against the wall. Ken Towery quickly wrote a carefully worded letter from Tower to Hank Brown, president of the Texas AFL – CIO, sidestepping and softening as best it could be done. The letter was widely publicized, at the leadership level, unruffling feathers fairly well, but Tower had provided Carr with some badly needed ammunition that he would use from time to time over the course of the campaign.

During the summer, campaign funds were tight and very little was done outside what had been budgeted originally; however, an innovative opportunity came along that was too good to ignore. Dave Campbell's *Texas Football* magazine, the Bible for the state's legions of rabid fans, offered a full-page ad adjacent to the table of contents, a coveted spot. But it was an expensive item outside the budget, leaving it apparently as a lost cause until Marvin Collins and the state headquarters staff decided to raise the money by seeking endorsements for Tower from former Southwest Conference stars. Tower supporter Weldon Smith, an oilman from Houston and avid football fan, agreed to serve as chairman of an ad hoc group known as "Boosters For Tower Committee," which sponsored the ad containing an action picture of Tower walking alone, taken directly in front of a camera. Some of the great names from the various SWC schools in the state (Houston had not yet entered the SWC at that time) appeared among a list of eighty-two players under a headline of UNI-

TED STATES SENATOR JOHN TOWER – A PROVEN WINNER FOR TEXAS, with a subheadline, "These proven winners urge you to join the lineup backing Senator John Tower's reelection campaign." Of special note were all-American Donny Anderson of Texas Tech, leading the alphabetized list that included Matty Bell, the revered former coach at SMU; Bill Glass, all-American at Baylor and a lay religious leader; Dallas Cowboys' Coach Tom Landry, already highly respected as an individual citizen as well as a coach; all-American Bobby Layne, the legendary quarterback at Texas and in the pros; Bob Lilly, TCU all-American who would become one of the all-time great Cowboys; and Froggy Williams, one of the favored Rice names of yesteryear. A political activist once said something like "You can take all the polls you want, but the best judge of your effectiveness is when you hear your opposition scream." Word in Lubbock, Carr's hometown, and in Austin, where such things were discussed, was that the football ad had a strong adverse impact on Carr's campaign. Donny Anderson was probably the best liked personality in Lubbock at the time, coming off an all-American season and preparing for a pro career at Green Bay. For him to endorse the opponent of the hometown candidate was a bitter pill indeed. The support of all the other well-known players, plus the renowned Landry, put Tower's campaign a little beyond the political context. For Weldon Smith and all others who put the ad together, it was a pleasure to see such names associated with Tower's campaign. It was a move that generated positive feedback among the grass roots supporters around the state.

After months of campaigning with attendant analysis, it was becoming clear in the summer to astute political observers that the pivotal battlegrounds of the race would probably be among the liberals and Mexican-Americans. Positions on the major issues had long been taken and forces were in progress that would more or less determine how most conservative Texans would vote, but leadership ranks among liberals and M-As were sharply divided, with the two-party system at issue. A classic confrontation occurred in a debate in Austin between Archer Fullingim, editor of the *Kountze News* in East Texas, and a longtime Ralph Yarborough supporter, and State Senator A. R. (Babe) Schwartz of Galveston, whose liberal-party loyalist credentials had long been established. According to an article in the *Fort Worth Star Telegram*, Fullingim said that by defeating Carr and reelecting Tower, liberal Democrats would defeat the conservative element in the Democratic Party, forcing it to move over and vote in future Republican primaries. To which Schwartz countered, "You can't force conservatives out of the Democratic party by voting against them. What you have to do is build a strong liberal element which will elect a liberal nominee in the primary." Fullingim said he couldn't accept Schwartz's "weird theory that the way the Democrats can strengthen their party in Texas is to eliminate the Republican Party so the Republicans will have to vote for conservatives in the Democratic primaries ... We [liberals] do not have to follow the suicidal course of continuing loyalty to the Democratic Party. We owe no loyalty to a name ... We owe loyalty to the philosophies of the National Democratic Party — not to the Democratic Party in Texas, which is nothing more than a group of lackeys for every big business interest in Texas."

Soon thereafter, *The Fort Worth Star-Telegram* observed in an editorial that read in part,

> Texas politics is in its usual form this year — wacky. It is the same but different.
>
> The liberal Democrats, erstwhile champions of strict party loyalty and party-line voting, seem to have a 'thing' for a conservative Republican — U.S. Senator John Tower ... and Senator Tower, darling of the rightist Americans for Constitutional Action and at least a dim prospect for GOP vice-presidential nominee, appears highly receptive to this liberal support, or in some cases, non-opposition. After all, it is better to have two wings in an election campaign than only one. When it comes to getting reelected, a vote is a vote is a vote ...

About that same time Ralph Yarborough, the senior senator and very much the top liberal leader in the state, again sent a signal — as he had in 1961. He was quoted as saying to supporters that, "I'm going to make as many speeches for Waggoner Carr in his campaign as he's made for me in my seven statewide campaigns," drawing laughter from the faithful. Yarborough said he had always voted the straight ticket, but that regarding patronage matters, Tower had been "very decent ... I have no personal (bad) feeling about Tower. As a matter of fact, I sort of like him."

Given all that, there was indeed a favorable climate for liberal activism against Carr. Its propaganda thrust came from an ad hoc group known as The Democratic Rebuilding Committee whose theme line was "Sometimes party loyalty asks too much," a quote from John F. Kennedy speaking about the Massachusetts Democratic Party. "Nothing can be done," Kennedy said, "until it is beaten ... badly beaten. Then there will be a chance for *rebuilding*." Those quotes, gleaned from a book by Arthur Schlesinger, Jr., entitled *A Thousand Days*, formed the basis from which this group would attack. Activists included Chuck Caldwell and Dave Shapiro, who had promoted Tower's election in 1961, plus Larry Goodwyn, one of the intellectuals who wrote for *The Texas Observer*. In addition to

the major argument for a two-party system based upon conservatives ultimately voting in the Republican Primary, this group went after all sorts
of political sins, including their distribution of a picture of Carr at a
segregationist rally and newspaper reprints about Carr's support for the
poll tax. Suitable for handouts or mailings, these one- page pieces were
known as flyers, or, in the parlance at Scholz Beer Garten, smear sheets.
The Rebuilding Committee also produced a bumper sticker with bold
letters proclaiming THIS CAR NOT FOR CARR, with a sub-line of,
"Sometimes party loyalty asks too much." But for the most emotional
appeal, they chose a picture of Father Antonio Gonzales, the Catholic
priest who was one of the leaders of the Valley Farm Workers March,
brandishing a crucifix toward Connally, Carr, and others who had met
the marchers near New Braunfels.

Under a hot August sun, the farm workers had been marching from
the Rio Grande Valley toward Austin with a target date of arriving at
the state capitol grounds on Labor Day. This 400 mile march had generated a tremendous amount of publicity, dramatizing the workers' call
for a $1.25 an hour state minimum wage. When the marchers had reached
New Braunfels, Connally, Carr, and a few other Democratic officials paid
them a visit which turned into something of a confrontation. A picture
was taken, showing Father Gonzales brandishing a crucifix at the politicians, who were not in support of the workers' cause. That picture was
widely distributed by the two-party liberals who alleged that Connally
and Carr were against a decent living wage for the workers. Though Connally was opposed to the minimum wage, there was some question whether
the liberal-labor element might apply sufficient pressure to secure a plank
in the Democratic State Convention platform, a move that would have
helped Carr tremendously. But neither party endorsed the minimum wage
per se, recognizing only that wages for farm workers should be higher.
That issue caused the only bit of friction for the GOP convention in San
Antonio. The platform committee, chaired by former State Representative
Dick Morgan of Dallas, heard extensive testimony from both sides on
the minimum wage issue, including remarks by Roy Evans, secretary-
treasurer of the Texas AFL – CIO, who was widely rumored to be sympa-
thetic to Tower's candidacy. But counter-pressure came from Tower's basic
conservative supporters, who saw no need to "out-Democrat the Democrats." The consensus hammered out was to express concern for farm
income and workers' wages, but refrain from taking a specific stand on
the $1.25 per hour proposal. With that issue resolved, the convention
became essentially a pep rally for Tower, who delivered the keynote speech.
Tower had surmised correctly — and early on — that Carr's major strategic

thrust would be to try to make the contest a partisan fight, which would, of course, work greatly to Carr's favor.

"My opponent," Tower told some 2,000 cheering Republicans in the Municipal Auditorium, "is trying desperately to divide the people of Texas on the basis of party versus party. He is failing in that effort ... The man who wins election to the United States Senate from Texas will not win because he is a member of a certain political party, but because he is the candidate who measures up in the eyes of Texas as the man who can serve Texas best ..."

Carr needed unity on his side, but it wasn't in the cards. The Texas Democrats had a stormy session in Austin, where about 200 liberals walked out, some of them shouting, "To hell with John Connally." They marched from the Municipal Auditorium on Town Lake up Congress Avenue to the capitol grounds where they passed a resolution favoring the minimum wage and one approving the idea of voting for Tower in November, though it stopped short of outright advocacy.

As Tower prepared for the stretch run of his campaign, three Republican congressional candidates were bearing down with chances to win. In the new Seventh District in Houston, George Bush was pulling ahead of Frank Briscoe, a strong conservative Democrat who had been a popular district attorney. Bush had the considerable benefit of superb campaign management from his old friend, Jim Allison, who hailed from Midland where Bush had been in the oil business.

Bob Price had an unusual break occur in his second contest with incumbent Walter Rogers for the Panhandle seat. With no advance warning or indication, Rogers withdrew from the race by sending letters to his supporters around the district over a weekend in August. Price's campaign manager, Jim Campbell of Pampa, was tipped off before the story was made public and summoned Price from a church service in order to brief him. Campbell contacted Tower and O'Donnell who were gathering at the Forty Acres Club in Austin for a weekly meeting. They discussed the matter with staff people, arriving at a consensus that Price should praise Rogers for his long service to the Panhandle and for withstanding arm-twisting by LBJ, implying a freshman Democrat couldn't possibly withstand the arm-twisting. That approach was used, rather than one suggested in the Panhandle that Price chide Rogers for quitting and for having been too susceptible to LBJ's liberal initiatives. Stunned Democrats scrambled to get Dee Miller, an Amarillo attorney, as their replacement but Price had the momentum, picking up support from many former Rogers backers before Miller could get organized.

In Dallas, Jim Collins had mounted a competitive campaign against incumbent Joe Pool, but Pool had a fairly strong conservative voting record that was hard for Collins to attack effectively and most observers gave the edge to Pool.

Facing the final crucial weeks of the campaign, Tower and his operatives worked hard to utilize resources to the maximum in reaching those people and places most likely to yield the most votes. Tower's campaign became a scheduling nightmare as he would move about in one part of the state, fulfilling tight campaign schedules while his attractive and energetic wife, Lou, would be conducting a bus tour in some other region. At times two aircraft, a DC-3 and a Twin Beach, would be in use along with a bus to accommodate the Tower Campaign, including staff and volunteers plus travelling political writers. The aircraft were slow but maneuverable, and easy to land on most airstrips. Bus tours were used in those parts of the state, such as East Texas and the Lower Rio Grande Valley, where clusters of towns could be reached more efficiently by ground transportation. Smartly costumed "Tower Belles," women volunteers, would accompany Tower on bus tours, distributing campaign literature while he was speaking or shaking hands around a town square.

The spadework done by Tower, with the assistance and guidance of Moreno from the inception and from Fuentes of late, plus the added impetus from the backlash liberals, was beginning to yield tangible results. In late September, Sam Kinch, Sr., covered a significant event in San Antonio, as reported in *The Fort Worth Star-Telegram*:

> Senator Tower got glowing reports of support from Latin Americans today.
>
> At a breakfast meeting sponsored by the Committee for a Two-Party Texas, he heard predictions that Texans of Mexican extraction will switch this year and elect Tower to another six-year term. That forecast came from M.P. Maldonado of Corpus Christi, chairman of Amigocrats for Tower. Maldonado was a delegate to the recent state Democratic convention.
>
> A victory prediction also was made by Albert Fuentes, Jr., Chairman of the Committee for a Two-Party Texas. [And former state chairman of PASO.]
>
> Fuentes introduced delegations from Victoria, Duval, Travis, Bexar, Nueces, Hidalgo, and Harris Counties and read telegrams from leaders in others.
>
> Present for the meeting were publishers of nine Latin American newspapers ...

Kinch reported that later on that day with Tower in San Antonio, "the icing on the cake was from greeting a group of young Democrats at St. Mary's University — all wearing Tower campaign buttons."

About that same time in late September, Dick Morehead of *The Dallas Morning News* also recognized Mexican-American movement toward Tower, pointing out that Mrs. Alonzo Benavides of Laredo — a longtime party leader — held a top GOP office, State Secretary, and Rudy Garza, the young Corpus Christi businessman who was the GOP nominee for state comptroller, was the only M-A on the statewide ticket for either party. Morehead described the confrontation at New Braunfels between Connally, Carr, and the farm workers as a serious political issue among M-A activists, and likely to cause problems for Carr. Morehead speculated that Tower might achieve a twenty percent M-A vote, which would be significant.

A few weeks later, a special brochure was completed, culminating a year and a half of work by Moreno, cajoling Mexican-American leaders to have their picture made with Tower, arranging for photographers, sometimes completing the process with only minutes to spare. In the October 6 edition of the *San Antonio Express*, these comments were made:

> An initial printing of more than 100,000 pieces of campaign literature extolling the merits of U.S. Sen. John Tower and aimed at the traditionally Democratic Mexican-American voter, made its appearance in San Antonio and South Texas Wednesday.
>
> The campaign brochure, in red, black, and white, carries 20 separate pictures of Tower, and in 19 of those pictures he's shown with Mexican-American leaders ... Among Mexican-Americans pictured, are: County Commissioner Albert Pena (of San Antonio) Albert Fuentes (also of San Antonio) past state chairman of PASO; William Bonilla, Corpus Christi lawyer; Manuel Cano, Corpus Christi chairman of Democrats for Tower; Alfredo Hernandez, LULAC national president; Roy Elizondo, PASO state chairman; Ruben Ruiz, American G. I. Forum state chairman; Roy Hinojosa, Bexar County PASO chairman; Father Antonio Gonzales, co-chairman of the Valley march; Bob Sanchez, Valley attorney (and liberal leader); Reynaldo Salinas, former Duval County justice of the peace, and U.S. Army Sgt. Felix Lopez, of McAllen, pinned with a purple heart by Tower on a recent Vietnam visit.

The brochure also contained extensive information on Tower's legislative record relating to Mexican-Americans. Though most of the leaders weren't endorsing Tower, the association was there and the brochure, designed by Charles Pantaze, was soon considered to be a potent campaign tool for Tower.

Carr's campaign countered with a strong tabloid entitled, *El Democrata*, which contained pictures of Carr with the late JFK, and LBJ, Ralph Yarborough, Congressman Henry B. Gonzalez of San Antonio, Father

Antonio Gonzales of the farm workers, and several more. It also contained a copy of LBJ's endorsement telegram to Carr which had been sent during the State Democratic Convention to Frank Erwin, the party wheelhorse who served as state chairman and national committeeman during the Connally – LBJ years. A picture of Tower with Goldwater was prominently displayed over a half-page of harsh, detailed criticism of Tower's voting record and public positions. Tower's remark of "eighty-five cents an hour is better than nothing" was prominently displayed and denounced. It was a well-conceived, hard-hitting campaign piece, designed to elicit emotional ties to the Democratic Party. But the fact that the leading Democrat in the state, Governor John Connally, was neither pictured nor mentioned, pointed to Carr's plight in trying to unify his party. Coupled with that problem, the best copy that could be conjured up for the picture with Ralph Yarborough, the state's leading liberal, was that Yarborough had informed Carr he would vote the straight Democratic ticket. Congressman Gonzalez, always a partisan, would take an active role for Carr as he had done for Blakley in 1961. Of Tower, Gonzalez remarked in late September, after lambasting his record as a senator, "And we all know he's a no-count skunk."

Joe Belden had continued to bedevil the Tower Campaign, and in August, the Texas Poll was released, showing the race to be Carr forty-nine percent, and Tower thirty-three percent, balance undecided. Such an allegedly hefty lead for Carr created another morale problem for Tower and the Republicans around the state who read the results from widespread newspaper distribution. Another statewide survey by John Kraft was commissioned by the Tower Campaign. In a personal letter to Tower dated September 26, Kraft reported his latest results were Tower forty-three percent, Carr forty-one percent, and not sure sixteen percent. Kraft's reflection upon those figures was hardly reassuring, "It's not much more than an edge, and allowing for standard statistical error, it would have to be said that it might be just the other way around. In short, it's a toss-up situation." However, Kraft reported Tower's image had become more "solid", which suggested "greater enthusiasm" for his campaign.

Insofar as the issue structure of the campaign was concerned, Kraft found Tower positioned about where he should be on the Vietnam War, perceived as a senator who understood U.S. policy, and who cared for the welfare of the troops. Inflation and the rising cost of living had become more prominent, reflecting again an issue where Tower was well-positioned, opposing non-essential federal spending on the domestic side. Kraft also put forth a point about voter perception regarding the power equation of Texas politics. "It should also be noted that there may be some room for Tower to make gains by stressing his independence of the administration, whereas Carr might end up being a rubber stamp for LBJ." Tower was also informed that among traditional Democratic voting groups, blacks, Mexican- American and Catholic, he had made some inroads, plus young people were trending his way. Even so, for ALL CONCERNED, it was a disappointing report. Tower had been campaigning effectively for more than a year and a half, making only that one mistake about minimum wage for farm workers. A tremendous amount of mass media soft sell promotion had been implemented, including outstanding television and newspaper material, plus direct mail. An extensive door-to-door canvass program had been conducted during the summer. Those in the program contacted the most likely voters in the conservative precincts of urban Texas. Professional voter surveys had evolved to the status of roadmaps for campaigns, and candidates rarely changed strategy without the guidance provided by survey research. Yet, each campaign is unique and complex, or as Carolyn Barta of *The Dallas Morning News* would write, "Each election year has its own dynamics." Moreover, the degree of change and the manner in which it is pursued can pose perplexing questions unto themselves. The right path may not be easily discernible, and at that uncertain moment in Tower's campaign, a sharp division developed among ALL CONCERNED over what strategic change Tower might make, if any. Tower and a few "doves" wanted to stay the course in a positive manner, believing that a solid image had been developed and any major change was too risky. Ken Towery was the unofficial leader of the "hawks" who wanted to attack Carr repeatedly through Tower and not rely solely on occasional potshots from O'Donnell and other third parties. Towery contended Tower's own supporters were bored with the campaign, needing something to spark enthusiasm. He said they were weary of Carr's charges, most of which were petty but nonetheless often went unchallenged. On the other hand, Tower felt comfortable with what had been accomplished and was reluctant to make any major changes. Yet, none could deny the race, as reported by Kraft, was too close to call at this late stage, and that was the best intelligence available from which to make a judgement. With that in mind, Towery wrote a blistering anti-Carr speech for Tower, who balked when confronted with it. A heated discussion ensued with Tower finally agreeing "to test" the speech the following day in Corpus Christi. Towery had structured the speech to open and carry until about midway with the usual litany and chronology of Tower's record, experience and position on the major issues. Then, it changed course sharply to state,

> Texans are now becoming aware that they must make a choice
> in November between promise and performance, between demagoguery

and dedication, between independence and ineffectiveness. The choice is between John Tower and Waggoner Carr. No stronger man's prestige is impaired when the voters in their wisdom reject a weaker man. [That line anticipated LBJ and Connally campaigning for Carr.]

Texans are now realizing that they will be called upon November 8th to cast their ballot either for a man who has honestly and effectively served them in the United States Senate for six years, or for a professional candidate who is so terribly weak that *he cannot even stand on his own two feet in the political arena.*

Texans are now realizing that they must decide between a strong, independent voice in the world's greatest deliberative body, or a puppet who had to go hat in hand begging for political support wherever he could find it, and who has confessed to a deal that callously sacrificed principle for promise of votes. I refer, of course, to Mr. Carr's confession that he attended a Houston racist rally to make a deal for votes in his race for Speaker of the Texas House against conservative Joe Burkett.

This gives rise to the question of what other deals have been made since that time. What deals are being made now? ... Texans deserve the answers. They are the ones who must choose between a dealer and a Senator.

Carr had said he would support use of nuclear weapons in Vietnam, and had pursued the line that Tower should not have gone to Vietnam. This was a subject about which Tower felt very strongly. He had no problem with the tough language in the speech.

Texans are now realizing that they must decide between a Senator who, in the line of duty, has visited their sons on the battlefields of the world, or a candidate who has said bluntly that he would support use of atomic weapons in Vietnam, but would not go personally to the battlefield to look after the welfare and morale of our sons. What sort of man could take this attitude? What sort of man could vote to send your sons to battle, could support the use of atom bombs and could — despite this — ridicule members of the Senate and House Armed Services Committees of both parties in the proper discharge of their duties? Obviously, the President of the United States does not share Mr. Carr's stated views on this matter. The President has been most courteous to those of us from both political parties who have gone to Vietnam for firsthand information, and has solicited our views on the subject. Yet, Mr. Carr said he would not go to Vietnam ...

Tower received a standing ovation upon completing the speech and a new phase of the campaign was underway. With time and campaign money running short, Towery contacted the GOP headquarters to determine how rapidly a new and larger anti-Carr brochure could be produced for statewide distribution to support Tower's personal campaigning. The crew was ready there, and the bomb bay was loaded. A new brochure was written overnight, based upon research provided by Lance Tarrance and Jerry Stephens. On issues, Tower's positions from the new speech were condensed, and some other anti-Carr swipes were added:

> INFLATION — COST OF LIVING ... Embraces 'creative federalism,' which means greater federal spending, greater deficits, more inflation, high taxes, higher living costs, higher interest rates and tighter money ... RIGHT TO WORK ... Lukewarm support. If elected, would be under heavy Administration pressure to repeal right-to-work ... INDEPENDENCE ... Running a coattail campaign, calling for his election on blind partisan basis ... EXPERIENCE ... Limited to state politics. Considered future candidate for Governor regardless of outcome of Senate race. THE FUTURE ... Take a chance on a 'six-months senator' whose ambition is to be governor.

The brochure contained six panels with pictures of Tower and positive copy but the focus was on the issue comparison between the two candidates. Charles Pantaze, the still photographer — graphics designer who printed the state party newspaper and supplied most of its other printed materials, was contracted to produce the late brochure for Tower. He would run 600,000 on his small presses on Brazos Street near the Capitol, keeping his shop running around the clock for three days. Though the state party staff produced the brochure, it was to be paid for by the Tower Campaign. When Pantaze made his delivery, he was informed payment would be spread out a bit, perhaps after the election. Pantaze inquired what would happen if Tower should lose. "Don't sweat it, Charley," he was told by Dick Elam, comptroller for Tower's campaign, "you shouldn't have any trouble collecting from an ex-senator with a wife and three children whose earning capacity in the classroom is about $5,000 a year." Pantaze shook his head, but delivered all the brochures which were rapidly distributed around the state.

Some vinegar had been poured on the spinach. There was no one who liked a political fight better than U.A. Hyde, who supplied purple prose on the matters against Carr for subsequent speeches and news conferences by Tower. Carr, Tower charged,

> ... has gone all over the state repeating the absolutely false assertion that I have imported the 'public relations team that helped Ronald Reagan win in California ...' In addition to being untrue the statement is absurd. In the first place, Reagan would not be likely to release

a winning public relations staff to me or anyone else while his [guber-natorial] campaign out there is still running full blast. In the second place, we don't need to import anyone. Mr. Carr knows we have an effective team already ... and in the third place, why doesn't someone ask him who he is talking about?

And Tower reminded Carr, who had said he had never lost Dallas County, that in 1960 Will Wilson had defeated him by more than 18,000 votes there in a race won statewide by Wilson for attorney general. Such issues appeared to be trivial, but they were threads in a whole cloth to discredit Carr.

In early October, as Carr tried hard to unify Democrats and gener-ate momentum for his campaign, he called a news conference in the state capitol to review major themes and issues. But he was hit by a barrage of antagonistic questions, the most difficult being about a picture of him at a White Citizens Council meeting taken several years previously — a picture reproduced and circulated widely by the anti-Carr liberal Dem-ocrats. From a front section article in *The Dallas Morning News* of October 11 by Dorothy Lillard, "Attorney General Waggoner Carr said here Monday that he attended a 1957 segregationist rally in Houston only to woo East Texas Legislators' votes during a race for Speaker of the Texas House ... 'I just wish it [the segregation problem] had gone away,' Carr lamented, and he said the 'far left wing' group mainly was an effort of *Texas Observer* editor Ronnie Dugger and Mrs. Frankie Randolph of Houston, leader among liberal Democrats." Next to the article in *The Morning News* was a picture of Carr with a cutline that read, "Atty. Gen. Waggoner Carr ... explains presence at a race rally." All that provided more ammunition that was distributed widely by the Democratic Rebuilding Committee.

Stung by the pointed nature of Tower's new line of attack, Carr responded with a drumfire of renewed charges against Tower; and feeling the sharp pressure from a divided party, he attacked the Democratic Rebuild-ing Committee by name on October 19. Tower, he charged, was pursu-ing "his master strategy of an unholy alliance between his right wing supporters and the left wing ultra liberals ..."

Having played a prominent role in saving the Texas right-to-work law, Tower had a credential with conservatives across the board. Among Republicans and independent conservatives, he seemed to be running well, and though conservative Democrats generally favored Carr, they found little to quarrel about in Tower's voting record. A major defection oc-curred when Will Wilson decided he had no future staying in the Dem-ocratic Party — endorsed Tower — then took an active role in the cam-paign. The former state Supreme Court judge and Carr's predecessor as attorney general brought prestige with those credentials, making him a natural to chair a special ad hoc committee, Attorneys for Tower. Various ad hoc committees were formed for business and professional groups to sponsor direct mail regarding Tower's record to their memberships. The undecided voters, determined from the canvass program, would receive a special letter signed by nine prominent Texans, including Wilson, Tom Landry, and Abner McCall, president of Baylor University. All that might have explained why, just a few days before the election, Connally spoke on behalf of Carr in Dallas, but qualified his remarks by saying he had nothing against Tower and was not trying to tell anyone how to vote. Late in the campaign, Jim Lehrer, political writer for *The Dallas Times-Herald* who would subsequently become a PBS-TV news anchorman, penned a column about the race that appeared on October 27. In the article Lehrer observed that the final stretch "can be the most interesting or the most frantic, or the most important part of any political season ... Tempers get short, schedules get fouled up, people scream at one another, money runs out, advice comes too fast and too often. And decisions become monumental.

"Both of the U.S. Senate candidates, John Tower and Waggoner Carr, are very much at this juncture right now. The decisions they make during the next few days could very well decide a lot — maybe all. The problem of execution gets critical because all indicators are that the results in their race are going to be close no matter who wins." Lehrer probably hit the mark when he observed that the ultimate perception among undecided voters toward Carr's support by LBJ and Connally could be pivotal. Tower, he noted, had already branded Carr a "coattail candidate" and was making a central issue of independence.

Tower was indeed hitting harder and harder. Finding favorable response to his central line that "My opponent can't stand on his own two feet in the political arena," Tower relished talking about LBJ and Connally shoring up Carr's "faltering campaign." When asked during a Houston appearance if the support of LBJ and Connally would bring victory to Carr, Tower cracked, *All the king's horses, and all the king's men could not put Humpty Dumpty together again.* In addition, Tower kept up a drumfire of criticism on Carr for having attended the segregationist rally.

On Sunday, November 6, two days prior to the election, another Texas Poll was published, with Joe Belden projecting the result to be fifty-three percent for Carr to forty-seven for Tower. On October 26, Tower released his final Kraft's Poll which showed the race, as of October 19 when Kraft completed that field survey, to be Tower forty-five percent, Carr forty-one percent, with fourteen percent undecided.

In an analysis of the race published November 6, Jimmy Banks of *The Dallas Morning News* mentioned conflicting polling results but bore down on a central issue. "Stripped of the swirling political currents, the race boils down mainly to this question: Is it better for Texas to be represented in the U.S. Senate by one Democrat and one Republican, or by two Democrats? Tower contends that 'Texas deserves representation in both major parties.' His ability to get votes on the Republican side of the aisle is vital to Texas on many issues ... Carr counters by saying, 'if you want to persuade President Johnson to favor the Texas position on an issue you don't send a Republican to sway him.' "As to probable voting results around the state, Banks wrote, "Most observers expect Tower to carry Dallas and Harris Counties along with the Panhandle and much of West Texas. Carr is expected to carry Deep East Texas, the Waco area and much of South Texas, along with El Paso. The Beaumont – Port Arthur area, heavily industrialized, will be watched with keen interest because of its heavy concentration of labor voters.

"But with its larger number of votes, Bexar County (San Antonio) could be pivotal. That is why Carr backers still hope the President may show up there Monday night. [For a Carr – Democratic rally — LBJ didn't show.]

"But Monday night may be too late for anyone to change many votes or even influence the size of the turnout Tuesday when the only poll that means anything will be taken."

Logic and voting history would support Banks's listing of how those regions and counties might vote, but the Tower operatives had their fingers crossed for the liberal-labor backlash against Carr to cause some substantial changes.

The final days of Tower's campaign went off without any major problems. Crowds were moderate to small, but at each stop where there was a television station, Bob Heller would direct a program with Tower talking to local people. Most of the programs were daytime and the topics were not of the nature of national and international issues, but rather such as how the price of a head of lettuce had increased. Tower would then explain why he opposed nonessential federal spending that causes inflation and higher prices. Major Texas newspapers had dispatched their political writers to cover Tower and Carr and they searched with little success for something new each day to enliven their copy. Mostly they heard the same themes time and again, but some of the younger writers, including Dave (Moose) McNeely of *The Houston Chronicle*, perceived that Tower's campaign had developed an edge in execution, working in more news-generating activities each day. In fact, Tower had received fair if not favorable treatment from the working press whose representatives had found him to be a refreshing candidate. Tower was open and accessible, with a wry sense of humor that he often expressed in understatements that made for interesting conversation if not copy. Editors, reflecting the conservative Democrat tradition of their newspapers' ownership, were not so kind to Tower. He received no outright endorsements from a metropolitan daily, although the two dailies in Dallas endorsed both candidates.

A dichotomy seemed to have developed during the year due to the forward thrust of the two-party movement having taken hold among some younger writers of liberal persuasion along with those who were trending toward the GOP, while the old guard owners and editors held to the notion that one-party government, dominated by conservatives, was established and effective, and shouldn't be changed. No editorial writer in Texas held more consistently to that line than Dick West, editorial editor of *The Dallas Morning News.* Late during the campaign, West stated it succinctly: "The active role taken by Connally in the general election is based on this premise: Those who vote for a Republican against a conservative or middle-of-the-road Democrat are voting to destroy control of the majority party by conservatives — therefore, they are indirectly voting for political domination of Texas by the [Ralph] Yarborough liberals."

If Tower had changed parties after his election to the Senate, he would have been welcomed with open arms in the board rooms of the state's largest-circulation newspapers along with those of business and industrial giants. But as a Republican, even though he was the incumbent, he was a minister without portfolio.

Tower was able to make some positive late announcements including word that the Administration was preparing to name a Mexican-American to the EEOC; that numerous college campus polls around the state all showed Tower to be leading by a substantial margin; and that the Secretary of State's office had reported Tower's list of contributors was the longest ever filed in Texas history. Some 20,000 Texans had contributed about $300,000 to Tower's campaign, or an average of $15 per contribution. On the other hand, Tower chided Carr, the Democratic nominee, who claimed to be the candidate of the people while receiving the support of only about 1,500 contributors who averaged some $125 apiece.

The only complaint from the traveling news media came during a late bus tour in East Texas during which Tower's father, Dr. Joe Z. Tower, the Methodist minister, joined the entourage, whereupon the senator forbade alcoholic beverages on the bus. The media people preferred riding in the DC-3 which, though often lumbering slowly against a head wind, was comfortable and accommodating for writing, playing cards, or enjoying conversation. Tower staffers, particularly Kay Sealy, often doubled as secretary and stewardess, typing news releases, making sure the traveling press each had one or two of the cold sandwiches brought on board at a recent stop plus a libation or two. On the last flight from East to West Texas, Tower drafted his monologue for the final telecast scheduled for broadcast Monday night, election eve at 7:00 P.M. After a stop in the Panhandle to plug Bob Price, Tower and his group arrived in Wichita Falls, where the political operation set up shop at the Trade Winds Motel. Tower's campaign-closing speech would be filmed in his living room at home with wife Lou and the daughters. Since a teleprompter couldn't be moved into their house, Friedheim and a few aides wrote in large letters the entire thirty-minute speech onto file folders that would be held and changed manually one by one for Tower to read. Such a procedure appeared to be a bit risky, but Tower, having written the speech and practiced it several times, was able to work right through it without faltering. The script called for Tower to introduce his family with a few brief remarks, then the camera would close on him tightly for a serious summation of the issues. When filming was completed that Sunday, November 6, several aides prepared to depart for Austin, their work having been completed. Tower stood on the porch of his modest home, bidding them farewell. "We have," he said, "accomplished what we set out to do. I'm convinced we're going to win."

Tower has often been alleged to be lucky. What transpired on election eve was almost as though Dame Fortune decided to deal him an extra card. Tower had been trying to establish the independence issue for weeks and his election eve performance was planned to reinforce Tower's independence. Not only did he review each theme and issue carefully, but he appeared alone, not relying on any others to plead his case. In addition, his closing remarks were aimed straight at the heart of any proud Texan who might be wondering how to vote in the race.

> Foremost in my reasons for seeking reelection is my love for our state and my desire to serve our people as unselfishly as I know how.
> Since boyhood, I have been impressed with the fierce native pride of our Texan people and with the profound love of liberty that was manifest in our state's infancy when Colonel Travis with his sword drew a line in the dust of the Alamo and invited all those who were prepared to stand and face almost certain death to cross the line. One hundred eighty-three men crossed the line and, after three assaults from a vastly superior force, on a bleak day in March in 1836, laid down

their lives because they had resolved that they had rather die as free men than live as slaves.

It is for our generation of Texans to carry on in this magnificent tradition. The preservation of our free institutions should and must be our constant concern. I pledge myself to that pursuit. In good conscience, I earnestly ask for your support at the polling place tomorrow, and I do not fear the judgement of the people.

Good night and God bless you.

No sooner had Tower's program gone off the air than Carr's followed. Tower had charged time and again that Carr "can't stand on his own two feet in the political arena," and Carr appeared in a big Democratic rally with mostly politicians assembled to praise him. Tower operatives believed the image contrast created by the election eve television program couldn't have been better for their side.

On election day, O'Donnell and Collins kept close tabs on reports of voter turnout. By mid-afternoon a pattern was becoming clear and clearly favorable — the more conservative areas were turning out fairly strong while the traditional Democratic areas were reported to be voting on a moderate to light basis. If the results of the door-to-door canvass were accurate, Tower should be enjoying an advantage. Tower's headquarters at the Trade Winds in Wichita Falls, and the state GOP office in the Littlefield Building in Austin, exchanged information during the long afternoon. Tension built slowly until seven o'clock when finally the long wait was over. A few minutes after seven, some absentee totals were reported, favorable to Tower, but none of the big urban boxes were reported early while the television networks were assembling their data from which to make projections. Many political analysts and writers had conditioned the public to anticipate a cliff-hanger. Texas Republicans were just assembling at various headquarters and hotels around the state when, with only thirty-six minutes having elapsed since the polls had closed, NBC suddenly made an incredible, electrifying announcement — Tower would win with fifty-seven percent of the vote. Shouts, cheers, and many a tear engulfed all those who had worked for Tower for such a long period of time, some of whom had been totally involved in the effort for more than a year. Around their vast state, Republicans in Texas breathed a long sigh of relief, knowing they had won a fight for survival by providing six more years for their rallying point, Senator John Tower. While celebrations commenced, a few of the Tower – GOP operatives hung by television sets, waiting for bolstering information. Exactly five minutes after NBC's break on the race, CBS picked Tower to win with fifty-four percent. Then, eight minutes later, ABC made it unanimous, projecting

Tower the winner by fifty-three percent. As more and more tangible results were reported from Tower and GOP sources, it became clear that NBC's high projection of fifty-seven percent would be right on target, producing a winning margin of almost 200,000 votes.

For the first time in this century, a candidate for a statewide office carried Texas, running on the Republican ticket, in a general election. It was a sweeping victory, far beyond the hopes and expectations of those involved, and completely reversed what Joe Belden's final Texas Poll had projected shortly before the election.

At the Trade Winds in Wichita Falls, John and Lou Tower accepted the accolades of victory before a crowd of cheering, relieved supporters. Then they enjoyed some time with old friends such as Paul Eggers, Bill Rector, Brad Streeter, and their wives. At 1:30 A.M. Tower called his staff members to his private quarters where he told them, "I have always maintained that a senator is more than one person. He is several. You, as members of my staff, have performed splendidly, and you have contributed in a vital way to our success tonight. We have taken on the most formidable political organization this state has ever seen, and we beat them. We return to Washington as free people, beholden to no one but the people of our state." Then, he broke, wiping his eyes with his handkerchief.

CHAPTER SIX

Special Wins in the Afterglow

In a strict historical perspective, Tower's 1966 victory could be relegated to a holding action. But by winning and winning decisively, the "fluke" of 1961, a man who had labored five and a half years under a cloud of uncertainty, established himself as a major fixture in the Texas political arena. The potential danger in the 1966 election had been evident to Republican activists across the state since digging out from the debris after the 1964 debacle. (Years later, Peter O'Donnell reflected upon what would have happened if Tower had lost. "It would," he stated flatly, "have been devastating.")

Tower's 1961 election had made national news and his reelection would cause national magazines to take note of his positive accomplishment and what some would describe as the first signs of LBJ losing his political grip.

In a postelection editorial, *The Dallas Morning News*, a staunch opponent of the Great Society, contended LBJ's "stock had declined drastically in Texas..and Tower profited ... Compared with the disaster of 1964, the comeback efforts of Dallas and Texas Republicans have been vigorous." The editorial was quick to point out that Connally and other conservative Democrats also fared well at the polls in Dallas.

In the raw figures, it was Tower 842,501 to Carr's 641,855. Some Democratic spokesmen contended that with a turnout of only about 1.5 million, too many Democrats were lulled into not voting and thereby the race was conceded to Tower by virtue of the fifty-percent "no-shows." Sam Kinch, Sr., veteran political writer for *The Fort Worth Star-Telegram*, would have none of that. "There is room," he wrote in an article published five days after the election, "for considerable doubt about the explanation by Democrats that they lost the U.S. Senate race because too few of their party turned out to vote." Kinch pointed out that Tower received about 400,000 votes from Democrats and independents, from people who "approved of Tower and saw no need to replace him, those who resented being told how to vote, those who wanted to speak out against state or national administrations and a number of other groups." In addition to all those factors, Kinch had been covering the race closely and observed, "One thing that has not been mentioned publicly is the fact that Carr did not offer as aggressive a campaign as Tower, or one as well organized."

Another little noticed factor was the tremendous volume of non-political news releases generated by Tower's Washington office alone, which accounted for more than 300 during 1965 – 1966. Add to that all those news releases from his Austin Senate office, plus his state campaign office, and those from the State GOP in his behalf, and one can understand why Tower-the-senator and Tower-the-candidate had portrayed a strong image of awareness and effectiveness during vigorous pursuit of both capacities.

Whatever the factors, the victory produced some interesting results. The top ten counties that gave Tower his greatest margin of votes, with principal city in parenthesis, included — as expected — Harris (Houston) with a plurality of 49,869. Then Dallas (Dallas) with 47,819, and Tarrant (Fort Worth) with 17,896. Two surprises included Jefferson (Beaumont) 11,254, and Travis (Austin) 9,575, followed by Bexar (San Antonio) 7,904, and El Paso (El Paso) 7,202. The liberal-labor backlash was evident in Jefferson and Travis Counties and the Tower Mexican-American program had scored in Bexar and El Paso Counties. In addition, Tower carried Nueces County (Corpus Christi) and the densely-populated Lower Rio Grande Valley counties of Cameron and Hidalgo (Brownsville, McAllen, Harlingen).

Tower's Mexican-American vote throughout Texas was estimated to be between thirty and thirty-five percent, but was higher in some areas targetted by Celso Moreno, such as El Paso County where, in thirty-seven Mexican-American dominated precincts, Tower received more than forty-three percent of the vote. Of the twenty-eight counties that contained at least forty percent of their population as M-A, Tower received forty-nine percent of the aggregate vote in those counties. In four target Bexar County precincts, the Tower M-A vote was estimated at near thirty percent but as one analyst put it, "Look what that does when you consider almost all those votes had consistently gone Democrat. Each one of those that was a new vote for a Republican is a 'two-factor vote.' One for the

Republican, one denied to the Democrat." The net result was a disaster for Carr who knew Tower would probably carry Harris, Dallas, Tarrant, and other areas of proven GOP strength. But to lose Bexar, El Paso, Nueces, and the Lower Rio Grande Valley, meant that he had sustained a defeat in depth, losing considerable turf which had been expected to vote Democratic.

In addition to those surprises, Tower carried sixteen counties that had never before voted for a Republican candidate, not even Eisenhower. Those included Bowie, Borden, Crane, Hardin, Hockley, Howard, Kleberg, Llano, Martin, Morris, Nolan, Orange, San Augustine, San Patricio, Titus, and Wichita. Of the state's 254 counties, Tower carried 141, besting Eisenhower's high of 136 and Tower's 57 percent surpassed Ike's Texas percentages in 1952 and 1956. Tower received a majority in all but one of the state's twenty-five most populous counties, McLennan (Waco).

There just wasn't any consolation for Carr. In his home county of Lubbock, he lost decisively 14,558 to 10,476.

The statewide voter turnout had been about fifty percent, but in strong conservative areas it was much higher, providing Tower with hefty margins. Precinct 1177 in Richardson, just north of Dallas, voted a whopping eighty-five percent Tower. In Bexar County, Joci Strauss counted a staggering nine to one margin in her Terrell Hills precinct. An item in the *San Antonio Express and News*, the Sunday following the election, gave credit to Tower's "new style" of campaigning with "modern in-depth polling" plus an "effective TV schedule of brief, hard-hitting spots" and the "GOP's well-tuned volunteer precinct machine." Further, the *Express/News* took a poke at one of the deepest thorns in the side of Tower's campaign. "So far as Republicans are concerned, one of the jolliest by-products of Sen. John Tower's victory last week was the slap it gave to Joe Belden's poll." After describing the series of Belden poll results versus those of Tower's pollster, John Kraft, the item ended with the observation that, "The little professor had the last word by taking a 57 percent slice of the vote."

Of the ten counties that gave Tower his highest percentages, five were in the Hill Country — Kendall, Gillespie, Edwards, Kerr, and Uvalde — all in excess of seventy percent. This was plus two counties in the Panhandle — Ochiltree at a staggering seventy-eight percent, and Gray with almost seventy percent. Also, two counties in West Texas, Ector at seventy-one percent and Midland at almost sixty-nine. Finally, there was Gregg in East Texas, with just over sixty-nine percent.

In the four most populous counties, results were revealing as to how the race was decided. Dallas County had the highest percentage with sixty-seven and a Tower plurality of 47,819. Tarrant County had the next best percentage at sixty-two with a margin of 17,896, followed by Harris County at sixty-one percent and a margin of 49,869, then Bexar with fifty-four percent and a margin of 7,904. That amounted to an aggregate of sixty-one percent and a Tower plurality of 123,488, which was about sixty-two percent of his entire margin of victory.

By regional vote, the Panhandle provided the highest percentage with an aggregate of twenty counties on the North Plains rolling up a sixty-three percent Tower edge, compared with the lowest, South Texas, where an aggregate of eighteen counties produced a Tower percentage just under forty-eight.

As expected, Tower did poorly among blacks. Selected precincts in Harris County revealed blacks voted less than fifteen percent for Tower, but unfortunately for Carr, the voter turnout among blacks was very light.

Some of the unsung heroes of the campaign were those who carried out the difficult task of raising funds, often operating under the discouraging cloud of a Belden Poll showing Tower well behind Carr. John M. Bennett, Jr., of San Antonio, a banker and retired general, was the State GOP finance chairman. He was assisted by Paul DesRochers, the director, who brought in thousands of new contributors by using creative direct mail pieces and follow-up procedures that left little to chance.

More than a year after the 1966 election, Belden would write Lance Tarrance, who had moved from the State GOP to the national party as assistant research director. Belden defended his Tower – Carr results in 1966, and his firm's methodology in arriving at these results until the final poll published two days prior to the election, projecting Carr to win with fifty-three percent. "Now," he wrote, "in the Tower – Carr race we really attempted a prediction, and we did a lousy job, we have been the first to admit."

Tarrance was one of those young political operatives who launched a long career from the 1966 Tower campaign, operating his own polling firm at the end of Tower's tenure. Others whose careers excelled, included Pete Roussel, who was with the Rives – Dyke advertising agency and ultimately became deputy press secretary to President Reagan, and Shirley Green, who left the State GOP public relations staff to join then-Congressman Price's Washington office and ultimately become deputy press secretary to Vice-President Bush.

For his part, Tower was unable to bask in the glory for long. There was a considerable debt and he wrote to an old friend on December 9, a month after the election, "I apologize for being so late with the reply. As you may have noted, I have spent most of the time on the circuit in Texas, trying to relieve our creditors. I've only managed a few days in Washington, catching up on the mail ..."

In the winning GOP congressional races, Bush took the Seventh district in Houston over Briscoe with more than fifty-seven percent, while in the Panhandle, Price rolled up more than fifty-nine percent over Miller. Jim Collins polled forty-seven percent against the incumbent Joe Pool to keep his political credibility alive, but the other GOP candidates didn't fare well enough to warrant reruns.

Hank Grover of Houston, a veteran conservative Democrat in the Texas House, changed parties to run for a strong conservative state senate district created in Harris County by redistricting. Grover became the first Republican in the Texas Senate since 1927 when he swamped his Democrat opponent, W.D. Miller, by more than 20,000 votes.

Ike Harris of Dallas, the former GOP member of the Texas House, made a spirited bid for a state senate seat, polling forty-nine and one-half percent against incumbent Democrat George Parkhouse, losing by only 596 votes out of more than 65,000 cast.

In the Texas House, "Lonesome Frank" Cahoon of Midland, who was easily reelected, received some company with the election of two Republicans — Malouf (Oofie) Abraham of Canadian, where he had served as mayor, and Chuck Scoggins of Corpus Christi, the only GOP House member defeated in 1964 to be reelected in 1966. Abraham won handily with almost sixty-one percent and Scoggins polled about fifty-five percent. Though legislative gains were meager, features of coming attractions were evident in Harris County where seven GOP legislative candidates polled between forty-four and forty-nine percent and in Dallas County where nine Republican legislative candidates received votes in the forty-four to forty-eight percent range.

Though Tower had won decisively, he would proceed from a weak political base in terms of Republicans holding elective offices. After the 1966 election, Democrats controlled all the 254 courthouses and the GOP only held thirty-six public offices throughout the state. However, volunteer participation had rapidly increased. In 1962, the Texas Federation of Republican Women (TFRW) had fifty clubs in twenty-four counties — following the 1966 election there were 130 clubs with a membership of more than 4,500. In 1960, the Texas Young Republicans (YRs) had only two federated clubs in Texas colleges, but in 1966, there were thirty-three with The University of Texas at Austin club included as the largest in the nation, with 1,100 members.

Statistics can be analyzed forever, but one subjective factor became evident to Texas Republicans in the months ahead — Tower's victory had generated the forward momentum their party desperately needed to pursue their dream of competitive status.

The momentum would soon be tested. A special election was called for January 7, 1967, to fill the vacancy caused by the resignation of State Representative George Cowden of Waco, to join the staff of Attorney General Crawford Martin. Those who would involve themselves soon spent a great deal more time politicking than Christmas shopping. The district contained McLennan County with its county seat of Waco as the only prominent population center. Of the top twenty-six most populous counties in Texas, McLennan was the only one not carried by Tower in 1966, though the senator had polled forty-nine percent. Tower's showing was remarkable since the average Democratic vote in the previous five presidential elections in McLennan County was more than sixty-one percent. Neither Jack Cox in 1962, nor George Bush in 1964, had been able to crack forty percent.

Carl McIntosh, politically unknown but an active church-civic leader in Waco, decided to run as the Republican candidate though there would be no party designation on the ballot. An engineer – businessman, McIntosh had strong contacts in the business community, but the Waco newspaper was steadfastly pro-Democrat. Six Democrats were in the running, including Tom Moore, Jr., former district attorney, and Frank McGregor, a former state representative. Out front, McIntosh, the newcomer, wasn't a polished politician such as Moore and McGregor, but he had an attractive "I'm just a concerned citizen" appeal that contrasted well against the seasoned Democrats. McIntosh issued his views from a mainstream conservative Republican philosophy compatible with that having been earlier articulated by Tower. In addition, McIntosh was a handsome man with an attractive wife and five children — all making an appealing picture in campaign literature.

Waco businessman Doug DeCluitt, the GOP county chairman, and Bill Sessions, a local attorney and chairman of McIntosh's campaign, employed the same procedures they had used in support of Tower. They mounted a well-organized campaign and stunned the community when McIntosh ran first on January 7 with forty-one percent of the vote, causing a February 4 runoff with Moore, who garnered thirty-three percent. Thomas E. Turner, Central Texas correspondent for *The Dallas Morning News*, termed McIntosh's showing as "the equivalent to a hard-shell Baptist finishing first in an election at Notre Dame. Not many years ago a local GOP candidate couldn't have outpolled Billie Sol Estes in McLennan County."

"The Republicans," said Moore, an articulate liberal, "are to be congratulated. They ran a quiet, well-organized and well-financed campaign
... [but] no Republican has ever carried McLennan County in my memory
... and I welcome the opportunity of representing the Democratic Party
in this runoff." Moore saw the Democratic turnout had been moderate
to light in the first round and that he must make sure the local Democrats knew McIntosh was a Republican in order to stimulate support
for his candidacy as the Democratic standard-bearer. Moore drew the battle line on a purely partisan basis ("How could a Republican possibly
be effective in Austin?") and began marshalling his various forces. Ultimately, he received help from a number of outside sources including Barbara
Jordan, the immensely popular black state senator from Houston who
would help energize the traditional Democratic liberal and black vote.

DeCluitt and Sessions had the considerable help of the State GOP
headquarters staff — fresh from its Tower Campaign experience — throughout the first campaign and runoff, assisting in organizational and media
work. A picture of Tower with McIntosh was arranged to be used in a
widely-distributed brochure that also contained a picture of McIntosh with
Abner McCall who, as president of Baylor University, was one of the
most widely respected citizens in the community. McCall also sent out
a letter of support for McIntosh in which he contended that Tower's reelection proved that a "majority of Texans, while classified variously as 'Democrat,' value their political independence and will judge a man on his
individual qualifications. They don't want their votes taken for granted."

For Texas Republicans, the race took on added significance when a
campaign fund-raising letter was sent out statewide on January 18 signed
by the top leadership of the State GOP – National Committee members
Al Fay and Barbara Man, State Chairman and Vice-Chairman, respectively, Peter O'Donnell, Jr., and Anne Armstrong. After reviewing the
"important election," their pitch came down to, "If the campaign is adequately financed, we stand a very good chance to win." In order to expedite cash flow, the letter asked that checks be sent directly to the campaign office in Waco.

As the February 4 runoff date approached, interest in the race intensified. The two television stations ran items and feature material each
day and the Waco newspaper was running front page articles almost daily.
Between all that and the hard general advertising thrust of Moore's "Vote
Democrat" campaign, the McIntosh Campaign saw its chances of winning start to move downward with a high voter turnout in prospect.
Finally, it was decided to raise the emotional issues of liquor-by-the-drink
and pari-mutuel gambling, both of which McIntosh opposed. Protestant

lay leaders sent out letters to that effect, implying Moore might be on the other side of "the drinking issue" since he had once represented an applicant for an off-premises license to sell alcoholic beverages. In heavily dry Waco, if there was a way to stem the tide of old-line Democratic voting, that might indeed be the route.

For election day organizational work, volunteers streamed into Waco from as far south as San Antonio and from Dallas to the north. These volunteers, mostly Young Republicans, bolstered the local organization, making sure every effort was made to turn out all possible McIntosh voters who had been located through extensive canvassing, phoning and from personal contact by McIntosh and his numerous supporters in churches, clubs, and other organizations. Some respondents to phone calls complained they'd already been contacted two or three times, but the campaign leadership believed it was more important to inadvertently over-contact a few people with an imperfect system rather than risk not having made contact with a prospective voter for McIntosh.

After the polls closed, early returns gave McIntosh a small lead that, as the night progressed, he maintained over Moore, but that lead never exceeded a few hundred votes. Volunteers, who had packed the GOP – McIntosh headquarters, stayed glued to phones and radios, learning that voting was heavy all over Waco. By ten o'clock, an astounding possibility was in prospect — McIntosh could win this special election, with nothing more on the ballot, *with a voter turnout in excess of that for the previous general election*. When all the Waco boxes had reported, McIntosh still held a slim lead, but all attention turned to the final box to report, from the little community of West, north of Waco. Sentiment in West remained strongly Democratic and its results crushed the candidate and his cadre of supporters — the West results reversed the lead, giving Moore the election by 254 votes out of 21,710 cast. That turnout did indeed exceed the Tower – Carr combined vote by 650, and was about 7,000 more than voted in the first round where there were seven candidates. McIntosh's forty-nine- and four-tenths percentage was identical to Tower's for McLennan County but McIntosh had received 315 more votes than Tower, a truly remarkable achievement.

In his postelection remarks, Moore observed, "These Republicans are getting rough. Whenever Republicans can raise more than 10,000 votes against a conservative like Waggoner Carr, and another 10,000 against an old liberal like me, you had better recognize the fact they are here to stay."

While the McIntosh Campaign went into the GOP record books as a nostalgic near miss, Tower, Bush and Price were settling in for their terms recently won. From a modest start with only 5,000 names on his mailing list, Tower had some 200,000 names on a general mailing list, plus thousands more in special categories. He produced a weekly radio report that was distributed regularly to some one hundred Texas radio stations, down a bit from the list during the campaign year. The same material presented in the radio report was rewritten into a column that was sent to every newspaper in Texas. A large volume of mail was being handled daily by Tower's office with an average of 850 letters received and a like number sent out. Most of the mail dealt with major legislation pending before the Senate, but a fair amount came from constituents with personal problems, such as requesting information regarding Social Security or a basic such as how to obtain a passport. The timely handling of "casework," as it is known in the offices of Congress, goes a long way toward determining the perception of efficiency among those many voters who seek assistance. Tower continued to benefit from the work of Jerry Friedheim, his aggressive press secretary, who kept a stream of news releases flowing from his office.

Reflecting the great potential national Republicans held for George Bush, the newly-elected congressman from Houston was rewarded with a seat on the House Ways and Means Committee. This key committee originates all tax legislation and oversees many of the laws affecting basic Texas industries such as oil and gas. Bush became the first freshman of either party to serve on Ways and Means since 1904. *The Houston Chronicle*, which supported Bush's opponent in the 1966 election, declared that through the Ways and Means appointment, "the GOP was able to point up to the state one benefit of a two-party system."

Price had pledged during his campaign to seek a seat on the Agriculture Committee which dealt with so much legislation vital to his Panhandle district. Price and his supporters were gratified to learn the House GOP leadership was in tune with their needs and saw to it that Price received the prime committee assignment he had sought.

As 1967 unfolded, the State GOP would redirect its thrust toward state government with no United States Senate race on tap for 1968, and the possibility that the unbeatable Connally might retire from the governor's office. With that in mind, plus the need to prepare for legislative races, O'Donnell created a Coordinating Committee composed of the top four party leaders, plus the four state legislators, Grover, Abraham, Cahoon, and Scoggins. They would oversee eight task force committees dealing with *Crime and Law Enforcement*, chaired by Will Wilson; *Job Opportunities and Economic Growth*, chaired by Jim Reese, an outstanding Odessa businessman on his way to becoming mayor of that city; *Clean Air and Water*, chaired by Dr. S. J. Skinner, a prominent Houston pathologist;

Education, chaired by Sproesser Wynn, the Fort Worth attorney active in civic leadership who had served as state chairman of "Texans For Tower Committee"; *Human Rights and Responsibilities*, chaired by Dr. William Rector of Wichita Falls, civic and political leader; *Agriculture*, chaired by Jim Campbell of Pampa, rancher – businessman who managed Bob Price's 1966 campaign; *Modernization of State and Local Government*, chaired by Robert Porter of Dallas, a knowledgeable attorney who would ultimately become a federal judge; and *Revenue and Fiscal Policy*, chaired by tax attorney Paul Eggers of Wichita Falls, prominent in the State Bar Association.

O'Donnell retained Vernon McGee of Austin, former Legislative Budget Board director, as a research consultant for the eight task forces which, he said, "will propose solutions to major state problems." McGee's involvement, plus that of such well known figures as Will Wilson, gave the program immediate credibility. In a June 2 newspaper article Stuart Long, veteran editor of the capitol-based Long News Service, commented on McGee's appointment: "Few Texans are as knowledgeable in state government as McGee, and his research work can provide a candidate for governor with plenty of ammunition." Several newspapers devoted long articles to the task force program, including an analysis in *The Dallas Morning News* on July 9, in which O'Donnell laid out objectives of the program, most importantly the building of a sound basis for the 1968 GOP state platform and presenting the image of the party as responsive and activist. A few days later *The Corpus Christi Caller* commented in an editorial that the concept of each task force gathering expert testimony, digesting it, then making public proposals is "an impressive one for strengthening the state's minority party, enlisting public interest in state problems, educating candidates ... It should strengthen the two party system in Texas, compel the Democratic Party to make a competitive effort, and in the long run serve to improve this state's government. The Republican task force plan in Texas ... should attract nationwide interest."

On other fronts, the State GOP pursued its wooing of Mexican-American voters in June with O'Donnell naming Hilary Sandoval of El Paso as assistant state chairman and chairman of an advisory committee that ultimately would be named Mexican-American Republicans of Texas (MART). Humberto Silex of Austin succeeded Celso Moreno, who had joined the Republican National Committee staff. Later in the year, ill health caused Sandoval to resign and he was replaced by Tony Rodriguez of San Antonio, a young businessman who had been active in Tower's 1966 campaign. Tower's support among M-As had produced a profound effect. In a news release on August 2 announcing the forthcoming PASO state convention, Roy Elizondo, the state chairman, made it clear his organization was not aligned with either party and, it was observed, "Senator Tower, who received a great deal of support from the Latin vote in his reelection, will make a major address to the Mexican-American delegates." In contrast, "PASO's growing dissatisfaction over the work of Governor Connally" was made quite evident. That sentiment was expressed, along with an anti-LBJ aspect, by Dr. George I. Sanchez, professor of Latin American education at The University of Texas and longtime champion of Mexican-American causes. He was quoted in *The Corpus Christi Caller* of August 24: "We 'Mexicanos' have had our fingers burned too often. As far as I am concerned, I will vote against LBJ and Connally. [Presuming they would run in 1968.] They haven't done anything for us and never will. Give me someone else, a Republican, Socialist or whatever. I don't care. Just give me competent opposition and I'll vote for them."

General dissatisfaction with LBJ's Administration was evident in various polling results published during the summer of 1967, prompting Republicans to work harder in preparation for 1968, and whomever the presidential nominee might be. A citizens' committee organized by James Drury, star of the television series *The Virginian*, had launched a trial balloon for Tower. Whatever chances such a movement might have had were not enhanced by Drury operating out of Los Angeles. Reagan had carried California handily in his 1966 gubernatorial campaign, and was preparing to be named that state's favorite son for the 1968 GOP National Convention. Tower eventually would adopt such a strategy, with most Texas Republicans knowing he would steer the delegation to Nixon.

Insofar as the governor's race was concerned, Connally left aspirants dangling for most of 1967. Lieutenant Governor Preston Smith of Lubbock sensed that Connally had had enough but wouldn't announce retiring in order to maintain political leverage during the year. Smith was a veteran of eighteen years in state government, six each in the House and Senate plus six as lieutenant governor. He knew the roads and paths, the twists and turns. He announced for governor early on, proceeding to secure secondary commitments from many Connally sources in the conservative Democrat establishment. Other aspirants, such as Dolph Briscoe and John Hill, pawed sand, waiting for Connally to announce his intentions.

In the late summer and early fall of 1967, an unusual number of vacancies occurred in the Legislature due to deaths and resignations. There was one in the Texas Senate and six in the Texas House. All of the special elections were called for November 11, and the hungry Republicans set out to make a run for all seven.

In each race the Republican candidate would identify with Tower, either by a picture with the senator or through a Tower endorsement letter, or both. If the earlier Tower vote could be regenerated in most of these districts, Republican candidates would have a fighting chance.

A coveted plum was the Eighth Senatorial District in Dallas, open by virtue of the death of George Parkhouse, the venerable conservative Democrat who had barely squeezed by Republican Ike Harris in the 1966 general election. Dallas Republicans had been smarting since 1964, when they lost their ten-year congressman, Bruce Alger, and they badly wanted to win this race. Having run such a close race in 1966, Harris believed he "had dubs" on GOP support in 1967, but such was not the case intitially. O'Donnell and Fred Agnich, the Dallas County GOP chairman, favored Tom James, a former conservative Democrat legislator who had made an unsuccessful bid for the Democratic nomination for attorney general. Horace Houston, a former GOP state representative, and Pat Holloway and Jack Paden also wanted to run. Except for Houston, there was consensus that the GOP should circle the wagons behind one candidate, but since it was a special election there was no nominating process. Finally, the aspirants, save Houston, agreed to a party caucus of the ninety-one precinct chairmen in the district at which those chairmen would decide whom they wanted to run. Ike Harris took a clear majority and became the party's "nominee." Republicans from all over Dallas worked for Harris's campaign which became one of the best organized in the county's history. Harris had seventeen opponents, including Houston, yet he rolled up seventy-one percent of the vote, winning easily without a runoff. Harris polled 15,105 votes to his nearest Democratic challenger who managed only 3,718. Houston finished third with 1,114 votes. Jim Lehrer, the political writer for *The Dallas Times Herald*, termed it a "sweeping victory ..."

> The unrealistic Democrats can play down the importance of this until they're blue in the face, but they're kidding nobody — probably not even themselves.
>
> Regardless of how small the turnout was, it created a Republican momentum, an enthusiasm both within and without the ranks ... Psychologically, it was quite a lift.

Indeed it was. Republican candidates had made it into runoffs for the six House seats, and word of Ike Harris's smashing victory was inspiring. The State GOP staff and Tower's political people worked diligently to provide whatever support they could for those campaigns that were mostly behind candidates who had never sought public office previously. Center stage belonged to the contest for a vacant seat in Travis County. There voters in the state capital were treated to a fierce showdown between Maurice Angly of Austin, a twenty-seven-year-old attorney running as a Republican versus Rogers Wilson, an attractive young Austin businessman with the full support of the ruling conservative Democratic establishment. Politically, Angly had been nothing more than a name in the phone book, but he was the beneficiary of a diligent GOP volunteer organization, exemplified by Dr. Elizabeth Paterson, that would rapidly swing into action for such a high challenge. This was a hardy group that had labored under the long political shadows of LBJ and Connally, losing by wide margins, but which had turned it around for Tower in 1966. These were experienced organizational people who knew precisely how to work their precincts. In a ten-candidate field, Angly had surprised the Democrats by taking first with forty-two percent to thirty-four percent for Wilson. The idea of a Republican winning in LBJ's backyard sent Frank Erwin and cohorts to their drawing boards, planning to unite the Democratic Party and increase the voter turnout for the runoff. The scenario was similar to the runoff between McIntosh and Moore in McLennan County. But Angly seemed to have some angels in his outfield — special, intangible factors going his way. At the core of the ruling conservative Democrat faction's ability to control legislative elections was the law requiring urban Texas House members to be elected from multi-member districts. This law brought about such absurd distortions as causing some Texas House members to represent more people than some members of Congress. It virtually guaranteed that in urban areas — where paid advertising was usually crucial to receiving adequate name identification to win — the best financed candidate would win. The power structure made sure which candidates were best financed. Had the media treated the Angly – Wilson runoff as a ho hum affair, Angly would have had little chance since he needed to become better known throughout Travis County, yet his advertising budget would allow only two nights of television commercials. But media attention was intense, not only from the local Austin media but from the Capitol Press Corps. The possibility of a Republican breaking into the capital area legislative delegation was indeed intriguing. Angly, as the upstart underdog, became the sentimental favorite among many political reporters who wanted to see a spirited fight. Each day during the runoff *The Austin American Statesman*, though editorially staunchly Democrat, would run at least one article on the race in the front section. Electronic coverage was widespread, including a radio call-in program on KVET during which Angly clearly upstaged

Wilson. Every time that Wilson would launch what might be a "homerun" attack, Angly, articulate and fast on his feet from courtroom experience, would manage to catch the ball before it cleared the fence. Several times Wilson would try to make a hit, but Angly would field the charge and throw it back harder than from whence it came. Despite being a Republican, a member of the "out party," Angly was better informed on state issues. The State GOP Research Director, Jerry Stephens, provided him with four well-written position papers dealing with current issues, including how to strengthen state government, of paramount concern in Austin. Further, a deal had been cut quietly between Angly's campaign and Robert Canino, a liberal Democrat candidate who said that if he didn't make the runoff he would support Angly for a similar commitment if Angly lost out. Canino, who had openly supported Tower in 1966, finished fourth with about 1,000 votes and proceeded to fulfill his end of the bargain, campaigning early and hard during the runoff for Angly in East Austin. That move rapidly enhanced Angly's position among Mexican-Americans, preventing Wilson from establishing a badly-needed edge in that important voting element. Wilson's campaign was keyed to "Vote Democrat" and it did succeed in boosting turnout, but Angly had too much going his way and on December 9 won by more than 3,000 votes out of 22,046 cast. This was 5,492 more than voted in the November 11 election with ten candidates. Despite the higher voter turnout, Angly won decisively, carrying fifty-nine of the county's eighty-two precincts. The story made national news with the UPI account appearing in the *The New York Times* and *Washington Post*, an article in which Peter O'Donnell proclaimed, "Angly's victory comes in Lyndon Johnson's old Congressional district, his seat of power, and is a sign Johnson is losing his grip in Texas ..." The article pointed out that Angly became the first Republican to be elected to the Texas Legislature from Travis County since 1872. It further stated that the Austin area, with its LBJ tradition, "has always been the core of Democratic strength in Texas." Ernest Stromberger, state capitol correspondent for *The Dallas Times Herald*, asserted that,

> ... Angly's victory gave the GOP a tremendous morale boost ... Angly
> proved on a local level what U.S. Sen. John Tower proved on a statewide
> level last year in beating Waggoner Carr: A Democrat can't expect
> to win simply by saying 'vote for me because I'm a Democrat!'

December 5 was a day of rejoicing for Harris County Republicans, reflected by the December 6 front page of the *The Houston Chronicle*'s Texas edition on which a huge headline appeared proclaiming, "GOP TAKES 2 SEATS" with a sub-headline, "Archer Changes to Republican." Sonny

Jones and Glenn Purcell had been elected handily to open seats in the Texas House from which the Democrats had also lost one of their rising stars, Bill Archer of Houston. The popular conservative Democrat had announced he would seek reelection as a Republican, not as a Democrat "when I would be forced to campaign in passive support for national Democratic policies which are opposite my own."

In the three other Texas House races, Republicans made credible showings but were defeated. Wayne Slone, a Bay City veterinarian – farmer, lost to Tom Uher in District 30, Matagorda and Wharton Counties; Manny Sanchez, a Brownsville businessman, lost to Henry Sanchez in District 47, Cameron County; and Eddie Paxton, a businessman – farmer from Levelland, lost to John Kendrick in District 75, composed of Bailey, Cochran, Hockley, Terry and Yoakum Counties. For 1967, "The year of the Special Elections," it was four wins for the GOP, and four for the Democrats. Not bad for a party that was on the ropes two years previously. And the Texas GOP had received a bonus with the change announced by Archer, who was considered to be one of the most articulate and effective legislators among the younger House members.

Perhaps the strongest tribute to the 1967 effort came not from exuberant Republicans, but from the inner sanctum of the conservative Democrat establishment that had been fighting the fledgling GOP for the previous six years. In a late year newsletter published by the Texas Manufacturers Association entitled *Executive Digest*, these observations were made.

> ... General conclusions can be drawn from the results of these special elections. First, that there is a statewide showing of a general tendency to rebel against 'Democrat.' And, second, the Republicans generally are better organized and more willing to work for their party ... More good strong candidates will be willing to offer themselves for Republican nomination when they see the willingness of party workers to put their shoulder to the wheel. This could very well reflect an even greater increase in the general election in 1968. The showing of rebellion evident in the returns might even bring out a Republican candidate for statewide office that would have a chance of winning in 1968, which is a presidential year ...

That final reference was a signal to the membership that the GOP was aiming for the governorship, the citadel of political and governmental power in Texas. Indeed, Republicans were looking longingly at the prospect, having laid groundwork with the task force program and enjoying the momentum and publicity generated by the special election victories, near misses and Archer's conversion.

Through most of 1967 no one had made a move toward running for governor except Preston Smith, whose early creative gamble and plodding follow-up had put him in the front-runner's spot the instant Connally announced on November 10 that he would not seek reelection. Other Democrats soon lined up for the enticing opportunity, including Dolph Briscoe, Waggoner Carr, John Hill, Eugene Locke, and Don Yarborough. Locke was Connally's candidate, and Yarborough once again carried the liberal banner. The others were more or less on their own.

Dallas attorney Preston Weathered, a venerable conservative Democrat who provided cogent advisory memos to his comrades-in-arms, observed in late November 1967, that with Connally's withdrawal, "Republicans, like the liberals, see in the present situation the best opportunity they have ever had for winning a Governor's race." Weathered reviewed the demands of such a statewide race and leaned toward Preston Smith. "From our information, his supporters are growing in number and his campaign finances are reasonably assured. He has been through a number of hotly contested races, district and statewide, none of which he has ever lost and in none of which has he ever sacrificed his conservative principles."

Jim Collins, the Dallas insurance executive who had run against incumbent Joe Pool for Congress, had taken a close look at the governor's race in the summer of 1967, but had decided to run again for Congress. Shortly after Connally's announcement, Margaret Mayer, Washington correspondent for *The Dallas Times Herald*, wrote an article that appeared in the November 16 edition, leading with a strong statement that, "Top Republican sources view Rep. George Bush as a virtually certain candidate for governor next year, but the Houston congressman still has serious doubts about making the race ... The possibility of Tower being the party's candidate for governor from the safety of five years remaining in his Senate term was also being kicked around. Tower, like Bush, said he would not close the door on any possibility ..." Such speculation may have served to ward off GOP candidates unsavory to the leadership, but the fact was the party had no one groomed and ready. Jim Lehrer of *The Dallas Times-Herald* had speculated in October that Senator Hank Grover might be favored in "high-level Republican circles" to head a ticket including State Representative Frank Cahoon for lieutenant governor and Dallas attorney Tom Crouch, a former candidate for state senator, for attorney general. Other names mentioned prominently for the gubernatorial race included Will Wilson and Al Fay. But none stepped forward to file because none had the backing of the "party leadership," Tower, O'Donnell et al. GOP operatives had pondered the enormous challenge of mounting a gubernatorial campaign with perhaps an unknown or little known candidate. Time alone was a paramount consideration in the strategic context. In mid-September, one of Tower's operatives had expressed the concern to the senator in a letter which read, in part, "I don't want to belabor the point, but Old Father Time seems to be closing in on us if we are to put the bits and pieces together in order to mount a winning gubernatorial campaign." But at year's end, as the major Democratic candidates were off and running, the Texas GOP was yet to place its consensus candidate in the starting blocks.

CHAPTER SEVEN

Gunning for Governor Again

John Trice, a thirty-five-year-old Dallas attorney and Wallace Sisk, thirty-eight, a Houston attorney, had filed for the GOP gubernatorial nomination, but by mid-January of 1968, nothing short of political paranoia gripped Texas Republicans. They knew that neither Trice nor Sisk wore the magic glass slipper, and they looked anxiously to the party leadership for a candidate while reading adverse publicity. On January 16, an article by Jimmy Banks of *The Dallas Morning News* had a particularly sharp needle when he wrote,

> Texas Republicans, apparently facing the best opportunity they've had in many years to win the governor's race, seem likely to snatch defeat from the jaws of victory ... Party leaders who gathered last weekend ... indicated they will probably back 'a new face,' an unknown without any political experience who would almost be a cinch to lose ... Bill Clements, Dallas oilman and chairman of the SMU board of trustees, reportedly had been agreed upon unofficially by Republican leaders ... but Clements said Monday he had 'never seriously considered' running ...

Jon Ford, the veteran capitol correspondent for the *San Antonio Express-News*, contended in a column appearing January 21 that there was more to the Clements boomlet than was widely known. Clements, he wrote,

> ... isn't leveling when he says he never considered the race. He was practically in, then unexpectedly pulled out, declaring he didn't really have the political background, instincts and drive necessary ... O'Donnell helped engineer the Clements draft ... [the GOP gubernatorial dilem-

120

ma revolved around the fact that] Republicans had just two pre-developed glamor candidates — Sen. John Tower and U.S. Rep. George Bush. Though mention of both as possible candidates for governor sent some GOP hearts aflutter, it was obvious from the start that neither ever really intended to run ... Former Atty. Gen. Will Wilson would run but doesn't really want to, and some party old guardsmen emphatically agree with him on the latter. Jack Cox, who ran a good race against Connally in 1962, would like to try again, but only if old scars resulting from the 1964 misunderstandings over the GOP senate primary have healed, which they probably haven't. Laredo oilman John Hurd remains a possibility ... Houston attorney and ex-football star Adrian Burk is again being courted. Kenedy County rancher Tobin Armstrong [husband of Anne Armstrong, soon to be elected the party's national committeewoman for Texas] was approached but said no ... Party brass expect to settle on the-man-who by midweek.

A few days before the filing deadline, the guessing game was over. The party leadership's choice was Paul Eggers, the forty-eight-year-old tax attorney from Wichita Falls, whose only political experience was at the local level as party chairman plus his role as chairman of one of the State GOP task forces. Eggers had an engaging personality which would win friends and supporters wherever he went, and word spread that he was a longtime personal friend of John Tower. However, the stark fact that he was a politically-unknown Republican, starting late in a Democratic-dominated state almost caused some important members of the Capitol Press Corps to write him off before he hit the trail.

On February 4, Bill Gardner, political affairs editor of *The Houston Post*, framed the situation in this manner,

> With seven or eight Democratic candidates for governor, that party could get pretty well split up in the primaries, and a good, strong, well known Republican just might have a chance of winning.
>
> So what does the GOP high command do? It comes up with Paul Eggers of Wichita Falls, a native of Indiana who never ran a political race or held a political office in his life. He seems to be a nice, clean-cut fellow ... [but]if he knows 2,000 Texans outside Wichita Falls, it would be surprising. And this, mind you, is the man the Republican organization is going to throw itself behind and sell to a majority of the four million Texas voters between now and November. A salesmanship feat comparable to disposing of paper plates in a forest fire, of NAACP memberships at a George Wallace rally ... Fresh faces and new blood are fine for a political party, but for a political unknown to win the top state race is more than a rarity, it's darn near a miracle. And 1968 doesn't look like a year for miracles.

Margaret Mayer wrote in *The Dallas Times Herald* on February 9, that LBJ's continuing presence as President had caused problems in the GOP gubernatorial situation. "Dallas Mayor Erik Jonsson, while he was seriously considering the role of Republican candidate for governor, is said to have telephoned Health, Education and Welfare Secretary John Gardner (also a Republican) for reassurance. He wanted Gardner's word that Dallas projects and institutions would not be punished by cuts in federal funds if he decided to challenge the Democratic party ... He reportedly got the reassurance he sought and fear of federal retribution was not his reason for failing to run."

Mayer pointed to other problems, including a Texas GOP allegedly holding too tight a rein on candidates for fear of embarrassment. "The difference between the two parties is the same difference that allows a self-assured man to wear a comfortable outdated suit to an elegant party while the newcomer buys a new suit for fear of making a bad impression.

"Political success can be no more achieved with a last-minute hand-picked candidate than can social success with a hastily bought new suit."

Such unfavorable newspaper comment didn't make Eggers's task easy. One capitol wag commented after Eggers's opening announcement that, "He'd better be a reincarnation of Silky Sullivan," a reference to the legendary racehorse that consistently fell far behind but often won with great finishes.

But all the press at that time wasn't unfavorable to Texas Republicans. Congressman George Bush, completing his first term, drew no Democratic opposition, prompting *The Houston Chronicle* to comment in an editorial, "Bush has become so politically formidable nobody cares to take him on." Upon learning that eighty-four Republicans had filed for the Texas Legislature, *The Beaumont Enterprise* commented, "Texas will become a two-party state, truly a desirable objective from the standpoint of all the people, only if the Republicans consistently offer candidates at the lower levels of government. Since the Texas Legislature is one of the best spots for building a party image and for expounding political principles, it is gratifying that a large number of voters will have an opportunity this year for choices between Democrats and Republicans ..."

Texas Republicans had been spoiled for years by John Tower's unusual ability to articulate his positions. Eggers was late-starting and unaccustomed to the demands of speaking in the political arena. He was pressing hard to catch up, and often gave the impression of not knowing his material well, because of halting speech and hesitation. But it was a problem he would overcome with time, along with many other problems. Marvin Collins, the former executive director of the State GOP, was Eggers's campaign manager. He set forth an aggressive plan that called for three broad phases: (1) Win the primary against the two opponents, using the time to become known among grass roots Republicans. This meant covering the top twenty-six most populous counties thoroughly where most of the GOP primary vote resides, attending coffees, precinct gatherings, GOP Womens Club meetings, virtually anywhere Republicans congregated. (2) The summer months, traveling by bus and auto throughout selected portions of the vast rural areas of Texas where voting statistics indicated his time would be well spent. (3) The fall months, September –October to election day, back into these key twenty-six counties, concentrating on the top four, Harris, Dallas, Bexar, and Tarrant. Augment personal campaigning with heavy media — particularly television — since Eggers was a handsome candidate with a vigorous personality.

Hoping lightning would strike, the State GOP fielded a full slate of statewide candidates to join Eggers. They included Waco businessman Doug DeCluitt for lieutenant governor; Fort Worth attorney Sproesser Wynn for attorney general; Manuel (Manny) Sanchez, Brownsville businessman for state treasurer; E. G. Schuhart of Dalhart, where he had served as mayor, for agriculture commissioner; John M. Bennett, Jr., the San Antonio banking executive and major general in the Air Force Reserve, for comptroller of public accounts; Jim Segrest, also of San Antonio, a former Democratic state legislator, for railroad commissioner; and Millard Neptune of New Ulm, a former oil and gas executive, for land commissioner. These weren't tokens. They were quality candidates who, with Eggers, were promoted as The Action Team For Texas by the State GOP. But in the harsh reality of the Texas political arena, it would have taken hundreds of thousands of dollars, that weren't available, to promote them into competitive status with their Democratic counterparts.

On the national scene, Tower and Bush were playing prominent roles. In late January several top Republicans in the Congress were chosen to present their comments on particular subjects during a thirty-minute prime time television program entitled *Republican Appraisal of the State of the Union*. Nine members of the House, including Bush, and eight members of the Senate, including Tower, were chosen. As a member of the Ways and Means Committee, Bush spoke on the economic situation, bearing down on the need to cut back on deficit spending. Tower spoke about Communist aggression and criticized LBJ's conduct of the Vietnam war.

> We note that in the last few months the Johnson Administration has been vigorously prosecuting the war in Vietnam. But, we also note that for far too long it followed a self-defeating policy of 'gradualism.' That 'gradualism' policy caused us to pull our punches; it prolonged the fighting; it cost American lives unnecessarily. This war could be

over today if the Johnson Administration had acted with determination instead of with vacillation ...

Tower, still enjoying high approval ratings following his 1966 reelection, was hitting on a nerve that was causing the demise of the LBJ Presidency. Once, the so-called hawks, such as Tower, had strongly supported LBJ's prosecution of the war, but as it dragged on, that element wanted more forthright military action while "the doves," anti-war from the start and mostly in the Democratic Party, were pressing LBJ to end United States involvement rapidly. LBJ, who had finessed many a political problem over his long career, was caught in an intractable situation where he could no longer prevail. Following Eugene McCarthy's media-hyped dovish challenge in the New Hampshire presidential primary of 1968, LBJ soon announced he would not seek reelection.

During the early years of Tower's Senate tenure, he struggled under the long political shadows cast over Texas by Connally and LBJ. In private conversations, after recognizing the difficulty one or the other posed to Republican advancement, Tower would often say something like, "When they're gone we're going to turn this state upside down." Within the span of a few months Connally and LBJ had announced they were relinquishing their powerful positions, rendering themselves in the spring of 1968, as lame ducks with rapidly waning power. Yet, Texas Republicans were not on the warpath with the zeal that conditions indicated they should be. In the presidential nominating sweepstakes, Nixon was favored but he was the pragmatic Nixon who never elicited the visceral response from conservatives that Goldwater evoked and Reagan rekindled. Much of the anti-Washington fire was being stoked not by Nixon but by George Wallace, the feisty Alabama populist-states righter who was aiming a third party movement, under the American Independent banner, which would cut into GOP potential in the South. Further, some longtime Texas Republicans, including the venerable Jack Porter, were strongly for Reagan, the unannounced conservative favorite, who, after winning the governorship of California by a wide margin in 1966, commanded widespread respect among conservatives throughout the nation. Moderate to liberal Republicans had hoped George Romney or Nelson Rockefeller could regenerate their cause into a formidable factor, but Nixon had sown the seeds carefully, convincing many middle-of-the-road Republicans that he alone had the appeal to win the election despite the Wallace problem.

Tower and O'Donnell devised a strategy which called for the fifty-six member Texas delegation to name Tower a favorite son for bargaining purposes at the convention. As the spring unfolded, it became increasingly evident that Nixon was building the kind of advantage that might put him over the line early; nonetheless the strategy was pursued.

On the gubernatorial trail, Eggers found that Texas Republicans, by and large, had a greater interest in national politics, particularly during a presidential election year, than at the state level. Also, he sustained the frustration of seeing most of the news media attention in the governor's race focused upon the Democratic Primary in which six contenders were flailing away.

Lieutenant Governor Preston Smith, because of his tenure in office and his early start, appeared to have the lead among conservative Democrats while Don Yarborough, the only liberal in the pack, was virtually assured a runoff spot because of that built-in base. In the middle scrambling about for votes were Waggoner Carr, with the remnants of his statewide organization; Dolph Briscoe, the amiable former state legislator from Uvalde, whose personal wealth insured a formidable media campaign; John Hill, secretary of state under Connally, an important credential; and Eugene Locke, a longtime operative in conservative Democrat politics — considered to be "Connally's candidate." Locke's campaign utilized a little jingle sung in an upbeat manner by a chorus of young women to the effect that, "Eugene Locke should be governor of Texas — the governor of Texas should be Eugene Locke." The airwaves were flooded with the jingle which caught on with youngsters, but most of the Democratic Primary pie had been too well committed at the inception and Locke wound up in fifth place, far behind the frontrunners, Yarborough and Smith, with Yarborough finishing over 40,000 votes ahead of Smith. Eggers, who had spent the spring working grass roots Republicans, won the GOP primary without a runoff, polling 62,003 votes to 27,630 for Trice and 9,781 for Sisk. The Eggers' camp hoped Yarborough would win the runoff, providing a clear philosophical difference, but Smith won, posing a race between Smith, the "caretaker of the stagnant one-party system," and Eggers, "the forward-looking conservative offering vigorous new leadership for Texas."

Eggers was soon making speeches that generated favorable response, particularly among young Texans whose perception of the state government had been lukewarm. Among the favored themes:

> In the one-party system, participants often lose sight of their public duty in order to advance themselves or to protect each other. As governor, I would infuse new ideas and new people into our state government — competent, qualified people who are not tied to past promises or mistakes ... Texans cannot afford standstill government. We must improve education, law enforcement and other important pro-

grams. By strengthening and improving state government, we can help stem the tide of federal intervention into problems that should be solved at the state level.

In late June, Eggers got a break. Another scandal in state government was reported. It was not of the magnitude to send top state officials packing, but embarrassing nonetheless. An investigation into practices of the Texas Liquor Control Board revealed, in the words of a *Corpus Christi Caller* editorial, that the board was "largely run by the industry it was assigned to regulate ... No wonder the LCB has been one of the most secretive of state agencies; it certainly had plenty to hide."

Eggers jumped on the scandal as fresh evidence of the political sins about which he had been referring in the abstract. His attack generated widespread newspaper coverage thanks to the wire service reports which also stimulated additional coverage on radio and television. A television commentator, Ray Conaway of Channel 13 (KTRK–TV) in Houston, chose to air an editorial which stated in part,

> Paul Eggers, who's running for Governor of Texas on the Republican ticket, made one of the best, and certainly one of the most apropos comments about the government of this state that we've seen in a long time. He was talking about the recent report on the LCB, which showed the board to be about as clean and effective as the operations of an honor system in a maximum security prison ... Eggers said that's what comes of having a one-party government. It grows stagnant, and gets in the habit of going along with almost anything that doesn't rock the boat, and the Lord knows the LCB was not rocking the boat.

After Jon Ford, the veteran capitol correspondent for the *San Antonio Express News*, had seen Eggers in action a few months, he wrote that despite all the problems surrounding the recruiting period, "Eggers, who is sincere and determined, may yet vindicate the choice." It had taken a while, but Eggers had established himself as a contender in the summer of 1968.

Eggers's gubernatorial route during the spring and early summer of 1968 had been rocky at times as was the presidential path taken by Tower and O'Donnell. They brought Jack Cox aboard to lead the drive for the favorite son designation for Tower, which was helpful. In addition to Jack Porter's thrusts for Reagan, John Trice repeatedly accused O'Donnell of dealing with Rockefeller, a charge O'Donnell flatly denied. As events moved toward the GOP state convention in mid-June — at which national delegates would be chosen — more and more talk was heard about Reagan support that might surface. At the convention held in Corpus Christi near the bay, Tower was able to secure his favorite son role with a modicum of unity when a rupture was averted by some behind-the-scenes maneuvering among Reagan supporters over the degree by which they would try to assert themselves. Jim Campbell, the Pampa rancher who had managed Bob Price's victory in 1966, was for Reagan but didn't want to embarrass Tower. He wrote a resolution commending, but not endorsing, Reagan, a resolution acceptable to Tower. However, a Houston Reaganite managed to change the language into an endorsement and almost had it presented to the convention, a move that would have indeed been disruptive. As it turned out, the Campbell resolution permitted the more militant Reagan supporters an opportunity to blow off steam with a noisy demonstration in which J. Evetts Haley waved a Reagan placard precariously close to Tower, according to an account written by Clyde Walter that appeared in the *Amarillo News Globe* of June 16.

The crucial language in the Tower resolution stated "that the Texas delegation be instructed to support the Honorable John G. Tower as favorite son nominee at the National Republican Convention until released after consultation with the delegation." Two weeks after that state convention, Tower released the delegation when it was obvious the national convention in Miami starting August 5 would nominate Nixon. Upon releasing the delegation, Tower made a clear endorsement of Nixon, who, he contended, would "provide the change from Democratic crisis, crime, and chaos, which Americans demand . . ." After Nixon secured the nomination and brought aboard Spiro Agnew as his running mate, Tower was named by Nixon to head a Washington key issues committee composed of several members of Congress. The group's purpose was to advise Nixon on such issues as urban affairs, financial stability, law enforcement, agriculture, education and job opportunity.

In addition to all the presidential clamor, the summer of 1968 was eventful for Eggers and local Republicans, particularly those in Dallas where two special elections were held. John Lowrance won a seat in the Texas House on June 1, and the death of Democratic Congressman Joe Pool caused a special election for his Third District seat. Jim Collins, who had run a competitive race against Pool in 1966, won the seat by a large margin in late August. Lowrance was the first Republican to win a Texas House seat in Dallas since the 1962 election, and Collins became the first Republican to serve Dallas in Congress since the defeat of Bruce Alger in 1964.

Eggers persuaded Will Wilson to serve as state chairman of the Eggers for Governor Committee, a move which lent some strength to Eggers's campaign, but a bad break occurred when Preston Smith went to Washington in late July to seek the endorsement of Senator Ralph

Yarborough. Smith had seen the liberal Democratic Rebuilding Committee cranking up again, and mindful of how it had been able to bushwhack Waggoner Carr in 1966, scurried to Washington for support from Yarborough and the Democratic members of the House with whom he met behind closed doors. According to an article in *The Houston Post* on July 25, a Texas congressman, who asked not to be identified, stated the following about the meeting: "Smith visited with us and urged us to present a unified front behind him and the other Democratic candidates in November. He said he was worried about the Rebuilding Committee and other splinter groups among the Democrats in Texas." Smith was able to secure unified support from Yarborough and the other Texas Democrats in Congress, including Bob Eckhardt of Houston, one of the old line legal reserve liberals who had been such a sparkplug during his years in the Texas Legislature.

Nonetheless, some of the liberal operatives in Texas were on the warpath again, renewing the Democratic Rebuilding Committee with its two-party theme of "Sometimes party loyalty asks too much," quoting JFK. Chief operatives were Tom Bones, whose specialty was organizational politics, and Patrick (Pat) Conway, former UPI state capitol bureau chief, both fresh from the Don Yarborough camp. Behind the scenes was the ubiquitous Dave Shapiro whose activities in this type of endeavor dated to Tower's first election in 1961. Archer Fullingim of Kountze, the weekly newspaper publisher from East Texas, served as a cochairman along with State Representative Curtis Graves, a black Democrat from Houston, and McAllen attorney Bob Sanchez, who, like Fullingim, supported Tower in 1966. Their task in 1968 would be more difficult since it was a presidential election year in which liberal-labor forces were accustomed to preaching straight ticket Democratic voting in order to minimize confusion. In 1961, 1962, and 1966, there had been no presidential race involved, plus, the Republican and Democratic nominees in the liberal backlash races were perceived about the same on the political philosophy scale. In the Eggers – Smith race there was a marked difference, with Eggers generally perceived as a moderate-conservative while Smith, according to most liberals, was a reactionary of the worst order. Shapiro framed the challenge in a memo to Eggers's operatives in the summer of 1968, "We have more [liberal] leadership types solidly on this program than ever before. There are even finks who were for Carr over Tower who will go for Eggers over Smith (but I fear that your side has finks who were for Tower over Carr, who will go for Smith over Eggers — it's those [expletive deleted] finks who are the bane of our mutual existences), and our problems are of an entirely different kind than in '66 and in '62. This time we've got to really take the message to the grass roots, rewrite the message into a ticket-splitting proposition instead of a go-fishin' deal, and it requires more hard work, resources and competence to pull this off ..." Cross-pressures were soon evident among liberal-labor ranks in which pro-Eggers sentiment was growing, but anti-Nixon sentiment was strong. Thus, ticket-splitting had to be promoted and that was not easy for so many leaders who had so often preached straight Democratic voting in presidential years.

On August 21 a new Gallup Poll was published showing Nixon, the Republican nominee, over Vice-President Hubert Humphrey, the expected Democratic nominee, by forty-five percent to twenty-nine percent. A Nixon – McCarthy pairing showed Nixon with forty-two percent to McCarthy's thirty-seven, probably reflecting anti-Vietnam LBJ policy sentiment attached to Humphrey. Nixon's unified convention had apparently enhanced his position throughout the nation and against Wallace in the South, of particular concern to Texas Republicans. Tower dispatched Ken Towery to Texas to run the Nixon campaign which Towery pulled together into a formidable force chaired by John Hurd, the Laredo oilman long active in party affairs. Ben Carpenter, Dallas entrepreneur and civic leader, was brought aboard as state chairman of a statewide Nixon committee designed for Democrats and independents. Nola Smith, who had won her political spurs during Tower's 1966 campaign, was Hurd's vice-chairman and director of women's activities. It appeared to have the ingredients for success except for Connally, who gave what O'Donnell described as "mixed signals" before finally endorsing Humphrey. Ralph Yarborough had continued his feud with Connally in the summer of 1968 after the governor had said he didn't know "what abilities or qualifications" Ted Kennedy might have to be named Democratic vice-presidential candidate. "Governor Connally's attack on Senator Edward Kennedy is shocking and disgraceful," Yarborough said. "President John F. Kennedy lifted John Connally from obscurity to prominence by appointing him Secretary of the Navy in 1961 and then in helping him to be elected governor in 1962 ..." Emotions revolving around the Kennedys were again running at a fever pitch in the wake of the assassination of Robert Kennedy in June 1968, plus, there was the emotional aftermath from the assassination of Martin Luther King which had occurred in the spring. Violence had rocked several cities as products of the unsettling climate in which the 1968 election was played out.

As the Nixon and Eggers campaigns prepared for the stretch runs, Wallace's candidacy hung heavy over both. If Nixon could carry Texas by a substantial margin, conventional GOP wisdom dictated that Eggers might coattail into the governor's chair. But as the bits and pieces of the jigsaw puzzle shifted, it became more likely that Wallace would pull enough votes from Nixon so that Eggers would run ahead of Nixon. Thus, if Eggers were to win the governorship, he'd have to win it more or less on his own. Eggers would benefit from the Nixon-oriented urban silk-stocking precincts, but those alone would not win in Texas. There had to be minority votes and perhaps even some Wallace votes in order to overcome the Democratic state tradition and Preston Smith's strong advantage throughout most of rural Texas. There was no denying that Wallace had fused two long-standing traditions in parts of rural Texas, populism and states rights, the latter often translating to anti-black, derived from Wallace's famous defiant stand against school integration. In parts of East, North Central, and Northwest Texas, populism and states rights were grounded deeply in the political thinking of the population — and higher voter turnout in those areas, stimulated by Wallace, pointed to a downside for Eggers because he was perceived as an "outsider, a Yankee," and worse than that, a "Republican." But in those same areas, Wallace's candidacy might be considered helpful to Nixon, denying Humphrey thousands of anti-Republican rural people who would have held their nose and voted for Humphrey were Wallace not on the ballot.

In other parts of the state, thousands of Anglo conservatives who were upset over what they perceived as Federal usurpation of power across the board, apparently were preparing to vent their frustrations by voting for Wallace. Had he not been on the ballot, those votes would have gone reluctantly to Nixon. Thus, it was a dicey situation from the start as Nixon and Humphrey tried to minimize their losses to Wallace in various sections and segments of the Texas electorate that could be crucial in determining which candidate carried the state. Few people believed Wallace could forge a leading plurality for himself, but he certainly held the balance of power between Nixon and Humphrey.

A new factor burst onto the Texas GOP scene in 1968, with the ascendancy of Mrs. Nancy Palm as party chairman of Harris County, the state's most populous county, and the scene of explosive growth. An attractive, resolute woman with auburn hair, she became to Harris County what O'Donnell had been in Dallas, the consummate organizer. But unlike O'Donnell, who was careful and measured in his public comments, Palm became known as "Napalm" for her blistering remarks toward adversaries whether they be within the GOP or among the Democrats. She became known as an authority on election laws and procedures to such an extent that Democratic officials connected with the election process learned they had better meet her at least halfway or be prepared to take a strafing in the media from Napalm. She was, as they say in media parlance, "good copy," and she had a politician's keen sense of timing as to when to fire a round. She would maintain a well-organized county headquarters stocked with volunteers, a place where many an aspiring candidate, campaign manager, and political operative would cut their teeth, including Molly Rockwood (later to be Molly Pryor) who would play a prominent role in the future. Palm was a leader of the strong conservative element in the Texas GOP that wanted Ronald Reagan for President and diligent, disciplined precinct organizations prepared to support candidates to their liking. In addition to Jack Porter, Palm's early backers in the local GOP with financial and/or political clout included J. R. (Butch) Butler and Jimmy Lyon. Above all, she was determined to build such an effective organization that it would help win local elections even when things weren't going well at the top of the ticket.

Another Republican woman figured prominently in Texas GOP history relating to 1968. Midland County Judge Barbara Culver presided over the first GOP-controlled courthouse in modern times when a vacancy filled that spring changed the court from Democrat to Republican.

On the Mexican-American front, the State GOP continued to expand its organizational program under the leadership of Tony Rodriguez, the aggressive young businessman from San Antonio who received staff support from Humberto (Bert) Silex. Rodriguez became a delegate to the GOP national convention, backed by alternate Eddie Garza, also of San Antonio. Since the party had another Mexican-American on its state ticket (Manny Sanchez of Brownsville) for state treasurer, State Representative Chuck Scoggins of Corpus Christi chided the Democrats for not ever nominating Mexican-Americans for statewide office. Such criticism might have had something to do with Connally appointing Roy Barrera, Sr., of San Antonio as secretary of state in 1968, a high honor for Barrera and a major breakthrough for Mexican-Americans in Texas.

In any event, Rodriguez claimed some credit for the appointment when he issued a statement contending "the initiative shown by the Republican Party in giving Mexican-Americans the opportunity for full participation in political affairs is changing the taken-for-granted attitude of the Democrats ... By asserting political independence and supporting the two-party system, Mexican-Americans have awakened to their important leadership role in making Texas government responsible to all the people ... Democrats are worried because Mexican-Americans will no longer tolerate the do-nothing, taken-for-granted attitude of Texas politicians ..."

Other Mexican-American leaders taking part in the State GOP organization included Leo Carrasco of Brownsville, Bocho Garcia of Roma, Solomon Garcia of Mission, J. R. Provencio and Conrad Ramirez of El Paso, and Brownie Trevino of Dallas. At the local level, more grass roots Mexican-

Americans were openly identifying with the GOP and making their sentiments known. In San Antonio, according to an article in the *San Antonio Express-News*, local Republican Precinct Chairman Richard Sanchez echoed Scoggins's remarks and said Congressman Henry B. Gonzalez was "the Democratic DMZ, de-Mexicanized zone, a buffer between the party and the people." Sanchez said whenever someone points out the lack of Mexican-American political power, "All the Democrats do is say, 'See Gonzalez, that's my Mexican.' "To which Gonzalez responded that Sanchez is "the Republicans' Number One professional Mexican. I know him so well I don't pay any attention to him." Gonzalez blasted Scoggins, contending the GOP was not providing important opportunities for Mexican-Americans. Such exchanges didn't do anything for the cause of statesmanship, but they did serve to inform the public that both major political parties were more aware of the growing impact and independence of the Mexican-American vote in Texas.

With Marvin Collins in charge as manager, the Eggers campaign staffed up with some of the best talent available among young GOP operatives, some of whom would be active for many years hence. They included Carlton Suiter, directing organization with Roger Wallace as the understudy; Pete Roussel, from the Tower 1966 campaign, as press secretary with Clint Dare as backup; Tom Gilliland, veteran of the 1964 Texas Goldwater campaign, head of scheduling; Jim Francis, who ultimately would manage a gubernatorial campaign, doing advance work; Gary Griffith and Jim Oberwetter involved with youth activities; and Steve Franklin, Jerry Stephens, and Harry Walsh in research. Those three produced seven comprehensive position papers that Eggers presented in news conferences at the state capitol, providing him with a strong vehicle to establish his knowledge and understanding of state government. They generated a great deal of media exposure in the process. The papers covered the gamut of current issues of high impact, including education, crime and law enforcement, fiscal policy, environment, special needs of minority groups and rural Texas, plus structural reforms for state government. Based to some extent on the comprehensive work done by the GOP task forces the previous year, these papers probably encompassed the most substantive material ever presented in a Texas gubernatorial campaign. Though that effort created a favorable impression in some key areas, including the Capitol Press Room, a successful campaign in Texas is dependent upon other major factors. This includes the necessary funding to run extensive paid media advertising, and a political organization with the muscle to generate those extra votes from each and every precinct worth working.

Throughout the Eggers campaign, Betty Bramblett and Eleanor Arnold helped keep the flow of material moving to support the entire effort. Despite adversity created from lack of campaign funding, Eggers maintained a vigorous pace. Though polling data continued to reflect a wide margin for Smith, by mid-September a few observers within and without the GOP began believing Eggers might be that rare political Silky Sullivan who could pull off the miracle in the finish.

The Rebuilding Committee redoubled its efforts, trying desperately to stem the tide of Democratic unity being promoted by Smith and LBJ behind Humphrey for President and the entire party ticket. PASO endorsed Eggers, largely by virtue of 1966 groundwork laid by Bob Sanchez and Celso Moreno, plus the 1968 diligence of Tom Bones and Patrick Conway who worked the convention. Bones and Conway were also working key areas of the state with liberals among the Anglo and Mexican-American communities. John Alaniz, a former Democratic state representative from San Antonio, was busy in that city, concentrating on the West Side where powerful County Commissioner Albert Pena maintained an ambivalent public stance toward the effort, thereby giving it tacit approval. In the black community, State Representative Curtis Graves, assisted by civil rights leader Booker T. Bonner, put forth the message that blacks should oppose Smith for having never helped their cause and having sometimes hindered it. From the Legislature, in addition to Graves, the Rebuilding Committee received help from Representative Rex Braun of Houston, another staunch liberal who favored Eggers. A strong environmentalist, Braun firmly believed that Eggers would be a better governor since the GOP candidate had made a forthright antipollution stand. In Austin, at Eggers state campaign headquarters on West Sixth Street, between Congress and Lamar, a casual observer might believe the place had been overtaken by political schizophrenia. On a given night that fall after dark, Braun, the strong liberal from the Gulf Coast, might ease by quietly to pass on some advice or information; then arriving a few moments later would be a hard-nosed conservative Democrat from the Panhandle, State Senator Grady Hazlewood of Canyon, who would pound his anti-Smith ideas into the mesh of material the Eggers camp would utilize. Hazlewood had been more discreet early on, specifying obscure meeting places where his involvement would be most unlikely to become known, but as the campaign heated up, the outspoken Hazlewood, whose long-standing feud with Smith was personal and political, would be more open about his intense desire to see Smith defeated. Smith, as lieutenant governor and presiding officer of the Senate had often "incurred the displeasure" of Hazlewood, a colorful character known as "The Gray Fox." He was as tough and weathered as the rugged country he represented, but he practiced protocol and conducted himself in the manner of a courtly gentleman. Among the many war stories about the veteran Hazlewood's feud with Smith was one about a reporter who was covering the Senate during a particularly fast, heated exchange between the two. When the rhetoric subsided, the reporter approached Hazlewood and inquired, "Senator, did I understand you correctly — that you were implying that the lieutenant governor is a liar?"

"No, sir," Hazlewood replied with the demeanor of a judge, having regained his composure. "I merely pointed out that the lieutenant governor had made a deliberate misstatement of fact."

In any event, there were substantial factors beyond the Republican base vote working for Eggers in the stretch run of his campaign, but in early October, polling data continued to show Smith with a commanding lead. Reagan had made a momentum-generating appearance for Eggers, and Tower did his part by campaigning for Eggers along with his strong support in Texas and elsewhere for the Nixon campaign. Among the reform themes hit most effectively by Eggers were his proposal for an Economy Commission, similar to that put into effect by Reagan in California, that had saved millions of dollars by removing waste and duplication, and the attack on the conference committee practices relating to appropriations. The arcane system permitted the Legislature to make a mockery of representative government. This allowed the conferees, five members from each chamber of the Legislature, to not only meet to iron out differences between the two bills passed by their respective bodies, but to add millions of dollars in spending for items that they inserted during their conference meetings, items that had not come through the legislative process. When they had finished inserting complex riders and all their special little projects, the ten members would return to their respective houses with the "conference committee bill." The remaining 171 members were then faced with accepting or rejecting the entire bill, including all the necessary expenditures to run the state government which had been worked through the tedious regular legislative process. A badly-inflated appropriations bill had been rammed through in the summer of 1968 "with nary a peep from Preston," the presiding officer of the Texas Senate. And when Eggers hammered home a specific issue such as this he always tied it back into the umbrella problem of a "stagnant one-party system unable to reform itself."

As the final weeks were played out, Eggers's campaign ran on a tight budget with less paid media than was desired and scaled-down efforts across the board, creating some bitterness and misunderstanding about how the campaign was supposed to have been funded. No great breaks occurred in the late stages, in fact the presidential campaigns seemed to be flat as they ended. Nixon won the Presidency but he lost Texas to Humphrey by 38,960, with more than three million voting and Wallace taking 584,269. Smith tallied 1,662,019 to 1,254,333 for Eggers whose total was more than 26,000 ahead of Nixon's tally in Texas. Of particular interest was the fact that Eggers carried three of the four most populous counties, and in Harris ran about 25,000 votes ahead of Nixon. This was due in part to Curtis Graves's efforts that produced black votes for Eggers well in excess of those received by Nixon. In the key Panhandle counties of Potter – Randall (Amarillo), Gray (Pampa), and Hutchinson (Borger), Eggers ran far ahead of Smith, reflecting the help of Hazlewood, and Eggers finished well ahead of Nixon in those key Panhandle areas. But the vote in rural Texas was high and highly Democratic, providing Smith with his victory margin.

Though Eggers had lost to Smith by a substantial margin, he reaped a bonanza of favorable publicity from veteran political writers who had virtually written him off at the outset. Bill Gardner, political affairs editor of *The Houston Post*, praised Eggers as a strong campaigner. "While he didn't muster enough votes to defeat Preston Smith, who is quite a campaigner himself, he did set a new record for Republican vote-getting in this state." Gardner pointed out Eggers tallied 80,000 votes more than the number George Bush had received in 1964, and had run ahead of Nixon. "One of the real surprises was Jefferson County (Beaumont – Port Arthur) where the labor vote is predominant. The fact that Eggers carried the county may be an indication that the Rebuilding Committee, which urged liberals to shun Smith and vote for Eggers, had some influence ... He criticized his opponent's record, as a challenger must, but all in all he ran a clean race with no mudslinging ... The odds are good ... that this impressive Republican newcomer with a knack for getting votes will be heard from again."

An editorial in the *Fort Worth Star-Telegram* entitled "Some Looked Good While Losing Races" singled out Eggers, "the easy-mannered, articulate Republican candidate for governor, who rolled up the record vote for a Texas GOP gubernatorial nominee and ran ahead of Nixon. "What

Mr. Eggers has gained, aside from making a highly respectable showing in his first essay into politics, is public exposure and recognition. He has earned the role of leading spokesman for the party in Texas, and not only will his name remain known but the state will benefit if he continues, as he has indicated, to speak out on public issues."

Shortly after the election, Garth Jones, veteran chief of the AP state capitol bureau, wrote that "Paul Eggers doesn't look like a ray of sunshine but he is to Texas Republicans still moaning over Hubert Humphrey's unexpected capture of Texas ..." Jones recounted Eggers's ascendancy from a survey that showed him with only twenty percent in July to setting records for a Republican in Texas. "Bush and Eggers," Jones wrote, "are the two most attractive young campaigners presently available with proven vote-getting ability."

Bo Byers, chief of *The Houston Chronicle* state capitol bureau, and one who understood the intrinsic dynamics of the two-party system, described Eggers as a threat to the status quo.

> Republican Paul Eggers, the political unknown, did so well in his race for governor against Lt. Gov. Preston Smith that it threw a scare into a great many Republicans as well as conservative Democrats.
>
> The reason for their being upset: They love to see Republicans win at the national level and even at the local level, but they are fearful of upsetting the status quo at the state level.
>
> This attitude was illustrated when Eggers visited a high-ranking official of a major industrial firm in Houston to solicit support ... 'We like you, Paul, and we like what you're saying, but we can't support you ... We've got too much invested in Preston Smith.' To elect Eggers or any other Republican as governor would tend to lure more of the conservative Democrats into the Republican Party.

And therein lay one of the major reasons for the inability of the Eggers Campaign to attract more funding — so many business and professional elements would support John Tower in the Senate, where the two-party system was structured and the GOP conservative-oriented, but at the state level, it was quite another matter. They wanted to keep it in conservative Democrat hands.

Eggers's campaign spent about $550,000, far below the $1 million that had been originally budgeted, but party leaders — including O'Donnell, Fay, and State Treasurer David Dorn — had to sign substantial notes just to keep it moving on a competitive basis. There was a general misconception in those days that "the Republicans" could raise huge sums of money which "the party leadership" would dispense according to however it deemed most appropriate at the time. The fact was, that such funds as were raised strictly in the name of the party could be dispensed as the party leadership so desired, after approval by the SREC in budget form, but so much of the money raised during a campaign year was raised in the name of a particular candidate. Those earmarked funds could not be used for purposes other than the direct benefit of those candidates. In 1968 the emphasis was on the presidential race and Eggers, the unknown with a late start, had those strikes against him plus the built-in problem of challenging the conservative Democrat establishment. It added up to a year-long uphill battle trying to earn the recognition and respect necessary to attract more campaign contributions.

At the congressional and legislative levels, 1968 was a washout for the Texas GOP. Retained were the three congressional seats — those of George Bush, Jim Collins and Bob Price — and two state senate seats — those of Hank Grover and Ike Harris — and eight seats in the Texas House. Malouf (Oofie) Abraham of Canadian, would return as the only GOP House member who had won in the 1966 general election. Frank Cahoon retired in Midland, being replaced by Tom Craddick. Chuck Scoggins of Corpus Christi, who had carried Nueces County twice but couldn't withstand the high Democratic presidential vote, was defeated by Frances (Sissy) Farenthold, later to become a statewide factor in the Democratic Party. Bill Archer and Sonny Jones were reelected easily in Harris County where two new GOP representatives were elected, Jim Earthman and Will Lee. Those victories offset losses elsewhere and established Harris County as a stronger force on the Republican legislative scene. Maurice Angly of Austin, who had shaken the Democratic establishment by winning a special election in 1967, led the Travis County ticket in 1968, outpolling Nixon and Eggers en route to winning reelection. Tom Christian, a rancher from Claude, became the second Republican member of the Texas House from the Panhandle, winning the right to serve the vast six-county District Seventy-five.

Nixon's victory brought to Texas Republicans that great big rock candy mountain known as federal patronage. The victory brought the vast array of high appointments and positions, plus just plain old good-paying jobs suddenly available, or hanging out there to be filled in the not-so-distant future. Having been out of power for eight years, the Republicans were ready for this political leverage that can make a marked difference in preparing for the next election. Eggers, the viable discovery in Texas of 1968, received a prestigious (though not politically visible) appointment as general counsel of the U.S. Treasury Department. From there he could watch events transpire in Texas during 1969, before making a decision about another governor's race.

Prior to the time Eggers received his appointment, O'Donnell had assumed the chairmanship of the Texas GOP patronage operation, a move that further strengthened his position in the SREC where a majority of its members would support his desire to replace Al Fay as national committeeman, which occurred in early May 1969. Though patronage is a power-enhancing element to a political party, it also has its downside. For each position filled, there are always several other aspirants who come away unhappy, along with their supporters. It's easy for feuds to develop over who is most qualified for a particular position or whether it's more a case of who had the stronger political leverage. Nancy Palm criticized O'Donnell in 1969 for allegedly not securing enough high appointments for Texans, a problem she contended stemmed from Nixon not carrying the state. She charged O'Donnell was guilty of providing no more than "seven years of inept leadership," and that Tower had won in 1966 with a separate campaign operation. Some observers believed Palm's recurring criticism of O'Donnell was based partly on her contention that the State GOP had allegedly neglected local and legislative elections, failing to build strong grass roots organizations. Plus there was the loss of fellow Houstonian Al Fay from his high party leadership position; and long-standing intra-party rivalry between Dallas and Houston that had been evident for years. In any event, Palm would keep things interesting within the Republican Party of Texas for years to come.

It took a while for the patronage operation to become organized and functional. O'Donnell headed a five-member committee which included Tower, Steger, Anne Armstrong, and Beryl Milburn. Jacque Irby served as staff director. Elaborate recommendations and screening systems were devised as large and small appointments were sought by longtime Texas Republicans and others in the state who had helped the party or some of its candidates along the way. Roger Hunsaker of Fort Worth, the Tarrant County GOP chairman, was an example of a level-headed leader who served in making some of the difficult decisions. He was chairman of the Post Office Committee for the O'Donnell committee, and by virtue of his long record of party service, was influential in decisions for other areas as well. In addition to the Eggers appointment, other highly visible appointments in 1969 included the Mexican-American leader from El Paso, and Tower's good friend, Hilary Sandoval, who became administrator of the Small Business Administration (SBA) and Will Wilson, the Democratic convert who had helped Tower and Eggers in their campaigns, who became a top assistant attorney general in the Justice Department. Bill Sessions, a prominent Waco attorney and member of the city council, was appointed a deputy assistant to the Attorney General, working with Will Wilson. The move launched Sessions on a course toward becoming a federal judge where he would serve with distinction. On the Washington scene, Tower's top aides moved into important positions elsewhere, with Ken Towery becoming deputy director of the United States Information Agency (USIA); Jerry Friedheim, deputy assistant secretary of defense and Tom Cole, Tower's legislative counsel, was named to the White House staff as deputy special assistant to the President. Those moves may have been beneficial to the Nixon Administration, but they removed the top hands who had guided the Tower Washington office so well for years, including through the crucial 1965 – 1966 election cycle. Towery, who had won a Pulitzer Prize for breaking the Veterans Land Scandal of the 1950s, was joined in the Nixon Administration by another Pulitzer Prize winner, Oscar Griffin, who had been honored in 1963 for exposing the Billie Sol Estes fraudulent empire. Griffin, who had been a White House correspondent for *The Houston Chronicle* and *Fort Worth Star-Telegram*, joined the U.S. Department of Transportation as deputy director of public information.

On the Mexican-American front, Tony Rodriguez, the assistant state chairman, resigned to accept a federal appointment as executive director of the U.S. Border Development and Friendship Commission, a move which eventually landed him on the White House staff. Rodriguez was replaced by Ed Yturri, a Corpus Christi attorney and native of San Luis Potosi, Mexico. A World War II veteran who served on Douglas MacArthur's staff, Yturri laid his cards on the table to the SREC when he said Mexican-Americans don't want a handout. "They want a helping hand. We need more than their votes. We need their actual involvement in the party ... They have been convinced they really weren't wanted ... It's up to us to convince them the party wants their support. . ." Yturri was soon able to point to more federal patronage to Texas Mexican-Americans who had been active in the GOP with Jesse Rios of Corpus Christi, Oscar J. Martinez of Uvalde, and Benjamin Martinez of Kingsville, receiving appointments. The state party in 1969 also attempted an outreach program for blacks, hiring L.B. Johnson of Dallas as director.

Bill Steger, the Tyler attorney who had been active in the party for years including having run for governor and Congress, succeeded O'Donnell as state chairman with Beryl Milburn, the veteran party organizer, as the new vice-chairman. Norman Newton was brought aboard as executive director, having earned his experience as a field representative for the

State GOP in 1964, and having been on Tower's staff. Among changes, a new program was devised to support the election (and reelection) of Republicans to the Legislature, patterned after the "Cal Plan" that had been successful in California, but which had been funded more from outside the regular party organization.

For Eggers, the path toward another governor's race was indeed uncertain. Texans had traditionally given their incumbent governors a second term without much question and that alone was a distinct barrier, along with the prospect of a financially demanding U.S. Senate campaign, relegating the governor's race to second fiddle. The last thing Eggers wanted was to endure another underfinanced campaign. In the summer of 1969, Eggers, along with a few of his top campaign aides from the previous year and television producer Bob Goodman, gathered for a seminar to review the race at Southern Illinois University at Carbondale. Keith Sanders, a communications professor from that school, had helped Eggers briefly in 1968 and wanted to see him try again. Debriefing the 1968 campaign thoroughly was productive for all of them, and the desire to run again was evident. By summer's end the news from Austin was certainly encouraging for the GOP, since the Democrats, in lopsided control, had made a mess of things, starting at the top. Governor Preston Smith received a harsh dose of how the public felt about three bitter sessions of the Legislature, two of them special, as described by Ernest Stromberger in *The Dallas Times Herald* of August 31:

> ... The noise Smith heard from among the 55,000 football fans when he stood in the middle of the Astrodome to toss the kickoff coin for the Cowboys – Oilers game ... was all too convincing ... The moment the Astrodome announcer finished pronouncing Smith's name in his introduction, the stadium instantaneously broke into a stunning chorus of boos which drowned out the scattered and light applause ...

A *San Antonio Express* editorial of September 11, laid it on the line:

> The legislature has ended its worst performance in modern times. It stemmed from a leadership breakdown, among other things. Texans paid for it with the cost of two special sessions.

The battles between Smith, Lieutenant Governor Ben Barnes and House Speaker Gus Mutscher had produced some strong issues such as the Senate passing a tax on groceries which caused such a tremendous public outcry that House members wouldn't touch it. Pork barrel spending was shoved through with impunity, prompting Texas Republicans in the Legislature to point out that state spending had doubled in just four years and had increased ten times faster than the population in the

1960s. The arcane conference committee system, under fire from Eggers in 1968, was the target of editorial criticism in 1969. For a change, state issues that were easy to explain were available. The State GOP, in promoting its legislative candidate support program, grouped those issues under the umbrella of "the old one-party machine" that is "unable to mold our state government into a modern, efficient operation. Lopsided Democratic domination promotes self-serving cliques, special interest influence and poorly-planned legislation ... Responsible, efficient government can be built only with competition provided by a strong two-party system." The State GOP plan was under the chairmanship of a special committee headed by Winston Wrinkle of Big Spring, a radio station owner and member of the SREC. Wrinkle's committee directed a program designed to (1) Determine which legislative races the GOP had a reasonable chance to win; (2) Help the party leadership in those target areas recruit qualified candidates; (3) Provide professional assistance and financial support for their campaigns. Some thirty-five races would eventually be on target for this ambitious, initial program to make substantial gains in the Legislature. For State GOP planners the strategic significance of the plan was the matter of redistricting after the 1970 census. Each Republican seat in the Legislature would become precious because that body not only redistricts for its own membership but redraws the lines for the congressional districts. Court cases inevitably result from this "fox in the henhouse" system, but each major political party wants to establish all the ground it possibly can during the legislative process. A major GOP thrust would ultimately center on changing the election of state representatives from multi-member districts to single-member districts. No single change in election law would greater benefit the GOP than achieving that goal. The absurdity of electing state representatives countywide was pointed out in a resolution by the SREC during a spring meeting of 1969. It read:

> WHEREAS multiple member legislative districts are confusing to the electorate and deprive the voters of a chance to observe at close range the actions of their elected officials; AND WHEREAS Dallas County Democrat Party Chairman Joe Rich, when asked recently to name the fifteen Dallas County Democrat legislators, was able to recall only six of them; AND WHEREAS at that time Mr. Rich was testifying in favor of multiple member districts; NOW THEREFORE BE IT RESOLVED that the Republican Executive Committee, which feels that multiple member districts are bad for democracy, does hereby convey to Joe Rich the message: We couldn't have stated the argument better ourselves.

An awkward moment occurred for the State GOP in early 1969 revolving around a special election for a Texas House seat in a district southwest of San Antonio. There was no party designation on the ballot, but John Poerner of Hondo indicated he was a Republican and accepted substantial support from the GOP, including a full-fledged effort by the state headquarters staff. After winning in late February, Poerner's victory was showcased in the state party magazine with a long article and picture of him being "welcomed to Republican ranks" in the Legislature by the GOP state representatives, Maurice Angly, Malouf Abraham, and Tom Craddick. A great deal of fanfare was also made in the news media since Poerner's victory was by a hefty sixty-three percent margin, and it had occurred in dusty, Democratic-dominated Southwest Texas, where Republicans had been about as prevalent as rain clouds. After looking over the Democratic dominance in the Legislature, Poerner burst the bubble by announcing that he would align with the Democrats in order to more effectively serve his district. Republicans screamed foul, but Poerner stuck by his decision.

One aspect of reform pursued by a Republican in the Legislature produced howls of pious protest from the ruling Democrats. Representative Maurice Angly of Austin discovered that a substantial amount of ticket-fixing for legislators, including some for moving violations, had been going on in Austin as an established practice. For raising the issue, Angly was roundly denounced as though he were a traitor improperly divulging information about his privileged colleagues. But the pressure he created by going public with the issue brought many of his outraged constituents to the realization that none of the Travis County Democrats had dared mention the practice. Angly's move was strong evidence of the value of the watchdog effect of two-party representation.

While Angly antagonized his colleagues over ticket-fixing, Archer was working with them to achieve the first statewide law authored by a Texas Republican, a measure establishing a reporting system for suspected cases of child abuse, signed by Governor Smith on May 14, 1969.

Also in the spring of 1969, O'Donnell sounded an ominous note about HEW bureaucrats rejecting desegregation plans in Texas that sought to preserve neighborhood schools. "These HEW officials are Democrats operating under guidelines established by the Democrats," O'Donnell charged, calling for policy changes to be effected by the new GOP administration. In an uncertain atmosphere, wary parents feared the advent of forced busing of their children.

In the spring of 1969, Texas Republicans felt a sense of stability subside with the death of Dwight Eisenhower and the resignation of

Ray Bliss, the party's national chairman during the rebuilding process of 1965 – 1966, and the presidential prelude to Nixon's victory in 1968. Eisenhower had never taken an active role in party affairs per se, but as a father figure to his party and his nation, he had no peers. Bliss had provided steady leadership during the GOP's most difficult years since World War II, presiding over the healing process from the searing split of 1964. Nixon's choice for Bliss's successor was Rogers Morton, a four-term congressman from Maryland who had served as Nixon's floor manager at the Republican National Convention in 1968. Morton was, of course, a loyal spokesman for the Administration and he had an amiable personality, but he could never match the organizational skill of the quiet man from Ohio.

Also in the national limelight was Ronald Reagan, who had been elected chairman of the Republican Governors Association, representing thirty governors in whose states resided about two-thirds of the United States population. Reagan said the 1970 issues would be the cost of government, taxes, violence, and anarchy on campuses.

Tower was becoming more important in national GOP circles, exemplified by his being named chairman of the Republican Senatorial Campaign Committee, the potent position that helped Barry Goldwater spring into national prominence. Though Tower didn't possess Goldwater's charismatic appeal, he propounded the conservative philosophy and supported conservative candidates in such a manner as to be an effective fund-raiser. His committee would raise and disburse tremendous sums of money into the Republican campaigns for U.S. Senate in 1970, and Tower made it clear early on that the other seat in Texas, held by Ralph Yarborough, should be a prime target.

Yarborough's supporters in Texas were indeed concerned about the possibility of Bush making the race. If there's an axiom that should be coined regarding longtime incumbents in Washington, it's, "The longer they serve, the more effective they become in discharging their duties in the capital while the less they become responsive to political demands at home." Yarborough's Texas operatives were proud of their senator's prestigious chairmanship of the Senate Labor Committee, but they wanted him to spend less time in Washington during 1969, and more time at the barbecues, rodeos, and commencement exercises across the vast Texas landscape. Texas Republicans were virtually united in their desire for Bush to make the race. He had run well statewide in 1964, won a tough race in 1966, and been reelected without opposition in 1968. He had a positive reputation in Washington, including a favorable rapport with Nixon at the top, on down through the ranks of GOP elements in the

Congress, party organizations, and the business-industrial interests which would be needed for campaign funding. Bush had a valuable ally in Tower as chairman of the GOP Senatorial Campaign Committee and his close personal friend, Jim Allison, was in a strategic spot as deputy chairman of the Republican National Committee. Bush received generally favorable treatment from the news media who appreciated his easy, open manner and they liked his new press secretary, Pete Roussel, who had served in that capacity for Eggers's recent campaign.

It was shaping up as an attractive match up from the GOP standpoint. Nixon was making moves which appeared to be winding down the Vietnam War, the economy was in fair condition and the many growth areas of the state were providing a potential GOP edge to help offset the Democrats' long-standing advantage in rural Texas. It would be Bush, the active, articulate congressman, versus Yarborough, the old liberal warhorse who had become a bit distant from his troops.

At year's end, the paradoxical nature of Eggers's situation was evident on the political page of *The Houston Chronicle* December 28. At the top of the page was an article from the *Chronicle*'s Washington bureau with an assertive headline, GOP MONEY TO BACK BUSH, NOT EGGERS. The article quoted an inside source in the Republican National Committee as saying Bush would have priority on funding and that the Texas GOP would probably put up only a token candidate for governor. However, on another part of that page was an AP story from Austin reporting on views of top Texas Republican leaders. Regarding Eggers, Tower was quoted, "He would run strong at the grass roots, and if he gets in the race I think he could win." Tower, according to the AP, said the Texas GOP could adequately finance candidates for the Senate and governor.

CHAPTER EIGHT

Double-Barreled Defeat

For 1970, Texas Republicans had bitten a big bullet — the task of electing a second United States Senator, the first governor in one hundred years, and increasing the party representation in the Legislature by twenty-five seats to a total of thirty-five. Bush and Eggers filed for office with high hopes, Bush having built a strong financial and political base in Houston, the state's largest city, from which to run. He chose as his campaign manager Marvin Collins, who had earned quite a reputation as manager of the 1968 Eggers campaign, and for having managed the 1969 campaign of Linwood Holton who was elected the first Republican governor of Virginia since Reconstruction. Eggers received substantial financial commitments, including the all-out support of Sam Wyly, the Dallas computer magnate. Wyly had set up a political consulting subsidiary headed by Bruce Merrill, a survey research analyst originally from Arizona, who would take over management of the Eggers campaign. The legislative program appeared to be promising since it was attracting more high caliber candidates than ever. They varied in political orientation from a Democrat incumbent state representative, (Jim Nowlin of San Antonio, who changed parties to run for the state senate) to Gary Bruner of Tyler,(one of those young men who had worked diligently in various GOP endeavors before trying the elective route as a candidate for state representative) to Tony Conde of El Paso. Conde was a young Mexican-American engineer with an attractive family, the type of new candidate the party needed badly in such areas.

The stakes were indeed high, with Bush representing one of seven new GOP seats needed to take control of the upper chamber, and Eggers seeking to lead a Republican revolution at the state capitol. State GOP Chairman Bill Steger stated in early spring that the party "has taken on one of its most ambitious programs in its history. It has accepted the responsibility of supporting major races for [the] United States Senate and [for] Governor. Our lead convinced the Republican Senatorial Campaign Committee and the Republican Governors Association to target both races ..." The bold Texas GOP program generated considerable attention in the Texas media. *The New York Times* ran a long article that recognized Republicans were employing advanced techniques for targetting precincts and direct mail programs. The article also pointed out that of the ten most populous states, only Texas did not have a GOP governor.

Republicans had their sights set on Yarborough ever since the veteran liberal had defeated Bush in 1964, and they were only mildly concerned when former Congressman Lloyd Bentsen, the Houston millionaire who had been dissuaded by LBJ from running in 1964, filed against Yarborough in the Democratic Primary. Since Bentsen had been absent from the political arena for sixteen years and had never made a statewide race, there was a tendency among political writers and observers to question whether he could mount the type of campaign needed to challenge the entrenched incumbent. But Bentsen had the strong support of Connally which meant instant credibility in the conservative Democrat establishment plus access to fast, heavy funding for a comprehensive media campaign to get Bentsen known statewide. Bentsen and his attractive wife, Beryl Ann, a former Democratic National Committeewoman for Texas, campaigned extensively, but it was the strident television commercials that made the difference. They keyed on emotional issues, such as riots and civil protest against U.S. involvement in the Vietnam War. The commercials were in concert with so much of what voters were seeing on their nightly newscasts and Bentsen was proclaiming his opposition to the radicals, implying that liberals such as Yarborough were egging them on. Reading the public mood correctly, Bentsen ran a strong conservative campaign and Yarborough, the lightning rod for Texas liberals all those years, was soon limping on the defensive. He had started late and couldn't reverse the momentum. Bentsen went on to claim an upset primary victory, causing Bush and his campaign to rethink their strategy completely for the general election.

Instead of the desired philosophical battle, it had suddenly become a personality contest to the average voter who viewed Bush and Bentsen as about equal on the liberal – conservative scale. Distinctions would be drawn more subtly relating to party affiliation and the ability of each to project on the campaign trail. Ask around the Capitol Press Room in Austin who would win and you'd find the group about evenly divided. In addition to similar political philosophies, both were combat pilots during World War II, successful businessmen living in Houston, and both had served in the Congress and were acceptable in WASP circles around Texas. Neither had any liberal credentials nor strong liberal support, which meant the liberal-labor attitude toward the race might be critical. This prompted Tower to send out a letter shortly after the primary, trying to shore up the morale of those many Texas Republicans who had wanted to take on Yarborough. His letter was quoted in a post-election article by Dick Morehead in *The Dallas Morning News*: "Republicans feel their chances were enhanced by the Democratic primary results. Liberal Texas Democrats have defected in the past to help elect conservative Republican John Tower to the U.S. Senate, and they will be expected to do the same this year for Bush and perhaps Eggers." Tower quoted national journals, including *Time* Magazine, that saw the primary results as favorable to the Bush candidacy, and Tower made it clear his commitment was firm: "As chairman of the Party's Senate Campaign Committee, I am doubly interested in the upcoming battle. An increase of seven seats will mean a Republican majority in the Senate ... This seat is one we are confident we can win ..."

Some surface logic was there to support Tower's optimism, but it was also true that Yarborough's defeat removed advantages beyond the obvious liberal – conservative aspect. Bentsen was acceptable virtually throughout rural Texas and he knew, from personal experience, how to turn out a strong vote in South Texas, which no other conservative Democrat on the scene could do in a non-presidential year. He was a product of Rio Grande Valley – South Texas politics, having served a vast congressional district in that part of the state where politics is indeed different. He knew how to deal with various political chiefs or *jefes*, Anglo and Mexican-American, whose degree of support determined the voter turnout in their given bailiwicks. All the modern campaign techniques are of little value even today in the vast and sparsely settled counties of South and Southwest Texas. The intrinsic key to success, as Bentsen knew, was to activate and energize the political machines that controlled the courthouses.

Going back to the drawing boards, Bush's operatives knew that Bentsen would capitalize on a theme Tower had used in 1966, that the state is better served by having a senator from each party, principally so that bipartisan support can be assured for projects and programs important to Texas. Bentsen would expand on the theme in Democratic-dominated areas of the state, such as South Texas, by hammering away to the effect that Republicans never had really represented those areas and it would be tragic to have no Democratic voice from Texas in the Senate. Bob Heller, who had devised much of the advertising for Tower in 1966, was Bentsen's advertising architect, so development of that theme was a natural. The Bentsen camp was also watching polling results that were showing a mild anti-Administration syndrome setting in over the economy and school integration policies, though this was not clearly defined. Bush's campaigners believed his close ties to the Nixon Administration would translate into greater effectiveness for Texas, embodied in a theme line of *He can do more*. Then, various subjects would be added to the line for advertising, such as "He can do more to get jobs in Texas."

A few in the Bush camp questioned that general approach because once advertising programs are set into motion they are extremely difficult to change and there was the concern that if Nixon should be unpopular at campaign's end, the theme line would become, "He can do more for Nixon," with obvious downsides. It was suggested that perhaps the line should be extended from the outset to be a conclusive, umbrella theme line of *He can do more for Texas*, similar to Tower's, "He's doing a good job for Texas," but that was unacceptable to the ad agency because it would prevent the line's adaptability to use for various subjects. Another general theme line was considered for Bush, *He's in step with today's Texas*, which would have contrasted the individual backgrounds, Bush with contemporary experience versus Bentsen, a voice from the past. But the ad agency prevailed and Bush went out to prove he could do more for the people in various areas of endeavor, thanks to his ties to the national administration.

Eggers opened his campaign in strong style, hitting themes he knew would score against Smith. "When our great State of Texas," he would proclaim with a flourish,

> ... with all its vast manpower and resources, can be mired in financial and economic crisis; when our governor cannot inspire the people or lead the Legislature; when our state government becomes more a tool of the lobby than a servant of the people; then it is time to change ... Texas needs sound leadership that will face the challenge of the seventies, unfettered by an ingrown political system that has become incapable of reform ... A governor can't sit back and hope things will fall into place. This approach has caused patchwork programs and created crisis after crisis in our state's financial situation ... It's going to take sound leadership and careful planning to improve education,

law enforcement and job opportunity, bring pollution under control,
and meet other challenges, within our financial means ...

Eggers's theme line for 1970 was, *You'll be proud of Paul Eggers as
Governor of Texas*. This keyed on his challenge of Smith who had been
taking his lumps trying to dodge so much adversity coming from the
Legislature.

In March 1970, Merrill brought in polling results that were indeed
encouraging. They showed the head count between the two as Smith with
forty percent, Eggers with thirty-seven and twenty-three percent undecided.
Smith's negative perception among voters was high and Eggers was not
perceived firmly one way or another. Merrill concluded his analysis of
the polling data with the statement, "The undecideds hold the key to
this election and will continue to do so until election day."

In addition to taking issue with Smith over many of the same
problems as existed in 1968, Eggers brought to the 1970 campaign the
issue of federal revenue-sharing, a Nixon program to distribute funds
to the states with few strings attached. It was an idea gaining acceptance
and though the state was in a financial bind, Smith opposed it. "I believe
very strongly," he said, "it could be courting disaster to turn the money
over to the state legislature which had absolutely no responsibility to
raise it." Lieutenant Governor Ben Barnes praised the plan, saying he
was "very optimistic" that Congress would adopt it.

In the spring of 1970, Eggers had the initiative and was building
momentum for the long months ahead, but his campaign began to sustain
serious internal problems. The economic downturn caused financial
commitments to be dropped or reduced drastically, and the relationship
with Merrill didn't work out. Eddie Mahe, former executive director
of the New Mexico GOP, was brought in to manage the campaign with
a reduced budget subject to further reduction. Mahe didn't know much
about Texas politics or the Republican leadership, but he learned fast
and was a strong competitor who bore down on the essentials to keep
the campaign from crumbling. Eggers's friend, Keith Sanders, the professor from Southern Illinois University, was aboard full-time as an advisor
and speech writer. Others of an intellectual bent who had been attracted
to the campaign included Griffin Smith, who wrote updated position
papers, and Doug Harlan, whose writing talent was made secondary to
the pressing task of helping raise desperately needed campaign funds.

In congressional races, Bill Archer had staked claim to Bush's seat
in Harris County, winning a bit of a tussle in the primary but favored
heavily in the general election. Collins and Price would hold their seats,
but gains appeared to be uphill propositions. The Twenty-first District,

over which Clark Fisher, the venerable conservative Democrat, had presided for years, drew a Republican challenge in the form of Dick Gill, a wealthy young San Antonian.

In legislative races, the GOP fielded many qualified candidates, mostly in urban districts which party leaders believed Bush and Eggers would have to carry in order to provide at least some coattail effect, particularly Eggers, since the legislative candidates would run to a great extent on the platform of the gubernatorial nominee. Opportunities were still greatly inhibited by the at-large election law for the urban counties, except Harris County, which was electing state representatives by congressional districts. Although that was helpful there, it still required a tremendous effort since Bush's district — the most favorable for the GOP — contained more than 600,000 people.

The party showcased the race by State Representative Jim Nowlin for a state senate seat in Bexar County against Democrat Glenn Kothmann. Nowlin's move was fresh fodder for San Antonio's veteran political writers, including Kemper Diehl and Jim McCrory of the *San Antonio Express-News* and Joe Carroll Rust of *The San Antonio Light*. Bexar County Republicans had been feuding among themselves for years which contributed to their inability to win a congressional or legislative race. Nowlin was a bright young attorney from a prominent San Antonio family who was considered by the news media the be the sharpest among the Bexar County legislators. Before he made the final decision to change parties, the two feuding factions of the local Republicans had to pass judgment, and their approval of Nowlin was unanimous except for a little grumbling from John H. Wood, the staunch veteran conservative destined for the federal bench. Wood reminded his colleagues that Nowlin had once been on the staff of Ralph Yarborough, thus his conservative credentials weren't quite in order. But Nowlin had established a fairly conservative voting record in the Texas House and for the most part, Bexar County Republicans, along with the State GOP, were gratified to find an upcoming young Democratic politician willing to change course and gamble his future with the GOP.

Republicans targetted the East Texas state senate seat being vacated by Jack Strong of Longview. They fielded John F. (Jack) Warren — a Tyler oilman long active in GOP affairs — against Lindley Beckworth, the former Democratic congressman from Gladewater, who had moved to Longview.

Another high hopes state senate race was the match between State Representative Malouf Abraham, the two-term Republican from Canadian, and Democrat Max Sherman of Amarillo, for the Panhandle seat from which Grady Hazlewood was retiring. Abraham's good friend, Tom Christian of Claude, would win reelection to his Panhandle seat in the Texas House without opposition. In other Texas House showdowns, Dallas County was running a full slate led by Fred Agnich who would pour a considerable amount of his personal wealth into his race, and in Harris County, the concentration was on seven races in Bush's congressional district. They included incumbents Jim Earthman, Sonny Jones, and Will Lee, plus challengers Bill Blythe, Sid Bowers, Walter Mengden, and Norman Reynolds, who was contesting a powerful Democrat incumbent, Jack Ogg. In Tarrant County such attractive candidates as Betty Andujar of Fort Worth faced the tremendous challenge of running countywide with a modest media budget. A sentimental favorite was Zack Fisher, a young Memphis, Texas, businessman – farmer, who challenged Bill Heatly, "The Duke of Paducah," the most controversial and powerful legislator of that time. He was chairman of the House Appropriations Committee and wielded almost total control over the process, which included the myriad state spending programs plus all the special pork barrel projects. Heatly's Northwest Texas district had a long Democratic tradition. However, Heatly adversaries from all over the state, including some lobbyists and former members of the Legislature, managed to help Fisher in some manner, most of it behind the scenes. Fisher needed all the help he could get because Heatly and his powerful cohorts brought financial pressure against Fisher and his friends as they had on Heatly's Democratic Primary opponent, Leon Williams. Williams still carried four of the nine counties of the district. In other parts of the state, incumbent Tom Craddick of Midland was expected to win handily, and incumbent Maurice Angly of Austin, was also expected to win. Angly was challenged by a potent conservative Democrat, Durward Curlee, who had strong ties to the financial community in the capital city, and who eventually became a powerful lobbyist for the savings and loan industry.

In the summer of 1970, Republican hopes were running high in Texas. Though Bentsen had removed the liberal target, his victory had made the two major statewide races as conservatives versus conservatives. Therefore, the Rebuilding Committee was back on the scene with a vigorous program, seeking vengeance against Bentsen plus the overthrow of the conservative Democrat dominance in the governor's office. Three of the top leaders from 1968 were back out front, Archer Fullingim, Curtis Graves, and Bob Sanchez, as cochairmen. Executive director was Tom Bones, a veteran of the 1968 operation, and director of organization was Dave Shapiro, he of the original pro-Tower liberals of 1961, who still believed that establishing a true two-party system was the most important goal of Texas liberals. Pitching in with Bones and Shapiro was Bill Hamilton, a savvy young writer who had been with *The Austin American-Statesman*. One of their first mailings, again on letterheads containing the JFK quote, *Sometimes Party Loyalty Asks Too Much*, played to the emotional aftermath of the Democratic Primary.

> ... We have all lost a great deal with the defeat of Senator Ralph Yarborough in the Democratic Primary. The multimillion dollar smear campaign carried out by Connally's stand-in would not have resulted in Senator Yarborough's defeat if Texas were a two-party state — in which nearly all conservatives vote in the Republican Primary and those of us who believe in the principles of the National Democratic Party are in the overwhelming majority in the Democratic Primary. Our objective is to create just such a two-party system ... Let's not be hoodwinked into believing that the Bentsen – Smith one-party machine will ever benefit the cause of a real Democratic Party in Texas which is dedicated to the great liberal traditions of Ralph Yarborough and John F. Kennedy ... The one-party system is the ideal atmosphere for Shivers – Connally – *Dallas News* candidates to clobber good Democrats like Senator Yarborough and that one-party system must be replaced by a competitive two-party system ... Let's start rebuilding the Democratic Party of Texas by establishing a two-party system ...

The work of this group undoubtedly made it difficult for Bentsen and Smith to move into certain leadership elements in liberal – labor circles and expect instant early support on a purely partisan basis. Many of the leaders temporized, waiting for a clearer picture to emerge as to what course of action might be most desirable.

Bush's campaign was running hard from its headquarters in Houston, where Marvin Collins directed a staff that included such veteran operatives as Carlton Suiter in organization, Pete Roussel as press secretary — and often on the road with the candidate — and Boone Vastine as research director. The state press office was in Austin, where Clint Dare ground out stacks of news releases. Bush was especially effective in his personal campaigning. Many hamburger suppers were arranged in medium-sized to smaller communities during which the candidate would mix and mingle in a casual manner. This was done throughout the summer, along with occasional stops in larger cities.

By the time of the GOP state convention at Fort Worth in September, the Bush Campaign was running on all cylinders, even though its operatives knew quite well that Bentsen had maintained a full head of steam since the Democratic Primary. The Eggers Campaign, on the other hand, was hurting. Funding was tight, to the point that advertising elements that had once been considered essential were being juggled or reduced. Further complicating fund-raising was the fact that Eggers had made some rather progressive stands on issues which didn't sit so well with some of the strong conservatives. They also didn't sit well with with the GOP nominee for lieutenant governor, Byron Fullerton, who opposed reducing the penalty for possession of a small amount of marijuana from a felony to a misdemeanor. Nancy Palm took aim at Eggers on that issue also, threatening a floor fight at the state convention if Eggers's stand were put into the platform. The news media seized upon the issue to create a controversy for the convention, but, as is usually the case, an up-or-down confrontation was averted so that neither Eggers nor Palm would lose face. But the publicity surrounding the "drug issue" certainly didn't enhance the fund-raising capabilities of Eggers among bedrock conservatives during the stretch run of his campaign.

As the Eggers campaign struggled to stay afloat, strain was created at the State GOP where its ambitious funding support program for legislative candidates was being reduced at the height of their needs. The economic downturn was manifesting itself. Too, it was known in party circles that Steger, the state chairman, would soon be named a federal judge, therefore he was, in effect, a lame duck with little leverage. As word spread of the severe problems being wrestled with by Eggers and the State GOP, those wondering where to concentrate their final resources generally gravitated to Bush. With such stalwarts as Fred Chambers pursuing campaign financing, and with Bush's background in the oil business, the funding for that campaign remained at a strong competitive level. Tower had certainly done his part, directing more than $70,000 from the fund-raising committee he had headed — tops in the nation — plus assisting in other ways. Bentsen, well aware that Bush could match him dollar for dollar or perhaps even surpass him, had proposed limiting campaign spending for the general election, an obvious ploy to take advantage of his high name identification that had been achieved in the primary.

Part of the final phase strategy for Bush and Eggers included trips to Texas by President Nixon and Vice-President Agnew, designed to rekindle enthusiasm among the thousands of volunteers and to demonstrate the effectiveness for Texas that would be gained by electing those close to the national administration. Bush had campaigned tirelessly across Texas for Nixon's major positions, including Vietnam and revenue sharing. Bush opposed forced busing and gun control while favoring voluntary prayer in public schools. He was, indeed, in step with majority thinking in Texas. But so was Bentsen, who, as a Democrat, could position himself on the emotional issues the same as Bush, yet take potshots at Nixon on a variety of items relating to the economy, including what he termed "the inflationary spiral." Bentsen rapped the visits by Nixon and Agnew as a "Republican power play." Joe Carroll Rust, political writer for *The San Antonio Light*, pointed to the Nixon and Agnew visits to Texas as being offset somewhat by LBJ headlining a major dinner for Bentsen in Houston, and Connally playing such a potent role in behalf of Bentsen. Rust concluded: "the major issue in the Bush – Bentsen contest is whether Texas should have two Republican senators," and that well may have been a key factor in the outcome.

Another factor looming ominously for Bush (and Eggers) was the liquor-by-drink proposal that was not discussed much by any major candidate because it was such a volatile issue. Sentiment varied literally by precincts and counties. The issue was to decide whether serving liquor-by-the-drink would be permitted after local option elections. In rural Texas, and among certain staunch anti-alcohol elements, the issue was framed as "open saloons" with a particularly adverse connotation. As a practical matter, the more rural vote that was stimulated to turn out for whatever reason, including the liquor-by-the-drink controversy, the less chance Bush and Eggers had to win because of the longstanding Democratic bias in rural Texas.

Though Eggers's campaign had struggled for months, it had also generated widespread publicity, and scored again in minority areas where Eggers had established some simpatico in 1968. Preston Smith had sustained embarrassment from hecklers in Houston and San Antonio who had branded him a racist. Smith's advisors generally kept him away from further such risks during the stretch run, and relied on announcers for his paid commercials that portrayed Smith in a bland manner as the quiet incumbent. That brought out Eggers's sense of humor, and he quipped in October 1970, that Smith wouldn't debate or even talk to the voters any more. "He has an announcer who does all his talking for him, so I'll be happy to debate his announcer."

The Rebuilding Committee fired off many a round during the 1970 campaign, causing Smith to duck and wince while Bentsen would respond publicly, contending his liberal detractors were in total cahoots with the Republicans.

When Nixon's late campaign swing to Texas was announced, Eddie Mahe, beleaguered campaign manager for Eggers, seized upon that as a vehicle to stimulate some late contributions to produce a special thirty-minute television program for Eggers. It was a desperate scramble to put together a multiscene, tightly-edited program in twenty-four hours, but it was done thanks to Forrest Moore of Dallas, who was the producer. He and three of Eggers's aides were up all night piecing together the program written by one of the aides on an airplane between Austin and Dallas. Major campaign themes were reviewed while Eggers was shown in various scenes, campaigning in a warm and friendly manner, which had been his long suit. There were a few serious scenes with Nixon and Tower. The program was on the air forty-eight hours prior to the election, giving the tired troops for Eggers something to talk about and perhaps moving some undecided voters to the challenger.

Despite the frantic last minute efforts by Eggers and the strong stretch run by Bush, a general anti-Administration syndrome, keyed somewhat by the strident campaigning by Agnew, had seemed to have set in over Texas in the fall of 1970, and it was manifested on election day. Bentsen defeated Bush by a vote of 1,194,069 to 1,035,794 while Smith won over Eggers by 1,197,726 to 1,037,723. Rounding off, Bush and Eggers each received forty-seven percent of the vote in their respective races. They both carried the aggregate urban vote in Texas, but the rural vote was heavy — heavily Democratic — and decisive, lending credence to the theory that the liquor-by-drink proposal (approved heavily by urban Texas) contributed substantially to the dual GOP defeat, certainly to the margin. In 1966, the total vote in the United States Senate race was less than 1.5 million, while in 1970, the total was more than 2.2 million. Even allowing for population growth, that higher turnout of more than 700,000 voters told part of the story. In any event, it was a crushing defeat for Bush, who had crafted a well-rounded campaign and whose polls (as well as those of others) had consistently shown him to be competitive, perhaps ready to win with a break. But a break never came. Eggers had seemed to be resigned to losing when his campaign financing collapsed, but he maintained his "game face" out front, exerting considerable pressure upon Smith.

For Texas Republicans, it was a bleak aftermath. The glamor races were lost and there were no gains from congressional races, nor those for the state senate. Nowlin, the bright new star from San Antonio, was defeated by Glenn Kothmann, and Abraham, widely popular in GOP circles, lost to Max Sherman, an outstanding Democratic candidate, in the Panhandle race. In Texas House races, gains were meager except for Harris County, where the Nancy Palm organization helped win three new seats with Bill Blythe, Sid Bowers, and Walter Mengden. Jim Earthman, Sonny Jones and Will Lee were reelected there, and Norman Reynolds pressed the favored Jack Ogg to the wall before losing with forty-nine percent. Fred Agnich managed to break through in Dallas County, but the rest of the slate there lost and no other gains were to be found around the state. Among the few bright spots was the reelection of Maurice Angly in Austin, who again led the GOP ticket, outpolling Bush and Eggers in his district. Angly's opponent, Durward Curlee, cut into traditional conservative areas of West and North Austin but Angly, who had tweaked the local establishment with his ticket-fixing issue, piled up votes in South Austin where the "pickup truck driver vote" went for the Republican underdog. Such emotional issues were few and far between for GOP candidates in 1970, who were unable to overcome the downsides of an unpopular national administration at the time of the election.

Failure of the party's legislative program could be laid to adverse conditions that had impacted upon the Eggers campaign as well, but if there was a lesson that should have been learned about the difficulty of winning legislative races, it was that considerable muscle, including money and organization, must be put behind Republican candidates running at that level. Even where Eggers ran ahead of Smith, most GOP legislative candidates were defeated. The notion of relying on a coattail effect was only wishful thinking. Texas was a long way from being a two-party state in which straight ticket voting would help the GOP as well as the Democratic Party, which had long been the beneficiary of straight ticket voting in the state. For any down-ballot GOP candidate, strength at the top of the ticket would always be helpful, but unless that lower level candidate had substantial name identification and organizational support, the opportunity to win would be remote indeed.

For Bush and Eggers, the Texas Republican fallen stars of 1970, the paths of the future would vary widely. Stung by defeat, but determined to pursue a career in public service, Bush would serve in various important capacities in the Nixon – Ford presidential years, including United States Ambassador to the United Nations, United States Envoy to Peking, and Director of the Central Intelligence Agency (CIA). In addition, he would serve a stint as chairman of the Republican National Committee, a choice spot from which a presidential aspirant could get to know so many important party people around the nation. For Eggers, it was back to civilian life as a practicing attorney who would relocate in Dallas, and play a relatively quiet role insofar as visible political activity was concerned.

CHAPTER NINE

Return of the Tower Touch

In early January 1971, another state scandal broke, high on the scale of political impact. It became known as "the Sharpstown stock fraud scandal" deriving from a Securities and Exchange Commission (SEC) probe of state officials who had received loans in 1969 from the Sharpstown State Bank in Houston, in order to purchase stock in National Bankers Life Insurance Company, both entities owned by Houston tycoon Frank Sharp. Fast profits were allegedly made in return for help in passing two bills beneficial to Sharp's interests, particularly legislation that would allow his bank to avoid certain federal scrutiny. Several former officials and officeholders were implicated, including Waggoner Carr who flatly denied any wrongdoing and fought it through successfully. Lieutanant Governor Ben Barnes was embarrassed because he was presiding officer of the Senate in 1969. Governor Preston Smith, who had participated in stock purchasing but had vetoed the bills, sustained adverse publicity but no legal problem. Gus Mutscher, the powerful speaker who ran the House to his liking, had been involved in the transactions, along with a House colleague, Tommy Shannon of Fort Worth, and an aide, Rush McGinty. They would come under intense scrutiny from the news media and a bedrock group of reform legislators, some thirty members in the 150-member Texas House, who never cared for Mutscher in the first place. A searing session of the Legislature ensued in the spring of 1971 with the "Dirty Thirty" coalition of Republicans and liberal Democrats challenging Mutscher to institute various ethics and reform measures. Mutscher, of course, had the votes to withstand such challenges, but legal questions surrounding his involvement in the Sharpstown scandal, plus the constant publicity generated by the Dirty Thirty, made for a divisive session. Mutscher responded in a vindictive manner, directing his cohorts to draw a redistricting plan that would eliminate many of the Dirty Thirty. That was done with a great deal of creative redrawing of the lines, prompting Nancy Palm to charge that "the sophisticated gerrymandering of the entire state to the whims of the speaker was used to dilute Republican strength as much as possible ... It is obvious that the hurried, dictatorial manner in which these redistricting measures were presented to the Legislature prevented any real study or analysis." A Harris County census tract had been lost in the Mutscher plan, a discovery Palm was using to threaten a lawsuit. Mutscher's plan had another flaw, cutting across twenty-three county lines, a practice in opposition to the Texas Constitution which calls for preserving county lines whenever possible. Mutscher's cohorts contended they had to comply with the new federal one-man – one-vote doctrine, causing the various county lines to be crossed.

Tom Craddick, the Republican representative from Midland, whose county had been divided, led the legal challenge, contending Mutscher's plan wantonly cut across county lines. Duncan Boeckman, the Dallas attorney who was legal counsel for the State GOP, presented a strong case before State District Judge Herman Jones in Austin. He put a seventeen-year-old Austin High School senior, Laura Shoop, on the stand to show the court that a redistricting plan she drew in less than twenty hours complied with the one-man – one-vote doctrine without splitting county lines. A Baylor University graduate student, Bill Adams, testified that a computer could produce hundreds of plans without splitting county lines such as Mutscher's plan had done. The case was clear. Judge Jones promptly declared Mutscher's plan unconstitutional, sending the task to the five-member state redistricting board composed of Barnes, Mutscher, Attorney General Crawford Martin, Land Commissioner Bob Armstrong, and Comptroller Robert Calvert. The board produced a Texas House redistricting plan that divided Harris County into twenty-three single-member districts but left the other urban counties with the same old ground rules of electing all their state representatives on a countywide basis.

Lawsuits were filed challenging the countywide elections for Bexar and Dallas Counties. They were combined, setting the stage for one case about which a pivotal change in the politics of the State of Texas would be argued. Few people understood the vast ramifications in prospect. If the status quo could be preserved, the ruling conservative Democrats knew they could much better ride out the adversity which was going to impact to some unknown but ominous extent in the 1972 elections in the wake of the Sharpstown scandal. Further, they would stave off problems in such as future speaker's races, being able to rely on their tried and trusted methods of keeping internal problems to a minimum. Though Republicans were all conservative, they tended to be more independent than conservative Democrats, a point often brought home to Republican candidates who would see lobby-generated money go to their conservative Democrat opponents. If the liberal Democrat – Republican coalition should win the lawsuit, it would ultimately break the back of conservative Democrat domination of legislative delegations in urban Texas. If single-member districts were ordered for Bexar and Dallas Counties — and they were already in effect for Harris County — it would only be a matter of time before they would be in effect throughout the urban areas of the state.

Another unsettling factor on the horizon for Anglo Democrats in general was La Raza Unida (The United Race), a militant MexicanAmerican movement led by José Angel Gutierrez of Crystal City, in South Texas. This movement was developing into a political party that would field statewide candidates, a migraine-inducing prospect for liberal Democrats in their party primary, where nominally loyal votes would be siphoned off, and for conservative Democrats in the general election, who might see thousands of usually straight-ticket Democratic votes wander off to answer the ethnic call. This major potential problem, along with those of the more traditional nature, were under deep consideration by the conservative Democrat leaders who prepared to do battle against the legal challenge from the outsiders, liberal Democrats and Republicans, in early January 1972.

Most of the people active in politics were preparing for the 1972 campaigns, but the legal drama would be played out in Austin at the Federal Courthouse before a special three-judge panel — Irving L. Goldberg of the Fifth Circuit, and two Federal district judges who would become well known, liberal Democrat William Wayne Justice of Tyler, for his controversial decisions on integration and prison reform, and conservative Republican John H. Wood of San Antonio, who would be assassinated after laying down tough decisions against drug trafficking.

The liberals had a battery of lawyers, led by State Senator Oscar Mauzy of Dallas, and sharp statisticians, notably Dan Weiser, also of Dal-

las, to set forth their thrust that countywide elections in Dallas discriminated against ethnic minorities.

The Republican case was presented by Tom Crouch, the Dallas County
GOP chairman who was an accomplished courtroom lawyer. At his side
was Tom Gee, longtime GOP attorney of Austin, who would become a
Federal judge. The thrust of the GOP case was that the enormous cost
of conducting countywide urban races rendered it virtually impossible
for an ordinary citizen to win. A candidate had to be blessed with a tremendous amount of money he could afford to spend himself, as Fred
Agnich testified to having done, or else be a handpicked part of some
slate bankrolled by special interests.

The conservative Democrats were on the defensive, relying more on
tradition than substantive rebuttal. It was difficult defending a system
that required an individual in Dallas to campaign before 1.3 million people
rather than 75,000 in order to win a relatively thankless job that didn't
pay a living wage. It did not sound like democracy's finest hour, but
their forces sent forth an imposing array of legal and political talent into
the courtroom, led by Frank Erwin and Leon Jaworski. They were playing out the high-stakes game as best they could.

In retrospect, the case seemed to have been clear-cut, but at the
time, there were no sure bets. Judicial restraint had been practiced regarding reapportionment suits since, as one judge had stated, courts could
enter into a "judicial thicket" in which precise guidelines would be difficult to determine. Writing about the uncertainty of the case in an inter-
pretive article for *The Dallas Morning News*, Sam Kinch, Jr., observed
that "the U.S. Supreme Court has set some stiff and difficult rules of
evidence for the proof of allegations that multi-member districts are discriminatory against racial and political minorities ..."

Regarding the stakes involved, Kinch noted that a plaintiff victory
"will affect the politics of the state for years," and observing the views
of Mauzy and Crouch, "would dramatically change the complexion of
the Legislature, both cosmetically and philosophically."

When confronted with the fact that Harris County (Houston), had
single-member legislative districts but the rest of the state did not, the
confident Jaworski, an imposing figure who was then president of the
American Bar Association, replied in what Kinch termed a "classic performance" that though the plan "is inconsistent doesn't matter, unless
you show it violates the Constitution." Jaworski held to the position that
the plaintiffs failed in their "awesome" burden of proving their case.

In addition to his points about the high cost of campaigning, Crouch hit a nerve when he referred to testimony by a leading Dallas conservative Democrat, William H. Clark III, who said that the conservative slate organization would back three blacks in 1972, rather than one as currently. "We have heard shocking testimony about three black candidates being slated for 1972," Crouch said. "Why can't the people decide like they will in Houston (with single-member districts)?"

David Richards, one of the top liberal lawyers, bolstered that point by contending the slate system freezes out blacks from the nominating process. The decisions, he said, were made by downtown business interests in Dallas that had few, if any, contacts in the black community. "Blacks are not entitled to black senators or representatives," Richards said. "They are entitled to full participation in the electoral process."

For Bexar County, the thrust of the plaintiffs' position was that Mexican-Americans had about fifty percent of the population, but had only one state representative — Bob Vale — whose surname was Anglo. A political scientist from Saint Mary's University, Dr. Charles L. Cotrell, contended that individual districts with about 74,000 constituents would open up representation as opposed to the countywide system. Young Mexican-Americans in San Antonio, he said, believed the whole electoral process was an "Anglo tool" to freeze them out. Bexar County Republicans also complained of gerrymandering in the state senate districting. But virtually all legal participants in the proceedings believed the judges were only interested in resolving the question of individual district elections as opposed to countywide elections for state representatives.

When the proceeding ended, a few of the Republican and liberal Democrat participants paused on the courthouse steps to reflect a moment. It was a cold January day. People wanted to head for their cars, but the prospect for victory, such a significant victory, kept them together for a few minutes, reviewing what had seemed to be the high moments during four days of tedious testimony. Their political philosophies on the liberal – conservative scale were worlds apart, but some of these veterans had worked together for their common goals since John Tower's first election in 1961, through the Rebuilding Committee programs for Tower, Bush, and Eggers, the "Dirty Thirty" battles of the previous spring, and into the federal courtroom for the case just concluded. It had been more than a decade since Tower's first election when the two disparate political elements had come together for the purpose of furthering the quest for a two-party system. No one spoke of it that day, but they seemed to sense the days of such coalitions were over. Indeed, they would be.

The court would rule in favor of the liberal Democrat – Republican side, opening a path for two-party advancement throughout urban Texas. It was the end of a political era, perhaps the most unlikely in the state's modern history, but also pivotal.

All the while the Sharpstown scandal, the "Dirty Thirty," and redistricting episodes were in progress, John Tower had been preparing for his second reelection campaign. Shortly after the 1970 elections were over, Tower heeded the thought expressed by one of his old friends, *Look cool and confident on the surface while running as hard as a scared jackrabbit*. Party morale was nowhere near as low as it had been following the 1964 debacle, but it needed shoring up after the defeats of Bush and Eggers. One encouraging early point in Tower's favor was the promotion of Anne Armstrong to the position of cochairman of the Republican National Committee. From there she could help the senior senator from Texas. But all was not pleasant for Tower in Washington, where Nixon tapped John Connally to be his cabinet Democrat as Secretary of the Treasury. This move miffed many Texas Republicans when they read that Tower had allegedly not been consulted. Tower also had found how difficult it could be to serve in the Senate and work with Texas conservative Democrat congressmen, yet be expected to operate as a party leader at home and support Republicans against those friends in Washington. Such had been the case in 1970, when Republican Dick Gill ran against Clark Fisher, the powerful pro-defense Democrat who represented the sprawling Twenty-first District that ran from North Bexar County through the Hill Country, deep into West Texas. Fisher put out a newsletter dated November 12, 1970, castigating Tower for his role in supporting Gill, who was branded as "Tower's boy." For the 1971 – 1972 election cycle, Tower would again adopt the posture of running his own campaign, asking no help from other candidates, nor offering assistance to them.

In the summer of 1970, Tower had received an offer from Austin businessman Julian Zimmerman to raise early funds for an off-year political program in 1971. Tower had accepted the offer and Zimmerman launched a fund-raising program under a committee banner of "Friends of John Tower." Zimmerman was a rare individual in Texas GOP politics, a savvy businessman and effective political fund-raiser, yet one who possessed considerable political acumen in general, including the ability to size up people and strategic situations accurately. He was president of Lumberman's Investment Corporation, a growing company in the Arthur Temple empire located in the Westgate Building directly west of the state capitol grounds. The Westgate Building was home of the Headliners Club, the most important gathering place in the political arena of Austin in those days.

The idea of Tower starting political activity early was brought about not only by the GOP adversity sustained in Texas in 1970, but by the fact that Tower's two previous victories had occurred in non-presidential elections. His only statewide race in a presidential year had been in 1960, when he lost to LBJ by a wide margin. Looking ahead to 1972 and Nixon's reelection campaign was an uncertain proposition indeed, but Tower knew for certain that the voter turnout in 1972 would be vastly higher than it was in 1966, his most recent election. Therefore, it was wise to start early and run hard with a strategic plan that contemplated his reelection campaign divided into two major phases. First would be the 1971 off-year with the incumbent doing an effective job for his state, representing the thinking of a majority of Texans. Much of that would be done from his Washington office by accelerated direct mail. For Tower's personal appearances, the 1971 phase would emphasize the gruelling, logistically-demanding task of appearing principally in the "cow counties" of rural Texas, in those many little communities where Bush and Eggers had been "nickeled and dimed to death." Appearances in those communities were thought to be particularly effective when a nonpartisan event of high community interest, such as the annual Chamber of Commerce banquet or commencement exercise, could be secured. Phase Two would be the general-election-1972 campaign, tailored when the opponent was determined, but stressing throughout the value of incumbency and bipartisan representation for Texas in the Senate, plus all the other favorable factors relating directly to his office, such as prominence on the Armed Services Committee.

To implement the two-year strategy, Tower had a strong Washington staff under the direction of his AA, Dick Agnich, son of the new state representative from Dallas, Fred Agnich. His Austin office was directed by Nola Smith, whose campaign and party experience made her ideal to work Tower's involvement in patronage along with liaison to the State GOP and preparation for the campaign. She was a strikingly attractive brunette who would have appeared at home on the cover of a glamor magazine, but who had a political personality derived from working in the medical auxillary and through the regular GOP organization in various capacities before joining Tower's staff. Tower made it clear that he was leaning toward naming her his state campaign manager, the first woman to hold such a position in a major statewide race in Texas, but a choice he knew would be well accepted in party circles. In any event, having strong leadership in those two offices was important to Tower in 1971, a year of preparation. Commitments were made to provide Tower with professional public relations assitance in the state, incuding Bob Heller and Jim Culberson of Houston, who had played prominent roles in the Tower 1966 campaign, and had formed their own public relations and advertising firm. A political office was utilized on Guadalupe Street, a few blocks from the Federal Building in Austin, so that no conflicts could be alleged. That office handled Tower's scheduling in Texas, under the direction of Carlton Suiter, and served as a repository for vast amounts of research data and other material that would be used in the forthcoming campaign. Marvin Collins was retained to direct preparations for a major fund-raising/publicity event, the "Decade of Service" dinner to be held in Dallas on May 27, commemorating the ten years since Tower had first been elected. Bill Clements was dinner chairman and, working with Zimmerman's committee, did a tremendous job selling tickets at $150 a piece together with special tables at higher prices per plate. That dinner served further notice that the Republican-liberal coalition was no longer necessary for Tower. His dinner received strong support from some top conservative Democrat leaders, including Allan Shivers of Austin, the former governor still potent in Texas politics; and such heavyweights in the Texas financial community as Ben Carpenter and Trammell Crow of Dallas, Hayden Head of Corpus Christi, Michael T. Halbouty of Houston, and Roy J. Smith of Killeen. Also of significance politically was the attendance of several key mayors, including Louie Welch of Houston, R.M. (Sharkey) Stovall of Fort Worth, Roy Butler of Austin, and Mayor Pro Tem Ted Holland of Dallas. Ron Calhoun, political writer for *The Dallas Times Herald*, and never one to pass out accolades casually, flatly termed the dinner at the Fairmont Hotel "the most successful fundraiser for a Republican in Texas history." The net proceeds for the dinner were in excess of $250,000 which, in those days, meant that it was a smashing success. In addition to the show of strength exhibited by all the Texas Republican faithful and the many friends of Tower from across the state, the aura of the event was enhanced considerably by the special guests, including United States Attorney General John Mitchell and Senators Bill Brock of Tennessee, Henry Bellmon of Oklahoma, Howard Baker of Tennessee, Paul Fannin of Arizona, Peter Dominick of Colorado, Roman Hruska of Nebraska, and Robert Griffin of Michigan. Videotaped messages were presented from President Nixon, Senator Barry Goldwater,

United Nations Ambassador George Bush and others. The AP story said that 1,600 friends of Tower "did him proud last night. They fed him a $150-a-plate dinner, heaped him with praise, and assured him of their backing as senior United States senator for Texas when he runs again next year ..." Calhoun chided Tower for being a bit "maudlin" in his speech but termed it "quite effective." The AP article noted that Tower praised the Senate as a great institution which he would not change although "some people think it is anachronistic. It has been a great ten years ... because it has given me an opportunity to serve." Invoking such Texas heroes as Stephen F. Austin, Sam Houston, and William Barret Travis, as well as his father and grandfather who were Methodist ministers, Tower said he thought his own contribution might be "pretty puny by comparison." Talking quietly of his great love for Texas, he adopted an almost poetic turn of phrase. He called the state "This great and happy and progressive land," and concluded, "My last thought will be for her. Tejas, Tejas, beautiful country." To a standing ovation, Tower wiped his eyes in a rare public display of emotion as everyone in the banquet hall, including the news media, concluded that the onetime "fluke" of Texas politics was indeed standing tall for reelection in 1972.

While Tower's political efforts in 1971 had been successful in Texas, the national Republican administration, to which his fortunes were tied in 1972, was not successful at all. In fact, it had become counterproductive. The Vietnam War dragged on, with its attendant cost in American lives, funding and anguish of her people, and a new issue, even more divisive, had developed. Zealous bureaucrats in the Department of Health, Education and Welfare (HEW) and the Justice Department were pressing for massive forced busing of school children, often for great distances, ostensibly as a means to remove the last vestiges of segregation, but proceeding to seek rigid ethnic quotas. In the view of conservative attorneys, "two wrongs don't make a right," and the new attacks were punitive and vindictive in nature. The zealots were substituting sociological theory for law, ignoring the fact that the United States Constitution is color blind. The heart of Nixon's support was in middle-America, Anglo-dominated white-collar sections of cities in which the tax-paying citizens took for granted that their nearby neighborhood public schools "came with the territory" in which they had invested their money to live and raise their families. These citizens were indeed upset at the proposition of a high-handed Federal government dictating such disruptive policies.

One of the most volatile cases occurred in Austin, a city with a moderate image and voting record, never one to have been accused of overt, conniving racial injustice during the emerging era of racial consciousness. A veteran Federal judge, Jack Roberts, tried repeatedly to work out a reasonable settlement with the bureaucrats and the local school board. But the zealots appeared determined to destroy the concept of neighborhood schools, no matter what the cost in resulting racial disharmony or citizen revulsion of such high-handed tactics. Austin attorney Bill Lynch, who had run an unsuccessful race for the Legislature on the GOP ticket, ran a highly successful campaign as chairman of the ad hoc Austin Anti-Busing League, gathering 20,000 signatures on a petition against forced busing which he hand delivered to elected officials in Washington.

Nixon responded to the public pressure by making strong antibusing statements, but many of the old-line Republicans didn't accept his pronouncements at first. After all, he had campaigned against forced busing, why couldn't he call off the dogs in his own administration? Dr. George Willeford of Austin, the new Republican state chairman who succeeded Steger, was incensed by the issue. He called the White House and other Republican power points in Washington, giving them the Texas position in no uncertain terms. He fired off a letter in the summer of 1971 to Republican National Chairman Robert Dole, the U.S. senator from Kansas, in which he stated:

> I can assure you that no single issue, be it Vietnam or the economy, has the attention of the people of Texas ahead of this busing issue. I suspect that if the President continues to be blamed for busing massive numbers of Texas children, he will be defeated in 1972 in this state. If we are strong-armed by a runaway department of HEW, Republicans will not work for Nixon, Conservative Democrats will not work for Nixon, and we will all suffer the consequences. As a State Chairman struggling to build a Republican organization in a state with almost 100 years of Democrat history, it is extremely discouraging to feel so out of touch with my Party's National Administration. I can frankly state that there is considerable feeling within the Republican Party of Texas that the Party on the state level should publicly and dramatically disassociate itself from the Nixon Administration and from the Republican National Party ...

That language may seem a bit tough in retrospect, but it was measured and mild compared to what grass roots Republicans were saying in Austin and other busing-impact communities. They believed they had been betrayed by Nixon. The fact that Nixon had allegedly ignored Tower when he named Connally to the cabinet was actually in Tower's favor in the summer of 1971. Tower might not have conveyed the aura of being an adroit politician with as much attendant power as surrounded Nixon and his entourage, but Tower remained perceived as trustworthy by his troops, a tie that binds in politics when all others might fail.

In the fall of 1971, it was rumored that a number of Democrats were aiming for Tower's seat. Most prominent early on was Ben Barnes, the boy wonder of Texas Democratic politics who had been annointed by LBJ to lead the flock. As lieutenant governor, Barnes wielded tremendous power and was the heir apparent to Connally's throne as leader of the moderate-conservative power structure for which Dick West still wrote many glowing editorials in the *Dallas Morning News*. A few key people in Tower's camp had developed something akin to paranoia about Barnes, fearing his youth and vote-getting ability would be too much for Tower. But there were also those who saw Barnes as something of a Waggoner Carr-type candidate, a successful state politician with no experience on the federal scene, one who would surely make mistakes on complex foreign policy issues. Plus, rightly or wrongly, Barnes had to bear some of the stigma from the Sharpstown scandal. In any event, Barnes opted for the governor's race where he was chewed up in the Democratic Primary, (along with Preston Smith, seeking another term), by Dolph Briscoe, the Uvalde rancher and onetime state legislator far removed from "that mess in Austin," and Frances (Sissy) Farenthold, a liberal state representative from Corpus Christi, who had been a leader in the "Dirty Thirty" coalition. The Sharpstown fallout had hit Barnes and Smith at the ballot box. Mutscher would eventually face prosecution by Travis County District Attorney Robert O. (Bob) Smith, a conservative Democrat, but not part and parcel of the ruling faction. Smith had judicial ambitions, and his decision to go after Mutscher was certainly risky to his political career, since the faction's power brokers had quite a stake in Mutscher. Smith's deft prosecution of Mutscher won a conviction, but Smith paid the price, losing his subsequent bid for a judicial position in the Democratic Primary. He ultimately changed to the GOP.

In the Republican Primary Hank Grover defeated Al Fay in a runoff for the gubernatorial nomination. Dave Reagan of Sherman, an Austin College adminstrator and newcomer as a candidate, made a spirited bid, but the two well known Republicans from Houston, with its high primary vote, were the front-runners. Grover and Fay had dealt with one another without bitterness during the primary, but Grover had been critical of the state party leadership, portending problems down the road.

When Barnes had chosen the gubernatorial route, that cleared the way for a newcomer on the statewide scene to carry the banner against Ralph Yarborough for the U.S. Senate nomination. That was Barefoot Sanders, a former state legislator from Dallas who could bridge the gap between liberal and conservative Democrat politics. Yarborough was favored due to his Senate experience and long-standing statewide political organization. But he was attempting a comeback as a product of an era in which oratorical harangues before old-fashioned gatherings, such as union picnics and county fairs, were integral to a winning campaign. In the new context, soft sell, carefully-crafted television commercials, usually portraying a personality more than positions on issues, were taking center stage. It was a multicandidate primary field and Yarborough managed to lead the pack going into a runoff with Sanders. But Sanders defeated Yarborough, a development that upset the Tower Campaign. Most of Tower's operatives, including Nola Smith, had assumed Yarborough would be their opponent and considerable research had been done with that prospect in mind. The day after Sanders won the runoff, she organized a fast trip to Washington for herself and a few top Tower advisors to have a hurried strategy session with the senator. Accepting the new challenge, the group could see problems that Yarborough wouldn't have presented. Barefoot was not a nickname, it was a family name that Sanders was indeed proud to bear. Most of his campaign material pictured him with an open collar and no coat, tousled hair, and a smile on his freckled face. It all added up to an advertising agency's dream for an image contrast with the "cool and aloof" Tower and his stiff collars, suspenders and pinstripe suits. It would be Huckleberry Finn versus Mr. Cool and Aloof, an unsavory prospect to contemplate, yet Tower's advisors agreed it would be dangerous to attack Sanders since Tower had to play the role of longtime incumbent, favored to win reelection. It was generally agreed that Tower should stay on the "high road," selling himself and his record, avoiding criticism of Sanders. But as the meeting in Tower's office broke up, the senator paused a moment before saying, "Can't argue with it now, but if he gets me into trouble, I'm going to hang Ramsey Clark around his neck." Sanders had won the Democratic nomination without many questions raised about his friendship and political association with the controversial former attorney general who had contributed to his campaign. Sanders had been able to run mostly an image campaign with few questions having been raised about his political philosophy which leaned liberal. But since he had defeated Yarborough, he was perceived by many people as a moderate or moderate-conservative.

Tower soon found that he not only had to contend with Sanders, but with a serious intra-party problem in the form of Hank Grover's candidacy for governor. Grover had run as something of a maverick, enjoying support from Nancy Palm in Houston, because of his frequent tweaks of the state GOP leadership with whom Palm had been feuding from time to time. When the Republican State Convention in June 1972 was held in Galveston, the situation became serious when Grover let it be known he was considering calling for the ouster of the party leadership, principally Willeford, the state chairman and long-standing Tower ally. In his suite at the Galvez Hotel across the street from the convention hall, Tower held strategy sessions with various of his supporters and liaison people to the other side. Tower met with Grover privately the night before the convention and believed that no serious split would occur, that he and Grover could cooperate as each pursued his own campaign. But for whatever substantive or subtle reasons, Grover went through with his threat the following day during a dramatic speech to the convention.

Peter O'Donnell, Fred Agnich and other longtime Texas Republican leaders were behind the stage when Grover made his demand for ousting the state GOP chairman. They knew they had the votes to ward off such a move which, according to procedures, should not have even been considered until the fall convention, and they were upset with Grover for creating a divisive situation during such a high-stakes election year. Tower appeared to take it in stride, but his longtime associates knew he was deeply concerned over a party division in the middle of a long election year in which he faced a stern challenge. Most of the state's political writers proceeded to write off Grover, believing the split he'd engendered would only work against him in terms of campaign funding and organizational support. They believed he would limp home far behind Briscoe, who had won the Democratic gubernatorial nomination.

By the summer of 1972, Nixon's reelection bid had evolved into a favorable factor for Tower. Some of the steam from the forced busing issue had been let out, or at least directed to some other source, such as Federal courts. Nixon convinced a majority of the American public that his Vietnam policy was the proper course to take, and perhaps most importantly, the Democrats were about to nominate Senator George McGovern of South Dakota, whose doctrinaire liberalism was anathema in most parts of Texas. The heavy liberal coloration of the Democratic national party made it all the easier for Zimmerman and his fund raising apparatus that included Brad O'Leary, a strong professional fund-raiser he had summoned from Missouri.

On the Mexican-American front, Tower had an effective operative in Humberto (Beto) Aguirre, a seasoned pro originally from Del Rio, who was based on Fifteenth Street in Austin following his departure from the staff of Governor Smith. He helped rekindle support from the faithful M-As from previous years, plus melded in new people who were ready to join the GOP or who saw some immediate advantage by aligning with President Nixon and Senator Tower, who appeared headed for reelection. Federal money flowed through a number of programs and the winners of the competition for those dollars often depended upon party allegiance. Aguirre kept close tabs on the progress of the Raza Unida candidates for U.S. Senate and governor, concluding that Flores Amaya, in the U.S. Senate race probably wouldn't draw a heavy vote but Ramsey Muniz, an articulate attorney and onetime Baylor football star, was indeed making inroads beyond the narrow base of purely ethnic loyalty.

In 1972, Nola Smith had a strong organization functioning in a large campaign headquarters on Fifteenth Street until suspected arson struck on May 9, burning down the building as well as some of the records and materials. She was able to secure a large headquarters building on Congress Avenue, two blocks south of the capitol grounds, and the operation went smoothly thereafter.

Heavy fund-raising was needed to fuel a large campaign organization with fifty-six paid employees and the high-priced media advertising. Much of the campaign's execution relied upon extensive research materials prepared under the direction of Jacque Irby, a veteran of several years' service for the State GOP. The campaign attracted many young people, some of whom would remain active in politics for years, including Richard English, K.C. McAlpin, and Sheila Wilkes. Some of Tower's Senate office staffers in Austin, including Jo Ann Allen, were converted to campaign duty. Lionel Rawlings and Marci Sauls ran a "Black Texans For Tower" program that was long on heart and effort but unable to turn a large percentage of blacks from their affinity to the Democratic Party.

For the fall state convention, Grover would withdraw his objection to Willeford's reelection as state chairman, smoothing over that problem for the short run, and Nixon's continuing strength seemed to be boosting Tower's chances. A fair amount of harmony existed among the major Republican elements operating in the state, including the campaign for Nixon and Tower and the Texas GOP operation, with Grover doing his own thing, running hard against Briscoe though largely ignored by the news media. But an irritant kept recurring when Nixon would appear to be more concerned with Connally's advice and presence in Texas than Tower's. The situation wasn't enhanced when former Congressman Joe Kilgore, Connally's longtime close friend and political associate, became state campaign chairman for Sanders and a strong Democrats for Nixon

Committee, inspired by Connally, made it clear two months prior to the election that its activities were for Nixon only, not Tower. Such as that, plus concern over symbolic points including whether Tower or Connally would deplane from *Air Force One* with Nixon on occasion, would upset some of Tower's campaign officials, including Nola Smith. Forrest Roan, a savvy young Connally ally who wanted to help Tower, found the atmosphere a bit chilly at the Tower state headquarters and didn't pursue his efforts.

A major plus factor for Tower was the conversion of Ed Clark, who personified the old power equation of Texas politics, having been close to LBJ for decades, including having served as his ambassador to Australia, plus having worked closely with many other prominent Texas Democratic politicians, including Ralph Yarborough. The veteran Austin lobbyist was a rotund attorney originally from East Texas, from which he derived a homespun demeanor and manner of speaking. In the shifting sands of the Texas political arena in the summer of 1972, he probably found the transition from Yarborough to Tower easier than expected thanks to the spadework done by the pragmatic Zimmerman. Apparently, Clark and many of his cohorts had been convinced by Tower's 1966 victory and recent show of strength, plus the virtual certainty of Nixon sweeping Texas in November. They wanted to ride the winner in both races. But there was the matter of making Clark's transition credible, so Tower offered Clark the chairmanship of his main campaign committee, "Texans For Tower," a move encouraged by Zimmerman and Nola Smith. The formal announcement was made at a news conference in the stately old Supreme Court Room in the state capitol, an august setting for the cagey Clark to extoll the virtues of Tower while condemning the evils of "McGovernism." It all went well until during the question and answer session when Sam Kinch, Jr., inquired of Clark what he would have done if Yarborough, his old friend, had won the Democratic nomination. To which Clark, in his inimitable twangy East Texas brogue replied, "Well, now, that is an 'iffy' question ... Such an iffy question that I just don't think I ought to have to answer that ..." Most politicians would have received follow up questions from the news media, but Clark had done such an obvious soft shoe that even the usually cynical and persistent Kinch had to chuckle and let him off the hook.

Among repeat programs from 1966 were the Lou Tower Tours, separate campaign appearances for the senator's popular wife, and another full-page ad in *Texas Football Magazine* with a long list of well known former football players endorsing Tower under the sponsorship of the ad hoc booster committee with Weldon Smith again serving as chairman. Organizational efforts were keyed to phone banks from which massive numbers of calls were made to locate voters favorable to Tower or undecided. When out personally campaigning in urban Texas, Tower would make it a point to stop by and visit with staff and volunteers at the phone banks where the daily grind was dull and tedious. Many of the phone banks were working for Nixon and Tower in tandem, and they were reliable sounding boards for projecting voter turnout in given areas.

About the time Ed Clark came aboard in the summer of 1972, a new statewide poll was received from Decision Making Information (DMI), a highly regarded polling firm based in Los Angeles. Vince Barraba, a sharp analyst from that firm, was the bearer of bad news. Incredibly, Sanders was leading Tower, forty-eight percent to thirty-six percent, with sixteen percent divided between undecided voters and those favoring Amaya. How, asked Tower, could he be twelve percent behind, after ten years of service in the Senate and so much favorable publicity generated in the past year and one-half? Tower was crestfallen, so distressed that he confided to Nola Smith that perhaps he should step aside, let someone else carry the party banner which he suddenly felt he wasn't carrying properly. As was the case following the 1964 elections, no one wanted Tower to step aside. The stern challenge was to determine what had caused such startling results and what course of action could be pursued to reverse them rapidly. Of paramount concern immediately was to keep strict security over the results. Only a trusted handful would know the favored Tower was well behind, and none of them wanted to predict the adverse effect if the results were leaked and published. Those conversant with the psychology of campaigning knew there would be a discouraging impact upon Tower's contributors and supporters that might be irreversible.

If ever the ephemeral nature of Texas politics had been exemplified, it was in the results of the DMI statewide poll in the summer of 1972. Sanders, riding the Huckleberry Finn image for all it was worth, had suddenly captured the imagination of a plurality of Texans who saw him as a "good guy" and really didn't know much about his political philosophy. In the summer afterglow of the primary runoff, Sanders was perceived as having defeated the "bad guy," the old liberal Yarborough who they were ready to see retired. When one looked closely beneath the results of the survey, Sanders was having his cake and eating it too. The real task of the Tower Campaign was to paint him as liberal as he could be painted, otherwise if it came down to a choice between acceptable candidates, Sanders would probably win. The sudden choices created a sharp division in the Tower Campaign. So much time and resources had been spent on the positive image-building of the incumbent, that to change strategy abruptly, with frontal attacks on the challenger, seemed to be a high risk choice. A prudent course of action would be to temporize, let things simmer down and hope that surely Sanders would lose some of that halo. A continuation of positive promotion of Tower might move the figures into better balance. While the question was being debated, Sanders launched a tough anti-Tower campaign, including allegations that Tower was a special interest senator who collected large sums of money in honoraria, then voted the interests of those who had paid them. Tower was also portrayed as being under the political direction of the "Kingpin of the lobbyists," Ed Clark. The anti-Tower material was so harsh that Sanders was promptly branded around the headquarters as "Barefoot *Slanders*." After hearing scorching anti-Tower radio commercials driving to work each morning, Nola Smith would come into the headquarters literally gritting her teeth. Zimmerman, who had been a hawk all along, bore down with the argument that it was time to counterattack, and do it with all guns firing. The number one target was Ramsey Clark, the controversial former attorney general and longtime associate of Sanders, who had given him $2,000 for the 1972 campaign. That was brought out in a radio spot, along with a hard-hitting commercial linking Sanders to McGovern, and still another that questioned Sanders for not endorsing Tower's constitutional amendment against forced busing. Sanders had waffled a bit on the busing issue, trying to hold his liberal support while contending with the irate middle class conservatives. He would find it was an issue that didn't lend itself to waffling.

Nola Smith had secured the services of Kyle Thompson, who left his position as state capitol bureau chief with United Press International (UPI), to become campaign press secretary with the promise that if Tower won reelection, Thompson would become the senator's press secretary in Washington. Jimmy Banks, former state capitol correspondent for *The Dallas Morning News*, had also come aboard. They proceeded to lambast Sanders with a barrage of charges in concert with those hard-hitting radio commercials.

By mid-September, Tower was hammering away. The AP quoted him as saying he "would never vote to confirm a government appointment for former United States Attorney General Ramsey Clark or anyone else who becomes a dupe for Communist propaganda ..." Tower said he was "glad that Ramsey Clark is supporting my opponent, an old crony of his ... Frankly, I do not invite the support of anyone who goes to Hanoi and condemns our country."

Some key people in the Austin political arena, not active in Tower's campaign, informed a few of Tower's operatives quietly that they thought the Tower Campaign had taken a downturn with the heavy attack on Sanders. They viewed the move as unorthodox strategy with Tower guilty of poor judgement, embarking on a course that would backfire and create sympathy for Sanders, who, they rightly surmised, was still perceived as the underdog. What they didn't know, of course, was the tightly held secret that Tower had been trailing. Within two weeks after the counterattack had been launched, spot polling results indicated the desired change was in progress. Television spots were then made with Tower talking directly to the viewers. These were used in concert with the material on the radio spots, though were not quite as hard-hitting.

Senator Lloyd Bentsen, whom Connally helped defeat George Bush in 1970, came out strong for Sanders in late September, a move that, along with the conservative Kilgore's role, gave Sanders needed conservative credentials. But the Tower Campaign had turned the momentum since the uncertain days following the DMI summer poll, and by late September, new DMI results showed Tower leading by forty-four- and one-half percent to thirty- and one-half percent with twenty-five percent spread among undecided and the Raza Unida candidate. Nola Smith released those poll results which helped fund-raising move toward the three million dollar mark before campaign's end. In the final weeks, Sanders was clearly perceived as liberal, on the wrong side of those emotional issues.

On election day reports drifted into the Tower state headquarters to the effect that voter turnout was heavy in conservative areas around the state. That was a positive sign with Nixon's strength and Tower's hope of having converted late his share of the undecided voters in conservative areas where he couldn't equal Nixon's vote but he would certainly benefit from it. As the hours dragged by that day, Nola Smith took a long walk down Congress Avenue in what she later described as a "total vacuum," with nothing to do at the headquarters but "wait and pray." Nola Smith had stood up well to the pressure of being the first woman in Texas to manage a major statewide campaign, and as a fierce competitor, she wanted the victory badly.

On election night, early indicators bore out what had been predicted — Nixon would carry Texas by a landslide in the range of sixty-six percent. Tower took an opening lead that showed solid trend lines, causing the networks to declare him a winner early by a safe margin, confusing a bit the manner percentages are usually reported because of the La Raza Unida candidate, but heading toward a 300,000 vote margin, about 100,000 wider numerically than his margin of 1966. Shortly after Tower had been declared the winner and the champagne was uncorked in his state headquarters, Ed Clark came ambling in at the proper moment to deliver an eloquent speech about the campaign, Tower's great future and a few other morsels. While the exuberant Nola Smith and her cohorts at the headquarters watched Tower on television from Wichita Falls make calm, cogent statements about his victory, Clark eased to the UPI tele-type where late results were forthcoming. Bells were ringing to indicate bulletin material. Clark peered down at the wire copy to read an incred-ible bulletin — Hank Grover, the maverick GOP nominee for governor whom the news media had long written off, was riding such a pro-Nixon voting spree in Texas, that one of the networks had projected him to defeat Briscoe. *"Gawd A-mighty!"* Clark exclaimed increduously, recoiling at the thought of an unharnessed Grover in the governor's chair, at the heart of power in Texas. "Wot's goin' on in this state?" As the night wore on, the late-reporting rural vote went heavily for Briscoe who ulti-mately won by about 100,000 votes, but Grover's competitive race im-planted him as a factor in the Texas political arena for years to come.

Another Republican statewide candidate who came in with a supris-ingly strong showing was State Representative Maurice Angly of Austin, who ran against the longtime incumbent state treasurer, Jesse James. Angly was able to spend only $120,000 but garnered a slightly higher percent-age than Grover, and came within three percentage points of winning. That race, like those for United States Senate and governor, had a Raza Unida candidate. A consolation for Angly was the fact that for three con-secutive general elections as a down-ballot candidate, he led the GOP ticket in Travis County. In 1972 he outpolled Nixon, Tower, and Grover.

Bonuses for the GOP from the 1972 election included Alan Steelman, the former Dallas County GOP executive director who defeated incum-bent conservative Democrat Earle Cabell for the Fifth congressional dis-trict seat in Dallas, plus Republican Betty Andujar of Fort Worth, who became the only woman in the state senate when she defeated State Rep-resentative Mike Moncrief. Moncrief bore the burden of having been a close ally of Gus Mutscher. Walter Mengden defeated two of his House colleagues en route to winning the state senate seat vacated by Grover. Breakthroughs in the Texas House were evident by virtue of the changes to single member districts. Jim Nowlin, the converted Democrat, made a successful comeback in Bexar County and Joe Sage, a retired Air Force colonel, won a seat there to give Bexar County Republicans a long needed shot of political adrenalin with their first state representatives in modern history. From only one member in the 1971 session, Fred Agnich, Dal-las County saw its GOP legislative delegation increased markedly by the addition of Bob Davis, Frank Gaston, Ray Hutchison, Al Korioth, Bob Maloney, and Richard Reynolds. Harris County also increased its delega-tion substantially with five new members, Kay Bailey, Ray Barnhart, Milton Fox, Don Henderson, and Larry Vick. The Federal court had final-ly opened the two-party door in the Texas House of Representatives where

GOP strength at seventeen didn't sound impressive per se in a 150-member body. But the sudden change in the state's two most populous counties was significant indeed.

On balance, 1972 had been a highly successful year for Texas Republicans. Their foremost goal, the reelection of Senator John Tower, had been acheived in style, securing his position in the Senate for six more years. Those would be six years they could depend upon to have a continuing figure around whom they could rally. The scare Grover threw into Briscoe was impressive, as was Angly's challenge for state treasurer. In 1972, Nixon became the first GOP presidential candidate to carry Texas since Eisenhower in 1956. Spirits were indeed high for the future. Particularly gratifying for the Tower Campaign was the fact that in the three categories covering all 254 counties in Texas, the senator ran steadily on target. In the category of the top twenty-seven most populous counties, Tower received fifty-four percent, the same as in the fifty-two medium counties. In the remaining 175 counties classified as rural, Tower received fifty-one percent. His "cow county" strategy had paid off. The ticket-splitting was obvious because Grover managed only thirty-two percent in the rural category, while the Houston-based candidate had won over forty-eight percent in the top twenty-seven category. In numerical terms, Tower had received 1,822,583 votes to 1,511,669 for Sanders, a Tower margin of better than 310,000 votes. Part of Briscoe's problem with Grover was revealed in the total vote of 214,118 for Ramsey Muniz, by far the highest among the Raza Unida statewide candidates. In the immediate postelection punditry from the Capitol Press Corps, this fact was not widely taken into account. Under closer study, some analysts would determine Muniz made it close because Grover, unlike Tower, had made little effort for the Mexican-American vote. Therefore, had Muniz not run, most of the votes he received would have gone to Briscoe. In such heavily populated Mexican-American counties as Bexar, El Paso, and Nueces, Tower ran far ahead of Grover whereas the Houstonian ran ahead of Tower in some parts of the Gulf Coast. The ticket-splitting between presidential, United States Senate, gubernatorial, and state treasurer races — augmented by the Raza Unida factor in the Texas contests — was unique fodder for political analysts to ponder for years to follow.

Also gratifying for Tower was the fact that his campaign set a record for number of contributors in Texas. There were some 30,000 whose average donations were moderate, and far from the perception of a few wealthy power brokers bankrolling a conservative campaign. Art Wiese of *The Houston Post* state capitol bureau summed it up in a postelection article that appeared on November 13, "Republican John G. Tower mounted the most expensive and possibly the most professional, sophisticated campaign in Texas political history ..."

CHAPTER TEN

The Long Shadow of Watergate

For Texas Republicans, the 1973 – 1974 election cycle actually started the day after the 1972 general election, since Grover made it clear he was running again. Tower and his lieutenants had considered Grover to be an irritating maverick during 1972. Now they viewed him as a clear threat, an unsettling factor who might wrest party control from Tower should he be elected governor. Yet none of those who opposed Grover in the 1972 primary seemed to be in a position for a repeat try, nor was there a big name waiting in the wings, despite the strong GOP afterglow from the sweeping victories by Nixon and Tower. One of those in the anti-Grover element who started taking dead aim on the gubernatorial race was Dr. Jim Granberry, the forty-one-year-old former mayor of Lubbock, and a prominent West Texas Republican who served on the SREC. About two weeks after the 1972 election, *The Lubbock Avalanche-Journal* ran a long article under the headline of WINDS OF CHANGE CHILL DEMOCRATS, in which it was pointed out that Grover, already running again, was the first GOP gubernatorial candidate to carry Lubbock County. But Granberry was described as "very popular" in Lubbock amd his "seeking the governorship seems to grow more likely by the day." Granberry's popularity derived to a great extent from his days as mayor in 1970 when a killer tornado devastated the city. His crisis management in the aftermath received high marks from various government agencies involved. The citizens of Lubbock were indeed proud of Granberry, including students at Texas Tech. An editorial feature in *The University Daily* that November endorsed the "young, ambitious" Granberry for governor, contending that Grover's "ultra-conservatism and reluctant party support could dim the dawning GOP light to a waning apathetic flicker."

Shortly after the first of the year, some of Granberry's close friends in Lubbock, including Joe Boerner, one of the few prominent attorneys there who had been openly identifying with the GOP, began a serious evaluation of the race. No one particularly liked the idea of formally launching a campaign a year or so before the next primary, but Grover posed a unique problem. Having gained credibility with his showing against Briscoe, he had a sizeable advantage and was already generating press coverage for another race. He was well known, though certainly not uniformly supported, by grass roots Republicans around the state. To cover the ground necessary to compete with Grover would indeed be a challenge for Granberry, who was not independently wealthy and would need to maintain his orthodontist practice while running. It was a tough decision to ponder, ecpecially since Granberry had not been annointed by any of the top party leaders such as Tower or O'Donnell.

On January 22, 1973, LBJ died, formally ending that decades-long era of power and influence in the Texas political arena, and not long thereafter, his most famous protegé, John Connally, formally joined the Republican Party. Though certainly not a surprise, Connally's move generated a tremendous amount of publicity, including a long interesting article in *The Houston Post* in which state capitol correspondent Art Wiese interviewed people from all over the political spectrum. As expected, Republican leaders were generally highly pleased to have their former powerful adversary on their side. There was a concern — unspoken publicly — among some about Connally making the move in order to succeed Nixon. Fred Agnich of Dallas, the state legislator who had succeeded O'Donnell as national committeeman, predicted that other Texans would follow Connally's example, "including a number of current and former officeholders who are now Democrats." Anne Armstrong, counselor to President Nixon, said Connally,

> ... is joining us because the political philosophy of the majority of Republicans and most Americans is far more closely allied to his own than the increasingly leftist philosophy of the National Democratic Party. He is certainly to be commended for joining the party at a time when difficulties [Watergate] are being experienced ...

George Willeford, the state GOP chairman, said Connally's change "can only be an asset. We expect this move to give our candidate recruitment and other programs a desirable boost." Ike Harris of Dallas, a savvy political operative who was fast becoming a fixture in the Texas Senate, saw a pragmatic effect with Connally as an immediate major force in the GOP who would make fund raising much easier for the party and its candidates.

As expected, liberal Democrats had some unkind things to say about Connally. A searing statement, written by Dave Shapiro, was issued by the old Democratic Rebuilding Committee under the names of two of its former cochairmen, Archer Fullingim and Bob Sanchez. Terming Connally's move to the "party of Wall Street and Watergate" as "good riddance," the statement expressed "hope that the tens of thousands of other Republicans who have voted in our Democratic Primary elections and dominated the government and politics of Texas, while flying the flag of the Democratic Party, will follow ..." Former Senator Ralph Yarborough, Connally's longtime bitter foe, quipped, "It's the first time in recorded history that a rat swam towards a sinking ship."

Lieutenant Governor Bill Hobby was the only major spokesman who reacted to the change without a strong slice either way. He joked that his party had swapped Connally for New York Mayor John Lindsey, who quit the GOP in 1972. Hobby claimed the Democrats would surely get "next year's first round draft choice and a senator to be named at a later date."

A formal welcoming of Connally into the Texas GOP was soon held in Austin. Tower, the long-standing leader of Texas Republicans, made the official induction speech before the former governor and his charming wife, Nellie. It was during a cocktail – reception hosted by the SREC and attended by most of the veteran Texas GOP leaders who were anxious to extend their welcome and to size up Connally in person.

There was a sense of high drama to this unrehearsed ceremony in which the powerful Connally — whose political legions had crushed many a Republican campaign in Texas over the years — was now joining his former adversaries. Tower's position was somewhat paradoxical. He was the veteran Texas GOP general, speaking to his field grade officers about the proud defector standing nearby who had held general's rank in the opposing army, and wasn't expecting anything remotely resembling sergeant's stripes. Tower, speaking before one of the state's all-time masterful orators, made a masterful speech himself, a circumspect discourse that was fascinating. Tower's speech was filled with historical perspectives about changing eras, and enriched with Biblical parables containing double entendres. When he finished with the formal welcome to Connally, a young observer was heard inquiring of Al Fay exactly what Tower had been driving at. To which Fay responded in his dour, deadpan manner, "Tower's saying Connally is welcome to join the church, but don't start out trying to lead the choir."

Connally's move bouyed the spirits of Texas Republicans at a time when Watergate was nettling, but not thought to be pervasive. However, Grover wasn't hesitating to speak of Nixon's problem, and was quoted in *The San Antonio Light* shortly after Connally's move, "I think some people are going to go to the penitentiary ... And it's up to the President to show that he was not involved." Such a statement may have been reflective of the mood of the general populace at the time, but to many of the dedicated Republican precinct workers, upon whose support Grover had to depend to win his party's nomination again, it was nothing short of heresy. They viewed the situation as their President being harassed and hounded by an overly zealous Washington press corps.

Though the political winds were uncertain in the early summer of 1973, Granberry decided he had better launch his long campaign of catch up with Grover. He announced his candidacy on June 21, at the state capitol. Sounding a historical note, he pointed out that,

> ... in 1974, Texas voters will have the responsibility of electing a governor for the first four-year term in this century ... Thus, their judgment in choosing that leader must be more careful than in previous elections. Four years is a long time in this era of rapid change and dynamic growth and that leader, during those four years, must be ready to meet the problems, the challenges and opportunities that lie ahead.

Drawing the difference in experience and orientation with Grover, without mentioning his name, he stated that "As mayor I gained valuable administrative experience in elected public office. I know what it means to work with people, to pull things together, and to make decisions." Granberry flew to Dallas, Fort Worth, Houston, and San Antonio that day to maximize publicity.

As Granberry moved about the state in the summer of 1973, the first warning of the potential political danger of Watergate to Republican candidates became evident in a special election for the state senate. Charles Herring of Austin, the longtime incumbent Democrat serving the Central Texas District Fourteen, resigned to become general manager of the Lower Colorado River Authority. In the special election, a large multi-candidate field included two former state representatives, Maurice Angly, the Republican, and Don Cavness, a conservative Democrat, plus Lloyd Doggett, a liberal Austin attorney making his first race. Cavness had been a supporter of Mutscher and Angly was a member of the party whose national leader was under a growing cloud of suspicion. Angly edged out Cavness to make a runoff with Doggett who defeated Angly by a decisive margin. Angly had led the Republican ticket in Travis County three times, and his longtime GOP supporters stayed with him. However, the periphery of ticket-splitters beyond that Republican base wanted a "clean, fresh face" which they hoped to get with Doggett on August 14, ending Angly's string of impressive vote-getting campaigns in his bailiwick. Some observers laid the blame to the uncharacteristically strident runoff campaign Angly conducted against Doggett, but the wide margin of defeat indicated that a Watergate-induced anti-GOP bias was also a major factor.

From the anti-Grover element in the Texas GOP, Granberry was able to pick up endorsements during the summer from a number of middle-level party leaders who considered him to be a viable alternative. But when Tower, Bush and others in the high command remained noncommittal, it became obvious they had something else in mind. A move was underway to encourage Bush to run, and he considered it seriously. According to *The Houston Chronicle* of November 14, 1973, Grover was asked what he would do if Bush entered the governor's race. "Beat the hell out of him," Grover replied, contending Bush was a fine man at the national level with "no qualifications for state government at all." Tower had long harbored gubernatorial ambitions, having once been restrained shortly before the filing deadline by close associates who were convinced he was where he belonged in the Senate. For a few weeks, Bush considered the gubernatorial race, then formally withdrew from consideration in mid-November. Tower never made any overt moves, though some of his supporters believed at one point that he was leaning toward running, prompting Zimmerman to contact him directly. Tower was not running, and Granberry could settle into a posture against Grover without the specter of Bush or Tower in the primary. However, while the Texas gubernatorial intrigues were in progress during the fall of 1973, the shadows of scandal were lengthening in Washington. Vice-President Spiro Agnew, under felony charges unrelated to Watergate, resigned and Nixon chose Gerald Ford, the longtime GOP House leader, as his new vice-president. About that development, Grover was quoted October 25, in *The Waco Tribune-Herald*, "I never believed he (Nixon) could be so politically stupid. Nixon clearly showed he was no more careful in selecting Agnew than George McGovern was in his selection of Tom Eagleton." (McGovern had dropped Eagleton as his running mate in 1972, upon learning that the Missouri senator had once undergone treatment for mental illness.) Grover said that Nixon should have nominated either Barry Goldwater or John Connally. "I'd say Goldwater over Connally, simply because he's such a man of integrity." Of Ford, he said, "He's a nice guy, but doesn't inspire any confidence in the people."

Though Bush and Tower were out of the picture, an element of the anti-Grover forces wouldn't accept Granberry. A group led by National Committeeman Fred Agnich encouraged State Representative Ray Hutchison of Dallas, to make the race. Julian Zimmerman, the warhorse who had been instrumental in turning Tower's 1972 potential disaster into a resounding victory, had endorsed Granberry and took a dim view of Hutchison's impending candidacy. It would simply divide the anti-Grover forces, he contended, enhancing Grover's opportunity to again win the nomination. With Hutchison poised to announce, Zimmerman issued a stinging statement, contending that "there is no justification for this handpicked candidacy other than the determination of Mr. Agnich and his small clique of power brokers to place someone in that they can control. The real reason they have rejected Jim Granberry is that he didn't go hat in hand and ask their permission to run ... If they are successful in getting Mr. Hutchison in the race, they will benefit Grover, but I'm convinced most Texas Republicans will reject this late bit of manipulation and rally behind Jim Granberry ..." Zimmerman also pointed out that elected party officials are supposed to be neutral in contested primaries. He commended Jack Warren for not having taken sides. Warren was the new state chairman who had succeeded Willeford. On December 11, the day after Zimmerman's blast appeared in the state's leading newspapers, Hutchison announced. Less than a month later, on January 4, 1974, he withdrew. He cited as one of his reasons that it had become "clear that there is a substantial feeling and opinion that my candidacy in and of itself created a divisiveness within the Republican Party totally contrary to that objective of unity which I envisioned in my original announcement." With Hutchison's withdrawal, Granberry again assumed the mantle for all the anti-Grover forces which had grown during the previous months, due, in some measure, to Grover's continuous potshots at Nixon, Tower and the State GOP.

Mike Smith and Jim Tosch, two former young aides to Granberry when he was mayor, had been co-directors of his campaign from its inception. In late February, Zimmerman became campaign chairman and brought aboard Norman Newton as manager. Several veteran GOP operatives were involved, including Jacque Irby for research, Buddy Ives in communications and Carlton Suiter for organization. Frances Fatheree, a former SREC member from the Panhandle, and Virginia Leigh, who had worked in scheduling in the 1972 Tower state headquarters, were also assembled into a campaign headquarters on South Congress Avenue in Austin. Stuart King and Lee Manross were two promising young writers attracted to the Granberry Campaign.

Former President Dwight D. Eisenhower, with Senator-elect John Tower and wife, Lou, at a dinner in Washington in early June of 1961, before Tower was sworn into the Senate to fill the seat vacated by LBJ.

After the celebration and hoopla of the 1966 victory, Tower thanks his staff while brushing back a tear.

— Photo by Jim Culberson

Harris County GOP Chairman Nancy Palm, left, preparing to assist Pat Nixon in Houston during the 1968 campaign. — Photo by Charles Pantaze

Among the few prominent Democratic converts to Tower in 1966 was Will Wilson, the former attorney general shown here with his wife and the newly reelected senator.
— Photo by Charles Pantaze

Jack Cox (left) helped Tower maintain leverage in the Texas GOP toward Nixon's nomination in 1968.

— Photo by Charles Pantaze

LBJ, the man he opposed in the 1960 general election, administers the oath of office to John Tower in June 1961, when he became the youngest member of the United States Senate.

Dominant party leader of the 1960s was Peter O'Donnell of Dallas.

— Photo by Charles Pantaze

Tower on the scene during army maneuvers at Fort Hood in Central Texas.

— Photo by Charles Pantaze

In the mid-1960s farm workers in the Rio Grande Valley banded together for improved working conditions. Tower listens to Father Antonio Gonzales, who led a farm workers march to Austin.

— Photo by Charles Pantaze

On state capitol grounds. Onetime attorney general of Texas and Tower's Democratic opponent of 1966, Waggoner Carr, with hand extended, leads a demonstration against Soviet invasion of Afghanistan. At right with dark glasses is GOP activist Burt Hurlbut of Austin.

— Photo by Bob Ward

Towering over Tower is Ernie Ladd, a star for the Houston Oilers in the mid-1960s.

Congressmen George Bush of Houston, and Bob Price of Pampa, with Celso Moreno of Corpus Christi, left, and Humberto (Bert) Silex, pioneer Mexican-American political operatives for Texas Republicans on the state level.

— Photo by Charles Pantaze

As a young congressman, George Bush projected a dynamic image that drew many young people to support his 1970 bid for U.S. Senate.

Bill Steger of Tyler, GOP state chairman who succeeded Peter O'Donnell. At Steger's left is Beryl Milburn of Austin, longtime GOP leader.

— Photo by Charles Pantaze

Paul Eggers, George Bush, John Tower, and Richard Nixon. Campaigning in Texas late in 1970.

— Photo by Charles Pantaze

Paul Eggers, left, the Texas GOP's gubernatorial nominee of 1968 and 1970, with the late Allan Shivers, one of the state's most popular and effective governors.

— Photo by Charles Pantaze

Prominent Texas GOP leaders of the 1960s and 1970s included R. F. (Rudy) Juedeman of Odessa, left, who managed a congressional breakthrough and served in several party positions, and Peter O'Donnell of Dallas, who served as state chairman and national committeeman.

— Photo by Charles Pantaze

Ike Harris, first Republican state senator from Dallas, elected in 1967, with wife, Ann.

— Photo by Charles Pantaze

Fred Agnich, only Republican elected to Texas House from Dallas in 1970.

— Photo by Charles Pantaze

Nancy Palm, Harris County GOP leader who feuded with state party leaders in the 1960s and 1970s, enjoys an affable moment with Tower.

— Photo by Jim Culberson

College Administrator Dave Reagan of Sherman, no relation to Ronald Reagan, was a fresh face in the GOP gubernatorial primary of 1972, won by Hank Grover.

Conferring with President Nixon before their 1972 campaigns were launched.

— White House Photo

In Dallas during the second state convention of 1972, Ellie Seelig of Seguin, prominent Tower supporter, enjoys a friendly chat with Hank Grover, the gubernatorial nominee, after Grover's intra-party challenge at the first convention in Galveston had settled down.

Tower in a moment of relaxation with State Representative Larry Vick of Houston.

Jim Granberry, the former mayor of Lubbock who carried the gubernatorial banner during the Watergate-impact year of 1974.

— Photo by Charles Pantaze

Providing leadership for the founding of the Associated Republicans of Texas (ART) in 1975, was Austin businessman Julian Zimmerman, who had been state finance chairman for Tower's 1972 reelection campaign.

— Photo by Charles Pantaze

State GOP Field Representative Buddy Hedges, left, during the 1968 campaign with the late Frank Crowley of Dallas, who was a popular Republican figure for many years, serving as county judge to the time of his death after having served as commissioner.

— Photo by Charles Pantaze

Tower with Ed Clark of Austin, the powerful lobbyist and longtime close associate of LBJ who shook the Texas political establishment in 1972 when he became chairman of Tower's reelection campaign.

— Photo by Charles Pantaze

The Tower family in 1972. The Senator and Lou with daughters, Jeanne, seated; Penny to her left, and Marian between her parents.

— Photo by Jim Culberson

Republican senators of the 1970s, from left, Walter Mengden of Houston, Betty Andujar of Fort Worth and O. H. (Ike) Harris of Dallas.

— Texas Senate Photo

Connally and Tower at a Fort Worth Gridiron Show. At Tower's right is Congressman Jim Wright of Fort Worth.

Reagan and Tower in a happy moment before they were on opposing sides in the 1976 presidential race in which Tower supported Ford.

— Photo by Charles Pantaze

As President and leader of the Republican Party, Richard Nixon encouraged George Bush to seek a United States Senate seat in 1970.

President Ford with Texas Republican leaders Anne Armstrong, left, and Beryl Milburn.

— Photo by Charles Pantaze

Texas GOP National Committeeman Ernie Angelo, the staunch Reagan leader who served as mayor of Midland.

— Photo by Charles Pantaze

Vice-President Bush surrounded by Mexican-American admirers during White House briefing.

— White House Photo

In the Legislature during the 1970s — Houstonians conferring on the Senate floor include Republicans Walter Mengden, senator at left, and Kay Bailey, state representative, with Jack Ogg, Democratic senator.

— State Senate Photo

The young senator being interviewed on Capital Eye *public affairs television program in Austin by Ernie Stromberger, left, and Winston Bode, the host.*

— Photo by Charles Pantaze

Among Tower's most effective staffers were Molly Pryor (left) of Houston, and Dottie de la Garza of Dallas.

— Photo by Bob Ward

Campaigning in 1980 in Austin, were veteran Republican Congressman Bill Archer of Houston and Anne Armstrong, preparing to speak.

— Photo by F. W. Schmidt

State Representative Clay Smothers of Dallas, who changed party affiliation to Republican.

— Photo by Bob Ward

George and Annette Strake greet supporters on election night in 1982 as Strake loses to incumbent Lieutenant Governor Bill Hobby.

— Photo by Bob Ward

At left is Polly Sowell, longtime GOP leader and member of the Clements' Administration, reviewing a State GOP publication with Rita Clements, who was active in the party long before she married Clements.

— Photo by Bob Ward

As governor in 1980, Clements introduces Reagan at the state capitol, and later played the leading role in the Reagan–Bush Texas Campaign that swept to victory over Carter in Texas.

— Photo by Bob Ward

Bush and Connally, prized bulls from Texas in the national GOP arena, both aiming for the 1980 presidential nomination.

— State GOP Photo

GOP State Chairman George Strake points to party-sponsored billboard after Governor Mark White passed a large tax increase.

— Photo by Bob Ward

Allen Clark of Austin, GOP candidate for state treasurer in 1982, with a young admirer.

John Leedom, newly-elected Republican state senator from Dallas in 1981.

— Photo by Bob Ward

Promoting GOP aspirants, such as Maurice Angly of Austin, in his first campaign for the Texas House in 1967.

— Photo by Charles Pantaze

Singer Pat Boone flanked by Mr. and Mrs. Chet Upham during the 1982 campaign.

— Photo by Bob Ward

Lance Tarrance of Houston, the GOP pollster who started as a researcher at the Republican State Headquarters, speaks to a workshop for party leaders.

— Photo by Bob Ward

Republican power gathered at a 1982 luncheon in Houston included seated, from left, Vice-President George Bush; Eddie Chiles, Fort Worth industrialist who coined the "I'm mad" campaign against Jimmy Carter in 1980; Mrs. Bush; standing, from left, State Chairman Chet Upham and Mrs. Upham; Mrs. Chiles, (Fran), national committee-woman; National Committeeman Ernie Angelo; and Bob Perry, prominent Houston busi-nessman.

— Photo by Bob Ward

Rick Rodgers, political director for the State GOP, is taking in mostly good news on elec-tion night 1980.

— Photo by Bob Ward

Top Texas GOP officials in 1980 — State Chairman Chet Upham of Mineral Wells behind State Senator Betty Andujar of Fort Worth, national committeewoman; Dorothy Doehne of San Antonio, state vice-chairman and Ernie Angelo of Midland, national committeeman.

— Photo by Bob Ward

Tower's 1984 co-chairman for the Reagan–Bush campaign was Martha Weisend of Dallas, praising massive volunteer efforts in her victory speech election night.

— Photo by Charles Pantaze

State Representative Terral Smith of Austin, riding on an elephant.

— Photo by Bob Ward

Judge Will Garwood, left, with Tower and the senator's longtime aide, Bob Estrada during an SREC meeting in Austin in 1980.

— Photo by Bob Ward

Governor and Mrs. Clements with Henry Kissinger.

— State GOP Photo

A happy moment for then-Governor Clements during the 1982 GOP state convention in Austin. Bitter defeat at the hands of Mark White would come in the general election.

— Photo by Bob Ward

On the Washington scene with then-Congressman Jim Collins of Dallas and Anne Armstrong, the Texan who would serve as United States Ambassador to Britain's Court of St. James's.

Republican Ricardo Hinojosa who lost a special election for state senate in the Rio Grande Valley but became a Federal judge.

— Photo by Bob Ward

Rick Montoya, Hispanic political operative for Governor Clements in 1982.

— Photo by Bob Ward

The opening of George Strake's 1982 state campaign headquarters in Austin for lieutenant governor drew the party faithful, including Travis County GOP Chairman Richard Box.

— Photo by Bob Ward

Those who made official the historic change of 1980. Electors, who were the technical winners of the November 4 balloting and who represented Texas in the Electoral College, are seen here with Texas Secretary of State George Strake and Republican Party State Chairman Chet Upham. Back row, from left: Strake, John Welty, Dunman Perry, Jerry Yost, Ross Brannian, Clymer Wright, Berry Burnett, Jane Pieper, Gloria Ribbeck, Nancy Gordon, Upham. Center row, from left: Marion Young, Jack Markham, Billy Gragg, C. R. Dollinger, James Sheldon, Mary Jane Smith, Ellen Garwood, Nancy Palm, Ila Jo Hart. Seated, from left: Roger Johnson, Bill Beckham, Terry Means, Jack Boggs, Douglas Harlan, Gladys Hamilton, George Otto and June Coe. These electors cast Texas, twenty-six electoral votes for President on December 15 in ceremonies at the state capitol.

The senator with the second Mrs. Tower at the state convention of the Texas Federation of Republican Women in Fort Worth in 1981.

— Photo by Bob Ward

Linden Kettlewell directed the vast volunteer organization for the Reagan–Bush Texas Campaign of 1984.

— Photo by Bob Ward

Senator Phil Gramm, who succeeded John Tower by swamping his primary and general election opponents in 1984.

As chairman for the 1984 Reagan–Bush ticket in Texas, Tower presents petitions for their names to be placed on the primary ballot to Holly Dechard of Austin, secretary for the Republican Party of Texas.

— Photo by Bob Ward

Cyndi Taylor Krier, San Antonio attorney and political protégé of John Tower, changed Bexar County politics dramatically by upsetting an incumbent Democrat in 1984 to become the first Republican state senator from that county in modern times, and the only woman in the Texas Senate's 1985 session.

— Photo by Charles Pantaze

By February 1974, Granberry had established himself as a leading spokesman for a right-to-work provision in the Texas Constitution whose revision was being considered by a convention composed of all state legislators as delegates, meeting in Austin. The genesis of this latest issue came from 1973, when an agency shop bill was reported from a committee of the Texas House. The bill didn't pass the Legislature, but it signaled to right-to-work supporters that their principle, embodied in Texas law, was in danger. Under agency shop, a union collects dues from nonmembers equal to what members pay. Thus, passage of agency shop legislation would undermine the right-to-work principle, though technically not nullifying or repealing the right-to-work law which guarantees the right to join or not to join a labor union in order to get or hold a job. Therefore, a central issue was raised by conservatives to place a right-to-work provision in the Texas Constitution with a ban on agency shop. Granberry took up that cause and received a substantial amount of publicity, especially since Briscoe, who was close politically to Harry Hubbard, president of the Texas AFL – CIO, would waffle with a widestep anytime a reporter asked his position on the matter. Briscoe would decline, claiming he didn't want to "dictate" to the convention. Though the right-to-work provision didn't pass the convention, it did provide Granberry with a vehicle by which he became better known to Republicans and the general populace.

In early March, past the filing deadline for candidates, Texas Republicans girded for a spirited stretch run battle between Granberry and Grover, but after all the sounds and all the fury, Grover abruptly withdrew from the race, blaming his old enemies, the State GOP et al. Tower and his cohorts certainly shed no tears over Grover's withdrawal, which may have been caused by self-destruction from having criticized so many GOP leaders, including Nixon, Tower, and Bush. Further, a careful review of his 1972 vote-getting pattern in the general election appeared to be revealing since he had received substantial "hard-hat" Wallace-type votes from people who wouldn't be voting in the GOP primary nor would they be for the right-to-work provision pushed by Granberry, popular with most Republicans. In any event, Grover's withdrawal left Granberry with minor opposition in Odell McBrayer, a Fort Worth attorney with solid civic credentials but little political strength. On the Democratic side, Governor Briscoe was in a rematch with Frances Farenthold and Ramsey Muniz was running again on the Raza Unida ticket.

Granberry and Briscoe won their primaries easily, but whatever flickering chances Granberry might have had in 1974 were snuffed out in the long summer days and nights with the final unravelling of the Watergate nightmare. By the time Nixon resigned on August 9, the Republican troops in Texas were weary. In 1964, the polls had predicted doom all year but the troops hung in there fighting in formation because of their faith in Goldwater and dedication to promote the conservative cause. Ten years later they were crestfallen, believing they had been betrayed by Nixon and his powerful associates who couldn't stand political prosperity. The level of contributors and volunteers in Texas was down markedly, portending serious problems at the polls. Those die-hards who would stay active were angry and irritated over various aspects of the Watergate situation as well as the aftermath, not the least of which was Ford, the new President, choosing Nelson Rockefeller, Goldwater's archenemy in 1964, as his vice-president. Jack Warren had been led to believe Bush would be named, buoying Texas Republican hopes briefly, only to be dashed with the news about Rockefeller.

For the September GOP state convention in Houston, Tower would take command as chairman plus oversee much of the strategic preparation regarding Granberry's interests, along with Ike Harris, who was named chairman of the platform committee. Tower and Harris agreed to run the convention essentially for Granberry's benefit by limiting the consideration of issues to those affecting state government. It was the "governor's convention," and limiting consideration was logical, particularly since there was no presidential nor U.S. Senate race that year. Further, that strategy would prevent the delegates from fighting over Watergate-related issues, such as Ford's pardon of Nixon which was being hotly debated among the troops. The Tower – Harris strategy drew some grumbling as delegates began assembling in Houston's Hyatt-Regency Hotel and other environs near the Sam Houston Coliseum, the convention hall. But for the most part, the strategy appeared to have the support necessary to prevail. A potential fight for state chairman between incumbent Jack Warren and challenger Ernie Angelo of Midland was looming as a potentially divisive problem, but after some deliberation, Angelo decided not to press his candidacy, in the interest of party unity.

On convention eve, Tower was holding a strategy session in his suite at the Hyatt-Regency when a phone call came from the White House. President Ford was about to announce a new plan granting amnesty to draft dodgers and deserters during the Vietnam War. Tower was furious. He was ingrained with a deep sense of duty from combat experience in World War II, and from close association with the military from his position on the Armed Services Committee. Ford's move put him in a difficult spot indeed. Despite his personal dislike for amnesty, he wanted to help Ford build public confidence during those uncertain early days following the changing of the guard. He also wanted to help rekindle sparks for Granberry's campaign. But he knew the amnesty issue soon would be tossed into the surrealistic atmosphere of the convention, sending the cauldron into a fast boil. As word spread of Ford's amnesty program, it became obvious that Tower and Harris would have their hands full holding to the original strategy. Granberry, feeling the heat, decided he could accept an exception to the strategy if it were confined to the amnesty issue. George Bush would make a strong keynote speech, with the aim to elevate the eyes of the delegates toward the future, rather than remain mired in the Watergate trauma. Granberry would present a well-conceived, acceptable state platform. The natives, however, were restless. Harris did his part, beating back several attempts at exceptions in Platform Committee hearings, but minority reports brought two nationally-oriented resolutions to the floor of the convention. The first, by Van Archer of San Antonio, praised Ford's pardon of Nixon. On a voice vote, the delegates shouted their *Ayes* and *Noes* resounding throughout the convention hall. It sounded fairly close, and when Tower ruled that Archer's resolution had failed, scattered boos and catcalls were heard from around the hall.

The second national-issue resolution was sponsored by State Representative Ray Barnhart of Pasadena. It expressed concern about the direction of the presidency, including amnesty and Rockefeller as vice-president. It was late in a long day, but the emotions of the weary delegates were still running high when Ike Harris stepped forward again, holding to the original game plan, contending the resolution was not truly germane to the delegates' responsibility. Barnhart hammered on the need to send a signal to Washington that the bedrock of the party was deeply concerned about liberal moves being made outside the context of conservative principles. Tower called for the voice vote which sounded about even for each side. And each side shouted long and hard. With a bit of flourish, Tower ruled that Barnhart had won and promptly adjourned the convention. Harris was visibly upset, believing his side had prevailed as it had at every other step of the way during the demanding process. When he approached Tower behind the stage, the senator smiled, "I'm sorry, Ike, but I had to throw them some raw meat." For Granberry and his tired operatives, the convention was a shambles which they knew would produce publicity regarding the emotional issues generated from Washington, D.C., far from the well-rounded state platform they had crafted to promote the gubernatorial campaign.

Of the Barnhart resolution, National Committeeman Fred Agnich commented, "It is extremely ill advised for the Texas Republican Party to take that kind of a position this early in the Ford Administration." Ron Calhoun of *The Dallas Times Herald* wrote that the delegates "could not shake off a lingering concern for national controversies. Fallout from the Watergate scandal, although never mentioned directly, seemed to hang over the gathering like fog which simply would not be dispelled by sunny rhetoric ... The idea was to put on a show of unity and gig the Democrats, but Texas Republicans wound up dividing their house and rebuking their President ..." In his post-convention analysis, Fred Bonavita of *The Houston Post* wrote that, "the mood of Texas Republicans, for the most part, is somewhere between unhappy and enraged over events that occurred since August 9 when Nixon resigned." Whether Barnhart actually had the winning margin was a subject of conjecture for some time, but he had undoubtedly hit upon the mood described by Bonavita. And that final resolution expressed the sentiment that would haunt Gerald Ford two years hence when he sought presidential delegates in Texas.

For all intents and purposes the gubernatorial race was over. A divided, disheartened group of Republicans gave Granberry lukewarm support in the final weeks that were uneventful. Briscoe knew he had a safe lead and played things cautiously, particualry since he also knew that Muniz, like Farenthold, was unable to regenerate the level of 1972 support. On election day Briscoe defeated Granberry by a vote of 1,016,334 to 514,725. As the trend became clear early on election night, one of Granberry's weary workers sighed, "The people had Sharpstown, then Watergate. They weren't even listening to us." Muniz, who polled more than 200,000 votes in 1972, polled only 93,295. A slate of statewide candidates had run with Granberry, none of whom had substantial name identification. Nick Rowe, a native of the Rio Grande Valley and a hero of the Vietnam War, generated considerable publicity in his race for state comptroller against Bob Bullock. Bullock, however, probably the shrewdest among the Democratic candidates, won by a wide margin as did the other Democrats. Bob Price, who had served four terms in Congress, lost the Panhandle seat to Democrat Jack Hightower, but Bill Archer, Jim Collins, and Alan Steelman held their seats in Congress. In the Texas House there was a net loss of one seat to sixteen, with new faces provided by Bob Close of Perryton in the Panhandle and Frank Hartung of Houston. There was a significant breakthrough at the local level with Republicans taking the county judge races in the state's two most populous counties, Harris with Jon Lindsay and Dallas with John Whittington. But on the statewide scene, 1974, an election year once projected to hold great promise, had turned into a disastrous reversal from 1972.

CHAPTER ELEVEN

Ford – Reagan Duel Splits Party

Fallout from the 1974 election hadn't settled before Zimmerman, Newton and a few others decided it was time for an ad hoc Republican organization to be formed in Texas to build from the grass roots by supporting legislative and local candidates. Debts from Granberry's campaign and other statewide races were to be retired as well as gathering funds for candidate support in 1976. Launching the Associated Republicans of Texas (ART) would not be an easy task. It would surely draw criticism from many people in the state party who would view such activities as distracting competition for funds. Tower's attitude would be crucial. If he would endorse the organization, it would have a fine chance of succeeding. Neutrality would mean "Maybe," and opposition would mean, "Don't even try." Zimmerman had the clout and credibility to approach Tower directly, which he did a few days prior to Christmas of 1974, during a trip to Washington. In a small, ornate room off the Senate floor, the two strong-willed veterans of the Texas political arena discussed the plan candidly. Tower took it under advisement and in the following weeks when he discussed it with trusted political allies, he found general support for the concept. So much money had been spent on the "glamor races," but not much had trickled down to help those at the lower levels. Money and technical assistance could indeed make a difference in those legislative races that determine who draws the new lines for Congress and the Legislature after each census. In early 1975, the 1980 census didn't seem that far down the road.

187

While Tower considered the ART program in early 1975, he was confronted by one of the highest local impact issues of his Senate career when the Army announced its intention to acquire 60,000 additional acres of land for expanding Fort Hood in Central Texas. That target area contained many homesteads on small farms and ranches, land that had been held by struggling families for generations. It became a pitched psychological battle between the Army and the landowners. After months of sharp protest by the landowners, Army Secretary Howard (Bo) Callaway contended in a Fort Worth news conference, reported in *The Star-Telegram* May 15, that the first "wave of emotionalism" was over. "I think now the majority of the people around Killeen, the merchants and property owners, see the need for this and will not fight us." But the landowners (organized as "Our Land Our Lives"), continued their opposition, calling on Tower for hearings in their bailiwick, preferably Gatesville, where the group was based. Major Texas newspapers intensified coverage of the controversy. Some, including *The Houston Post*, editorialized against the acquisition plan on the basis of that region losing a substantiial part of its tax base. Tower, with his strong ties to the military, was expected by many observers to come down on that side, but after conducting hearings himself on the scene, Tower sided with the landowners, effectively killing the acquisition proposal.

Alan Steelman, the sharp young GOP congressman from Dallas, was pawing the sand in the spring of 1975, considering a Senate race against the one-term incumbent, Lloyd Bentsen. With public interest piqued by the Fort Hood controversy, Steelman wrote a feature article for *The Dallas Times Herald* in which he plugged "land-use planning." This was a new approach calling for states, "in concert with city and county government, to make land-use decisions of greater than local scope. Thus, a state would make its voice heard in decisions affecting the siting of power plants, highways, airports, and other large-scale developments, but not of individual housing developments ..."

In arguing his case, Steelman pointed out the "United States is currently using land more intensively than ever before, with little or no thought to the consequences. This intense and unplanned use has led not only to an increasing concentration of our nation's population in urban areas [estimates are that seventy-five percent of the people live on about one- and one-half percent of the land] but also to a growing consumption of natural resources." Steelman was making waves, but he waited months before making his decision regarding the Senate race.

Tower made his decision to formally endorse the Associated Republicans of Texas in the spring of 1975, giving the group the boost it needed to expand membership and raise funds rapidly during the year.

Also in the spring of 1975, Tower continued to maintain a close rapport with his base of Mexican-American supporters. He was the featured speaker at a statewide meeting of Mexican-American Republicans of Texas (MART) in San Antonio, where its state chairman, Eddie Garza, had a large mariachi band playing for his arrival. Brownie Trevino, Tina Villanueva and many of the longtime Tower M-A supporters were there to greet him in a festive atmosphere. Tower assured them that MART held his support as an official arm of the party, there being a rival M-A GOP organization on the scene known as the Hispanic Assembly. San Antonio Republicans, whether Anglo or Mexican-American, had a tendency to snipe at one another from factional vantage points, but Tower could count on solid support from almost all Texas M-A Republicans. Louie Terrazas and Art Troilo might not be best of friends with Eddie Garza, but they would work for Tower, who remained the only true rallying point. Garza and his friend, Alfredo Cardenas, would try to expand MART membership in 1976. Their efforts, like those throughout the party in Texas, would be impacted upon substantially by a gathering storm. In 1976, the Bicentennial Celebration would consume the energy of many Texans, but those involved in Republican politics were in for a special showdown, the first bona fide primary contest for presidential delegates between strong contenders. Incumbent President Gerald Ford was being challenged by former Governor Ronald Reagan of California, a contest in which most active Republicans would take sides. Texas, the hub of the Southwest, would become a battleground. Most of the longtime party regulars were for Ford, wanting to proceed against the Democrats without a divisive internal fight. They believed he had handled the post-Watergate trauma effectively en route to warranting his party's nomination to try for an elected term. Reagan's dedicated supporters considered Ford to be a political aberration, an accidental President who had never even run a statewide race. They had fervently wanted Reagan to be President for years and had no intention of backing away from their opportunity. Tower was strongly behind Ford, serving as state chairman for his Texas campaign. His longtime associates, Beryl Milburn as director, and Roger Wallace as manager, would run the state headquarters located in North Austin. Jacque Irby, who had been research director for Tower's 1972 campaign, was deputy campaign manager and Pete Roussel, veteran media operative, would join the Texas group from Ford's national headquarters.

Reagan's top leaders were Ernie Angelo, the former mayor of Midland who had seriously considered running for GOP state chairman in

1974; Ray Barnhart, former state representative from Pasadena who had sponsored the anti-Ford resolution that closed out the 1974 Republican State Convention; and Miller Hicks, an Austin businessman making his first appearance at such a visible level. The Harris County stalwarts, including Grover and Nancy Palm, were for Reagan along with other staunch conservative leaders elsewhere, such as John Leedom, the former Dallas County GOP Chairman. In late February, Ford campaign officials and organizers gathered in Austin for a briefing at which Tower was quoted, "I feel very good about Texas. We have a splendid organization here — made up of some of the party's best people. We have a lot of blue chip people running as Ford delegate candidates ... Things are going our way everywhere, but we cannot travel on assumptions."

On the same day that Tower was quoted with his favorable assessment for Ford's campaign in Texas, a serious intra-party fight came into focus with a sharp attack sounded by Ray Hutchison, the Dallas County state representative who had succeeded Jack Warren as GOP state chairman. According to an article by Jon Ford, political editor of *The Austin American-Statesman*, that appeared on February 29, Hutchison was after the scalp of the Associated Republicans of Texas (ART). He contended that some contributors to ART "think they are contributing to the party. They have not been furnished any information" on ART's spending. "If it means my instant demise as chairman, I am not going to permit outstanding people to continue to be taken down the path — when their money could go to help the party," Hutchison charged. Ford's article said ART's 1975 financial report showed it raised $111,798 in contributions and spent $125,865 during its first ten months of operation. Hutchison complained that ART Executive Director Norman Newton received $27,917 in retainers and expense reimbursements and that $19,944 went to retire Granberry's campaign debt. Hutchison said more than $12,000 of Granberry's new resources went to repay loans held by Newton and another ART member. "I don't want any more money to go to these old debts," Hutchison said. "I have asked for information on A.R.T.'s bank account privately, and if I don't get it, I will ask publicly ... What A.R.T ought to do now is dissolve and work with the party organization ..." Asked by Ford to comment, Zimmerman termed Hutchison's remarks a "cheap shot." He added that Hutchison "may be asking for one right between his [expletive deleted] eyes." The controversy had become intense as the intra-party power equation had become clearer with the growing clout of ART. The organization had announced almost 700 members as of December 15, 1975, with many prominent middle-echelon Texas Republicans in the fold. Well-known party stalwarts included Paul Eggers of Dallas, Wilton Fair of Tyler, Rudy Juedeman of Odessa, Lee McMillan of Corpus Christi, and Bill Rector of Wichita Falls.

In addition to the charges made by Hutchison, Ray Barnhart had been sniping at ART and many State GOP activists wanted to know more about the organization and its intentions, there being a lingering doubt as to whether it would complement the efforts of the party regulars. In an effort to rein in the controversy, Hutchison and Zimmerman met privately. Zimmerman believed he had a commitment from Hutchison that an impending SREC meeting would discuss ART behind closed doors only, and that a committee of SREC members would be named to meet with representatives of ART. When the SREC meeting resulted in more harsh public criticism of ART, Zimmerman determined the very life of his organization was on the line, and he girded for war. On March 10, he sent a letter to Hutchison, with copies to the Capitol Press Room, contending that,

> ... since you failed to honor your commitment, you have left me no choice but to defend ART's position publically, which I shall do forthrightly... You have stated our program should be brought under control of the SREC. You have implied we have used deceptive practices, among many derogatory remarks you have made... In the past few years, I have never been accused of deceptive practices until your recent outburst. Let me make it clear that we have no apologies to make and nothing to hide... In assessing carefully the budgets of our respective organizations, I find that your charges against ART must have been made from frustration and failure since your debt structure suggests that you will be unable to support candidates this year. Further, the transfer of large sums of money from your campaign committees to cover state headquarters operating expenses suggests you have been raising money under the guise of candidate support when, in fact, much of the money was used to cover operating expenses... It's obvious that ART is in a better position to support candidates than the State GOP headquarters. Therefore, we will pursue our program as planned, and I suggest that you concentrate on rebuilding a grass roots organization rather than promoting intra-party conflict.

A cease-fire ensued, allowing ART to pursue its program of candidate support. ART had originated with the pledge to stay out of contested primaries for nominations and contests for party offices, limiting its mission to assisting GOP nominees for legislative and local offices. That posture was essential for 1976, the fledgling year for the fragile operation, because after the Zimmerman – Hutchison exchanges simmered down, Texas Republicans lined up for a brass knuckle brawl between the forces of Ford and Reagan. ART had its share of partisans from both camps, but they rarely discussed presidential politics when they came together. Their task was to meld carefully the divergent elements in order to work steadily for the common goals. More credibility, experience and leadership capability were needed. They came to ART in the form of Jim Allison, who had returned to Midland to become publisher of the family newspaper, *The Midland Reporter-Telegram*. In his work with George Bush and with the GOP at the national level, Allison had earned a remarkable reputation for effectiveness while becoming everyone's candidate for Nice Guy of the Year. He assumed chairmanship of the crucial ART Candidates Committee which would develop a sound methodology for determining how to target and assist campaigns, and how to deploy the resources wisely. Assisting Allison closely on that committee were Shirley Green, who had moved to San Antonio; Gordon Knight, of Marble Falls, a retired Army officer; and Forrest Moore, the veteran public relations executive from Dallas. Jack Borchers, a New Braunfels attorney, brought firsthand experience as a former legislative candidate who knew how hard it was to obtain campaign funding as a GOP challenger. Other dedicated Republicans serving on the ART committee evaluating campaigns included Dr. Sam Nixon of Houston, onetime GOP chairman of Wilson County in South Texas, where the 1960s were tough going indeed; Verne Philips, an Austin attorney who had worked in the state campaign headquarters for Granberry as a volunteer; and Jim Blythe of Fort Worth, (one of the youngest ART members) who had a knack for analyzing election statistics.

Others who would devote long hours of work and travel at their own expense for numerous ART Candidates Committee meetings over the years included Bob Barnes, former mayor of McAllen; Joe Boerner of Lubbock; Bill Hale of Floydada; and Nathan White of Plano, then county judge of Collin County.

A successful fund-raising program was essential for ART to accomplish its goals. Taking another crucial leadership position was John Hurd as chairman of the organization's Finance Committee. Hurd had longstanding credentials in Republican ranks dating to Peter O'Donnell's time as state party chairman. He had also served as Nixon's ambassador to South Africa, and was well known among independent oil operators, that core group for GOP fund-raising in Texas.

ART funds certainly weren't going for lavish offices. The original headquarters was located at 500 Chicon Street in the heart of East Austin, the lowest income area of the city. It was in an old warehouse owned by Bob and Patsy Ehrlich, dedicated Republicans who wanted to see ART succeed. In the warehouse offices, Newton and Mary Wellburn, the diligent secretary – bookkeeper who cut her teeth in politics during the Granberry Campaign, were the only full-time paid people during the early development of ART. As the campaign year unfolded, many volunteers would assist at the headquarters or at meetings elsewhere, plus a few, such as Frank Erwin, provided some assistance from well behind the scenes. Erwin was one of several key conservative Democrats who were frustrated by the fact that Connally had seen no chance to be nominated for President by the Democratic Party, and Bentsen had thought he had a chance, but his bid had floundered, causing further frustration.

After a few weeks, Tower's early optimism for Ford's campaign in Texas had turned into apprehension. Reagan had begun hitting on raw nerves of conservatives with such as his attack on the "giveaway" of the Panama Canal and various aspects of Henry Kissinger's record and pronouncements. Reagan was implying the United States was weak on defense, a charge that hurt in military-minded Texas. Reagan's populist-conservatism was also reaching beyond the regular Republican core group that voted in the GOP primary in Texas to supporters of George Wallace, who had nowhere else to go. No GOP primary in Texas had ever attracted a voter turnout in excess of 150,000, but the intensity of the contest in progress, plus the potentially strong Wallace factor, were strong indicators that this primary would indeed produce an all-time record vote.

Tower considered some Reagan charges to be irresponsible. At a spring news conference at the state capitol, he hammered away at Reagan, pointedly questioning his qualifications for the office he sought. Following the conference, Roussel, who had worked with Tower in his 1966 campaign, shook his head. "I never heard him hit Waggoner Carr that hard." On April 15, about two weeks before the election, one of Tower's top operatives sent him a cautionary memo stating in part, "Reports of probable Wallace crossover voting continue to pour in from around the state. In order to win, we're going to have to squeeze all the Tower supporters among Republicans, plus attract substantial numbers of independent conservatives who have supported you in general elections in the past. A 300,000 turnout wouldn't surprise me one bit, but we can no longer count on numerical progression to necessarily favor Ford ..."

Reacting to pressure from Reagan, Tower bore down hard with speeches and through advertising, trying to shore up doubting Republicans and conservatives. "Since becoming President nineteen months ago," Tower said, "Gerald Ford has restored confidence in our system of government, has strengthened our economy and has sent to the Congress the strongest defense bill in the history of our nation ... We simply cannot afford to gamble; President Ford represents the best opportunity to elect a conservative this November ..." Though Reagan had generated momentum, Ford's campaign had certainly not faltered. It was well organized; in fact some thought too well organized. All the strategic and many tactical shots were called from Washington or elsewhere. Texas, of all states, is indeed more diverse. It has various indigenous political elements that are unaccustomed to taking orders from afar, or from some "jet jockey" fresh off the plane from Washington or some other distant point. M-A Ford supporters were unhappy with a Hispanic jet jockey calling the shots, and they were crestfallen when Ford, during a stop in San Antonio, bit into a tamale without peeling the shuck. News media people traveling with Ford found it worth no more than a chuckling line or two in their daily reports, but to Ford's M-A supporters in Texas, it was a damaging gaffe. It was evidence that the candidate from Michigan knew little about the Spanish – Mexican culture of the Southwest.

It almost seemed as though Dame Fortune were dealing all the cards to Reagan. The inflexibility of Ford's campaign was made more obvious in the final days. Spending limits applied to both campaigns equally un-less some person or persons, completely independent from the campaign, chose to spend their money for advertising to promote the candidate of their choice. Such "independent expenditures" provided a big edge for Reagan when Hank Grover bounced around the state purchasing, inde-pendently of Reagan's campaign, large amounts of media advertising in behalf of Reagan's candidacy. It was frosting on the Reagan cake, which had been baked with his superior television delivery and a diligent army of volunteers who contacted and recontacted their potential voters. Ford's campaign had a strong organization also, but it wasn't fueled by the high-octane emotional power generated by Reagan.

Up for grabs on primary day, Saturday May 1, were ninety-six del-egates to the national convention, four from each of the state's twenty-four congressional districts with each district putting up slates of four delegate candidates for Ford and Reagan. An additional four at-large del-egates would be chosen later by convention. In most districts, Tower's forces had recruited top Republican names to be on the slate, old faith-fuls such as Paul Eggers, now in Dallas, Hal DeMoss in Houston, State Representative Jim Nowlin in San Antonio, Roger Hunsaker and Sproess-er Wynn in Fort Worth, Doug DeCluitt in Waco, Beryl Milburn in Austin, Fred Hervey in El Paso, Lee McMillan in Corpus Christi, Jim Allison in Midland, Vidal Cantu in Laredo, Ellie Selig in Seguin, Zack Fisher in Northwest Texas, Shep McKeithen on the Gulf Coast, Leon Richardson in Beaumont, Wally Wilkerson in Conroe, and many others.

Tower, the beleaguered general, had his best troops on the front line with more than the state's GOP presidential delegation at stake. This bitter confrontation had developed into a fight for control of the Republican Party of Texas.

In additon to Angelo, Barnhart, and Hicks, the Reagan slates contained such well known Republicans as Betty Andujar of Fort Worth, and Walter Mengden of Houston, both serving in the Texas Senate, plus Leedom, who was serving on the city council in Dallas. Many of the others had been active for years, carrying the banner for the more conservative candidates, such as Reagan and Grover. Some believed that Tower had caused Grover's campaign to be underfinanced in 1972, and therefore lost when it could have been won. They believed Tower had "frozen" Grover out of the 1974 primary and should be punished for these sinister deeds. This was their opportunity to vent years of frustration over being dominated by Tower's desires and Tower's people running the state party and the conventions. They were all highly motivated for Reagan and many of them were about equally motivated against Tower.

At Ford's state headquarters on primary election night, elaborate scoreboards were on the walls to chart the course of each congressional district. A few spot early encouraging reports were soon washed away by a roaring Reagan tide that swept the state, carrying all of his delegate candidates in every district. A total of 456,822 voted in the Republican Primary, breaking the old record set in 1964 by more than 300,000 votes.

From his home in Wichita Falls, Tower drafted his concession statement which alluded to the Wallace factor and to "erroneous" perceptions of Ford's foreign and defense policies. "The unanswered question is whether this victory gives Governor Reagan viable momentum or whether national perception of him as a result of this campaign makes his victory a Pyrrhic one. In any case, I congratulate Governor Reagan on a victory in Texas that can only be described as decisive. I continue to believe that President Ford will be nominated and elected." Tower's statement proved to be prophetic, but poor politics. Unfortunately for him, some of the news media keyed on his idea of a Pyrrhic victory — a term seldom used to describe a political situation — resulting in short broadcast items making it sound as though Tower had branded Reagan's victory as winning a big battle at ruinous loss before losing a war. Reagan's victorious forces, celebrating around the state on election night, were infuriated to hear their nemesis relegating their Texas triumph to virtually meaningless status in the long haul to the presidential nomination.

In his column that appeared in *The Austin American-Statesman* of May 9, Jon Ford fanned the fire when he wrote that, "The worst of times may be looming for hari-kari bent Texas Republicans ... Ronald Reagan forces, demonstrating sore winner tendencies, seem determined to lend credibility to Senator John Tower's prediction their May Day Massacre may be a Pyrrhic victory." Ford pointed out that Tower would be denied an at-large delegate spot, completely freezing out the titular head of the state party at his party's national convention. Ford termed the intra-party split the worst since 1952, portending a bad general election year.

At the state GOP convention in June, Ernie Angelo was elected national committeeman, ousting Tower's old ally, Fred Agnich, and Betty Andujar was named national committeewoman. Led by Barnhart, Texas delegates gathered in August at the Glenwood Manor Motor Hotel in Overland Park, a suburb to Kansas City, host for the national convention. John Tower, the dominant figure in Texas GOP politics since his election to the United States Senate, had been banished from the fold, and took residence at the Crown Central Hotel where Ford was headquartered. He would observe the swirling convention activity from the rarified atmosphere of a sky box high above the Kemper Arena during a time when he was mired in a quagmire of hostility with those Texas delegates below, who represented the new bedrock of the party he had led for fifteen years. These were people who would, to some unknown extent, control his political destiny and among whom there was gossip about mounting a primary challenge to him two years hence. Tower's political problem was indeed severe.

Connally, who had remained neutral during the primary shootout, had asked Peter O'Donnell to lead a drive for the vice-presidential nomination, which appeared to be up for grabs. O'Donnell, with the assistance of Mary Jester, his longtime executive secretary, set up an efficient operation for Connally in the Muhlbach Hotel. But O'Donnell found the conditions were far from ideal, with little base from which to work with his old Texas party constituency, and Connally had no real base within that delegation. Connally was believed to have many delegates elsewhere interested in his potential candidacy, if and when Ford would pass the word, but apparently the former Texas governor wasn't high on Ford's list.

The Texas delegation seemed to be interested only in promoting Reagan and a strongly worded conservative platform, but the Californian couldn't muster the needed votes elsewhere. A ploy was carried out whereby Reagan named his vice-presidential choice, Senator Richard Schweiker of Pennsylvania, perceived as a liberal, well before the actual presidential nominating started. His backers tried to force Ford to also name his choice ahead of the presidential balloting, but Ford refused, believing he had the votes to win the nomination, which he did. However, long before the convention, conservative pressure had forced Ford to back away from offering Rockefeller as a continued choice for vice-president. Anne Armstrong, the outstanding Texan who had become widely known by virtue of various party offices and was then serving as United States Ambassador to Great Britian's Court of St. James, was under serious consideration by Ford. Articulate and attractive, she might have made a positive impact upon the forthcoming campaign. Instead, Ford chose Senator Robert Dole of Kansas, who Reagan had reportedly said would be a favorable choice.

After the convention ended and the fallout settled, almost all Texas Republicans, from Tower down to the precinct workers who put up campaign signs, wondered who would benefit. Tower came out on the right side of his party's national convention with Ford the nominee to face Jimmy Carter's challenge, but he had lost control of his party in Texas, the base from which he must run for reelection in two years. Reagan's forces had enjoyed their Pyrrhic primary victory, but their standard-bearer had lost the big prize and shown an unsettling side of expediency by taking a liberal running-mate in the process. They would take over nominal control of the state party, but what would they do with it? They had no statewide candidates around whom to rally, nor any in the stable being groomed, with the possible exception of Grover. Ford and Steelman would be unable to regenerate the adrenalin that had pumped through their veins with Reagan's all-out conservative campaign. Anne Armstrong and John Connally, two "glamor" possibilities, either of whom would make a difference in Texas voting, had been passed over for the vice-presidential nomination. The net result of all this was that the Texas GOP, still a minority party far from competitive status, was limping warily into the fall campaigns, weary from disappointment and torn by division in the ranks over personalities and political ideology.

Some calming of the waters seemed to have occurred by the time the state GOP convention was held in Austin on September 11. Hutchison, who had been neutral in the presidential fight, was reelected state chairman, despite a strong challenge from Barnhart, who had succeeded Nancy Palm as chairman of the Harris County GOP. Polly Sowell, the state vice-chairman who was a protegé of O'Donnell and a longtime Tower ally, was also reelected. Though Tower certainly no longer maintained control, the leadership lineup was not out to persecute him with Angelo, Andujar, Hutchison, and Sowell in control for the time being. The Reagan forces had not remained totally aligned behind Barnhart. They did adopt a number of strong conservative resolutions including one that made it clear support for ERA expressed by the national convention was not shared by the state delegates assembled in Texas.

In the fall campaign some of the division over the Ford – Reagan fight eased up a bit as Alan Steelman moved his campaign onto center stage. Steelman had formally announced his candidacy on January 5 of 1976, and from a strategic standpoint, that was one of his problems. For a newcomer on the statewide scene, that was something of a late start, but he campaigned vigorously to catch up. For many Republicans and Texans in general, Steelman was a breath of fresh air in the political arena. At thirty-four, he was boyishly handsome and he had a deep, smooth voice with which to articulate his political philosophy. He was conservative on fiscal policy, but concerned about land use and all aspects of the environment. He became a champion of preserving the Big Thicket in East Texas, and was a leader in the defeat of the Trinity River canal project, which he termed "the biggest piece of pork barrel legislation ever." He was defending the individual against the collective forces of concentrated power in government, business, and labor, sounding a distant note from a theme in an Ayn Rand novel. And he would zero in on what he termed Bentsen's incessant use of his Senate office to further narrow special interests.

Steelman, the two-term congressman, was out to upset Bentsen, who was completing his first term in the Senate. Steelman assembled a small but strong campaign organization that included, at the top, Fred Meyer, the Dallas business executive who would ultimately become a highly effective county chairman for the party. Marvin Collins served as Steelman's AA in Washington, then assisted campaign manager Anson Franklin, a transplanted Virginian with whom he had helped elect Linwood Holton as the first GOP governor of Virginia in modern times. For Steelman's statewide campaign headquarters, they operated from offices in Dallas while Lujet McCullough ran the state press office in Austin, two blocks west of the capitol where Steelman held frequent news conferences. Steelman would hammer away at two central themes: the American economic system was no longer open to the average citizen — and Bentsen was the "very epitome of an elitist, special interest Senator." To the first theme, "the domination of our system by the big government, big labor, big business establishment has left our free enterprise system of competiton subject to the whims of these large impersonal special interests." To the second, "his loading the tax bill with special breaks that benefit a few of his out-of-state campaign contributors and himself ... his authorship of the New York bailout proposal, his failures to fully disclose his personal finances ... his six years in the Senate are distinguished, not by service to the people of Texas, but by narrow personal ambition, neglect of Texas for three years to run for the Presidency, and betrayal of everything he said he stood for when he ran in 1970."

Steelman was a game, hard-working candidate who gave it all he had, but the conditions weren't there. Though gestures of unity were being made, a political syndrome loosely defined as "Watergate residue" hung over Texas Republicans who had fought bitterly in the primary and many of whom, along with independent conservatives, couldn't forgive Ford's pardon of Nixon nor the heresy of having named Rockefeller vice-president. Further, Steelman couldn't raise the campaign funds necessary to compete with the entrenched Bentsen who, though embarrassed by his poor showing in the presidential sweepstakes, nonetheless maintained a powerful following in the business-industrial community in Texas, and to some extent the nation. He placed many a call on their "PACs," political action committees organized to funnel campaign funds to candidates.

Steelman's television commercials, produced by Bob Goodman, were effective, and his small, but loyal organization, backed his shoe leather, door-knocking personal campaign around the state. A number of active Democrats openly identified with the GOP candidate under the banner of "Democrats for Steelman," directed by Les Weisbrod of Dallas, former staff director of the House Study Group in Austin. One of the Democrats, Wes Masters of Austin, a member of the Jimmy Carter delegate selection committee for Travis County, tossed a hard pitch when he quoted Jimmy Carter as having said of Steelman's opponent, "I don't think Bentsen likes to work. He goes to a few very small receptions that are held for very wealthy people, most of whom are Republicans. And he will very quietly slip out of the community without making any sort of effort to reach the political consciousness of the community." Masters concluded, "I believe many Carter supporters will join me in voting for Alan Steelman." From the conservative Democrat side, Dennis Goehring of College Station, a banker who had been state treasurer for Phil Gramm's primary race against Bentsen: "He [Steelman] believes in sound principles of government which most Texans support, and I appreciate his record of fiscal responsibility, which is one of the best in Congress." It all sounded encouraging early on, but there wasn't a Rebuilding Committee to exploit liberal Democrat backlash nor even adequate funds to promote a Mexican-American program, badly needed to produce anything near the vote pattern attained by Tower in 1966 and 1972.

In the Ford Texas Campaign, O'Donnell provided leadership for the state operation with a staff that included Doug Lewis, taking a leave of absence from his position as executive director of the State GOP; Patrick Conway, former Rebuilding Committee operative who had changed to the GOP; and Cathi Villalpando, who led a belated effort to reach Mexican-American voters. Actually, all the Ford fall efforts were somewhat belated because by the time the September state convention was over, less than two months remained for the general election campaign, hardly the time needed to stitch together a well-rounded, effective statewide operation.

Ford's campaign would gain ground in the stretch run, but the inevitable was played out in the final days of the long, dismal election year. Carter defeated Ford in Texas by a vote of 2,082,319 to 1,953,300 and Bentsen defeated Steelman by a vote of 2,199,956 to 1,636,370. In its first election cycle, ART found it difficult to win when the top of the ticket was a negative or neutral factor. There were a few pleasant developments, including the election to the Texas House of Bill Blanton of Carrollton, Bill Ceverha and Lee Jackson of Dallas, plus Bob McFarland, a sharp young attorney from Arlington, whose campaign manager made it clear that ART's support was decisive in a tight race. New faces in the Texas House from Houston included Chase Untermeyer and Brad Wright, who had won a 1976 special election and was reelected in the general election, while Joe Robbins broke a Democratic tradition by winning a seat in Lubbock. Three other ART-backed legislative candidates in 1976, Bob Leonard of Fort Worth, Joe McComb of Corpus Christi, and John Smithee of Amarillo, lost their bids but were launched into viable status their first time out and subsequently would be elected to public office. The heartbreaker was the ART showcase race for state senate in Dallas between Republican Tom Pauken and incumbent Bill Braecklein. The District Sixteen contest, in which ART poured thousands of dollars, went right down to the wire with Pauken barely being edged out. Several ART-backed local races were won, including election of the first Republican in the Travis County Courthouse since Reconstruction, Bill Burnette of Austin as tax assessor-collector. In any event, it was enough to encourage the membership of ART to saddle up for another round in 1978 when the participants, whether they had been for Ford or Reagan, wanted to see an end to the bitter intra-party fighting that had been so debilitating during 1976.

CHAPTER TWELVE

Clements and Tower Win Barnburners

In 1977, Tower was licking his political wounds, wondering what the fallout would produce, particularly regarding his relationship with the State GOP. He'd been in the Senate for sixteen years and might survive without party help in the 1978 election. But he and the party leadership knew, after adverse election results in 1974 and 1976, that it would be of mutual benefit to bend their swords into plowshares. In the meantime it was doubly important for him and his Senate staff to function at full capacity during the first year of an election cycle before turning over the reins to a campaign operation. One major reason Tower had been successful as a member of the minority party serving the vast, diverse State of Texas was that he maintained a constant conservative voting record which accurately reflected the views of a majority of Texans. Another major reason was his skilled staff, many of whom had been on board for years. In 1977, his Washington office had as AA Carolyn Bacon, who had served there in other capacities before assuming the top position. She was supported by such longtime staffers as Dave Martinez, a native of San Antonio, the executive assistant who handled matters relating to minorities and who would eventually become AA; Pam Turner, a sharp legislative assistant who would ultimately join the White House staff after Jimmy Carter departed; Allen Balch, press secretary; Tom Fahey, who kept the flow of mail under control and whose wife, Rosemary, had only recently left the staff after many years in Washington, and after once having worked at the GOP state headquarters in Austin; plus several others who kept the large volume of constituent and legislative work moving along its way. In addition to the Washington office, there were branch offices in Dallas, Houston and Austin, the political hub where Bill Keener was director, assisted by Wini Chapoton, and where Monica Hearn and Joyce Thompson (later to be Sibley) had done so much constituent casework for many years, assisting individual citizens with their problems with some part of the federal bureaucracy. In Dallas, Larry Combest was in charge and Dottie de la Garza directed Tower publicity in the state. Martha Kirkendall, who served through many years, was in that office from which Phil Charles, longtime personal aide to Tower, also operated. Shan Pickard handled a load of constituent casework there, including matters relating to Social Security, passports, and visas. In Tower's new Houston office, the director was Cyndi Taylor, a bright young attorney who had served on the Washington staff and would eventually be elected as Cyndi Taylor Krier to the Texas Senate. Combest was destined for Congress, following in the steps of Tom Loeffler, who served on Tower's staff before joining the Ford White House staff, then returning to Texas to run for Congress, Twenty-first District, in 1978. Keener would wind up in Bill Clements's campaign and Fred McClure, another sharp young attorney, would serve in various capacities as would Bob Estrada, who started with the State GOP. Several members of the staff interrelated well with political activity, but their most important overall role in the pre-election year was to serve as the senator's steady conduit to his constituents. Through direct mail, phone calls and personal contact, these Tower offices were communicating with hundreds of Texans daily, not to mention the newsletters and special group mailings that reached thousands. The strength of the staff meant a great deal to an incumbent senator and Tower generally could count on effective people at the skill positions. Senate funds allocated for travel were skimpy, thus travel expenses for Tower and his staff were often paid from private funds raised and administered by the Tower Senate Club, whose chairman was Ed Clark.

ART, which had weaved through the 1975 — 1976 election cycle with bumps and bruises, received a big boost in the spring of 1977 when George Bush agreed to lend his name to a major fund-raising event in Austin. This was brought about largely through the efforts of Jim Allison, Bush's longtime friend and prominent ART leader. It was billed as a "Welcome Home George Bush" dinner May 13 at the Sheraton Crest Hotel. ART Chairman Julian Zimmerman said, "We're proud to host the first statewide function at which George Bush will be honored since this distinguished leader has returned to Texas after years of outstanding service ..." The atmosphere for the dinner was charged by the wave of rumors emanating from Houston that Bush was seriously considering the presidential race of 1980. Thus, this dinner was an unwritten kickoff of sorts, though many pro-Reagan people would attend. It was a highly successful event. The more than 500 attending, at $125 per ticket, and $75 for ART members, were greeted by a seven-piece mariachi band at the reception. Four former GOP state chairmen purchased tickets; Thad Hutcheson of Houston, and Tad Smith of El Paso, from the pioneer days, and George Willeford and Jack Warren of Austin, from more recent vintage. Hutcheson was unable to attend, but sent a congratulatory telegram as did Senator Tower and Paul Eggers. Jim Baker, who had managed the strong stretch run of Gerald Ford's 1976 campaign, was well received, amid rumors he might make a run for attorney general. Congressman Jim Collins of Dallas came to praise Bush as did many others, including Al Fay, the former national committeeman who had recently returned from his post as United States Ambassador to Trinidad. Showcasing ART-supported winners from 1976, State Representative Bob McFarland of Arlington spoke, along with Bill Burnette, the new Travis County tax assessor-collector. Winston Bode, longtime producer-host of *Capital Eye*, a television program dealing with public affairs, noted that it was indeed an interesting event. There was so much GOP partisanship yet Frank Erwin, one of the state's most prominent conservative Democrats, had been supportive of the dinner and Dave Shapiro, the veteran liberal activist, was there, as always talking of the need for a two-party system in near reverent tones. The movers and shakers in Texas politics made note of Erwin's support and the active ART support of Ike Harris, who was becoming more prominent in the Texas Senate. Harris's Senate colleague, Walter Mengden of Houston, had also subscribed to the ART grass roots approach and he joined Harris at the head table for the dinner. After a shaky start, ART was moving into a strong position in the scheme of things, but Allison, whose role was critical in the early establishment of the organization, contracted cancer and would die the following year. Forrest Moore of Dallas would succeed Allison as chairman of the committee which still bears his name, "Allison Candidates Committee," and his widow, Linda, pursued the tradition by serving on the committee.

The Texas GOP hosted a major dinner in June 1977, honoring Bush and four other Texans who had participated in the Ford Administration, including Anne Armstrong, Jim Baker, Bill Clements and Ed Vetter, who replaced Baker in the Department of Commerce position when Baker took over Ford's campaign. That dinner was held in Dallas at the Apparel Mart Great Hall.

In the winter of 1977, Tower began putting together his 1978 reelection campaign in earnest when he retained Nola Smith Haerle to organize the first phase, including the kick off tour in January. Having managed Tower's 1972 campaign, she knew the state, the party and the challenge of such an endeavor. She retained two advertising agencies, Bob Goodman's which had extensive experience in Texas, and Ed Yardang and Associates of San Antonio, an upbeat new agency whose principals were Bev Coiner, Lionel Sosa, and Warren Stewart. Goodman's designated role was essentially producing television, while Yardang would produce all the other material, including that for a special Mexican-American program entitled, "Nosotros con Tower" (We're with Tower). Brad O'Leary was on board again to raise funds, assisted by Libba Barnes and Ramona Seeligson. Taber Ward, who had been serving as acting executive director of the State GOP, joined the campaign staff as media director and was instrumental in working out many of the details for the kick off tour. Ward had served under the new State GOP Chairman, Ray Barnhart, who succeeded Ray Hutchison, the first major candidate for the Republican gubernatorial nomination.

Barnhart, whose relationship with Tower had improved over the months since the tempest of 1976, would bring Wayne Thorburn as executive director of the State GOP. Calm and studious, Thornburn, who held a doctoral degree, would add to the note of stability and unity that had been established during 1977, and would help Tower and other GOP candidates during the 1978 campaigns. There was a new aspect to Tower's modus operandi in 1977 in the form of his second wife, Lilla, a Washington attorney whom he married in May of that year following a divorce from his first wife, Lou, in December 1976. The second Mrs. Tower would take an active part in the senator's campaign, a factor which didn't sit so well with some of Tower's top operatives who often found her role to be more intrusive than instructive.

There was cause for optimism in December 1977 when the Texas GOP captured the state senate seat in the Texas Panhandle for the first time. Bob Price of Pampa, the former congressman, won a special election to fill the vacancy created by the resignation of Max Sherman. Another special election boost came a week prior to Price's victory when S. L. Abbott became the first Republican to be elected to the Legislature from El Paso. Riding momentum from the Bush dinner, ART had been a big factor. As expressed by Zimmerman, "Our organization played a leading role in these elections by sending ART funds to the candidates and by assisting them in raising additional funds. ART was again the largest single financial source for both campaigns."

For Tower's campaign kick off on January 11, 1978, Ed Clark set the defensive position in which the senator would be cast during 1978, no matter how many speeches and paid television commercials would be presented to extoll his virtues of seniority, service, experience and effectiveness. "Although we have a great deal of confidence in our senator," Clark intoned to the faithful gathered at the same large headquarters from the 1972 campaign at Ninth and Congress near the capitol grounds,

> ... there are those who are calling for a new senator. They are saying that our senior senator is 'ineffective' and that his name is not prominent as the author of legislation. These voices are deceptive. Let me remind them that the role of a senator in the opposition party is not as a creator of legislation. They know full well that the party in power in the Senate controls the makeup of the committees, the chairmanship of each committee and indeed, the course of legislation. They know this and they know our senator's party has never controlled the Senate during his tenure, yet they continue crying out that our senior senator does not have his name appearing as the author of legislation.
>
> Let me remind them also that the role of a senator in the opposition party is to refine legislation by debating and offering amendments, or if a particular piece of legislation is not in the public interest, by fighting to defeat it with all his strength ... And I believe that most Texans are weary of more and more legislation, regulation and nonessential spending — Texans want less, not more, controls from Washington ... So let's not be fooled by the coyote calls from our detractors. Let's set forth in a positive manner the admiration and respect we hold for our senator for the steadfast manner in which he has fulfilled his duties and responsibilities.

A tightly-scheduled three-day statewide tour was to be taken after the headquarters ceremony with the senator and his wife accompanied by Taber Ward and Pat Oxford, an affable young Houston attorney who would provide legal advice to the campaign. The weather was a harbinger for the campaign when an ice storm in Dallas caused a delay with attendant anxiety and confusion. But the reelection tour was carried out, with Tower briefly on center stage before the Democratic candidates, Congressman Robert Krueger of New Braunfels, and former State Senator Joe Christie of El Paso, took the limelight for the primary battle. As the filing deadline neared, rumors persisted from Houston that Hank Grover would run against Tower for the GOP nomination. In Tower's camp, this was considered to be a dangerous proposition, not as a threat to defeating Tower in the primary, but as a certain means of reopening the 1976 wounds, making Tower more vulnerable in the general election. Instead, at the last minute, Grover filed his intention to run for the Senate as an independent — a potentially deadly proposition for Tower, if Grover could qualify for the general election ballot. He had until July to gather some 20,000 signatures of qualified voters who didn't vote in either party primary or runoffs therefrom. Since Grover had run a strong statewide race, the proposition was feasible if he had maintained an organization that was essentially loyal to him. If he qualified for the ballot and ran a hard-nosed conservative campaign on issues spliced with potshots at Tower's anti-Reagan heresy in 1976, virtually all the votes he would receive would come out of Tower's hip pocket. Tower contended Grover wasn't a great threat, but his advisors found the situation serious indeed, with estimates of Grover's potential ranging from three to nine percent. In a close race between Tower and his Democratic opponent, Grover's vote could easily be decisive. Grover, the Republican maverick, had become a renegade. It was too much for some of his longtime supporters, including the venerable Nancy Palm who came to Tower's state headquarters on March 4 of 1978, to confirm that she would help Tower any way she could to hold the seat for the Republican Party.

In the spring of 1978, Tower divided his time between Washington and Texas, maintaining visiblility though he wasn't pressed by an opponent at the moment. He continued to score political points by identifying with sports when the Texas Longhorn basketball team won the National Invitational Tournament, the first time for a Southwest Conference team to win the title in the forty-one year history of the tournament. Tower sent a telegram to Coach Abe Lemons and his team that was quoted in part by most major newspapers in the state.

THE EYES OF TEXAS, AND INDEED THE NATION, ARE UPON YOU FOR THE EXEMPLARY MANNER IN WHICH YOU PERFORMED IN WINNING THE NIT CHAMPION-SHIP.

Later in the year Tower would gain benefit from another full-page endorsement ad in *Texas Football* magazine, with Tom Landry as chairman of the ad hoc sponsoring committee.

As the primary campaigns were getting underway, Ken Towery, who had returned from service in the Nixon — Ford Administration, assumed the manager's role for Tower, replacing Nola Smith Haerle who had been hired to manage Bill Clements's gubernatorial bid — a bid that was bold and impressive. The former Deputy Secretary of Defense had considered such a race in 1968, when Paul Eggers became the nominee. Then and for the 1978 race, the ubiquitous O'Donnell wanted Clements. O'Donnell was prominent in this campaign from the inception with superb talent that could get things moving rapidly, not the least of whom was Clements's wife, Rita, who knew politics from the precinct level upward. They ran their primary campaign out of Dallas since it provided home strength and also was Hutchison's home base from where he had served as a state legislator. From his time in that capacity plus his role as state GOP chairman, Hutchison had a strong line of contacts around the state and was considered to be the early on favorite. But Clements had a trump card known as the mother's milk of politics, money, and lots of it; a personal fortune from which he would draw millions of dollars. And he struck a note with Republicans throughout the state when he would say, "We will not run out of gas in the fourth quarter." Those tired troops who had fought so hard for Jack Cox, Paul Eggers and other GOP gubernatorial nominees knew exactly what that meant. Lance Tarrance, the Houston-based Republican pollster who worked for Clements and Tower, found Clements brought another unusual appeal to the race that would bode well for the general election — he was perceived as having "just enough" governmental experience to handle the job of governor, yet he could run against "the professional politicians" who were messing things up in Austin. He was perceived more as a tough, self-made successful businessman who would provide leadership and management, a desired image contrast from the six bland years of incumbent Dolph Briscoe, who was seeking four more years in office. Having had four years of Washington experience, Clements spoke with authority when he criticized the Carter Administration, particularly about defense and energy policies. Clements hit issues with directness and clarity, such as his view of the state's fiscal situation.

> ... State spending has increased seventy-six percent in the last six years, but our income hasn't come up. A few years ago we had a $3 billion surplus — today it is $21 million. Our state bureaucracy has increased twenty-three percent these last few years giving Texas the fastest growing bureaucracy of any state in the nation ... We currently are spending forty-seven percent of a year's budget of over $8 billion in education, yet Texas school systems overall rank in the lower third nationally. I consider this a disgrace and a disservice to our children ...

Well-conceived television commercials, showing Clements from early days working in the oilfields to the present, were shown repeatedly to develop the desired image. Clements wasn't bashful in backing them up. "I started my business [SEDCO] with two used drilling rigs and built it into the largest company of its kind in the world." Regarding his tour with the Defense Department, he proclaimed that congressional leaders "said they had never had an administrator who handled the defense budget as efficiently as I did." The Clements — Hutchison contest was energizing Texas Republicans, but center stage belonged to Briscoe and challenger John Hill, the attorney general who had lost out, along with Briscoe, in the 1968 Democratic Primary race for governor. The first round of the contest to replace Hill was between Price Daniel, Jr., former Speaker of the Texas House, and former Secretary of State Mark White. It was spirited indeed, with the winner sure to face a stern challenge from Republican Jim Baker in the general election. Briscoe and Daniel had been early favorites but in the stretch run both races were believed to be close. Despite strong support from the AFL — CIO and liberal elements, Christie had fallen behind and most observers picked the well-financed Krueger to win the Senate nomination by a fairly wide margin.

On primary day, Tower and his wife had a relatively relaxed schedule, thanks to friends in Wichita Falls, including Jacque Allen and the Maxfields. That night, however, Tower found himself much in demand by news media people calling his suite at the Trade Winds for comment on his impending race with Krueger and what impact might be in store from the other Democratic races. Tower spoke cautiously, with only the one major variable sorted out for him — Krueger was his opponent. But Tower stayed on a positive note that night, reemphasizing his intention to run on his record. Though Clements had come out of Chute Number One riding hard, and had won the Republican gubernatorial nomination by a wide margin, the Texas news media still generally regarded the Democratic gubernatorial nomination as tantamount to election. In a bitter, divisive race, John Hill upset the incumbent Democratic governor. The praise heaped on him that night helped cause Hill to make the strategic political blunder of the decade — he failed to take Clements seriously for a critical period of time.

White's victory was a bad break for Baker, who many observers believed could have defeated Daniel in something of a conservative — liberal contest, whereas White wouldn't present such an opportunity. While Hill was resting on his laurels, talking about who he might appoint after his inauguration, Clements proceeded to execute his strategic plan. A key element was "Project 230." This was a summer-long campaign to reach 230 counties of rural Texas, with Clements and his wife often traveling in a mobile home to cover the vast distances involved to reach the grass roots people in hundreds of small towns. In sweltering heat, they greeted farmers and ranchers who appreciated such a concerted effort. That personal touch was crucial to slice into what otherwise would have been a decisive Democratic margin. Further, the gathering storm was advanced by Briscoe's reluctance to unite with Hill. The primary had been bitter, leaving deep wounds. Thanks in a large measure to David Dean, a key Briscoe operative, many Briscoe county campaign chairmen would rally to Clements's banner. This helped the Clements Campaign greatly in rural Texas, and in achieving another strategic tenet as well, that of painting Hill as a liberal.

In the summer of 1978, Tower's campaign girded for battle from its state headquarters near the capitol, the same large two-story building that had been used for that purpose in 1972. With strong cash flow generating a multimillion dollar campaign, Tower could afford a large staff which was assembled under the direction of Towery, the manager. As in previous campaigns, major emphasis would go to paid media and political organization, keyed to urban Texas where phone banks and other activities would be used to generate pro-Tower voter turnout. Some of the old pros involved included Janelle McArthur and Polly Sowell in the state headquarters with Molly Rockwood (soon to be Pryor) in Houston, Carol Reed in Dallas, Cyndi Taylor (to be Krier) having moved to San Antonio, Nora Ray in Fort Worth, and Anita Atkison in Austin. In developing certain aspects of organizational activity, such as helping find locations for campaign signs and bolstering crowds for Tower's appearances, the realtors around the state had been helpful. This was due in large part to their state leadership, particularly Hub Bechtol of Austin, and their lobbyist, Gerhardt Schulle, who functioned as a political operative, helping various campaigns, when the Legislature was not in session. Plus the realtors provided considerable amounts of campaign contributions as did many other organized interest groups, such as the medical profession and various business interests. John Davis, the campaign treasurer, would double as organizational director. Young people attracted to the campaign included Maggie Bray, Kevin Burnette, Herb Butram, and Kevin Moomaw, who would remain active in political capacities for years, plus Mac Sweeney, who would eventually be elected to Congress. Burnette and Moomaw ran an aggressive program under the banner of "Young Texans for Tower," assisted by Kendyl Daugherty. One of their most effective weapons on campuses was Jeanne Tower, the senator's youngest daughter who had recently graduated from Southern Methodist University. She took to personal campaigning more enthusiastically than did her father. The Mexican-American program, Nosotros con Tower, was directed by Isaac Olivares, a former member of the San Angelo City Commission (Council), assisted by Theresa Vasquez and Ernest Olivas, who would eventually serve on the staff of Vice-President Bush. Arnold Tompkins was research director, dividing time with a program for black Texans for Tower. Tompkins was assisted by Sweeney and Jeff Dunn. The press section was directed by Bruce Neeley, assisted by Suzanne Majors.

"Pollmanship" would be played in the Texas political arena of 1978 as it had never been played before. Polling, or "survey research" as it's known in the profession, is generally used more for planning strategy and tactics of a campaign rather than as a propaganda tool to one-up the opponent at points during the game. But the bandwagon psychology is so coveted in politics that modern campaigns seize on bits and pieces of polling data to try to impress upon the news media that an important finding or trend is being revealed. Perhaps Texas is more subject to such tactics because of its diverse electorate which is very difficult to assess by most political writers who are only conversant with the particular city or region which they cover on a regular basis. In any event, the 1978 campaigns would be influenced from time to time by what was reported by a particular polling entity. With Tarrance advising Tower and Clements, there would be continuity of methodology though the races were as different as night and day. For instance, Tarrance believed that to survey less than 1,000 qualified voters was wasting money on a statewide poll because the degree of accuracy would be too uncertain to warrant confidence in campaign planning. In late June, Tarrance's firm reported a statewide survey to Tower's Campaign that showed a ten-point lead over Krueger, but projected a tough contest. The poll reported thirty-eight percent of the M-A vote leaned to Tower, but that was not expected to hold that high after a full-scale attack from Krueger. Blacks again were strongly Democratic, favoring the Carter Administration with which Krueger would align in that community. M-As were trending more to two-party politics, but blacks were staying hitched strongly to the Democratic Party.

Tower's positive posture for the campaign was obvious — key on incumbency with its seniority and benefits to the state, including being able to provide bipartisan support for measures important to Texas, stress particular value attached to his membership on the Armed Services Committee, vital to the nation's defense and to the state's economy; and remind Texans of a voting record consistent with majority thinking, pointing out specific votes to various groups affected. What wasn't obvious was how to posture against an opponent who would pose more difficult problems than any of his previous Democratic opponents in statewide contests.

Krueger was a two-term congressman who had pursued an academic career at Duke University where he had reached high levels in administration before his first venture into the political arena in 1974. At that time he ran for the Twenty-first Congressional District seat being vacated by the retiring Clark Fisher. Nelson Wolff of San Antonio, then a popular state senator, was the favorite to win the Democratic Primary with Fisher's endorsement, but the native son of New Braunfels forced a runoff and swept to an upset victory. Krueger had maintained a relentless attack on Wolff's record as a senator plus he had conjured up a cloud of dislike in the far-flung district by portraying Wolff as a tool of heavy-handed business interests in San Antonio. Garry Mauro, a young liberal political operative with experience gained in campaigns for Ralph Yarborough and George McGovern, was the campaign manager for Krueger, and manipulator of much of the anti-Wolff material that proved to be decisive. Roy Spence, who would attain the Mondale creative account in 1984, was the whiz kid television producer in 1974 who could portray Krueger however he needed to be portrayed along the way. After winning the nomination, Krueger defeated Doug Harlan, the San Antonio Republican making his second try, in the general election. Harlan carefully laid out to Tower's top campaign operatives the reason why Krueger was such a difficult opponent. He was one who took half-truths and twisted them further if he thought it would pay off with a net plus at the polls. During the Democratic Primary in 1978, Joe Christie branded Krueger as "a politician in the worst sense of the word — a politician who is willing to bend the rules, shave the facts and skate close to the edge." One of Krueger's former colleagues at Duke University, Professor Victor Strandberg, told a *Dallas Times Herald* reporter what he thought about Krueger's surprising success as a politician in Texas: "He's proven what some of us here have suspected all along, and that is that he is one of the more coldblooded people you will ever meet. He will use people to advance his ambition. Krueger is almost like an electric calculating machine. He has an almost inhuman desire for power. You can never tell what he might do to get more."

With all that in mind, Tower's campaign was apprehensive about posturing since a longtime incumbent, sitting on a nice lead in the polls, has no business attacking the underdog. Yet, the Tower Campaign knew the senator would soon come under constant fire from the campaign of a chameleon who had no political convictions, attacking and responding with situation ethics and expediency as the only guidelines. One of Tower's top operatives, after reviewing all the Krueger material, penned a memo in late June which said in part, "From this time forward, Tower's personal posture vs. his opponent should be reviewed carefully and often since we anticipate a series of strong, personal attacks from Krueger." A follow-up confidential memo to Tower, dated August 4, laid out an explicit warning,

> I see some thunderheads on the horizon ... Krueger et al are a team of hardball players. They're more aggressive, clever and resourceful than those we faced in your prior two campaigns. Their game plan is now clear. It's attack constantly, establish doubts about your legis-

lative record and leadership ability. It's hit-and-run, day in, day out. They're relentless and somewhat ruthless, playing fast and easy with the facts and conclusions ... As I read the Krueger — Wolff race, it was about the same as ours. Though it was an open congressional seat, Krueger chewed on Wolff's state legislative record and took advantage of the underdog role. Wolff's decision to return the fire came too late and Krueger pulled a major upset.

The memo urged Tower to prepare for counterattacking soon, since "you may have already slid into a defensive position without knowing it." The memo further urged the Tower Campaign to develop anti-Krueger issues relating to the opponent's voting record and poor attendance during recent sessions of Congress.

An item in the July edition of Tower's campaign newsletter said it all about a favorable turn of events, "Hank Grover's move out of the Senatorial race brought a sigh of relief to Senator Tower's campaign staff and to his many diligent supporters, but Mr. Krueger was not as excited. He shouldn't be, because his own staff estimated that about three percent more people will be voting for the Senator, and that's important because every little bit counts." The Democratic nominee was also concerned about the presence on the ballot of a La Raza Unida candidate for Senate, Luis de Leon of Leander. De Leon claimed repeatedly that one of Krueger's operatives offered him a bribe to get out of the race, but no legal action was taken.

For his part, Krueger had pursued vigorous personal campaigning in Texas, throwing his congressional attendance to the wind. Some of his appeals before different groups were often blatant or maudlin. Before the AFL — CIO, Krueger assured organized labor it could rely on him "not to promise what I can't deliver, but maybe to deliver more than I can promise." He pledged "to be there when you really need me ..." All of which helped earn him vast coverage in the AFL — CIO publications, including a two-page spread in the July edition of the Texas AFL — CIO newspaper. But after Tower hit Krueger for having voted six times for AFL — CIO supported legislation designed to undermine right-to-work, Krueger ran out with strong statements claiming he was a longtime supporter of right-to-work and even ran an item in the summer edition of "The Krueger Report," his congressional district newsletter, under a headline, "Right to Work Must Stand." Further, his campaign sent a strongly worded pro right-to-work mailing to 30,000 Texas business leaders. It was an incredible performance considering the fact that right-to-work legislation per se wasn't even being considered by the Congress, and Krueger had assiduously courted the AFL-CIO which hates right-to-work more than any legislation. Tower's chairman, Ed Clark, promptly accused Krueger of waffling on the issue, but in an appearance on Winston Bode's *Capital Eye* television program, Krueger refused to answer Clark's charge. Appearing before a Mexican-American audience in San Antonio, Krueger gushed, "My name is German but my heart is Mexican." About which a Mexican-American Tower supporter quipped, "The way Krueger's running, he'll change Wurstfest [an annual celebration in New Braunfels] to Tacofest."

In the battle for the Mexican-American vote, Tower's program, directed by Isaac Olivares, showed promise with the acceptance of state chairmanship by Pete Diaz, a highly regarded businessman in the Rio Grande Valley. Two prominent M-A organizations, American GI Forum and IMAGE, honored Tower with special awards for sponsoring programs beneficial to their objectives. Two former national presidents of LULAC, William D. (Willie) Bonilla of Corpus Christi, and Manuel Gonzales of Waco, endorsed Tower early on and late in the campaign the senator would be endorsed by Juan Garcia, state vice-president of the GI Forum. Bob Estrada was often travelling with Tower, providing liaison with M-As all over the state. Tower had a litany and chronology regarding legislation and appointments favorable to the M-A community of Texas, including his role in securing the appointment of the first Hispanic American in history to head the Small Business Administration, the late Hilary Sandoval of El Paso. According to the Southwest Voter Registration Project, a repository of Hispanic voting data located in San Antonio, Gerald Ford had received only thirteen percent of the 1976 M-A vote in Texas. Tower was out to get a much higher percentage or he would face the results sustained by Ford. Tower had also begun pointing up waffling being done by Krueger, including the issue of a national ID card for all employees, and criminal penalties for the employer who hires undocumented workers — an issue, according to news reports, on which Krueger was on both sides.

Tower and his campaign people had decided to fight back when deceptive, irresponsible charges were made, but often the responses were not as widely covered as the charge nor was it easy to determine rapidly how widespread coverage of a new charge might have been. The hit and run charges by Krueger made only in individual locations around the state were extremely difficult to counter, since the nature and timing of the charge might not filter back for a day or two. Increasingly, the broad attacks were of a personal nature, violating an unwritten law in the Texas political arena that a candidate doesn't attack an officeholder's personal life or that of his family unless there is substantial evidence that some personal or family problem adversely affects discharge of public duties.

Tower was incensed by Krueger's snide remark that Tower voted for a congressional pay raise (which wasn't true anyway) in order to supply money for his daughters to shop at Neiman-Marcus. Further, Krueger was demanding that Tower's wife, Lilla, disclose her financial holdings, prompting questions from the news media to which Tower replied that he didn't know her holdings, that they had agreed before marriage to maintain separate estates, and that she was entitled to her privacy. Rarely had longtime associates seen an angered Tower respond as harshly as he did when he branded Krueger as a "lame duck Congressman and a dead duck politician. His campaign is foundering for lack of public support, so he is resorting to personal attacks and mudslinging ..." Krueger, a bachelor at the time, "knows little about marriage, and knows nothing of the sensitivity involved in a marriage between two people with children and long-standing careers." Pointing to his wife's professional career and defending her right to privacy, Tower branded Krueger as "this Little Lord Fauntleroy, a beneficiary of inherited wealth," who was attacking her for no just cause. "When a woman marries a man, she doesn't give up her rights to privacy even if she marries a senator."

The Houston Post reported from its Washington bureau on August 6, that "The flap over John G. Tower's refusal to make public his wife Lilla's finances is rooted primarily in her opposition to doing so, according to several sources ... It is just another example, the sources claim, of why grumbling continues within the Tower camp about her role in the Texas Republican's reelection effort. The senator obviously regards his wife as a political asset and indeed she appears to have been an unqualified hit on the campaign trail. Even critics acknowledge her genuine charm and her abilities as a polished speaker. But behind-the-scenes, she has crossed swords numerous times with Tower aides over strategy, personnel and other matters ..." The *Post* article pointed out that the Senate Ethics Committee seems "perfectly satisfied with Tower's statement."

As the financial disclosure issue simmered down, Mrs. Tower became the focal point of news again. From *The Dallas Times Herald* of August 22, an article by Paul West with a Washington dateline reported that Tower's AA, Carolyn Bacon, "has abruptly left her post as the top-ranking member of the Texas Republican's staff. Sources said Ms. Bacon, an eleven-year veteran of Tower's Washington office, was forced to resign her job because of pressure from the senator's wife."

Lilla Tower denied any role, and Carolyn Bacon refused to discuss it, but the article went on to state, "In a similar incident last fall, Houston advertising executive Robert S. Heller, who had handled the advertising in all of Tower's successful campaigns since 1961, was replaced following complaints from Mrs. Tower that he 'never captured the real John Tower.'"Such news, less than three months before the election, didn't exactly convey an aura of stability for Tower during the rough and tumble contest with Krueger. Ken Towery, the campaign manager and a longtime friend of Carolyn Bacon, was terribly upset over the turn of events and expressed his views forthrightly to the senator. Towery's relationship with Mrs. Tower, which had been tenuous for some time, became so strained that they didn't speak for the duration of the campaign.

At the same time the Bacon incident occurred, Tower's campaign finance arm was flexing its muscle. Chairman Hayden Head of Corpus Christi reported some 62,500 contributors had donated to the campaign, raising nearly $3 million. Dinners and other fund-raising functions accounted for big infusions while direct mail pieces, such as a highly successful letter by former Governor Allan Shivers, motivated thousands of respondents to contribute in the ten- to twenty-five dollar range.

While Tower divided his time between Washington and Texas, Clements bore down throughout the summer to carry out his rural campaign plan. William Murchison of *The Dallas Morning News* editorial staff had written after the primary,

> ... Now comes Bill Clements, with sleeves rolled up and fire in his eyes. If he has not already, John Hill should gird for battle. The Democratic nomination in 1978 is tantamount to heartburn.

There were many of the Capitol Press Corps who had not seen much of Clements yet, having concentrated on the Democratic Primary, and they still didn't consider him to be competitive to Hill. Though he spent most of his time in rural areas during the summer, Clements made one memorable appearance in Amarillo. He had vowed he was going to hang Jimmy Carter around John Hill's neck like "a dead chicken." During a nonpartisan function at which Hill was present, Clements took the occasion to produce a rubber chicken from a brown paper bag and tossed it in the direction of Hill. The chicken landed in the plate of Mrs. Hodge, wife of the Amarillo mayor, Jerry Hodge, causing some consternation at the time, but the incident certainly stirred publicity about Clements.

Throughout Texas, Clements's campaign operation was working day and night to close the long gap with Hill. Top advisors included Tom Reed and Stu Spencer, plus O'Donnell, who knew no peer in organizational politics. Nola Haerle, the manager, would marshall the troops in a remarkable campaign that would claim 25,000 volunteers by its end. David Dean, formerly a close associate of Briscoe, provided tangible evidence of the efforts of Clements to attract Briscoe voters, a program enhanced by the work of Omar Harvey. Jim Francis, former executive director of the Dallas County Republican Party, was Clements's finance director and Bill Keener, the veteran former Tower staffer, handled scheduling. Mark Heckmann, formerly with *The Houston Chronicle*, was in charge of the press operation and George Steffes, a Californian close to Ronald Reagan, provided assistance as a volunteer. On the other side, Hill's campaign was managed by easygoing John Rogers, a former newspaperman who had spent some time with the AFL — CIO in communications and political activity. Rogers was a no-nonsense organization specialist who fulfilled his role in a low key manner, about the opposite to Krueger's manager, Mauro. Hill and Rogers were in a difficult spot in September, seeing evidence of Clements's campaign gaining some momentum, but Hill was still perceived as virtually elected and their strategy was to avoid giving Clements any added recognition. Hill would launch a well-rounded media program devised by Bob Heller, the veteran Houston advertising executive, but the melding of the major campaign elements in the fall never matched the effectiveness of the spring.

In addition to building a large well-rounded organization, effective television commercials were essential for Clements to gain the identification and acceptance necessary to attain competitive status. With millions to spend, advertising was extensive indeed. In addition to well-conceived commercials portraying Clements as a self-made Texan with deep native roots, an image contrast was developed between the management-oriented conservative versus the plaintiff lawyer on the liberal side. Clements was aiming at a coalition of Republicans and conservative Democrats. He was aiming at Briscoe Democrats spread all over rural Texas, far from the gleaming vote-rich cities of Houston and Dallas. None of this would be effective overnight. It required diligent pursuit by all cylinders of his campaign to bring Clements gradually into focus to the crucial urban ticket-splitters who were starting to tune into the race by September.

In late August, Tower saw the serious nature of polling manipulation being practiced by Krueger, or more accurately, Mauro, his campaign manager. A statewide poll with only 600 interviews had been taken for Krueger with Pat Caddell, the noted Democratic pollster, signing off on the methodology and conclusions that showed the race about even. Tower commissioned a 1,000-survey statewide poll that Lance Tarrance had insisted was needed to insure accuracy. Tarrance enjoyed playing hardball and welcomed an opportunity to present his results and chide the Caddell poll, which he did at a news conference in the state capitol on August 31. He was introduced by Tower, spotlighting the importance his campaign placed on the propaganda revolving around the release of polling data. Tarrance reported his survey showed Tower leading by thirteen points, fifty to thirty-seven, with the balance spread between un-decided and the La Raza Unida candidate. The credibility of Tarrance was placed against Caddell, and Tarrance made sure the reporters attending understood his methodology compared with that of Krueger's poll-ster. "The Krueger people," Tarrance charged, "are using research data farther than it should be used," implying the use was for propaganda purposes. Stung perhaps, but not undaunted, Mauro sent out a mailing contending the race was a "dead heat," according to *The Houston Post* when, in point of fact stated by Towery, *The Houston Post* had not run any such poll. The newspaper had simply reported what Krueger claimed from Krueger's poll. Mauro apparently received some adverse feedback regarding that small sample size since the next statewide poll he announced would be taken with 1,200 interviews, twice the number in the poll denounced by Tarrance. Increasingly, the race had evolved into a contest between Mauro and Towery. Mauro would initiate some charge or maneu-ver, and Towery would respond rapidly, trying to blunt the effectiveness of devious tactics that often could only be viewed as deliberate decep-tion. But some people in the news media had begun taking a closer look for such tactics. Jim Craig of *The Houston Post* Washington bureau pointed out that in an interview published in *The Dallas Times Herald*, Mrs. Tower was quoted as saying she was "exclusive in whom I see socially." Recent Krueger literature, Craig continued, included a passage that implied Tower, not his wife, said he was "exclusive in whom I see." The campaign liter-ature dropped the word "socially" and did not attribute it to Mrs. Tower. The material Craig referred to was indeed deceptive with a headline, "Do You Have a Key to John Tower's Exclusive Club?" then the altered quote plus numerous charges aimed at portraying Tower as a snob in politics allegedly consistent with his social life. Nowhere was there any indica-tion other than that the quote was attributed to the senator. Pursuing his drumfire of slashing personal attacks, Mauro sent a letter to *The Dal-las Morning News*, published in mid-September, in which he complained about coverage given to Tower for having served as honorary chairman of a telethon for the United Negro College Fund. Tower, Mauro charged, is "a man who has stood against everything that black Americans stand for." To which H. Rhett James, chairman of the fund and longtime black leader in Dallas, responded in part,

> ... It is tragic that the Krueger campaign has attempted to politicize our UNCF telethon by unworthy criticism. Senator Tower has consis-tently supported and helped black colleges throughout Texas and was selected to serve in the honorary post based on his longstanding com-mitment to meeting the needs of these institutions.

What really incensed Ken Towery was reading Krueger campaign material poking fun at Tower for not having achieved greater than enlisted status in the Navy. Nothing rankles a combat veteran worse than one who has never shouldered a rifle taking advantage of American liberty and prosperity without holding due respect for those who have put their lives on the line. Ken Towery wrote a blistering speech which he delivered in San Antonio, reported in the *San Antonio Express* of September 28, by Jim McCrory. "The fact that U.S. Rep. Bob Krueger didn't serve in the military or a civilian service group has come under attack" from Towery, indicating weapons in the U.S. Senate race were "going from pea shooters to howitzers." After reviewing Towery's contempt for Krueger's material about Tower's enlisted status, McCrory quoted Towery: "He had to spend his time hiding out in academe, studying poetry, while his peers were being called to the colors by the thousands ... Perhaps he can explain to the people why he was never called up, or better yet, why he never volunteered for his country ... And if some physical impairment kept him from the service he could have at least joined the USO and gone abroad and entertained the troops with poetry readings." On October 4, McCrory had a follow-up story with Krueger contending asthma prevented him from serving in the military. On that same date a new Krueger poll, with 1,200 respondents, was reported. This showed the race to be a dead heat, but with approximately half of those respondents identified as "most likely" to vote, breaking out as forty-seven to forty-one percent in favor of Krueger, the balance undecided and Raza Unida.

On television, positive commercials for Krueger portrayed him as an effective and intelligent Congressman who was a warm and sensitive individual, trying to create an image contrast to Tower whom Krueger's campaign was painting as an ineffective senator who was aloof and exclusive as an individual. Roy Spence's image spots promoting Krueger were excellent, providing a definite advantage over Tower's first positive spots which were weighty and uninspiring. These spots had been filmed in a replica of the original Senate chamber with Tower giving monologues. But Bob Goodman came up with an effective "zinger" as he termed short negative TV spots, when he produced a commercial attacking Krueger's recent congressional attendance which had dropped below twenty-five percent while he was out campaigning. Goodman's spot contained a series of people-on-the-street interviews, one of which had the announcer inquire, "How would you like to show up for work twenty-five percent of the time and still get paid $57,500 per year ... One hundred percent of the time?" In mid-September Sam Kinch, Jr., wrote an article in *The*

Dallas Morning News about the spot which he contended "finally had drawn blood from the camp of Democratic challenger Bob Krueger."

Unfortunately for Tower, Spence produced a devastating negative TV spot based upon the specious argument that Ed Clark had warned about when the campaign began — Tower hadn't authored major legislation. Simulating Tower signing a piece of paper with a tight camera shot on a hand only, the voice intoned, "After seventeen long years, there still is not one piece of major legislation called the John Tower bill." Tower's campaign theme, "He Stands For Texas," had been reproduced widely on materials with a bold Tower signature underneath or alongside. The spot hit at the heart of those graphics as though Tower had been signing off on a long record of ineffectiveness. That spot hurt Tower's campaign more than any other single thrust. To blunt it properly, a well-reasoned explanation would have been required about partisan organization of the Senate in which Tower had served all of his seventeen years in the minority party. The majority party always controlled the legislative process, but all of that amounted to a cumbersome, impossible rebuttal to a tight, thirty-second spot which would be shown widely and absorbed by those thousands of voters who knew little about the legislative process in the Senate.

Krueger had the initial advantage on television which was certainly important, but his tightrope act to hold conservative voters was becoming almost impossible. Tower hit hard, opposing the Constitutional amendment to give the District of Columbia full congressional representation, including two United States Senators. For a conservative representing a large state, the idea of giving Washington, D.C., two senators — liberals elected from the federal enclave who would cancel out Texas's senators on most votes — was nothing short of absurd. Yet Krueger had voted for it and slammed Tower, trying to paint him as anti-black. Some heavy headlines resulted, including an eight-column banner in the *San Antonio Express* of September 1, under which Jim McCrory detailed the clash between Tower and Krueger with Tower branding Krueger's attempt to make a racial issue as "blatant demagoguery." Tower pointed out that D.C. is "a one-industry town, and that industry is the federal government. What we are talking about here is giving the federal bureaucracy itself voting representation."

Krueger had stepped into a trap. Unlike the AFL — CIO issue about which he waffled in a hurry, Krueger stood by his vote and it was clearly against the majority view in Texas. It was further embarrassing to him on September 14 when Ron Calhoun of *The Dallas Times Herald* reported that John Hill, certainly not perceived as a hard-nosed conservative, came out against D.C. representation with the statement, "It was never my concept that the district be given two senators. That conjures up in my mind statehood." Calhoun pointed out that Hill's position matched that of Tower, at odds with Krueger. The issue had another positive effect for Tower — unifying the party behind him. State Chairman Ray Barnhart issued a strong statement blasting Krueger's support as "a sellout to the liberal wing of the Democrat Party ..." He called on "all Republican candidates to bring this issue before the voters and to join Senator Tower in continuing the fight ..." Republican Senator Walter Mengden of Houston, known to ramble at times in debates, came down hard and fast on the issue, "Washington, D.C. is not a state, it is a city. If it needs representation in the U.S. Senate, then the people should be allowed to vote for U.S. senators from Virginia, but not have two all of their own ... U.S. Senator John Tower should be congratulated for his vote against this measure ... " The weakness of Krueger's position was proven seven years later when the deadline for ratification passed with only sixteen of the fifty states voting for the D.C. proposal, far short of the thirty-eight needed. Texas was not among those sixteen, nor was California or New York.

While Tower was under heavy siege from Krueger's campaign, the State GOP leadership supported him steadfastly, but there were still rumblings from the grass roots indicating a residue of anti-Tower animosity remained from the Ford — Reagan fight of 1976. For the Tower Campaign, it was a subjective factor about which to be concerned, but there wasn't much to do about it other than stay the course and hope for a few breaks along the way.

Tower enjoyed another positive step when former Congressman Clark Fisher, a conservative Democrat whom Krueger succeeded with Fisher's support in the 1974 general election, endorsed Tower on October 2, based upon what he termed was the single most important yardstick, a careful comparison of the voting records.

By that time, Clements's campaign was in high gear with the candidate and his attractive wife, Rita, out front leading a large organization. Lance Tarrance was providing guidance with polling information indicating Clements was indeed closing the gap. Phone bank whiz Nancy Brataas of Minnesota had been retained to oversee the massive program of contacting potential voters and preparing to recontact them prior to the election. Except in Dallas, few people reporting for metropolitan newspapers had given Clements much coverage or credibility. Joe Nolan, political editor of *The Houston Chronicle*, was among the first when his column of September 25 appeared with the lead paragraph, "It's time someone admitted that Bill Clements really does have a chance of pulling it off and becoming the first Republican governor of Texas since Reconstruction."

Nolan reviewed the primary victories by Clements and Hill, then pointed to one of the key elements involved, Clements had been campaigning steadily for almost a year, building momentum while Hill's campaign had eased off after defeating the incumbent governor. "It's almost as if Hill's people think the only unfinished piece of campaign business is the swearing-in ceremony." Projecting the spending process out, Nolan surmised Clements would spend at least $2 million more than Hill. Fred Bonavita of *The Houston Post* state capitol bureau reported in late September that Clements was working from a new Lance Tarrance poll showing he had thirty-one percent to Hill's thirty-three, balance undecided. Rogers, Hill's manager, said their latest poll showed a twenty-one point lead for Hill. Bonavita also reported Hill had accepted a joint appearance with Clements and would probably work out more, a sure sign that Hill was finally feeling the pressure. Soon after that article appeared, Dave Montgomery of *The Dallas Times Herald* reported that Briscoe's wife, Janey, would follow her husband's lead and vote Democratic but that she believed Clements "would make a better governor than Hill." That story sent shock waves through the Hill camp — now the so-called Briscoe factor was on the table. That development prompted Bo Byers, the veteran chief of *The Houston Chronicle* Austin bureau, to analyze the contest closely in a column that appeared October 10, in which he reviewed the historical perspectives leading into the race in progress. He concluded that the well-financed pitch of Clements to conservatives against a moderate-loyalist Democrat might indeed carry the day.

So much of the Tower — Krueger race had been slugging in the center of the political arena, a battle of hardball news releases in the Capitol Press Room, while so much of the Clements — Hill contest had been much more subdued. But the net result of vastly increased news coverage of Clements in late September and early October meant the governor's race was competitive going into the stretch run. Clements had climbed into the center of the arena.

In the Senate race, Tower had already sustained a long hard volley of attacks relating to his legislative record and his personal life. But the worst was yet to come. To Texas newspaper editors the Krueger campaign circulated a column written by Tom Anderson, a controversial politician in Tennessee, in which an unnamed U.S. Senator was castigated for drinking and womanizing. On top of the reported column was a note stating, "Dear editor: Thought you might be interested in this unusually candid description of Bob Krueger's opponent in the U.S. Senate race, John Tower." The mailing contained the standard Krueger disclaimer and Krueger confirmed later that Mauro made the decision to distribute it. Texas reporters pursued the matter, finding that the columnist wouldn't name whom he had in mind and there was no credible evidence whatsoever indicating Tower was the target of the column. Tower was terribly upset by the publicity surrounding the episode. On October 16, he cancelled four joint television appearances with Krueger, agreeing to fulfill only an impending appearance before the Houston Press Club. In a sharply-worded statement, Ken Towery stated that Tower "decided that Krueger's campaign has taken on such a personal attack and mudslinging basis that he will not give Krueger opportunities to vilify him on television ... We are seriously considering a libel suit against the Krueger Campaign for distributing this column to newspapers across the state ... It's gutter politics, and we're not going to help Krueger spread this sort of thing."

It may have been gutter politics but it was effective. It reinforced doubts about the senator who had been around so long and couldn't even pass a bill with his name on it as the author. The Senator who was exclusive, insensitive to the needs of the poor and the minorities, a senator who needed to be replaced by the intelligent, dynamic, warm, sensitive young congressman named Krueger.

On October 17, at the Press Club luncheon in Houston's Whitehall Hotel, Krueger ambled up to a seated Tower and offered to shake his hand. Tower turned away, refusing, both instances caught in perfect sequence by *Houston Post* photographer King Chou Wong. The pictures were relayed by wire across the state and nation, receiving widespread coverage. Jane Ely of *The Post* was on hand, reporting that Tower considered Krueger to be employing "a contemptible means of campaigning"which is "a sign of desperation, if you can't win by fair means, then try to by foul." In Houston and those places where some explanation was given of Tower's refusal, the feedback was not unfavorable to Tower, but in many media markets where the pictures were run without Tower's views, or details of the recent Krueger mailing, the feedback was decidedly anti-Tower. He was perceived as the snob, the poor sport who was unable to hold his own with the young challenger. Many unfavorable phone calls were fielded at Tower's state headquarters, including those from his supporters who were distressed and upset that he had committed such a social and political blunder.

Morale at Tower's state headquarters and among his supporters had been shaken by the series of personal attacks by Krueger and Mauro. It fell drastically due to the sudden turn of events that cast Tower in such an unfavorable light. Ken Towery was reflective, yet resolute about the incident — it had to be turned around. He drafted a statement for Tower that was released on October 20, and he laid it on the line:

> For months, my opponent has continued a campaign of unabated distortion and deception. I think he has engaged in scurrilous campaign activities which Texans do not admire. He is a man who has no loyalties and no convictions. As many others have observed, including newspaper writers, he seems to be a man who is fired only by personal ambition, and will do or say anything to try to achieve that ambition ... I was brought up to believe that a handshake was, and is, a symbol of friendship and respect. I was not brought up to believe that a handshake is a meaningless and hypocritical act done for public display ... I think under the circumstances that I should not have dignified him by shaking his hand after what he has been engaged in ...

On the following day, the lead headline on the front page of *The Austin American-Statesman* was POLL HAS KRUEGER LEADING TOWER, spotlighting a new *Texas Monthly* and *American-Statesman* statewide poll of 1,000 registered voters that gave Krueger the lead by almost four percentage points. Krueger had indeed established considerable momentum, reflected in the new polling data reported publicly and from that data reported privately to Tower from Tarrance's tracking polling data. He had also gone too far with the irresponsible personal attacks. Cactus Pryor, the noted humorist, wrote an item that appeared in *The Austin American-Statesman* in October "I think the voters are familiar with your knowledge of Shakespeare, Congressman Krueger ... but don't you think it's a bit much to use the paraphrase, 'I come to bury Tower, not to praise him?'"Ben Sergeant, the Pulitzer prizewinning cartoonist of *The American-Statesman*, known for his liberal bent, drew a damaging cartoon of Krueger being caught by Tower writing on a men's room wall, *John Tower wants only women and whiske*, the *y* incompletely drawn because Krueger has spotted Tower walking in. *The American-Statesman* hit another lick with an editorial on October 18, denouncing Krueger for distributing the controversial column, which it branded a "sleazy thing ... Krueger would be well advised to get back to the issues." Further, the political editor, Jon Ford, termed the column distribution "an irresponsible act . . ." William Murchison, writing in *The Dallas Morning News*, lamented that, "For all the bad taste involved in Krueger's questioning of Tower's private life, the issues are what matter in the race." In the same newspaper, Carolyn Barta wrote a column that appeared on October 26, one of many emanating from the handshake refusal, "Believe it or not, the elusive handshake incident has turned into the most notable event of the contest

... While Krueger is milking the incident for all it's worth, reaction to the Houston handshake episode is cutting both ways."

While the Tower Campaign was trying to contend with fallout from the handshake refusal, another hard personal shot was fired at the senator. On October 23, a "news item"was run on Channel 11 in Houston, reporting that "Congressman Krueger accused Senator John Tower of being, quote, a drunk ... The Democratic senatorial nominee said Tower had been seen drinking seven mixed drinks in the space of an hour and half in a Capitol Hill bar." No credible evidence was presented nor witnesses named to substantiate Krueger's charge. The item even stated that "We have found no evidence so far, however, that drinking has affected Tower's performance in the Senate." Those who knew Tower well could attest to the fact that he hadn't been drinking any hard liquor in more than a year, but answering such an irresponsible charge would only attract more attention to it, causing the matter to inure further to Krueger's benefit. Towery protested in a no-win situation, wondering how such a flimsy piece of broadcast journalism had been instigated on a major television station. To their credit other news media outlets let the story alone.

On October 27, Norman Baxter reported in *The Houston Chronicle* that Krueger had changed his mind about the column distribution, now saying it was a mistake made by his staff and "my own choice would have been not to release it." He also said he was "wrong in saying Tower had voted for a congressional pay raise so he could afford to pay for clothes purchased by his daughters at Neiman-Marcus." At this point the polling data coming in to both camps and elsewhere indicated a Krueger trend, prompting him to become courteous and pious toward Tower, believing the damage had been done and it was time to ease toward victory without playing high-risk politics. Jim Loyd, a sharp young analyst for Tarrance, was in charge of "tracking"polling, which was nightly monitoring of the contest by phone around the state. Loyd would call from Houston to Tower's top campaign operatives in Austin each night to report immediately the results, which, during October, were uncertain, often discouraging for Tower. But having current data upon which to make decisions was invaluable, leading the Tower Campaign to face the harsh reality that the fairly comfortable lead it once enjoyed was gone. In his final written communication to the Tower Campaign, Tarrance laid out, in a terse confidential memo, the gravity of the situation as of October 25. Tower's support had grown soft, instead of solidified as desired. Too many voters were beginning to see the race as partisan, which was a boost for Krueger, the Democrat. Some of that softness was in areas where Tower had to run strong, such as West Texas and Dallas — Fort Worth. "If that trend persists, we cannot make up the vote deficits caused by South, Central, and East-rural Texas. Houston is the next big battleground. If Krueger can cut up Tower in the vote-rich 'Southwest Houston' area (after already minimizing his losses in DFW and advantageously using his San Antonio Twenty-first District base), Tower will not be able to win statewide ... The election today hangs in a balance between defeat and victory ..." On November 2, Roland Lindsey, veteran UPI state capitol bureau chief, led off his political roundup with the observation that Tower "appears in jeopardy of losing Nov. 7, and his refusal to shake hands with his challenger may be a key to the outcome." On the following day, UPI reported that Krueger's Texas polling firm, Henson, Hopkins and Shipley, projected Krueger to win with 52.5 percent of the vote. At the Tower headquarters, there was indeed apprehension in the closing days. Charlene Darr, a veteran Republican political operative, came by a few days before the election, after participating in phone banks for Clements and Tower. Fighting back tears, she reported that she believed, "We're going to finally elect a governor, but we're going to lose our senator."

In the political arena, perception is reality. Tower had one last round to fire, an emotional shot aimed at the very bedrock of the Texan mentality, a gut appeal to righteous indignation. Krueger's devious personal attacks could be portrayed as a sneak Pearl Harbor type assault on Tower and his family whom he felt compelled to defend from a sense of honor. If that potent message could be conveyed to Texas voters convincingly, the Krueger trend might yet be reversed in the final days, perhaps hours, of the long turbulent battle. To answer all of Krueger's charges was out of the question. It came down to centering on the handshake refusal as the focal point for the final Tower TV commercial, a thirty second spot composed of ideas and wording condensed from the statement released October 20. On October 27, in San Antonio, at a studio-production facility on the Hemisfair grounds, Tower, his wife, a few aides and two executives from the Yardang ad agency, Bev Coiner and Lionel Sosa, gathered for the final, perhaps pivotal, major thrust of the Tower Campaign. In addition to the thirty second handshake spot, a five minute monologue would be produced, with Tower giving a summation of his record, position on issues in the campaign, and a look toward the future. No one questioned his ability to deliver that script in a logical, measured manner, but the handshake refusal spot required stage presence, perfect physical execution plus particularly convincing eye contact with the viewers. It was early morning, and Tower had been up until five that morning, going over the scripts and other matters relating to the campaign. He must have practiced the short script time and again riding from the La Mansion del Norte Hotel on Loop 410, to the production facility near the Alamo. The Alamo was a symbolic location for the beleaguered Tower to make a stand. The senator's performance was vintage Tower, most effective on television with few props or distractions, hitting the issue head-on. The script called for the opening shot of Tower leaning in front of a desk, holding *The Houston Post* edition with the large pictures of Krueger offering to shake hands and his refusal, clearly visible. "Perhaps you've seen this picture of my refusal to shake my opponent's hand," Tower said, with a note of disdain in his voice as he tossed the newspaper aside and the camera moved in tight on him. Then, in a strong, direct voice,

> I was brought up to believe that a handshake is a symbol of friendship or respect. Not a meaningless, hypocritical gesture. My opponent has slurred my wife, my daughters, and falsified my record. My kind of Texan doesn't shake the hand of that kind of man. Integrity is one Texas tradition you can count on me to uphold.

Coiner, the writer with a gifted touch for scripting, had fine-tuned the wording and Sosa had provided solid direction. When the commercials were completed, one of Tower's aides commented, "This will turn it around, or it's his last hurrah." When Tower walked from the studio that day, confident he had performed to his utmost, one of the aides waved, "Once more unto the breach." No one suggested additional last-minute ideas. They were pleased with his performance, hopeful it would rekindle sparks in a campaign that needed a shot of something akin to adrenalin. How well the spot would be received in the turmoil of the final days and nights was the central question for Tower's campaign. The senator maintained a rapid pace in the countdown as did Krueger, whose conservative credentials, like his attendance record in Congress, were ignored or distorted, depending upon the audience or location, in the final quest for votes. Radio spots by Ted Kennedy were beamed around South Texas, while Krueger campaigned elsewhere with Ralph Yarborough and Harry Hubbard, president of the Texas AFL — CIO. According to *The Corpus Christi Caller-Times* of October 26, Krueger said all doctors should be required to serve two years in an area designated by the federal government. That — from the conservative champion of individual rights, including the right-to-work. The chameleon was performing for various audiences with a more conservative pitch in conservative areas of the state. He had been challenged from time to time by the aggressive Tower youth leaders, Kevin Burnette and Kevin Moomaw, who enjoyed playing hardball with Mauro every step of the way. They constantly produced hard-hitting flyers and reprints to point up Krueger's flip-flop on issues or liberal stands taken only in liberal areas. Tower's organization throughout Texas, including the Mexican-American program, was working hard, right down to the wire. A late campaign bus tour in the Lower Rio Grande Valley was considered to be successful. Tower campaigned vigorously through numerous appearances in clusters of towns, clad in slacks and a Mexican shirt, conveying a far different image from that insensitive old aloof Tower at whom Krueger and Mauro had been flailing away. For the third consecutive campaign, Tower was keying on potential areas of positive response in the M-A community of Texas, the Lower Valley, and San Antonio, El Paso, and Corpus Christi. Tower knew his opponent would carry the vast areas of South and Southwest Texas, but Krueger would have to combine with Hill and work all-out to maximize voter turnout in those areas in a non-presidential year. Tower had conceded that ground, denying Krueger the benefit of increased turnout from a visibly hot contest. In Houston, and the Dallas — Fort Worth area, Tower believed he would receive substantial support from M-As amalgamated into the socioeconomic life of those high growth regions.

In the gubernatorial race, Clements had closed the gap by late October. He capitalized literally on his assets, using heavy financing to fuel an effective media program along with the tremendous campaign apparatus, keyed to phone banks. On November 4, three days prior to the election, Roland Lindsey filed a report for UPI in which he stated,

> Republicans show an unprecedented optimism that Dallas millionaire Bill Clements can upset Attorney General John Hill and become the state's first GOP governor this century, but are concerned about the chances for survival of their only current statewide officeholder, Sen. John G. Tower, R-Texas. Hill appeared an easy winner in the governor's race after his upset of Gov. Dolph Briscoe in the Democratic Primary, but Clements, aided by a $6.4 million campaign that shattered all previous spending records in Texas political races, has closed the gap.

For the time and the place, Clements had conducted an almost flawless campaign. The development of themes and issues had been well-conceived and skillfully executed, through personal appearances bolstered by television and various forms of advertising. The latter included a strong tabloid, *The Texas Spectator*, with a 500,000 press run. The tabloid plugged Clements while branding Hill as a liberal tied to Jimmy Carter, whose administration was unpopular in Texas. Clements fared well in late-campaign debates with Hill, forums that made it clear the race was competitive. From after the primary until the election, Clements's campaign stressed the involvement of conservative Democrats, the key element to his projected victory. As the gubernatorial and United States Senate campaigns wound down, Texans had been blessed — or cursed depending upon one's views — with unique, spirited statewide contests that would impact markedly on the future.

On election day, November 7, a last look at polling estimates appeared in an article written by Felton West, chief of *The Houston Post* Austin bureau. Henson, Hopkins, and Shipley, polling for the top three Democratic candidates, predicted Hill would win with 53.5 percent or more, Krueger with 52.5 percent or better and Mark White would defeat Jim Baker with fifty-six percent or more. Lance Tarrance, polling for Tower and Clements, was cautious, reporting only that his tracking polls showed both races to be extremely close. Dr. Richard Murray of the University of Houston, a noted academic pollster, reported he found in a six-day survey ending October 30, that Hill was leading Clements by eleven percent, but Krueger and Tower were in a dead heat. "The Senate race is pretty volatile," he said. "I would guess Tower has a slight advantage." The least scientific poll, that taken by Democratic State Senator Glenn Kothmann of San Antonio, stirred interest. Although Kothmann only polled in what he considered to be bellwether precincts in Bexar County, he had managed to produce accurate reflections that applied statewide. He had predicted the upsets by Hill and White in the Democratic Primary, West pointed out, and Kothmann raised eyebrows in the fall by announcing that he found Tower and Clements to be leading.

Krueger's campaign people had become confident in the final days, exemplified by one of their top operatives who, after reviewing their late polling data, contacted the Tower headquarters with an offer of a sizeable wager. The bet was covered by three of Tower's campaigners who viewed the race as a toss-up.

On the afternoon of November 7, some of Tower's campaign staff gathered for the last time at Don Politico's, a tavern on East Sixth Street near Congress Avenue, a few blocks from the senator's headquarters. During the long hot days of the summer and early fall, the attacks and counterattacks of the campaign had been discussed over cold beer in front of walls covered by political posters and paraphernalia. Patrick Conway, former UPI state capitol bureau chief, and his friend, Jim Walls, owned the tavern that had a bipartisan appeal. With all the tension building before the time for returns to be reported, a badly needed note of levity was sounded by one of Tower's staffers who remarked with a wry smile, "Well, I don't know whether I feel like I've been through a U.S. Senate race or a sheriff's race in a rural county."

When the long wait finally ended, first returns weren't indicative of a trend, but when the initial results from Dallas County were posted in Tower's headquarters, trained eyes were indeed concerned. Clements was running strong in Dallas, but that old Tower stronghold was not producing nearly as well for him. Jack Warren, the former Republican state chairman, noted quietly that if such a trend were true in Harris County (Houston), Tower probably wouldn't win. Some Harris County results were soon posted, showing the opposite of Dallas with Tower running ahead of Clements, but both doing well. As the night wore on, Mark White would be declared the winner over Jim Baker, but the races for governor and United States Senator were too close to call, prompting anxious Tower staffers to seek any favorable bits and pieces from areas which were reporting slowly. When the Texas Election Bureau closed down after midnight, weary Tower campaign people retired for a few hours of restless sleep in a highly charged atmosphere of anxiety.

When they returned to the headquarters early the next day, they found that the issue was still in doubt. About midmorning, the wire services finally declared a GOP jackpot with victories for Clements and Tower. Texas Republicans had elected their first governor during the twentieth century, and had withstood the most serious challenge to their longtime U.S. Senator since his election seventeen years previously.

Most of the Austin campaign staffers for Clements and Tower were almost too tired to celebrate. But they, along with hundreds of Republicans and other well-wishers, jammed the capitol to welcome their champions later that day. "My election marks a new day for Texas," Clements declared. "We literally have turned a page in history, and the political scene in Texas will never be the same." Indeed, it was a historic moment to see the GOP finally claim the governorship after so many years of bitter frustration. For Tower, it meant another six-year term in which to accrue valuable seniority and experience to benefit his state and party. Perhaps it would be a term in which he might achieve chairmanship of a major committee in his beloved Senate. Sifting through the results, Clements won by a margin of 16,860 out of a total vote cast of 2,369,764. Tower won by a margin of 12,227 out of a total vote cast of 2,312,540, there having been 57,224 less votes cast in the Senate race.

Thanks to the handshake incident having occurred in Houston, and a superb organizational effort led by Molly Rockwood, Tower achieved more than fifty-five percent of the vote in Harris County. Tower also received higher percentages than Clements in several other urban counties, including Bexar, El Paso, Travis, Hidalgo, Nueces, Jefferson, Lubbock, and Cameron. In the aggregate of the top twenty-five most populous counties, Tower had a lead of 71,000 votes over Krueger. Clements, in that grouping, had a 66,000-vote lead over Hill. Those were interesting figures to consider since Mauro contended that Clements's phone banks, which were concentrated in the densely-populated areas of Texas, were what put Tower across the line. The truth was that Tower ran well in urban Texas on his own, but did not campaign as extensively as he had in the past in rural Texas. There was no "cow county" plan for 1977, as there had been for 1971, and it showed up markedly in the results. On the other hand, Clements's heavy personal campaigning in rural Texas during the summer of 1978, combined with the tacit support of Briscoe, paid off. Clements ran better than Tower throughout most of rural Texas. The two campaigns appeared to have complemented one another. The phone banks of the Clements Campaign energized the urban conservatives and Tower's old ties to the Mexican-American community prevented that door from being closed to Clements as solidly Democratic. In a post-election analysis by Art Wiese in the November 9 edition of *The Houston Post*, Ken Towery pointed to the Krueger Campaign's personal attacks on Tower as a "monumental mistake," probably pivotal to the outcome. For the final edge in Tower's race, Tarrance singled out television. Soon after the election he was quoted in *The Dallas Times Herald*, "It was TV that did it, all right. Whether it's luck or not, the Tower people finally got their act together. If I could use a basketball analogy, it was like they never played up to par all through the game, but in the last minute, they hit four straight baskets, and won by two points. They got hot." Tarrance's last preelection communication to the Tower Campaign had expressed concern about Krueger's gaining in urban areas and his apparent strength in his Twenty-first congressional district. Tower held his own in urban Texas and smashed Krueger by 20,000 votes in his own district in which Tower carried Krueger's home county of Comal. Tower's campaign had fired a barrage of strong anti-Krueger ads against his votes for the AFL — CIO proposals and for giving two United States senators to D.C. Krueger's conservative facade had finally been shattered in his home base.

    The victory for Clements prompted some strong conclusions from the news media in Texas. In the November 9 *Houston Post*, Jane Ely wrote that "a stunning page of Texas history was turned Wednesday." Carolyn Barta, on the same date in *The Dallas Morning News*, wrote that "the Clements phenomenon is not a feat to take lightly. It brings about a brave new world in Texas politics — the opportunity almost overnight for a real two-party state." A *Fort Worth Star-Telegram* editorial on that date pointed out "Texas voters — mainly Democrats — call his win stunning, shocking, unbelievable ... A new day for Texas? You better believe it. Republicans now have a grip on that two-party Texas they've been after ... Texans have decided to follow a different drummer. It will take some time, some steps to begin to get a clearer view of exactly where it's going to lead."

On the lighter side, the inevitable jokes sprang up about Clements's campaign financing. These included one circulated in Austin to the effect that, "Well, he bought it fair and square." But Texas Republicans didn't mind a gig here and there in the warm afterglow of such an achievement.

A long era of frustration ended for Republicans in the Twenty-first congressional district which Krueger had vacated. The district had a longstanding conservative voting history including for Tower and GOP presidential candidates, but it had eluded the local Republicans until 1978. Tom Loeffler, the former aide to Tower and Ford, won the race by a decisive margin over Nelson Wolff, whom Krueger had defeated four years previously. The GOP regained a Gulf Coast congressional seat when Ron Paul edged out Bob Gammage. Gammage had previously taken the Twenty-second district seat from Paul.

In the Legislature, the GOP Texas House total rose to twenty-two, with a net gain of three seats. Ed Emmett of Kingwood, Fort Worth attorneys Bob Leonard and Bob Ware, plus Tom DeLay of Wallis, in the Gulf Coast area, were newcomers, while incumbent S.L. Abbott of El Paso was defeated by a narrow margin. Nolan (Buzz) Robnett retained the Lubbock seat that Joe Robbins had vacated in order to run for the state senate seat being vacated by Kent Hance. Robbins was defeated by Democratic Representative E.L. Short of Tahoka. Gerald Geistweidt of Mason, a cousin of Loeffler's, won a special election for a Hill County seat while the Legislature was in session, bringing the House total to twenty-three. In the Texas Senate the GOP strength remained at four with incumbent Betty Andujar fighting off a strong challenge from Democratic Representative Roy English of Fort Worth.

So much energy and resources had been expended on the statewide races that the legislative and local candidates didn't receive the support that might have made the difference in some races. But each election cycle is unique. The 1977 — 1978 period had been the most demanding, yet most productive in the history of Texas Republicans.

CHAPTER THIRTEEN

Reagan – Bush Potent Team in Texas

Bill Clements's victory, and the awesome manner in which it was achieved, had a profound impact in the Texas political arena. It had proved, finally, that a Republican could capture the fulcrum of power in state government. There was a further air of anticipation surrounding the new governor's inauguration because he was perceived as an activist, far from the mold of his predecessors, Dolph Briscoe and Preston Smith. He would be a strong administrator and manager of the government. He would also vigorously pursue leadership of his political party.

Between his election victory and the swearing-in ceremony, political observers pored over his every word, searching through the post-campaign rhetoric for clues as to what might lie ahead. There weren't any surprises to be found, but there was a key expressed in his comment regarding leadership.

> What can you expect from me? You can expect leadership, because in my opinion, leadership is perhaps the most important power of the governor.

Consistent with his campaign, Clements made it clear that he would be a fiscal conservative, seeking reductions in taxes and government bureaucracy in Texas, while playing the role of advocate for the state in Washington on such key issues as energy and defense. He would place priorities on improving education and strengthening law enforcement. He would become the leader of the Republican Party of Texas, but not

232

lead the party in a narrow path postured in a partisan basis against the Democrats — the door was open to conservative Democrats and independents.

> ... For us to achieve a two-party system in Texas, for us to continue building our party, we must demonstrate to all Texans that their interests and that their causes are our causes ...

On Inaugural Day, Rita Clements was quoted, answering a question as to two-party status in light of the historic victory by her husband: "I've always felt that we cannot become a genuine two-party state until we do have a [Republican] governor because there are a lot of benefits accrued on having one. I think we are definitely moving in the right direction, but I think we have to look realistically at the figures as far as the number of Republican legislators we have as well as the number of local officials. It would not be right to say that we are there but we're certainly making progress."

An attractive, comprehensive, twelve-page edition of *The Texas Advocate* newspaper, edited by Media Director Gary Hoitsma, and including a full-page color picture of Bill and Rita Clements, was published by the State GOP for the occasion. Inauguration ceremonies were impressive, billed under an umbrella group named "Texas Inaugural Committee" with honorary chairmen, George Bush, John Connally, and John Tower; with cochairmen including Bum Bright of Dallas, and Beryl Milburn of Austin. Of the twenty-eight committee members, only one, Dick Morgan of Dallas, was a former GOP state legislator. He had been elected sixteen years previously on the ticket with Jack Cox, Connally's GOP opponent in the 1962 gubernatorial contest. Morgan was all smiles that day as he milled with the huge crowd on the south mall of the capitol grounds during the formal swearing-in ceremony, complete with cannon salutes, and followed by a big barbecue. Republicans had literally taken over the Capitol, munching barbecue in the halls while exchanging stories of times past, leading to the celebration they so deeply enjoyed that day. Following an inaugural parade, nighttime festivities featured the Texas Inaugural Gala with balls at the Frank Erwin Center and two hotels downtown, the Driskill and Sheraton Crest, plus other balls at the Municipal Auditorium and the City Coliseum. Governor and Mrs. Clements made the rounds that night, appearing at all the festivities, mingling with thousands of proud Texans who danced and celebrated well into the night.

Clements brought forth a strong staff operation that included Allen Clark, vice-president of a bank in Dallas and former Green Beret officer in Vietnam. Clark would serve as special assistant for administration with duties including day to day management of the governor's office. Tobin Armstrong, prominent South Texas rancher and husband of Anne Armstrong, would serve as special assistant for appointments and personnel, in charge of the vast patronage system that would recommend people to fill approximately 4,200 gubernatorial appointments to state boards and commissions over the following four years. Linda Underwood would serve as staff director under Armstrong, followed two years later by Pat Oles, Jr. David Dean, who had served as legal counsel to then-Governor Briscoe, would return to that post for Clements. Among the highly visible choices were George Strake, Jr., Clements's campaign leader from Houston, as secretary of state, and as press secretary, Jon Ford, the highly respected political editor of *The Austin American-Statesman*, longtime veteran of the Capitol Press Room with that newspaper and previously with the *San Antonio Express-News*. Sheila Wilkes would apply her campaign experience to the scheduling of the governor, perhaps the most tedious task of them all, with constantly changing variables to contend with under tremendous pressure of time. In dealing with the Legislature, Clements knew he must maintain a bipartisan posture, keyed to conservative Democrats. To direct legislative liaison, he appointed Jim Kaster of El Paso, a former conservative Democrat legislator who would be assisted by two others, Don Cavness of Austin, and Hilary Doran of Del Rio. Ray Hutchison, the former State GOP chairman who had served as a state legislator from Dallas, assisted the Clements Administration early on as a volunteer. Clements would also maintain a strong political arm, "The Governor Clements Committee," located on Brazos Street a few blocks from the capitol. It would be directed by Jim Francis, who had been active in the Clements campaign, assisted by Karl Rove, fresh from the George Bush operation, and Herb Butram. That committee would raise and expend funds in behalf of Clements's political fortunes, separate and aside from the conduct of the governor's office.

For almost eighteen years, Tower had been the titular leader of the Texas GOP. As Clements assumed the mantle, it was interesting for longtime Texas Republicans to note that in both instances, Tower's victory in 1961, and Clements's historic upset of 1978, Peter O'Donnell was close at hand. Clements moved to consolidate his leadership position by appointing State GOP Chairman Ray Barnhart as a member of the Texas Highway and Public Transportation Commission, creating the party post vacancy. Clements let it be known that he favored Chet Upham, an independent oilman from Mineral Wells with long-standing ties to Tower and O'Donnell. Some grumbling ensued among SREC members, but the once faction-ridden Texas GOP wanted its governor to move ahead and Upham was named to succeed Barnhart.

Clements soon found the rough-and-tumble of a hot campaign could be matched or exceeded when an emotionally-charged issue was injected into that gathering of 181 ego-driven politicians known as the Texas Legislature. Add to that consideration an entrenched presiding officer of the Senate, Lieutenant Governor Bill Hobby, who had become accustomed to having his way in an office with more Constitutional power than that of governor. In the spring of 1979, conservative Democrat strategists were looking at a worst case scenario producing nothing short of a migraine headache. The Carter Administration was unpopular in Texas, a condition that probably would intensify, ripening the climate for an enormous, record voter turnout in the Republican Primary in 1980. That prospective turnout would be enhanced if likely contenders George Bush, John Connally, and Ronald Reagan were in the running. Since the 1976 presidential primary had produced almost a half-million turnout with the Ford — Reagan contest, putting two popular Texans in there along with Reagan, whom everyone knew retained a strong organization, caused estimates in the one million range not to be taken lightly. Most of those hundreds of thousands of Texans voting in the Republican Primary for the first time would be "Connallycrats," conservative Democrats whose votes were needed in the Democratic Primary to maintain leverage long established there by leaders of the business-industrial community of Texas.

A one-million vote GOP primary would deny conservative voting strength in the Democratic Primary to such extent that liberal elements might well attain virtual total control. This could polarize in perpetuity liberal control of the Democratic Party to be opposed by a strong Republican Party dominated by conservatives. The stakes were nothing short of a quantum jump toward a true two-party system.

To address their problem, conservative Democrats rallied behind a "split primary" concept in which voters would be allowed to vote in a GOP presidential primary, then still cast votes in the regular Democratic Primary. Such a scheme would also benefit Connally whose large following of conservative Democrats would be much more at ease voting for him in the GOP Primary if they knew they could also protect their interests by voting for their favorites for other offices in the Democratic Primary. ART Chairman Julian Zimmerman branded the scheme as blatantly against the two-party system. "This is modern Texas, virtually a two-party state in which the people who participate should determine their nominees through a process with party discipline, deliberation, and voting ... Permitting voters to participate in nominating a Republican presidential candidate and nominating Democrats for other offices is like cheering for both Texas and Texas A & M when they square off."

Tremendous pressure was being exerted from powerful interests to adopt the measure however, and Hobby appeared to be adamant to ram it through. There were intrigues, variables and nuances involved, but the issue evolved to Hobby versus twelve moderate to liberal senators who became known as the "Killer Bees," a nickname Hobby had applied early on in the session to some of the liberals who would mount impromptu filibusters on other issues. Late in the session, the Killer Bees found themselves convinced Hobby would break a filibuster on the primary bill, so they conjured up a unique and unlikely strategy. They would hide out for a few days — until forty-eight hours prior to the end of the session if necessary — denying Hobby a quorum in his thirty-one member Senate. Within forty-eight hours of the end, the rules were such that the Killer Bees would prevail. The twelve senators vanished. Nine hid out in a West Austin apartment, while the other three maneuvered secretly near their homes or elsewhere, avoiding detection by officers of the Department of Public Safety (DPS) called out by Hobby to search for the "fugitives." The nine who holed up in Austin were Ron Clower of Garland, Lloyd Doggett of Austin, Glenn Kothmann of San Antonio, Oscar Mauzy of Dallas, Carl Parker of Port Arthur, Bill Patman of Ganado, A.R.(Babe) Schwartz of Galveston, Carlos Truan of Corpus Christi, and Bob Vale of San Antonio. Out and about were Chet Brooks of Pasadena, Gene Jones of Houston, and Raul Longoria, who represented the Lower Rio Grande Valley.

Robert Heard, former AP capitol correspondent, wrote an earthy book, *The Miracle of the Killer Bees*, which details the frantic five days during which the drama unfolded, including the types of food consumed in the Austin apartment and the fact that it contained a stifling odor of cigarette smoke while the cramped senators sweated out their daring move. The Killer Bees generated intense news coverage statewide and made considerable national news. But it was difficult for the Texan on the street to sort out the split-primary issue with its subjective potential ramifications amid all the hoopla attached to the aspect of twelve state senators hiding out beyond the reach of their furious presiding officer. Liberal political activists certainly knew the score and they cheered for the Killer Bees. Most Republicans were opposed to the split primary, but they were divided over approving the drastic tactics of the Killer Bees.

Clements didn't advocate a split primary, but he sided with Hobby to the effect that the "truants" were neglecting their duty. Clements and

Hobby spoke of dire measures such as stripping committee assignments, even declaring their seats vacant, requiring special elections. Bluff, bluster, and derision reigned from Clements, Hobby, and the "Worker Bees," the nineteen other senators who were angered by the prospect of some of their pet legislation dying because of Senate business being held in abeyance. But the five-day phantom strike proved to be effective with the Killer Bees causing Hobby to allow them to return unscathed with the split primary dead for the session.

In September following that session, Anita Hill, a Democratic state representative from Garland, decided to cast her lot with the GOP, and Clay Smothers, a black state legislator from Dallas, made the same decision a month later.

Later in 1979, the conservative Democrats' migraine appeared to be developing on schedule as Connally prepared for his presidential campaign with such building blocks as retaining Lance Tarrance, who had done some polling for Reagan in 1976. Connally assembled a formidable organization for the Texas effort, including such experienced political associates as Wales Madden of Amarillo, a prominent conservative Democrat with statewide connections and Jim Campbell, veteran Republican leader in the Panhandle who had previously supported Reagan. Political consultant-lobbyist George Christian, who had served Connally and LBJ as press secretary, and longtime Connally political associate Larry Temple, both of Austin, were set to participate along with Ken Towery of Austin, the political consultant who had managed campaigns in Texas for Nixon and Tower. Towery brought with him Kevin Moomaw, who had headed the Tower youth program of 1978, assigned to organize campus support for Connally. By the time early spring of 1980 rolled around, however, Connally's campaign had sustained too many defeats elsewhere, and he withdrew his candidacy. This left the Texas showdown between Bush and Reagan set for May 3.

Conservative Democrats may have breathed a sigh of relief, but Texas Republicans were preoccupied with choosing sides between Bush and Reagan. Though Bush was making his first try for national office, he had entered the sweepstakes with a working knowledge of the Republican Party across the country, having served as national chairman. Jim Baker, the Houston attorney who lost his bid as a candidate for attorney general in 1978, was impressing political pros around the nation with the adroit manner in which he was managing Bush's national campaign. In addition, Hal DeMoss of Houston was a respected leader of the Texas effort.

Reagan had a potent organization rekindled in Texas, nurtured from the grass roots since his decisive victory in 1976. Ernie Angelo, the soft-spoken GOP national committeeman, was out front again for Reagan, but Barnhart, the outspoken Reagan leader for so many years, was on the sidelines after his appointment. Clements, Tower, and the new party chairman, Chet Upham, were neutral in the primary contest. Fresh in their minds was the memory of how divisive the 1976 Ford – Reagan shootout had been. They were concerned that perhaps 1980 would develop into an even more divisive battle since Bush claimed Texas as home turf against a charismatic candidate who had swamped an incumbent Republican President on that same turf. But the dynamics of 1980 were far from those of 1976. Watergate residue was finally gone, leaving a clear focus on which candidate could garner more national convention delegates en route to the foremost objective, replacing Jimmy Carter. Ford had never run in Texas prior to 1976, a problem that contributed to poor judgement and an occasional gaffe. His political organization had not really been his; it was an amalgam of Tower's people plus those who believed Reagan was too conservative for their tastes but had nowhere else to go. Bush had run two statewide races in Texas, winning countless friends at the grass roots level, some of whom might opt for Reagan, but held Bush in high esteem. Reagan's forces smelled the nomination in 1980, a position from which they wanted to promote harmony to enhance their candidate's opportunity to carry the state in the general election. Also, there was the fact that Bush and Reagan had developed a friendly rivalry over the tedious months of campaigning around the nation. It all added up to conditions in which the Bush – Reagan contest generated a tremendous effort in behalf of the two candidates who were popular among Texas Republicans, but there was little of the animosity and divisiveness that had consumed the 1976 primary between Ford and Reagan.

Reagan was favored but he and his forces took nothing for granted, working hard at the grass roots where Bush also displayed strength. When the votes were tallied, Reagan had won the popular vote with about fifty-two percent from a record voter turnout of 526,769. He also took the majority of delegates but Bush had run such a competitive race that when Clements soon endorsed Reagan, he hinted Bush would make a fine vice-presidential choice. With the Texas victory, Reagan had about sewed up the nomination and many Republican campaign operatives, not in the presidential campaign, turned their eyes toward races for the Congress and Legislature. Though the Connally candidacy didn't impact upon the GOP primary, the record turnout had nonetheless sown important seeds in the changing dynamics of the Texas political arena.

For the first time, more people voted in the GOP primary over the Democratic in the state's two most populous counties, Harris (Houston) and Dallas. In the combined vote of five metropolitan counties, including those two plus Bexar (San Antonio), Tarrant (Fort Worth) and Travis (Austin), the GOP led the Democrats by almost 70,000 votes. The high Republican turnout impacted upon a number of races, including that for State Senator Bill Moore of Bryan, a conservative Democrat, who lost his primary to challenger Kent Caperton, a liberal, partly because in vote-rich Montgomery County, most of the conservatives voted in the GOP primary. Senator Babe Schwartz, a leader of the Killer Bees, had a deceptively easy primary win over former State Representative Dean Neugent of Texas City, due in part to the scarcity of conservatives available for Neugent in the Democratic Primary.

The sands were indeed shifting, but few conservative political operatives in Austin, accustomed to playing their chips in the Democratic Primary, seemed willing to face the new reality. For so many years in so many districts, the contests for the Legislature were decided in that primary. Now, they were faced with more liberal nominees and no particular faith in Republicans to stem the tide. Yet, these operatives represented the business-industrial-professional community of Texas and they weren't supposed to sit still for the Killer Bee-types becoming stronger in state government. In ART parlance, those operatives were known as the "lobby-PAC crowd," composed of lobbyists who controlled distribution of campaign funds from political action committees (PACs), funds contributed by members of special interest groups. Among the largest were TexPac representing the state's physicians, and TrePac, the funding arm for the realtors of Texas. The liberal-labor operatives weren't interested in any of the Republican candidates for Senate, their favorites having cleared the Democratic Primary and would be supported by such as the plaintiff trial lawyers' political action committee, LIFT, and various union funds from the AFL–CIO and other labor organizations.

The loss of the venerable Moore, dean of the Senate, had been a shocker. Two other vacancies would be decided in the general election, and there were a few races in which the lobby-PAC crowd was keenly aware that united Republican forces would make their decisions more difficult than before. There was new GOP pressure being exerted by Clements, who made it clear that he, along with Tower, would support the ART program by helping raise money. The State GOP was also prepared to support candidates with substantial amounts of cash and technical assistance. It was shaping up as a year in which Texas Republicans could break another barrier, that of never having defeated an incumbent Democratic state senator in modern times. The near miss by Ike Harris against George Parkhouse in 1966, and the razor-thin loss by Tom Pauken to

Bill Braecklein a decade later were the closest GOP bids through the long years of frustration.

Defeating an incumbent congressman had been achieved back in 1962 with Ed Foreman's upset of J.T. Rutherford and included the defeat of a fairly popular entrenched incumbent when Alan Steelman outpolled Earle Cabell in 1972. But the Texas Senate is a unique political entity in that campaigns to get there may cost as much as a congressional race, but funding for Republicans had been much more difficult. Not only had the lobby-PAC crowd preferred to deal with Democrats, but the presiding officer of the Senate had always been a Democrat, along with the governor, until the election of Clements. Further, issues in the Senate were rarely of the Killer Bees nature. Usually, they were dull or esoteric to the general public which receives more television coverage regarding local news and the network national and international news. Since the level of awareness of state issues had never been as high as national, typical urban Republican voters and GOP contributors were usually not terribly enthused about state senate races, particularly if their incumbent Democratic senator was perceived as a conservative. But 1980 was unique in another sense crucial to Texas Republicans — it was the last general election prior to the next redistricting process. Each winnable race for the Texas Senate and House should be contested vigorously, and on that point GOP leaders and operatives could agree, since those legislators elected in 1980 would redraw their own district lines in addition to those for the Texas members of the United States House of Representatives. There would be some disagreements about which races would be "winnable," but once a race was targetted as winnable by ART, it was supported with as much funding and technical assistance as could be brought to bear. The same basic procedures were used by the State GOP, but there would not be as much funding available.

Large doses of psychology were being applied in the summer of 1980 in Austin, attempting to tilt sentiment in a somewhat fluid situation in which several Senate contests would be weighed out carefully. After Krueger's defeat, Garry Mauro became executive director of the Texas Democratic Party. Although party officials and staff are supposed to be neutral in such matters as contested primaries, he played a significant role in Caperton's win over Moore, providing campaign financing at a crucial time. Enjoying the liberal primary showing, Mauro looked confidently to the general election Senate races against Republicans. In June 1980, he was quoted in an article by Scott Bennett in *Texas Business* magazine, "I think we can pick up seats in Dallas and the Panhandle, but for the life of me, I don't see where the Republicans are going to pick up any." Either Mauro wasn't aware of the changing conditions and voting data that ART operatives were reviewing, or he was churning out nothing more than hollow partisan propaganda. Of seven state senate districts targetted by ART, John Tower carried five in 1978 and Bill Clements had carried four. In varying degrees the targetted districts contained growth patterns which usually were trending GOP, plus in five of the districts the Republican Primary had drawn heavy turnouts, a sure sign that GOP turnout in those districts would be high in the general election. The district in Dallas Mauro said he expected to pick up was a seat vacated by Braecklein, who had changed parties to the GOP but who had not sought reelection. Clements carried that district in 1978 by fifty-eight percent and the Republican nominee was John Leedom, former city council member and GOP county chairman who knew his precincts like the palm of his hand. He faced a tough race against former Democratic County Chairman Ron Kessler, but the Republican operatives believed that one was prime.

In the Panhandle, Republican incumbent Bob Price was indeed in trouble — politically from the previous session of the Legislature, and from severe personal financial problems. He faced a stiff challenge from Bill Sarpalius of Amarillo, a new face on the scene. In the other contests targetted by ART, Dee Travis of Garland, a former aide to Congressman Jim Collins, was taking on incumbent Democrat Ron Clower in the Dallas suburban area district which contained some rural counties south of Dallas. Mike Richards of Houston, with strong support from Bob Perry, the highly successful builder, was challenging incumbent Democrat Gene Jones; Richard (Rick) Parker, Houston attorney and onetime legislative aide to Tower, was trying to upset incumbent Democrat Jack Ogg; Jay Brummett, Republican nominee from Cleburne, was working to win the Northwest Texas seat vacated by Tom Creighton, matched against Democrat Bob Glasgow of Stephenville; and J.E. (Buster) Brown, a Lake Jackson attorney, was the GOP nominee against Babe Schwartz, whom *Texas Monthly* magazine had dubbed the "Godfather of the Killer Bees." The State GOP targetted the same races, but added Republican Marco Eugenio, a Corpus Christi surgeon challenging incumbent Democrat Carlos Truan.

In the early days of ART, a $1,000 contribution to a campaign was considered significant, particularly since before, there had been so few purely Republican dollars flowing into races for the Texas Senate and House. By 1980, thanks to diligent fund-raising efforts by Julian Zimmerman, John Hurd and Norman Newton — bolstered by Clements and Tower — ART was targetting state senate races with cash infusions in mind of $20,000 and upwards, depending on needs as the campaigns unfolded. For the 1980 elections, ART had embarked upon its program with a sophisticated base of information, developed in 1979 and continuously updated, upon which to make decisions. Political consultant Don MacIver had provided guidance for targetting through the study of past elections, growth patterns, and demographic data. The Tarrance polling firm had produced current survey research for the various state senate districts considered to be possible targets. All this information had been weighed by the ART Candidates Committee which was charged with deciding which districts to target and how much money to allocate per district. Though the emphasis was on the state senate, at least thirty-five House races would be targetted. The usual procedure was for the candidate and his or her manager to appear before the committee to lay out their game plan. If targetted, it didn't mean arbitrary funding at given levels throughout. Each campaign was reviewed constantly to determine if it was progressing as planned. If not, funding might be held in abeyance until corrections were made. Or, if a GOP targetted race became a cinch winner, money allocated there would be shifted elsewhere, according to need. Most of the original ART Candidates Committee (Allison Committee) had stayed the course. They had been joined by Lubbock attorney Joe Boerner, who had long been active in GOP campaigns in his area.

A mark of ART's growing potent role was the greater attention paid by the Capitol Press Corps in 1980, with several articles being devoted in whole or in part to the group's activities, including long in-depth pieces by Bo Byers of *The Houston Chronicle*, and Dave McNeely of *The Austin American-Statesman*. Byers noted Clements's support shown in a recent fund-raising letter to more than 25,000 on Clements's contributor lists urging them to join "a group of my friends (ART) who're working to elect to the Legislature more supporters of my program." For such projects as the mailing, Karl Rove, a savvy young Clements political operative, provided steady liaison with ART. McNeely noted the thorough screening process. "Candidates are studied to see whether they have the skill, personality, background and desire necessary to get them elected. 'We can be arbitrary as hell,' Zimmerman says." Zimmerman had always maintained that ART could be most effective because it was not subjected to the pressures inherent in a regular party organization which must fulfill its statutory duties, including the holding of primaries and conventions, before it can turn to candidate support.

There were about forty-five operatives in the Austin lobby-PAC community who were constantly concerned about trends and developments in legislative races, particularly those affecting the competitive state senate races. Their decisions would determine the placement of hundreds of thousands of dollars into campaigns in which they must try to set aside personal or party bias. To build a stronger rapport with them, ART Executive Director Norman Newton and other ART operatives would often meet with some of them informally in attempts to influence where they would direct their PAC funds. In addition, and on a more formal basis, ART-supported candidates for the Texas Senate and House were brought before them at late afternoon receptions usually held in downtown Austin private clubs, The Headliners which had relocated from the Westgate Building near the Capitol to the American Bank Tower, and The Citadel in the Driskill Hotel. At those receptions candidates would set forth their game plans, keyed to that all-important final element of achieving victory. Lobby-PAC people often gathered for their own informal sessions at the Quorum Club, then located on Red River Street, eventually to be relocated in the United Bank Tower on Fifteenth Street. The ART headquarters was located in a small North Austin office building on Hancock Drive, next door to Jorge's Mexican Restaurant where many a strategy session was held over spicy enchiladas and cold beer. The State GOP was located in the First Texas Building on Congress Avenue just south of the Capitol grounds and near the Clements political offices on Brazos Street. Ken Towery's offices were also in the First Texas Building from where the Connally Texas Campaign had been seeded. Towery, answering a summons from Lyn Nofzinger, joined Reagan's campaign in Washington, after a brief stint as an ART consultant in the state senate campaigns during the summer of 1980.

The old stereotype of an Austin lobbyist was long gone. Instead of a rotund character flailing the air with a big cigar, the lobbyist of 1980 would easily meld into any meeting of business and professional people whom they represented. They ranged in demeanor from the ubiquitous, talkative type, such as Clint Smith, then with Southwestern Bell, to the quiet, soft-spoken Dick Brown of the Texas Municipal League to the stoic Gene Palmer, who might ease in and out of a reception without being noticed, having gathered some bit of political intelligence of interest to one of his clients. If there was a guru in the group it was Gene Fondren, a former state legislator who represented the state's automobile dealers. Having been a candidate gave him an edge in the crucial process of sizing up potential winners, an ability to judge intangibles after all the statistical information had been bandied about. Other former legislators included Gerhardt Schulle of the realtors and J.P. Word, who had served in the state senate and had several clients. There was an unwritten rule that lobbyists stayed with "friendly incumbents," those legislators who had voted more or less along the lines of what their clients wanted. In the other races, there was room for consideration and pressure from such as Republican challengers. The critical nature of some of those decisions in 1980 might come down to a well-heeled PAC with a representative trying to decide on whom to bet in a hotly-contested race for a state senate seat. If there had been $10,000 allocated for that race, the decision actually became a $20,000 one with the $10,000 going to one candidate whose opponent was, in effect, denied $10,000 he might have thought was coming his way. The competition for such funds was indeed intense.

On the national scene, Texans were prominent at the Republican National Convention in Detroit where Reagan's nomination was a formality, but suspense reigned about his vice-presidential choice. Tower was named to chair the Platform Committee, a prestigious role among the movers and shakers. Clements and Connally were on the scene, attracting television cameras, and Fran Chiles was officially installed as national committeewoman from Texas. But for Texas Republicans, the magic moment came when Reagan dropped the idea of naming Ford his running mate, and summoned George Bush, thereby melding the ideal ticket for the Lone Star State. For the campaign, Clements assumed the leadership for Texas, including the raising of necessary funds. Longtime Reagan leader Ernie Angelo was again functioning out front, along with many of those Reagan backers in Texas who had worked for years to see their standard-bearer finally making the formal run for President of the United States.

On September 5 — 6, the GOP state convention was held in San Antonio at the Hemisfair Arena, a gathering notable for pursuing the unity forged behind the Reagan — Bush ticket in Detroit. About the only hint of contests were reelection ads in the convention program for State Chairman Chet Upham and State Vice-Chairman Dorothy Doehne, along with her fellow San Antonians Libba Barnes and Jane Pieper, state committeewomen. Rounding out the state officers were Bruce Calder of Dallas, finance chairman; Robert McCaig, also of Dallas, treasurer, and Holly Dechard of Austin, secretary. Delegates were somewhat weary from all the speech-making at the convention, but they were united in their dedication to carry the state for the Reagan — Bush ticket and to help in varying degrees the many other candidates carrying the Republican banner around the state.

In addition to the Reagan – Bush ticket, the party fielded four other candidates for statewide offices led by Judge Will Garwood of Austin, a Clements appointee to the Texas Supreme Court, running for a six-year term. A highly respected jurist, Garwood would draw strong support, but he would find the longstanding Democratic bias for such offices still firmly in place. Jim Brady of Houston, a trial lawyer of long tenure, was also a GOP candidate for the state supreme court and after losing, would change parties to win a judicial post as a Democrat. H.J. (Doc) Blanchard, a former Democratic state senator from Lubbock, and Hank Grover, the perennial candidate, were running for the Railroad Commission.

To fuel the Texas engine for Reagan—Bush, a tremendous fundraising event was held in Houston on September 16. Billed as the "Lone Star Tribute," a picture appearing in the *Republican Party of Texas 1980 Yearbook*, written and produced by Media Director Bob Ward, told the story of political strength and popularity gathered at the head table. Pictured from left to right: former President Ford; Reagan, the recently named nominee for President; Governor Clements; Bush, the nominee for Vice-President; former Ambassador Anne Armstrong; former Governor Connally; and Senator Tower. Some 2,500 enthused supporters paid $1,000 a plate for the full-dress dinner. Many more bought tickets who couldn't attend, all of which netted more than $2.8 million for the Texas Victory Committee, the State GOP's major contribution to the Reagan—Bush campaign. The *Yearbook* quoted the party's finance director, Jan Naylor, as contending the event "made political history in the U.S. in that it was the biggest political fundraiser ever held."

At about the time of that dinner John Mashek, veteran political writer for *U.S. News & World Report*, came to Austin during his journey through the South and Southwest studying indicators for the presidential election. In private conversations he concluded, and would soon write, that Reagan was en route to a convincing victory. Many other analysts clung to the belief that the race was competitive throughout the fall, but Mashek, and a few others, had found too many signs that Carter's base of 1976 had been eroded substantially among blue collar workers and Hispanics. In addition, the Reagan—Bush ticket had energized urban Anglo voters with enthusiasm likely to generate higher margins than Ford was able to achieve in 1976. Part of this was due to the religious right movement producing such dedicated pro-Reagan workers throughout the South, taking their anti-abortion and pro-school prayer stands before voters in the precincts. Plus in Texas, there was a strong mesh of thousands of veteran Reagan and Bush volunteers who had amalgamated after the primary. The ingredients were there for substantial top-of-the-ticket strength in most areas of the state, essential for providing the climate in which marginal state senate races could be won. This was a climate in which thousands of conservative ticket-splitters, who had tended toward voting Democratic in state races previously, might vote Republican in those contests, for a change. Most Republican campaign operatives knew in October that, barring some strange turn of events, the Reagan—Bush ticket would carry the target areas handily. They sought every means available to improve chances for the down-ballot candidates, such as endorsement mailings from Reagan for legislative candidates engineered by the State GOP program.

Based upon assessments that the Reagan – Bush ticket would ride high in the stretch run, ART redoubled its efforts to help effect an historic breakthrough in the Texas Senate. Veteran GOP Senator Ike Harris of Dallas played a leading role in rallying support and raising funds. The State GOP picked up its pace thanks to direction from Upham, Thorburn, and Rick Rodgers, the political director whose father, Pepper, had long been a fixture as a collegiate football coach who would eventually wind up in the pros. Backing up Rodgers were John Tindall, the research director and Terry Glaser, the field representative who worked directly with campaigns.

All of ART's targetted Senate races weren't falling together as hoped and planned. Incumbent Bob Price sustained some pointedly adverse publicity about his financial problems, assisting his opponent toward a convincing win. Republican Jay Brummett was a popular campaigner, but Bob Glasgow was an equally effective campaigner and as a Democrat seized the advantage and would win the race to succeed Tom Creighton. Rick Parker had a well-organized campaign put together by his manager, Pam Hazen, but he had sustained some bad wounds in a rough-and-tumble primary with O.J. Striegler, and he tried to paint Jack Ogg as a tool of special interest PACs. The problem was that in so doing, Parker identified many popular Houston businesses and industries whose employees knew for certain their allegiance probably should be with Ogg.

In only one of the ART targets did the lobby-PAC community unite behind the Republican — the Sixteenth District in which Dee Travis used that support effectively along with a Jim Collins "bowl 'em over" precinct organization directed by Jan Patterson. Travis rolled up fifty-four percent in replacing incumbent Ron Clower. Mike Richards mounted a hard-hitting campaign, keying on incumbent Gene Jones's legal problems over allegedly using Senate office machines and personnel in an illegal manner for his campaign. Paul Caprio, Richards's manager, kept up a drumfire of charges through news releases and paid advertising that helped propel Richards to a victory by about 6,000 votes out of more than 140,000 cast. In the other Dallas area race, John Leedom, with assistance from Kay Copeland, out-organized Ron Kessler and won a spirited contest by just under 6,000 votes.

The cliffhanger was the showcase showdown with Buster Brown of Lake Jackson, the young GOP challenger trying to unseat that cagey veteran, Babe Schwartz, the venerable liberal leader who would become Dean of the Texas Senate if reelected. As if the match-up itself weren't enough of a challenge, the district was about as difficult as one could devise for television advertising. It meandered from a small part of southern Harris County (near Houston) down the Gulf Coast (including Galveston), to its southernmost boundary of Aransas County, near Corpus Christi. The cost of reaching voters living all over that district with extensive television advertising was prohibitive to Brown's campaign. To cover all that turf thoroughly by personal campaigning was physically demanding and logistically tedious. The district contained various bedroom communities feeding into Houston, Galveston, and Corpus Christi, developments and towns with diverse communities of interest that were not always easily discernible. To reinforce his personal campaigning in those communities, Brown would need to tailor his advertising accordingly through means other than television. Yet television had to be considered for limited use to provide a general awareness of Brown in the Houston – Galveston media coverage area, including Brazoria County, where Brown could offset the Galveston advantage that would go to Schwartz.

Brown was strongly supported by Clements, Tower, ART, the State GOP, and Senator Ike Harris, a stronger force the lobby-PAC crowd could foresee dealing with since he was expected to succeed the retiring Creighton as chairman of the powerful Economic Development Committee. But Schwartz had a longstanding winning tradition going for him, along with the backing of Hobby, his presiding officer in the Senate, plus the support of Attorney General Mark White, and most of the Democratic-oriented political power that could be mustered on the Gulf Coast. Schwartz had not only the traditional liberal-labor forces, but a number of prominent business and industrial leaders in Houston who presumed they were betting on a winner.

Pressure was indeed intense in the lobby-PAC community over this race. Most wanted to see Schwartz defeated, but it was a high risk decision to oppose Schwartz with his entrenched incumbency and his long memory regarding adversaries. Few believed that Brown could win and those who thought he might have a chance hesitated, weighing the risk of incurring the wrath of Schwartz should their hope not materialize. The only ones who decided to take the plunge for Brown were Gene Fondren, representing the automobile dealers, Gerhardt Schulle of the realtors, and Randy Ransdell of General Telephone.

A major reason the ART operatives had placed so much faith in Brown was that he functioned as a candidate much as a fine point guard operates on a basketball team — he knew exactly where he was on the court, as well as where the other players were, throughout the game. Calm and resourceful, he was the type most likely to weave his way through a pressure-packed showdown without making a major mistake. He presented the desired image contrast to Schwartz, projecting relative youth near forty and a measured way of articulating his views versus the gray, aging Senate veteran known for his acerbic outbursts, perhaps having grown out of touch. At his side Brown had an attractive wife, Jill, who was helpful in planning important aspects of the campaign. Young people rallied to his banner, including Tom Hockaday, the manager, and Andy Sansom, a sharp operative who kept a close pulse on the scene, relaying information to Austin where constant adjustments were being made. Molly Pryor, who directed Tower's Houston office, assisted in various aspects, including a key role in convincing Tower early on that the race was winnable. Nancy Canion, the Galveston County chairman, was redoubling efforts to maximize voter turnout in key pro-Brown areas, employing the Nancy Palm methods proven to be successful on the Gulf Coast. Jim Loyd of the Tarrance polling firm, who had guided the 1978 Tower Campaign with crucial late tracking data, indicated the race was winnable for Brown because thirty-six percent of Neugent's Democratic Party primary vote was so firmly anti-Schwartz that it would likely go to Brown in the general election. That anti-Schwartz vote, the GOP primary vote in that district, plus the added vote expected for Reagan — Bush in November, all added up to a projected toss-up — a toss-up if Brown continued to perform well as an individual and attracted enough campaign funds for paid media necessary to make him better known by election day. All campaign materials were developed by the Yardang Agency, the San Antonio group that worked for Tower in 1978, and had opened a Houston office directed by Ray Rodriguez, a former Tower staffer in Washington. Rodriguez was a gifted writer who gave a fine touch to Brown's material that suffered a few times from under-funding. Instead of filming called for in television scripts, color slides were substituted in order to effect substantial savings, preserving more money for purchasing time rather than spending it on production. Some of Brown's advisors had questioned the use of television commercials in the first place because the tremendous prices for time are based upon the enormous coverage of the Houston stations and Brown's district was only a relatively small portion of that coverage. Nonetheless, other than personal appearances, only television could portray the image contrasts favorable to Brown, so his campaign bit the bullet and expended a heavy portion of the budget on a limited showing of TV spots. Brown maintained a steady pace, hoping for a break which he received on October 20, when Schwartz threw a well-publicized punch at another attorney in a Galveston courtroom. Ike Harris, Gene Fondren, and Gerhardt Schulle worked closely with the

ART operation to expedite last minute fundraising to take advantage of the break. Brown desperately needed more money for late TV, since the most recent polling data, provided by Loyd, showed Brown closing, but still trailing. By campaign's end, ART had poured about $50,000 into Brown's campaign and assisted in raising much more toward his total expenditure of about $160,000. On election night returns came in at an agonizing rate, with Brown edging slightly ahead by midnight. At 3:00 A.M., it remained undecided with Brown leading by less than one percent and six precincts still out. It was, in the words of Brown's manager, Tom Hockaday, "utter hell" trying to nail down the final vote, and several of those following closely grabbed a few hours of sleep. On the morning after the election, jubilation abounded at the ART headquarters when word was received that Schwartz had conceded. When the final tally was made, Brown had won by 778 votes out of 142,772. His campaign had peaked on election eve, or perhaps it hadn't quite peaked but was still on an upswing sufficient to edge out Schwartz. In any event, it was a tremendous victory for Texas Republicans, a strong echo to the Clements trumpet sounded two years previously.

Two days after the election, a long article with a Galveston dateline appeared in *The Houston Post* by Tupper Hull with a graphic description of the Democrats' mood there: "Public officials and party stalwarts were a picture of collective despair here Wednesday in the wake of the defeat of their long-time champion ... It wasn't so much grief at the loss of a friendly senator as it was shock at a change no one really expected." To his credit, Schwartz didn't place all the blame for losing on someone else's phone banks, or the weather, or other factors. "I still say Buster Brown is the best person I came up against in twenty years," he was quoted in the same article about his political tenure, adding that Brown was "young and intelligent" but something of a "captive Clements candidate." For his part, Brown refused to refer to his election as a surprise or an upset. "When you know what you're supposed to do," he was quoted in the *Post* article, "you do it, and it works. You're pleased, not surprised."

Brown's stunning victory brought to four the number of GOP state senate wins in 1980, including the defeat of three Democratic incumbents, the first time any incumbent Democratic state senator had been defeated by the opposition party. Most importantly in a strategic context, the balance of power in the two most populous counties had suddenly been flipped on a partisan basis. Of the seven senate seats claimed by the GOP, the Houston and Dallas areas each had three seats, substantial clout for those crucial areas in the redistricting wars to come. ART alone had spread more than $100,000 into those four winning races, and had provided considerable assistance in raising more and in conducting the races. Thus, it was sobering to contemplate that despite all the work and heavy campaign funding, only Brown of the GOP senate candidates was able to exceed the Tower percentage in his district, and that Tower percentage was attained in 1978 when the senator barely squeezed by.

The Democratic bias for state offices remained strong elsewhere, exemplified in the defeat of Judge Will Garwood for the state supreme court. Despite the heavy margin scored by the Reagan–Bush ticket in Texas, Garwood and the other statewide Republican candidates were defeated. But in addition to the state senate, the targetting process carried out by ART and the State GOP paid off in races for the Texas House in which the party elected thirteen new members, losing only one incumbent, for a gain of up to thirty-six members. The new Republican legislators included Jerry Cockerham of Monahans, Frank Eikenburg of Plano, Jim Horn of Denton, Rollin Khoury of Waco, Mike Martin of Longview, Kae Patrick of San Antonio, Randy Pennington of Houston, Ken Riley of Corpus Christi, Jay Reynolds of Floresville, Alan Schoolcraft of San Antonio, Terral Smith of Austin, Chip Staniswalis of Amarillo, and Jack Vowell of El Paso. Anita Hill of Garland announced a change in party affiliation in 1979 and was reelected as a Republican in 1980, while Dan Downey of Houston won a special election in the summer of 1980, but was defeated in the general election. Ashley Smith won a special election to replace Untermeyer, who resigned to join George Bush's staff, and he was sworn in on January 27, 1981.

Another positive factor in the GOP's major gains of 1980 at the legislative level was the support of *The Dallas Morning News*. Since Dick West had retired from directing the editorial page, the newspaper no longer favored conservative Democrats per se for state offices. Under Jim Wright as director, editorial endorsements of *The News* for 1980 were weighted toward the GOP in almost all marginal races except the Senate Sixteenth, in which Democrat Ron Kessler was endorsed, but Republican John Leedom was described as "a tough, no-nonsense conservative who has proved his ability on the Dallas City Council."

Another big plus for the Texas GOP was the election of Jack Fields of Humble, to the Eighth congressional seat held by Bob Eckhardt, the liberal leader from Houston of long-standing. Texas liberals had enjoyed many results of the primary in 1980 but the general election, particularly in the Harris County area, was a disaster for them with the loss of Eckhardt and Schwartz, plus several other lesser known figures among the liberal-labor forces.

Beyond the borders of Texas, the Reagan — Bush ticket had done so well that it helped bring about another stunning change, Republican control of the United States Senate. That meant that after fifteen years of tenure on the Armed Services Committee, Senator Tower would become chairman, a big bonus for him and Texas.

The massive effort for the Reagan — Bush ticket in Texas paid off with fifty-six percent of the vote, a hefty 700,000-vote margin out of a record turnout of 4.5 million voters, or almost seventy percent of the registered voters. That helped in a number of local races with Republicans electing 155 county officials to complement the substantial breakthroughs in the Legislature.

A postelection feature story in *The Houston Chronicle* by Jim Barlow paid homage to Nancy Palm, one of the twenty-four Texan electors who would cast an official ballot in the Electoral College for Ronald Reagan. Though ailing from high blood pressure and a heart condition, she still spoke of the party efforts and challenges. Commenting on her nickname, "Napalm," that was heard often during her heyday as Harris County GOP chairman, she quipped, "Compared to some of the things I was called, I guess it was appropriate."

Chet Upham, the GOP state chairman, proclaimed the election "indicates that Texas isn't becoming a two-party state anymore, it *is* a two-party state." Babe Schwartz, licking his wounds and viewing Democratic debris around him in the Gulf Coast area, stated flatly, "We now have a two-party system in Texas," as quoted in a November 9 article by Bo Byers, veteran chief of the Austin bureau of *The Houston Chronicle*. Byers wasn't convinced. "... We have the first strong indication that Texas is developing into a two-party state but still has a way to go ... I have advocated the need for a strong two-party system for Texas the past thirty-five years. I see the possibility, but not the certainty, that it may be near at hand."

CHAPTER FOURTEEN

The Integral Calculus of Politics

"Redistricting is the integral calculus of politics," Richard Reeves, the columnist, wrote in 1981. "Few people understand it, but those who do often have more impact on who is elected and who isn't than famous speeches and fancy television commercials.

"Many, many elections are decided long before candidates are selected; they are won and lost on the basis of who is allowed to vote in a district."

After each decennial federal census, redistricting is required for every state's Congressional delegation and their Legislatures. The purpose is to adjust population changes into redrawn districts of relatively equal population, drawn in a manner not to dilute voting impact of ethnic minorities, defined in Texas as blacks and Hispanics. In 1981, for the first time, Texas Republicans entered the legislative process of redistricting with tangible political leverage. Clements let it be known that as governor, he would honor tradition which dictates that members of each chamber redistrict their own chamber without interference from him or the other chamber. In Congressional redistricting, Clements would take an active role in seeking a conservative plan to be hammered out by a coalition of Republicans and conservative Democrats in each chamber. Clements spoke softly, but carried a big stick, the threat of a veto of a redistricting bill and perhaps problems on other legislation if his goal wasn't achieved.

The stakes in the Congressional fight were high indeed with the state having received three additional seats, bringing the Texas total to twenty-seven by virtue of population increase over the past decade from 11,196,730 in 1970 — to 14,228,383 in 1980. To equalize the districts perfectly would require each to contain 526,977, but courts have long held that small population deviations are permissable for logical reasons. The inside players knew that minor changes and so-called fine-tuning of plans could make a substantial difference in the winnability factors for ethnic groups and political parties. They knew the process would be tedious and time-consuming. A Hollywood scriptwriter, however, couldn't have crafted a more dramatic scenario than that which was played out in Congressional redistricting that summer.

In addition to the guidelines of equal population and protection for ethnic minorities, state representatives retained constitutional protection against unwarranted cutting of county lines, the provision that Tom Craddick of Midland had used to nullify the Mutscher Texas House redistricting bill in the previous redistricting. Craddick was one of the few Republicans with experience in the legislative process, joined in the House by Fred Agnich of Dallas and Bill Blythe of Houston. Ike Harris of Dallas was the only GOP senator returning from the 1971 redistricting, though Walter Mengden of Houston had been in the House at the time. Republican numbers weren't impressive in 1981, seven in the thirty-one-member Senate and thirty-five in the 150-member House, but they were sufficient to form effective coalitions with conservative Democrats at various points in the process, particularly for Congressional redistricting.

A great deal of pious rhetoric is bandied about regarding community of interest, drawing compact districts and other desirable objectives, but when it comes down to the actual drawing, redrawing and voting, redistricting is the most partisan process the Legislature undertakes. It is also the most selfish, because 181 foxes in the henhouse look out for themselves first, which means trying to enhance any special winnability factors for their districts. If one or more members of the Legislature develops Congressional ambitions for the same district, the fighting over every inch of the map becomes even more intense as variables are weighed carefully, yet often rapidly, since so much redistricting work is in progress along with the regular work of a legislative session. Add to all that the fact that Republicans and Democrats have an intense partisan interest, particularly in the Congressional redistricting since the United States House of Representatives is organized on partisan lines whereas the Legislature has never organized along partisan lines. Most legislators approach the process with a sequence in mind — use all the skill and guile that can be brought to bear to feather one's own nest and those of friends if needed, then direct all energies toward partisan or philosophical goals according to party affiliation and objectives. However, the process has other considerations brought into play that may divert partisan plans, such as an ethnic minority may find its voting history to have been Democratic, but its current needs in the redistricting process to require an alignment with Republicans. Such alignments might occur for a given district or several districts or for an entire plan. Therefore, when a plan is altered in any substantial manner, the revised plan may cause changes in support by a faction, party or ethnic minority.

Redistricting has also been described as a "legislative nightmare" and a "judicial thicket" because invariably much of the blood shed to arrive at a plan during the legislative process winds up on the cutting room floor in a courthouse. In addition to clearing the Legislature and the governor, plans are subject to review by the United States Department of Justice for its interpretation as to whether they comply with the Voting Rights Act. It is almost certain that when a plan clears the legislative process it will be challenged in state and/or federal court. Also if a Texas House or Senate plan passes but runs aground by gubernatorial veto or court challenges under certain timing, a special five-member board comes into being to handle the task. That redistricting board is composed of the lieutenant governor, speaker of the Texas House of Representatives, attorney general, comptroller, and land commissioner.

The term "gerrymandering" is still in use to describe the act of diluting a political party's voting strength through "creative cartography," a clever drawing of maps to further that purpose. However, the term, "packing" is in wider use since this method is used often to achieve the same purpose by what might also be described as "inverse gerrymandering." For instance, if a given area warrants seven Texas House seats, and that area's voting history is about fifty-fifty Democrat – Republican, the packing process can be devastating, depending on the location of the party voting patterns and their susceptibility to manipulation. It may be possible to "pack" two districts with heavy Republican majorities in order to leave five probable Democratic seats. Dallas County Republicans have been bitter for years over their county's continuous GOP voting history, yet they have only one Congressional seat, the heavily packed Third District, while the Democrats control the county's other two districts. In the judicial thicket of redistricting, courts have been reluctant to tackle the issue of partisan gerrymandering until very recently. Guidelines, if any, are not expected until an Indiana case is heard by the United States Supreme Court after the time of this writing.

Some incumbents, whose districts have been packed and repacked over the years, don't mind the process at all, but for party leaders, seeking maximum numbers of seats attainable, it is a procedure they would like very much to see curtailed. "Pairing" means placing two incumbents in the same redrawn district, an unsavory but occasionally unavoidable procedure. Even apparently harmless minor changes on a plan sometimes prove to be frustrating by causing a ripple effect that tips the balance that had been achieved between districts covering a considerable amount of territory.

During the spring of 1981, the pulling and tugging over Congressional redistricting had become bitter and divisive. Clements advocated a plan that was conservative yet provided a new black district in Dallas County, the net effect of which would also provide an additional Republican-oriented district. The liberal-loyalist Democrats dug in to divide the minority vote into two Anglo Democratic-leaning districts in order to maintain their incumbents, Martin Frost and Jim Mattox, in those seats. Other parts of the state were fought over but the struggle over the Dallas turf was the focal point which couldn't be resolved in the regular session.

While legislative leaders stewed over how to resolve the redistricting impasse, Senator John Tower passed milestones of twenty years since his first election to the Senate on May 27, 1961, and two decades since he actually took office the following June 15. Several feature articles appeared, including one by Jack Kneece written from the Washington bureau of *The Dallas Morning News* under a headline of HIS NAME IS TOWER AND NOW HE DOES, playing off on the old Tower one-liner about his short physical stature. The article traced Tower's career from an obscure political science professor to the presently held position of high esteem in the Senate, including chairman of the Armed Services Committee, chairman of the Republican Policy Committee and second most senior Republican member. Governor Clements termed Tower "a fine, high-quality conservative senator ... who has demonstrated his good judgment in his service to this state as well as to the country." Not so charitable were comments by Ronnie Dugger, liberal author and longtime central figure of *The Texas Observer*, who said Tower "is obviously a very good politician. Nobody with a record as bad as his could have survived otherwise ... He is against the people and for big industry." Kneece conducted a thorough interview with Tower during which the senator recalled major points in his political career. These included the low spot of the 1964 election that "left him more depressed than he had ever been," and such humorous moments as "he laughed uproariously when recalling how he dressed up in a Superman suit at a Dallas Gridiron Show and Dinner." Asked whom Tower thought the greatest man of the century would be, his response was predictable. "I would say Winston Churchill ... I certainly think he was the most heroic figure of the century." Tower acknowledged he had been interested in the secretary of defense position, but "I have the privilege of continuing to represent the greatest state in the union." A longtime Tower associate commented on that remark, "All senators say that about their states, but when he says it, you can carve it in stone."

Most of the material written about Tower's twenty-year milestones failed to develop his crucial role as party leader in Texas during those seventeen years prior to the election of Clements, years when he was the only rallying point for Texas Republicans. One writer even compared the 1966 campaign to 1961 as another fluke based upon liberal backlash. In fact, the 1966 campaign took advantage of liberal backlash, but it was probably the most carefully planned and skillfully executed of the five statewide races Tower had conducted. It also spawned such initiatives as the Mexican-American outreach program launched in 1965. That tradition had been pursued all those years, and in the summer of 1981, Tower was the featured speaker at a successful roast for his longtime aide, Bob Estrada, who was gearing down political activity in order to attend law school at The University of Texas. At the State GOP, the M-A program was being pursued under the direction of Cathi Villalpando, an effective organizer who would eventually join the White House staff.

With the conflicting sides poised for another battle over Congressional redistricting, Clements called a special session of the Legislature in the summer of 1981. On the liberal-loyalist Democratic side most prominently was the Democratic State Chairman, Bob Slagle, who never seemed to miss any of the legislative action or corridor conflabs; Harry Hubbard, president of the Texas AFL–CIO, whose computers were used extensively behind the scenes; and a bevy of attorneys who were experienced and were prepared to offer advice to legislators along the way. In the Senate, Lloyd Doggett of Austin, Oscar Mauzy of Dallas, and Peyton McKnight of Tyler, were outspoken in their thrusts against "the Republican Plan" or "the Clements Plan," or what would ultimately become known as "the Wilson Plan." Lining up for Clements's approach was House Speaker Bill Clayton, a cagey conservative Democrat whose support made prospects in the House much better than in the Senate where Lieutenant Governor Bill Hobby often appeared to be ambivalent, caught between the party loyalty pressures exerted upon a statewide Democratic officeholder, yet sensitive to the idea of providing a black district in Dallas County. Added pressure was brought to bear by an ad hoc committee known as "Texans For A Conservative Congress," a powerful bipartisan pro-Clements group composed of forty-three prominent figures, including such potent conservative Democrat campaign financiers as Hayden Head of Corpus Christi, Walter Mischer of Houston, and H.B. Zachry of San Antonio. One of the cochairmen was Wales Madden of Amarillo, probably the most influential individual in the Panhandle who had maintained statewide political connections dating from the time Connally was governor. Madden's group would settle upon supporting a plan drawn by Senator John Wilson, a conservative Democrat from LaGrange, and the views of that group were not to be ignored.

In the summer of 1981 Texas legislators were weary of the hassle but acutely aware of how close the votes had been. They were wary of any changes in strategy. Jan Jarboe, writing in the *San Antonio Express News*, observed a summer session of the Texas Senate:

> One by one, the long-faced senators took their seats, looking as though they were about to take the dose of castor oil that comes once every ten years when they go behind the rail to decide what kind of political representation you'll get for the next decade.
> This process is called redistricting. Here are some of the phrases used by politicians to describe it: 'A necessary evil,' 'A pain in the neck,' 'A bitter pill to swallow,' and other unprintable variations on that theme.

A prominent figure had literally been brought to tears. State Representative Tim Von Dohlen, a conservative Democrat from Goliad, had served as Clayton's chairman of the House redistricting committee through the rough-and-tumble process. On August 11, Virginia Ellis reported on his speech in a *Dallas Times Herald* article,

> For many weeks, Tim Von Dohlen has been the man in the pressure cooker. He's been called a traitor to his party, a pawn of the special interests, a waterboy for House Speaker Billy Clayton and a political opportunist. And on Monday, he cried. 'Each of us now realizes that redistricting is a virtually impossible legislative process. Whenever you make a change, you please one and make another unhappy.'...
> Von Dohlen insisted he had been 'open and aboveboard, candid and truthful,' while some of his fellow legislators had not. He said they had privately made deals with him while they were publicly flogging him for being unfair and disloyal to his party. Von Dohlen said he withstood the temptation to go public with their behind-the-scenes maneuvering although he kept careful track of their duplicity in a private diary.

The article stated that Von Dohlen's voice broke as he concluded his remarks and that House members had given him a standing ovation, "while several members hurried to comfort him at his desk where he still sobbed quietly."

Turning up the heat under the cauldron were other various elements in addition to the political parties and the Madden group. Eddie Chiles, the Fort Worth industrialist and owner of the Texas Rangers baseball club, had some of his people involved, including Jay Banks on virtually a full-time basis that summer. Within the Senate, Ike Harris's office became the staging area for the Republicans with his veteran AA, Margaret Bacon, and staffer Tim Hendricks providing steady support to the effort. Other Republican senate staffers who were particularly active in this process included Terry Glaser with Senator Buster Brown, Danny Jensen with Senator Mike Richards, and Kevin Moomaw with Senator Dee Travis. Since Bill Meier, the veteran conservative senator from Euless in Tarrant County, had changed parties after the regular session, Harris could count on a bedrock of eight GOP senators. This was a potent force for circling the wagons under certain rules and half of the sixteen needed to achieve majority votes in the thirty-one member Senate. But even that wasn't a certainty since Hobby convened the Senate for redistricting under the Committee of the Whole rule under which he could vote any time, not restricted to breaking ties as under the regular rules. Providing liaison between the Senate and House and the governor's office were Hilary Doran, the former state representative from Del Rio, and Karl Rove, who had served previously in the Governor Clements Committee political operation.

In the Texas House, Republican redistricting leaders included Bob Davis of Irving (Dallas County), Ed Emmett of Kingwood (Harris County), and Bob McFarland of Arlington (Tarrant County). Jim Nowlin of San Antonio was another effective GOP operative, making his last hurrah in the Legislature. He would become a federal district judge while Will Garwood of Austin would join the Fifth U.S. Circuit with such distinguished judges as Tom Gee, also of Austin, one of those pioneer Republican attorneys willing to identify with the party in the uphill era of the 1960s.

For the Congressional redistricting fight in the House, Speaker Clayton's office was used as the staging area with the strategy calling for conservative Democrats to be out front, such as Bill Messer of Belton, who could help persuade marginal Democrats to join Clayton's effort.

Another factor through the redistricting process was the concerted effort of a consortium of civil rights organizations promoting Mexican-American interests. These included the Texas Rural Legal Aid group (TRLA), the Mexican-American Legal Defense and Educational Fund

(MALDEF), and the Southwest Voter Registration and Education Project, whose director, Willie Velasquez oversaw the collection and analysis of vast amounts of population data and voting history. The organizations were located in the Petroleum Commerce Building in downtown San Antonio from where for years they had been preparing their versions of favorable cartography and support material. Joaquin Avila, a MALDEF attorney, and Raul Noriega, a computer-cartography expert for TRLA, would make frequent appearances in Austin, pressing for measures to maximize opportunities for Mexican-American voting impact. Their interests were usually not incompatible with those of the GOP.

The Republican State Headquarters maintained a busy redistricting division where map revisions and computer-generated data were constantly updated in support of the efforts of GOP legislators and ultimately for lawsuits. Tom Hockaday took over as political director from Rick Rodgers and directed most of the processing endeavors that included extensive revisions by Lou Traycik, supported by several staffers from time to time, including Reta Cooke who kept the flow of information moving in the redistricting department and Teddi deClairmont, who was her counterpart to the remainder of the state headquarters staff on another floor.

With the July heat engulfing the capitol area each day, the 181 legislators and Hobby wrangled about all sorts of alternatives. Wilson, a game competitor undergoing treatment for terminal cancer, plugged away with his plan that had drawn near unified conservative support.

Jack Ogg, the conservative Democrat from Houston, had been prominent in the process throughout but his position wasn't always easily discernible at points along the way. He had voted on both sides of the issue in the regular session when he was a member of the conference committee. In Capitol corridors, he received the nickname of "The Wizard of Ogg" with rampant speculation as to what his next move might be during a series of close votes expected in the special session. On July 15, Ogg and Hobby surprised many observers by voting with Wilson to achieve a seventeen to fourteen margin on a crucial test vote, liberal Senator Kent Caperton being absent at the time. When he returned, and other liberals dug in for heavy combat, the result was six tense days of tedious maneuvering, causing close votes for and against Wilson's concept and other plans, as well as various amendments. Finally, the Senate cleared Wilson's plan on a nineteen to twelve tally.

The plan went to the House where Clayton knew the liberal-loyalist Democrats were in a feisty mood. Test votes in the Von Dohlen committee often deadlocked at nine to nine with one abstaining, and it took clever maneuvering, some of it engineered by Republican Bob Davis, to finally squeeze a bill from committee. On Saturday, August 8, Clayton laid the bill before the House, triggering one of the longest, most spirited battles ever waged in that chamber. Through hours of heated debate and parliamentary maneuvering, Clayton cooly kept the pressure on, working toward passing his version of the Wilson bill, a bit more conservative than that which had passed the Senate. In the evening, it was becoming difficult to keep members on the floor at all times and at one point, the anti-Clayton forces appeared to have won a major breakthrough with an amendment that carried by one vote. But Clayton quickly rounded up more of his votes and reversed the temporary defeat. With Bill Messer taking most of the heat at the microphone as the night wore on, the Clayton forces seemed to have established a small working majority that could prevail on most key votes. Clayton wanted to keep working his way through variations, maneuverings, amendments, delay tactics, in order to pass his bill that night, but the rules required a two-hour break at midnight.

During the break, the anti-Clayton forces decided upon a Killer Bee maneuver whereby they would boycott the resumption at 2:00 A.M. If more than fifty members were absent, Clayton would be denied a quorem and couldn't pass his bill. When 2:00 A.M. arrived, more than fifty of the anti-Clayton members among the 150 representatives had disappeared. Undaunted, Clayton promptly slapped a "Call on the House," empowering the sergeant-at-arms and Department of Public Safety officers to round up the truants from anywhere they could be found. From 2:00 A.M. until 4:30 A.M., the House stood at ease while a few truants returned. Clayton's loyalists remained loyal all right, but by 3:00 A.M., some of them were indeed weary, having had a few libations somewhere near the floor of the House. One in particular had required assistance in finding his desk button for voting during the hassle around midnight. During those unlikely morning hours, many of those following the proceedings searched the Capitol for the most precious commodity that could be found, a fresh pot of coffee. At 4:32 A.M., a quorum of one hundred members was present and Clayton rammed home his bill, sending it to the Senate for debate the following day. On August 10, the Senate considered the Wilson bill with Clayton fine-tuning and again, it was down to the wire. On the key test vote, it was sixteen to fifteen with The Wizard of Ogg again a deciding factor, voting for the conservative side. In the endless speculation as to motives, it was believed that Ogg responded to the Madden group, particularly Mischer, since Ogg had ambitions to run for attorney general and couldn't afford to incur Mischer's disfavor. Whatever the reason, that vote paved the way for an eighteen to thirteen vote, accepting Clayton's changes and sending the bill to Clements for his welcome signature. Dave McNeely, the veteran political writer of *The Austin American-Statesman* who had covered the entire process, termed it a "stunning victory" for Clements.

Veteran Republican operatives reflected upon how many close votes had been involved in the Congressional redistricting battle, particularly in the Senate. If the GOP breakthrough hadn't been scored in 1980, providing that net gain of two seats, the battle never could have been won by the conservative side.

Clayton also took care of the House Republicans to their satisfaction with their own districts, but in Hobby's Senate, the GOP would take a battering. From a strategic sense, the Senate redistricting was more complex than that for the Congressional redistricting, since there had been only twenty-four incumbents to contend with in the Congressional (with three new seats) while in the Senate there were thirty-one incumbents with whom to divide the state (and no additional seats).

Population configurations were such that it was difficult to redistrict the Senate even with pure motives. Add all the chicanery and political lusting involved and it became a bitter, divisive struggle. Unlike the Congressional redistricting, Clements stayed out, as he said he would, and there was no ad hoc committee involved such as the Madden group. Partisan anti-Republican hardball was played throughout the process but the Republicans contributed to their problems when rumors abounded that three incumbents would seek other offices, Walter Mengden for United States Senate, Mike Richards for state comptroller, and Dee Travis for Congress. Further, the GOP convert-to-be, Bill Meier, was headed toward a statewide race and Betty Andujar was rumored to be retiring. After Meier's change, Ike Harris could muster eight solid GOP votes for Congressional redistricting in the summer of 1981, half of the working conservative coalition, but he, along with freshmen Buster Brown and John Leedom, were the only Republican senators who appeared to be stable in their seats.

Therefore, with so few Republicans fighting to protect their seats, the partisan Democrats could maneuver more effectively to gerrymander the other GOP-oriented districts. The plan they adopted was so blatantly anti-urban and anti-GOP that Clements vetoed it, but subsequent redistricting board action produced a similar anti-Republican plan which withstood extensive court challenges by ART and the State GOP. The plan not only diluted Republican strength, but made a mockery of principles of equitable reapportionment by ignoring high growth areas, shat-

tering county lines with impunity, and dividing communities of interest. It was an example of partisanship at its worst.

In the afterglow of the Congressional redistricting, most observers
believed the plan would stand up in court, or at worst might require
minor fine-tuning in South Texas, far from the battlefield in Dallas. But
the anti-Clements forces brought suit in federal court, winding up before
William Wayne Justice, the liberal activist, along with two other Democrat judges, Sam Johnson and Robert Parker.

Justice was a veteran of such litigation, having participated in the
landmark decision in 1972 that changed urban areas from countywide
elections of state representatives to single member districts. The thrust
of his decision was to give ethnic minorities more opportunities to elect
their own to the Legislature. But that was in 1972. In 1982 he was receptive to a completely contradictory argument put forth by the partisan
Democrats who wanted to make sure blacks didn't upset their applecart
in the Dallas County Congressional delegation. The Democrats' plan had
the effect of excluding blacks, yet Justice and Johnson ruled in favor of
the partisan Democrats, creating bitter reaction in Dallas from blacks,
plus people in the news media who had been following the issue closely.
On March 3, an article by Jim Schutze appeared in *The Dallas Times
Herald*, taking Justice to task.

> In his separate opinion explaining why Dallas blacks don't need
> their own congressman, Justice said the minority district plan had a
> 'deliberate invidious purpose, to discriminate against minority residents
> of Dallas, by packing them into one district and eliminating any influ-
> ence they might have in another.' That's a lie. This district didn't
> come about because someone wanted to pull a trick on gullible blacks.
> A strong coalition of Dallas black leaders joined with the only white
> allies they could find, Republicans, and fought hard in the Legislature
> for their own congressional district ... What Justice is really express-
> ing is white liberal Democratic paternalism of the kind he grew up
> with in East Texas. This school of thought finally holds that it is noble
> of white liberals, even martyrly, to help blacks because blacks are not
> capable of helping themselves. It is, as [black leader John Wiley] Price
> says so often and so bitterly, 'the last oppression.'... This is a painful
> experience for white liberals, too. It isn't easy for them to see one of
> their champions, Wayne Justice, corrupting his own considerable skills
> to spin out absurdly camouflaged rationalizations for a political assault
> on black liberty.

An April 7 editorial in *The Dallas Morning News* stated that,

As every schoolboy knows, the federal government is composed of three coordinate and coequal branches — the judiciary, the judiciary, and the judiciary. Or does it merely seem that way sometimes, owing to the arrogance of federal judges like William Wayne Justice and Sam Johnson? Justice and Johnson, with Judge Robert Parker dissenting, have decreed that, never mind what the Texas Legislature says, nor even what the U.S. Supreme Court thinks, Dallas County will elect its congressmen this year from districts gerrymandered by Justice and Johnson ...

Among political activists, one of the most disappointed was Dallas County Republican Chairman Fred Meyer, who had been in the forefront of encouraging black participation in the political process with the GOP.

After several adverse decisions, a Republican redistricting operative reported to party leaders in a memo stating,

It's interesting to note that two of the three plans produced by the Legislature, Congressional and Texas House, were supported by us. What we had won during the legislative process was lost through administrative or judicial fiat. On that score, since the three plans left the legislative process, they have been under the scrutiny of twenty-two people, including federal and state judges and the five members of the Legislative Redistricting Board. All twenty-two are Democrats and every decision has been adverse to our interests. Anyone who believes that black robes and fancy titles dilute partisan blood may as well expect Santa Claus to arrive at high noon on July 4 ...

Republicans would carry the Congressional redistricting fight to the U.S. Supreme Court where hopeful signs were received, but delays and interference with the election process made the entire effort awkward and tedious at times, assisting the Wayne Justice-partisan Democrat position in Dallas to prevail for the decade. However, in the scheme of things, Republicans would wreak some vengeance at the polls in 1984, partly due to the Democrats' failure to have projected growth patterns that proved to be decisive in defeats of some of their incumbents who appeared to have been protected in 1981.

Outside the unsettling redistricting wars, Texas Republicans were prospering with Clements as a strong governor and the entrenched Tower apparently aiming toward another reelection bid. In January 1982, Clements introduced Tower warmly at a highly successful fund-raising dinner in Dallas honoring him for two decades of Senate service. Some ten years previously, Clements, then a political unknown, had chaired the "Decade of Service" dinner for Tower, also in Dallas. Tower's fund-raiser,

Brad O'Leary, reported the 1982 dinner raised more than $1.1 million of which sixty percent came from "new contributors."

The State GOP expanded its staff in early 1982, preparing for a larger support role for the slate of statewide candidates. Terry Glaser, who had been Senator Buster Brown's AA, became the finance director, assisted by James Hight, the veteran comptroller. Judy De Leo and Betsy Hurley signed on as organization director and auxiliaries coordinator, respectively. Melanie McIntosh kept the flow of memos and materials moving throughout the headquarters, directed by Wayne Thorburn, who had been brought to that position by State Chairman Ray Barnhart and was retained by Barnhart's successor, Chet Upham. Thorburn would move the state headquarters from the Congress Avenue location to 1300 Guadalupe, two blocks west of the Capitol.

With his part of redistricting out of the way, Clements turned to his reelection campaign, a sure bet to be extensive and well-financed. He chose Jim Francis, his veteran political operative, to be the manager, replacing him at the Governor Clements Committee with George Bayoud, his personal aide. When George Strake resigned as secretary of state to run for lieutenant governor, Clements replaced him with David Dean, his legal counsel who was replaced by David Herndon. Bob Close, the popular former GOP legislator from the Panhandle, had joined the legislative liaison staff and Sheila Wilkes and Pat Oles were involved in various forms of patronage, federal and state. Clements's image as an active and accessible governor had been enhanced through the work of Jon Ford, his press secretary who for so many years had been a part of the Capitol Press Corps.

In general, Clements was perceived by most observers as a formidable incumbent, favored to win reelection. With that in mind, Texas Republicans pressed for a slate of statewide candidates, believing Clements could lead a sweep of those offices they had not often contested in the past. Republican temptations were enhanced by the fact that conservative Democrats could no longer control their primary, with four liberals nominated for statewide office — Jim Mattox for attorney general, Jim Hightower for agriculture commissioner, Garry Mauro for land commissioner, and Ann Richards for state treasurer. Of that development, Kyle Thompson, editor of the editorial page of *The Fort Worth Star-Telegram*, wrote on June 20, 1982,

> The domination of more liberals of the 1982 Democratic ticket for the general election thus is a watershed in Texas politics. While the party slate by no means is wholly liberal, it is much more liberal than any state ticket offered in modern times. And if it is not wholly

liberal-loyalist, many veteran political observers feel it is in the final stages of so becoming.

Thompson traced the origin of realignment to Allan Shivers's support of Dwight Eisenhower three decades past, planting the rebuilding seeds for liberal Democrats to purify their party from conservative domination. Ronnie Dugger was quoted in the *San Antonio Express* of July 15, 1982, "Nothing like this has happened since I began following Texas politics in the late 1940s." The election of Clements and the other dynamics of two-party development had indeed markedly changed the Texas political landscape.

Joining Clements on the state ticket were George Strake for lieutenant governor, Bill Meier for attorney general, Allen Clark of Austin for treasurer, Mike Richards for comptroller, Woody Glasscock, former mayor of Hondo for land commissioner, Dr. Fred Thornberry, former supervisor in the Texas Agricultural Extension Service at Texas A & M for agriculture commissioner, John T. Henderson of Austin for railroad commissioner, and candidates for two high judicial offices, John Bates of Waco for Supreme Court and Ray Moses of Houston for Court of Criminal Appeals.

In the wake of liberals Ann Richards and Jim Hightower being nominated in the Democratic Primary, Clark and Thornberry were recruited to challenge them by replacing stalking horse candidates who had filed and been nominated in the GOP primary, Millard Neptune of Austin, former GOP Travis County chairman, for treasurer, and Donald Hebert, a Waller County rice farmer, for agriculture commissioner. The Democrats screamed foul play, but the procedure was legal until they changed the law in a subsequent session of the Legislature. Clark was a favorite of Clements, having served on his staff, and when Clark announced he was replacing Neptune, the news media took it as a sure sign that Texas Republicans were serious about such down-ballot races they had rarely contested before. In addition to his qualifications in finance-related endeavors, Clark was a highly decorated Vietnam veteran, who had lost both legs below the knees as a result of wounds sustained on his final scheduled day of duty there. A fast learner and strong organizer, Clark was a steadfast competitor who covered more ground on artificial legs than most people do on their own. He also had the marked disadvantage of starting as a new candidate on the statewide scene only five months prior to the election. Most new candidates who win statewide races start running more than a year before a general election.

Though Clements was governor of Texas and leader of his party, he would appear on the ballot below the U.S. Senate and Congressional nominees. Instead of a compatible relationship with the U.S. Senate campaign, as there had been in 1978 with Tower, a fundamental conflict developed that would haunt the two races. On November 13, 1980, Clements was quoted as having "dismissed the idea that U.S. Sen. Lloyd M. Bentsen, D-Texas, is a liberal and therefore a legitimate target for a right wing group's political 'hit list' for the 1982 elections." The article referred to the National Conservative Action Committee (NCPAC, which carried the slang pronunciation of "Nik-Pak") that claimed credit for defeating several prominent liberal senators in 1980, including Frank Church of Idaho, and George McGovern of South Dakota. Since the group did not formally align with campaigns, it qualified to make unlimited "independent expenditures," meaning it could pour hundreds of thousands of dollars into slashing negative advertising to tear down a liberal incumbent while the conservative challenger could devote more time and resources to selling his or her positive virtues.

No one paid much attention to the remark made by Clements since it was made at a point distant from the 1982 campaign. But as the primary later unfolded, observers began following more closely the campaign of Congressman Jim Collins of Dallas for the GOP U.S. Senate nomination. A fourteen-year veteran of the House, Collins at sixty-six showed his age with sparse gray hair on a balding head and a heavily wrinkled face. However, he was slender and agile, almost athletic, having kept himself in top physical condition over the years. He campaigned with an evangelical spirit, plugging hard for the conservative views he had espoused in Dallas and Washington. During the primary campaign, Collins virtually ignored his GOP opponents, including longtime State Senator Walter Mengden of Houston, while he hammered away at Bentsen for allegedly being a liberal. Many Republicans believed that was a fairly sound strategy to stir up the troops during the primary, but that a balanced campaign would be required in the fall, selling Collins as an individual while attacking certain liberal votes in Bentsen's record. Like Krueger, Bentsen had voted for giving two Senators to D.C., and for the so-called Panama Canal giveaway. Plus, he had taken some out-of-perception liberal positions during his ill-fated bid for the Democratic presidential nomination. All of which was fair game, but the idea of making "Lloyd Bentsen is a liberal" the centerpiece for the general election campaign was not considered to be sound strategy at all.

For twelve years, since he defeated liberal Ralph Yarborough, Bentsen had been perceived generally in Texas as a conservative or moderate-conservative. To change that perception, almost solely through the use of mass media advertising, was a proposition many believed to be based upon a false premise. However, Collins would embark upon just such a quixotic course. The top strategist for Collins's campaign was Arthur Finkelstein of New York, who had been prominent in the NCPAC scheme of things. For Collins, he was pollster, political consultant, and director of advertising. He convinced Collins and his key people that the race would be won largely through the simple expedient of branding Bentsen as a liberal, utilizing a multimillion dollar campaign whose advertising he would produce. This was apparently the NCPAC format used in 1980 to defeat liberal senators elsewhere. But this was 1982, and Bentsen was not perceived anything like McGovern had been, plus Texas is no sparsely populated political unit such as South Dakota. Politically, it is a million light years from the silk-stocking Republican precincts of North Dallas to the mesquite-shrouded barrios of South Texas. It was an arbitrary, inflexible approach, promoted by slashing television spots that ran against the grain of the vast majority of moderate-conservative Texans they were designed to reach, yet were perfect for motivating labor-liberal Democratic voters who might otherwise have remained dormant.

From the state headquarters in Dallas, Dee Travis, the campaign manager, spent most of his time running a strong grass roots organization, a traditional Collins asset. Lisette McSoud, the press secretary, generated news releases from her Austin office to the Capitol Press Corps, assisted by Marjorie Tellez. It was a game effort to promote a proud old Republican warhorse, but they were singing the wrong tune. Only the solid conservative base, which Collins had for the taking, would respond to the strident anti-Bentsen advertising proclaiming he was liberal.

By June 1982, Finkelstein had succeeded in bringing news media focus to his concept, but it was hardly encouraging to the GOP cause. On June 17, an editorial in *The Abilene Reporter-News*, quoting *Congressional Quarterly*, contended that "Bentsen voted with President Reagan more frequently than any other Democratic senator last year. Throughout his tenure in the Senate, Bentsen has been regarded as a moderate conservative — not only by his colleagues, but also, as recent polls indicate, by Texas voters."

On that same day, a front page article in *The Austin American-Statesman* reported on a $400,000 NCPAC campaign launched in Texas against Bentsen following a Finkelstein poll showing Bentsen as vulnerable. Bentsen raised the issue that Finkelstein couldn't be working for NCPAC and Collins simultaneously, yet NCPAC remain "independent" to pour such money against him. Bentsen didn't win his point legally, but he continued to complain publicly about the vast amounts of money being used to brand him as a liberal. On June 20, for Clements, the nerve was hit again. A *Fort Worth Star-Telegram* article reported that Collins "is getting no help from Clements in his efforts to brand Sen. Lloyd Bentsen as a liberal ...'I have never viewed Lloyd Bentsen as what my definition of a liberal is ... I've always looked on Lloyd Bentsen as a moderate. He certainly is no conservative,' " Clements said.

George Kuempel, Austin bureau chief for *The Dallas Morning News*, followed with an article which contended that "high-ranking Republicans concede privately that GOP U.S. Rep. Jim Collins has failed dismally in his efforts to portray U.S. Sen. Lloyd Bentsen as a flaming liberal. His attempts to do so, they say, have so strained his credibility he has virtually no chance of unseating the veteran Democrat ..." The ill-fated course led into more troubling water for Collins when he was implicated with a publication of the John Birch Society in a UPI dispatch from Houston, dated July 10: "The Republican challenger for Sen. Lloyd Bentsen's seat is using an article published by the controversial John Birch Society as proof that his Democratic opponent is a liberal ..." Such as that prompted humorist Cactus Pryor's crack in *The Austin American Statesman* of July 23: "Of course, Lloyd Bentsen is a liberal. Just as I told that commie Barry Goldwater ..."

The relationship between Collins and Clements was further strained when the results of a Finkelstein poll in August were released, showing Collins gaining on Bentsen, and Clements having fallen behind Mark White. Release of the polling data caused intense internal friction in Collins's campaign in which some longtime Republicans felt that undercutting the party's governor in order to help establish credibility for Collins was an underhanded way of conducting political business. When asked for reaction to release of the polling data, Clements was quoted by the AP on September 1: "I consider it a breach of good taste and a breach of etiquette for someone to dip into my race. Mr. White can do what he wants. He's my competitor. But I don't like someone else dipping into my race."

Though the incompatability with Collins was an early irritant, Clements had a strong campaign going for him. Republicans, conservative Democrats and independent conservatives related to his tough, uncompromising personality, not beholden to any particular interest groups. Further, he was supported by those who had held the office as Democrats with endorsements by Allan Shivers, John Connally, and Preston Smith. Clements had brought vigorous leadership and sound management skills to the office plus his major programs were generally supported — improving education, including basic curriculum and increased teacher salaries; and strengthening law enforcement, particularly the antidrug thrust. Yet, unrelated to his performance, he faced a serious problem in the economic downturn which had caused parts of the state to be hit hard, creating animosity toward President Reagan and Clements, the man who had played such a prominent role in carrying Texas for him. A staggering peso devaluation had further depressed border areas, creating an anti-Republican climate about which GOP candidates could only grit their teeth. Further, though the Clements campaign was massive, well-organized and heavily financed to the tune of thirteen million dollars, it seemed to lack the central focus and momentum which it had in 1978.

Everyone who ever participated in a losing political campaign has twenty-twenty hindsight, and the Clements 1982 campaign would draw its share of criticism. The general image problem was concluded to have been that too many people perceived Clements to be arrogant and caustic, yet most of his supporters admired his forthright stands and determination to support them. Part of the problem of general perception relating to the governor's record was caused by the fact that twenty-two separate television commercials were aired in the 1982 campaign, a disparate number for the attention and retention spans of most viewers. And even though there was a disparity of themes regarding his record, Clements probably would have achieved better results had he kept the focus on the record rather than let it drift over into a personality clash with White from time to time. In addition, some grass roots Republican leaders complained that the campaign was too oriented toward top-heavy endorsements, mass media advertising, and phone banks with little opportunity for volunteer involvement elsewhere.

On the Mexican-American front, Clements had a remarkable record, having appointed some 170 M-As to important state positions, including eleven to judicial posts, more than any previous governor. He had functioned as a one-man State Department with five meetings with Mexican President Lopez Portillo and two with President-elect Miguel de la Madrid. He had visited the capitals of the four Mexican border states which share a common border with Texas, and had hosted the governors of those states in Austin. Rick Montoya and Eddie Eurispa were M-A operatives beating campaign drums for Clements, along with Jim Richardson, an M-A with an Anglo name. They were working in a favorable atmosphere through half of 1982, building long lists of endorsements for Clements in the M-A community. Brenda Lee Huerta ground out many news releases counting names and statements in favor of Clements, including such familiar Tower supporters as Pete Diaz and Isaac Olivares in the Valley, Clemente Garcia of Corpus Christi, and Tony Salinas, mayor of Hebronville in South Texas. Also, a whole new cadre came aboard for Clements, including such prominent leaders as Ruben Sandoval, civil rights director for national LULAC who denounced "the Bonillas for prostituting themselves" by supporting Mark White. Sandoval lost his job for supporting Clements.

Feelings were running high among Mexican-Americans who had studied the records. Clements, a conservative Republican, had a positive record, particularly in the key area of meaningful appointments, while White, as secretary of state, had opposed the Voting Rights Act and bilingual education, two of the highest-impact issues in the Mexican-American community. Such prominent liberal M-A leaders as Carlos Truan, state senator from Corpus Christi, had scored White when Truan stated in 1978 that "if it had been up to Mark White, Texas would not have been included in the Voting Rights Act." Also quoted in campaign material for Clements were comments adverse to White made by Willie Velasquez, director of the Southwest Voter Registration Project and Ben Reyes, state representative from Houston. But heavy cross pressure came down upon the M-A rank and file from Democratic candidates who bombarded their communities with anti-Reagan, anti-Republican, anti-Clements rhetoric during the hard economic times in South Texas. The combined and cumulative effect created a tide that would turn against Clements.

Willie Nelson reportedly once accused Mark White, the colorless candidate, of having undergone "a charisma bypass." But in 1982, White was glib, coiffured and had suddenly become a populist who would rattle off his points with the regimen of an experienced trial lawyer, repeating endlessly the same evidence. In image, style and political views, he was a total contrast to Clements and he chalked up political mileage accordingly. A Clements campaign tabloid carried an item about White having been arrested for drunken driving when he was a Baylor University law student. Most people in the news media considered that to be a cheap shot and White seized upon it to claim that Clements had dragged the campaign into the gutter, even though White never denied the story.

White would find his pot of political gold through populist-oriented railing against utility companies, contending his election would result in lower rates for consumers. Such pronouncements caused arched eyebrows among some of his close supporters, but he was on a roll with that pitch which his polls showed was scoring with those many thousands of Texans feeling the pinch from high utility bills.

White also promised that he wouldn't raise taxes, a position apparently spawned from ignorance or a total disregard of salient fiscal information at hand. White charged all ills to Clements and promised a big rock candy mountain to every group that would listen. By mid-October he had maneuvered himself into a competitive position though many Democrats were uncomfortable with the type of campaign he was conducting. Dave McNeely, political editor of *The Austin American-Statesman*, certainly no bastion of Republicanism, wrote a column published October 17, that stated, "If Mark White beats Bill Clements for governor, it will be because White is a Democrat in a Democratic year. Even Democrats who want badly to vote for White are hard-pressed for reasons to do so. They look at his lackluster record, listen to his promises he can fix everything without costing taxpayers an additional cent, and shake their heads." McNeely proceeded to compare the candidates. "Clements. He's a pretty good manager, and stands for something, even if it is big business. All White stands for is election ... Clements. He has made some appointments of hard-nosed business folk who can get the job done, while White will appoint political drones whose chief qualification is that they supported him for governor ... White has a lackluster record as attorney general, and is even more demagogic than Clements and Reagan. He's criticizing high utility and interest rates, and talking about protecting consumers, when he never let loose a peep about any of those subjects when it might have made some difference." Still, McNeely could see a strong possibility that "Clements's ornery demeanor, high unemployment, and other problems, against a backdrop of Reaganomics and a Texas Democratic tradition, will push White across."

Those adverse factors were certainly there for Clements but there was another factor developing that would be perhaps even more damaging in the final analysis. Despite almost unanimous denunciation from the news media, Collins pursued the strident liberal label attack against Bentsen. Jan Jarboe observed tartly in the *San Antonio Express* of October 3, "the idea that Bentsen is a liberal is laughable ... All these kinds of advertisements do is reinforce the prevailing view that political candidates, as a class, can't be trusted." Molly Ivins commented on Collins's campaign in her column in *The Dallas Times Herald* of October 26: "The major premise of his campaign — that Lloyd Bentsen is a liberal — is just plain silly. Some days, I seem to be the only human being in the state who publicly admits to being a liberal; so take it from me, Lloyd Bentsen is not a liberal." On the same day an AP article from Austin appeared with the comment that "it would be a stunning political coup if Collins convinced Texas voters that Bentsen is a Kennedy liberal." For his part, Bentsen was hammering back at Collins for being an "extremist" supported by the John Birch Society, NCPAC and the "radical right."

More importantly, the extensive anti-Bentsen advertising had energized the South Texas courthouses where Bentsen alone, among the Democratic candidates, could maximize voter turnout.

About the only blip on Bentsen's radar screen in the closing weeks
came not from Collins but from the Texas Conservative Union. The chairman, Richard Harvey of Tyler, reopened an old wound; he contended
that Bentsen and members of his family had cheated the federal government out of a considerable amount of money through a land scam implemented in the 1950s and 1960s under the Soil Bank Reserve Program.
The AP and some of the large newspapers gave the charge some attention, but Bentsen's spokesmen fogged it up with righteous rhetoric —
more than facts — and Collins let it ride without comment.

Lance Tarrance was again polling for the Clements Campaign and
one reason his 1982 projections would turn out to be well off the mark
is that ordinary polling methodology doesn't always work in vast areas
of South and Southwest Texas. Only those who run the courthouse know
the intensity of their get-out-the-vote effort in a particular race. In 1978,
neither Hill nor Krueger could generate a heavy South Texas vote, but
in 1982 with Bentsen threatened, a heavier Democratic turnout would
be achieved, handing White a big bonus he couldn't have attained otherwise.

George Strake's campaign for lieutenant governor had wobbled at
times like an uncertain hurricane in the Gulf of Mexico. The campaign
started its thrust on a course similar to that of Collins, with Strake branding Hobby as a liberal, but he had pulled down that unlikely line before
the stretch run. Though Strake had been unable to establish a theme or
issue that was generating much support among undecided voters, his handsome appearance and upbeat personality had attracted a strong group of
supporters, plus he had substantial campaign funding available with which
to purchase extensive television advertising. Feeling pressure, Hobby
responded by conducting an all-out campaign, combining forces with
Bentsen and White, who all benefitted from the liberal down-ballot candidates who had built their own followings and thus strengthened their
entire ticket. The situation had its paradoxical side. Some conservative
contributors were pouring their money behind Clements, Bentsen, and
Hobby — with the money going to Bentsen and Hobby being used,
in effect, to defeat Clements. All the factors had melded together to form
a Democratic juggernaut with a full head of steam that was rolling across
the Texas political landscape in October of 1982.

On the Republican side, each candidate for a statewide office conducted his own campaign. There was no ticket, nor cluster of candidates

working together except the State GOP supported them as a team with publicity, including widespread mailings, and considerable amounts of cash. The party's campaign committee, chaired by Russell Pryor of Houston, would place almost a million dollars into various campaigns and the party's staff would provide technical assistance to many candidates. Clements stirred things up a bit on October 21, when he forecast victory for Bill Meier in the attorney general's race and Allen Clark in the race for state treasurer. The other GOP statewide candidates didn't take kindly to being, in effect, written off by the governor, but Clements managed to soften his remarks in response to subsequent questioning.

Tower campaigned five days with Clements during the stretch run and the governor received substantial help on the trail from sports stars, including golf legend Byron Nelson, Dallas Cowboy greats Roger Staubach, Walt Garrison, Billy Joe Dupree, Cliff Harris, and Charlie Waters, whose coach Tom Landry had been campaigning for Clements before the season opened; and Judge Olin Underwood, formerly of the Houston Oilers and Texas Longhorns. John Sammons, mayor of Temple, had organized sixty-four mayors around the state to support Clements, including many in small towns where Republican candidates usually fare poorly. Newspaper support for Clements was widespread, including almost all those in the most populous cities of the state. But so much of the focus of the race was on the personalities of the individuals. An article in *The Dallas Morning News* of October 17, by Sam Attlesey and Sam Kinch, Jr., described the contest as "money-mad, media-wise and mean." It pointed out that White branded Clements as "mean, arrogant and insensitive." Clements had often tagged White as "an incompetent attorney general." Janis Monger of *The Beaumont Enterprise* followed with an article printed on October 24, in which Clements bore down hard on White. "If you're sick and need a doctor, you want a doctor — not some quack. Make no mistake about it, the competency of my opponent is the issue in this campaign." That may have been foremost in Clements's mind but the unified Democrats made it a party against party contest with political winds blowing their way.

On election day, White defeated Clements by a vote of 1,697,870 to 1,465,937, or a margin of 231,933. Bentsen coasted by Collins with a vote of 1,818,223 to 1,256,759, or a margin of 561,464. About the Senate race, Kyle Thompson, editor of *The Fort Worth Star-Telegram* editorial page, had these postelection comments printed on November 21: "By making a major attack on Bentsen, Collins triggered one of the most powerful state political organizations into an all-out effort. As a result, the Democrats were able to get together as they not been able to do in decades. Collins used the wrong tactics and the wrong issues ... He campaigned solidly on the single issue that Bentsen is a super liberal, when Bentsen in fact is looked on by Texans as a moderate at the most, and leaning toward conservatism by many ..." In his postmortem published in *Texas Business* magazine in December, Scott Bennett branded the Collins campaign as "silly, misdirected and frequently outlandish ..." He contended that had the GOP run a campaign similar to that waged in 1976 by Alan Steelman which carried Dallas and Harris Counties, "Clement's totals could have been large enough to carry him to victory."

Saralee Tiede of the Austin bureau of *The Dallas Times-Herald* wrote an interpretative article that appeared on December 20, pointing out that "almost twice as many Hispanics voted in the 1982 governor's race as voted in 1978, and more of them voted for Democrats than had before ..." Though White was the least popular among the Democratic statewide candidates, he still garnered eighty-six percent of the estimated M-A vote in the study that exceeded 300,000. That was based upon an analysis of M-A votes in 262 precincts where eighty percent to 100 percent of the registered voters had Spanish surnames in thirty-six counties of South and Southwest Texas. The study had been conducted by the Willie Velasquez organization in San Antonio.

Within forty-eight hours of the election, Mark White was explaining that he really couldn't lower utility rates, but that he hoped the Public Utility Commission and the Legislature would read his victory as cause for action. And he would not only ignore his no-tax increase pledge but he would ram a record tax bill through the Legislature. But in the bitter aftermath of the 1982 elections, weary GOP workers weren't taking consolation from White's self-created credibility problems, they were licking their wounds and worrying about regrouping for the next election.

So much effort and resources had been put into the various down-ballot statewide campaigns, yet none attained more than forty-two percent of the vote. Adding salt to Republican wounds were Congressional results in which all three of the new seats went to Democrats. Former Arlington Mayor Tom Vandergriff defeated Jim Bradshaw of Fort Worth in the so-called mid-cities district containing densely populated areas between Dallas and Fort Worth; Mike Andrews defeated Mike Faubion in the Houston area district; and Solomon Ortiz of Corpus Christi defeated Jason Luby, former mayor of Corpus Christi, in the South Texas district dominated by that coastal city. Also defeated was Republican Jeff Wentworth of San Antonio, a Bexar County commissioner who was given a good chance of unseating longtime Congressman Abraham (Chick) Kazen of Laredo in the South Texas Twenty-third District stretching between those two cities.

Clinton Manges had promoted Garry Mauro with $50,000 and he financed campaigns against a number of Republicans, including the defeat of Judge John Clark of San Antonio, a fine appellate judge appointed by Clements. Clark's district covered a considerable amount of territory outside San Antonio, but four of the Clements appointees as district judges in Bexar County withstood the Democratic tide. Roy Barrera, Jr., David Berchelmann, David Peoples, and Tom Rickhoff were elected to terms as reform judges, not beholden to the old one-party corrupting political system that had ruled Bexar County for decades.

Former Dallas City Councilman Steve Bartlett replaced Jim Collins in the Third Congressional District, having won the primary runoff, tantamount to election, over Kay Bailey Hutchison, a former state representative from Houston. Dede Casad, Dee Travis, and Dallas County Commissioner Jim Jackson had been squeezed out by Bartlett and Hutchison. Don Henderson defeated House colleague Frank Hartung to succeed Mengden in the Houston state senate district and Bob McFarland succeeded Betty Andujar who had retired. For the election cycle, the Texas GOP held its own in the Congressional delegation but lost a net of three seats in the Senate where the blatant gerrymandering by the Democrats was effective. In the Texas House the delegation showed a net gain of one seat to thirty-seven, thanks to the 1981 changes from Democrat to Republican by prominent incumbent House members Ray Keller of Duncanville in Dallas County, and George Pierce of San Antonio. They became new members of the GOP delegation along with Barry Connelly, Bob Echols, Talmadge Heflin, Paul Hilbert and Mike Toomey from the Houston — Harris County area; Bill Hammond, Patricia Hill and Gwyn Shea from Dallas County; and Jan McKenna from nearby Arlington; Arves Jones, Sr., of El Paso, and Edmund Kuempel of Seguin.

Though losing the governorship was a crushing blow, along with all the other statewide races, the 1982 election was not a defeat in depth as some in the past had been. For the future, the Republican base in Texas was secure.

CHAPTER FIFTEEN

A Memorable Last Hurrah

For four years Tower had been out of the burning spotlight of party leadership in the vast State of Texas. Suddenly, he was there again as lightning rod and spokesman for Texas Republicans whose morale had been shattered by the defeat of Bill Clements. Yet, Tower was now fifty-seven, and his responsibilities in Washington — particularly as chairman of the Armed Services Committee — required him to spend more time there. Time was too precious a commodity to be used constantly riding the "red eyes," going back and forth on late-night weekend flights in order to promote party activities and candidates.

The high and middle-echelon party leaders understood full well that Tower's role was vital in 1983 to keep the party together, and that he must be reelected in 1984 when there would be no opportunity to recapture the governor's chair. Nancy Palm, with improving health, had reemerged in a party leadership position, as a member of the SREC from Harris County where she had served as such an effective county chairman. She spoke out with a call, echoed by Republicans all over the state, that the GOP must circle the wagons around Tower again, even while grumbling mounted over the party's state chairman, Chet Upham, who was Clements's choice and Tower's friend.

Few people entertained the idea that Tower would not seek reelection. In the fall of 1982, on a ranch near Austin, Tower had hosted a big barbecue. This was a festive function for current staff and spouses, plus people who had previously worked on his campaign or Senate operations, with their spouses. There were hundreds of "Tower people" there,

276

ostensibly to begin thinking about another reelection campaign. He had hosted a similar function prior to his 1978 campaign, also well in advance of the usual starting time. In addition, Brad O'Leary, the professional GOP fund-raiser, had been socking in heavy cash to the Tower Senate Club fund whose contributors were under the distinct impression that their money would be used for a 1984 reelection campaign. Further, President Reagan had agreed to do a fund-raising event in Houston that would raise a million dollars. The visible indicators were evident that Tower was aiming for another term, but a few insiders were concerned about his Texas visits in 1983, mostly to large cities. There was no "cow county" strategy of reaching rural Texas, the deficiency that almost lost the 1978 race. Perhaps, they surmised, Tower was just being stretched too thin and would have to rely on a strong metro-urban strategy to win another term.

While Texas Republicans circled the wagons around Tower, another potential star suddenly appeared. Phil Gramm, the "Boll Weevil" conservative Democrat congressman from College Station, had been chastised by the House Democratic leadership for having worked closely with the Reagan Administration for passage of its economic program. Boll Weevil was a term describing those Southern Democratic members of Congress who broke with their partisan leadership to support Reagan's program. Gramm was among the most vocal and most closely associated with the Administration. For his sins, he was stripped of his seat on the House Budget Committee in January 1983, whereupon he resigned his Congressional seat in a dramatic gesture, declared himself a Republican and proceeded to win a special election on Lincoln's birthday, February 12.

Since Gramm's district was marginal Republican country, the special election drew substantial media coverage as a test of Reagan's strength as well as Gramm's bold move. The extensive coverage not only helped him win the House seat as a Republican, but it gave him strong statewide identification in the event Tower decided not to seek reelection. Gramm, a forty-one-year-old former economics professor at Texas A & M, brought to political life extensive experience and expertise in his field. He coauthored the Gramm – Latta Budget, mandating heavy spending reduction in fiscal years 1982 – 1984, and several other measures designed to reduce federal spending, initiatives almost all Republicans would approve. His effective leadership in pursuing Reagan's three-year tax cut placed him at the top of the list of the most productive Boll Weevils. His 1983 quickie reelection campaign was as much against Tip O'Neill as it was for Phil Gramm, which was sound strategy in that most Republicans considered Speaker O'Neill to be an anti-Reagan anachronism presiding over a House he wouldn't admit had become more conservative, even though the GOP had taken the Presidency and control of the Senate. Gramm appeared to be one of those few politicians who learn fast and don't repeat mistakes. In 1976, he had challenged the incumbent Lloyd Bentsen in the Democratic Primary for United States Senate and had taken a tremendous drubbing, receiving only about thirty percent of the vote. But in 1978, he was elected to the House and proceeded to build a strong base. As a candidate after votes or an officeholder in pursuit of legislative objectives, Gramm was perceived somewhat as an irrepressible hound dog, never breaking stride or missing a scent along the trail until the end of a successful hunt.

In the spring of 1983, an agreement was worked out whereby Chet Upham and Dorothy Doehne, chairman and vice-chairman respectively of the State GOP, would resign and be replaced by George Strake and Diana Denman of San Antonio. That change brought about the departure from the state GOP headquarters of Wayne Thorburn, the veteran executive director. During Tower's tenure in the Senate, only two executive directors had been able to survive in that hot spot for more than a couple of years, Thorburn and Marvin Collins, who each were there about five years. Richard Box and Kay Danks, longtime Travis County GOP leaders, were cochairmen for a roast honoring Thorburn on June 18 in Austin. The fact that three people who held the office of state chairman — Ray Barnhart, Chet Upham, and George Strake — came to poke fun and pay tribute to Thorburn was testimony to their appreciation of his effectiveness. He was replaced by John Maxwell, a GOP operative from Iowa. Between January and August, speculation abounded as to how Tower would structure his reelection campaign and whom he might draw for a Democratic opponent. Any primary opponent who might file against him would have no chance of generating a battle in the uncertain climate that existed following the defeat of Clements. The Reagan fund-raiser in Houston in late April not only netted Tower's campaign fund in the range of a million dollars but it generated a substantial amount of positive publicity, underscoring the close working relationship that existed between the senator and the Reagan Administration. But all subsequent news media coverage wasn't of a positive nature. There was a long feature article by Mark Nelson of *The Dallas Morning News*, Washington bureau, which appeared on June 27, under a headline of TOWER BACKERS NERVOUS, PROBLEMS PLAGUE 1984 CAMPAIGN. Nelson contended that despite all the heavy fund-raising efforts, Tower had not reactivated a campaign organization in the state. It was noted that his longtime advisor and former campaign manager, Ken Towery, would not be available. "Some members of the Tower organization believe Towery thought the senator's wife, Lilla, had too much influence in the 1978 race," Nelson wrote. "Towery refused to comment on those statements." Nelson pointed out that Krueger was campaigning as the frontrunner for the Democratic nomination with State Senator Lloyd Doggett of Austin, a liberal and outspoken consumer advocate, announced and running. This was in addition to Dolph Briscoe and Congressman Kent Hance, a Boll Weevil from Lubbock, who were pawing the sand in the background.

By logical standards, Krueger was the frontrunner at the moment, with name identification from the previous race. However, life out front early in a political campaign means one becomes the target for potshots from all sorts of quarters. Kyle Thompson, editorial page editor of the *Fort Worth Star-Telegram*, wrote a biting column that appeared June 19, taking Krueger to task for waffling on issues, recalling the 1978 waffle on his pro AFL – CIO votes, and detailing a 1983 waffle on developing nuclear energy. A onetime exponent of such projects, Krueger had recently changed stands, prompting Thompson to comment: "Perhaps the forty-eight-year-old New Braunfels bachelor could get Jane Fonda to come to Texas on his behalf this time in view of his recent stand against nuclear power." In an article that appeared in the July 18 edition of *The Dallas Morning News*, Sam Attlesey pointed out that Doggett, though short of money and name identification, had some strong factors going for him "because of the more progressive bent Democratic primary voters have followed in recent years ..." He quoted John White, longtime Texas Democratic political figure and former Democratic National Chairman: "The dynamics of our primary now lend themselves to Doggett ..."

On how to defeat Tower, Democratic State Chairman Bob Slagle had a quick fix. In mid-August he was quoted in a *Wichita Falls Times* article by Michelle Locke: "The only way Tower's been able to hang in all these years is that he's been able to cut into the Hispanic vote. We're going to be turning out the voters in droves in the fall of 1984." In point of fact, Tower's Mexican-American base, particularly among young business executives and professionals, had continued to grow. Oscar Gomez of San Angelo, a telephone company executive and president of the school board, was an example of many who openly supported Tower from philosophical conviction, trust, community concern, or combinations thereof. Goodfellow Air Force Base stood within the bedrock of the San Angelo economy and Tower had been instrumental in keeping it open when the outlook hadn't been all that upbeat. The same was true in Corpus Christi, where the Naval Air Station remained at full strength and the economy of San Antonio was dependent upon various military installations remaining open and well-funded. That was Tower's mission and more people in those high-impact areas understood it. With the chairmanship of the Armed Services Committee, Tower was at the zenith of his power during his tenure in the Senate.

From a general strategic standpoint, Tower's longtime associates viewed him as being in a strong position for 1984, assuming a reasonably productive economy would propel the Reagan – Bush ticket to another victory in Texas. However, early on the morning of August 23, Tower was in the vortex of a storm about to explode in the Texas political arena.

Tower's longtime political associates in Austin were swamped with calls from Republicans and people in the news media trying to verify a story that had appeared in *The Houston Post* to the effect that Tower would not seek reelection. Wire services had picked up the story that morning, causing it to be heard on the early morning radio newscasts. Tower had called a news conference in the state capitol for 1:00 P.M. that day, the purpose of which had not been announced. Since he was unavailable for comment prior to the news conference, and his staff refused to comment on the story, it was presumed to be true.

As word spread around the capital city and the state, Tower and his wife, Lilla, plus a few staff members came to the Capitol for the news conference. Old friends and political associates, such as Hub Bechtol, the Austin realtor, and Ken Towery, the longtime advisor, trudged in with long faces, showing strain and lines of concern and disbelief. A Texas political legend was about to self-destruct before their eyes and they were none too anxious to witness it.

A large crowd gathered in the chamber of the Texas House of Representatives where Tower and his wife were seated, and hundreds more were in the gallery upstairs. Of the capitol correspondents who had covered Tower in 1960 when he made his first statewide race, only two had been there through all those intervening years, Garth Jones of AP and Lee Jones, no relation, with the *Fort Worth Star-Telegram*, formerly with AP. Of the news photographers, only Ted Powers of AP was still on the scene.

Tower's statement was short and to the point. He would retire after the end of his present term "at the peak of my productivity" in order to "pursue other avenues of endeavor." Tower praised Texans for having given him the privilege of serving after four election victories.

> To those who have given me their encouragement, support, dedication, and friendship, I will never be able to adequately express my profound appreciation. I also wish to thank my colleagues who have entrusted me with positions of leadership in the Senate. These respon-

sibilities I have attempted to meet to the best of my ability. The confidence and trust they have placed in me have been a source of strength and satisfaction that few who enter public service come to know.

I have informed President Reagan of my decision and have volunteered to serve in an appropriate position in his reelection campaign.

In the question and answer period, Tower contended he had no health problems nor fear of losing a forthcoming campaign.

... The longer you stay around, [the more you] run the risk of getting maybe a little cynical and not having as much vigor for your job. I still have a great deal of vigor for my job [and] a great deal of enthusiasm for it. I think that is the time to leave. I've seen some of my colleagues stay around longer than I believe they should have.

Ken Towery had been sitting in the gallery, chewing on a cigar and stewing over what was said. When the news conference ended, he marched from the gallery to the floor near the Towers. One of his friends, upon seeing the angry expression on Towery's face, detained him for a moment as he began commenting in stern tones about the decision. Seconds later, a few reporters converged upon Towery, who continued his adverse comments. *The Houston Post* carried an article the following day that said Towery "stopped just short of accusing the senator of committing political treason by abruptly bowing out of his reelection race next year. 'I don't believe all that stuff,' a grim-faced Ken Towery grumbled after listening to the senator list the reasons he would not seek a fifth term in office. 'I think the real reason is sitting at his right arm,' Towery said of the senator's wife, Lilla ..."

Party leaders and political operatives were puzzled by the decision since they knew Tower enjoyed high standing in the Senate and in public opinion polls. Some simply accepted the theory that he was "burnt out" from the grueling pace and the fact that the Senate was no longer the reflective, deliberative body that it was when Everett Dirksen and his like were the leaders. State GOP Chairman George Strake said he was

... indeed shocked when Senator Tower informed me last evening of his decision ... I was also saddened to think of the loss, to Texas and to the United States, of the leadership of John Tower ... He is synonymous with strong national defense and Texas jobs ... He has pioneered the Republican effort into the Hispanic community of Texas and they will have lost a good friend when the Senate convenes in 1985 ... Whatever endeavor he chooses to follow in the future, I will be cheering him on ...

Letters, telegrams, and phone calls poured into Tower's offices, recalling times past and wishing him well. Wrote Lance Tarrance,

> I want you to know that the reason I stayed in politics after the defeat of Barry Goldwater in 1964 was my brief association with you during that campaign as a very young man and later in your reelection effort in 1966. That election was a great 'political comeback' as opponents, journalists, and Democrats thought we were going to lose ... Your personal and political history has touched my life in many ways and I want to thank you very, very much for your direct and indirect guidance ...

From a longtime political associate came a note commenting on the withdrawal,

> You surely do possess the unique power to create a hurricane far from the Gulf ...

And on the farewell to arms,

> I had relished the opportunity of a rematch with Krueger, but I'm beginning to believe that [expletive deleted] won't be nominated again — Doggett is dogging him unmercifully on issues and Hance has cut off a lot of potential funding ...

Every front page in the state carried its version of Tower's withdrawal. To the mark, Ron Hutcheson of the *Fort Worth Star-Telegram* Austin bureau led his story:

> For more than two decades, John Tower broke the rules of Texas politics by running — and winning — as a Republican in a state full of Democrats. On Tuesday, he quit while he was ahead.

Most editorial comment and feature stories were favorable. On August 25, *The Dallas Morning News* proclaimed,

> Throughout Tower's tenure in the Senate, Texas's basic conservatism never has lacked representation. There are conservatives, to be sure, who fault the senator for this or that political infidelity. Yet Tower's voting record as a whole is overwhelmingly hostile to Big Government, overwhelmingly friendly to private enterprise and the requirements of a strong national defense ... John Tower, for twenty-two years, has made Texas an energetic and principled senator. He deserves much gratitude, of which we're pleased to accord him a portion.

The Lubbock Avalanche-Journal of August 24, commented editorially,

Texas should pause for a moment to salute Senator Tower and the job he has done in the Senate for twenty-two years. He is unique in Texas history. As the first and only Republican elected statewide until Bill Clements became governor in 1978, Tower has been in tune with the prevailing Texas philosophy throughout his tenure in Washington ... To say the least, his conservative voice in the Senate will be missed.

The Midland Reporter-Telegram of August 25, commented that Tower's tenure leading to the election of Clements brought about the moment that

... Texas was confirmed as a two-party state ... The Republican Party in Texas will miss Tower, too, regardless of what party officials claim or Tower suggests. It's entirely true that during the past several years the party has gained in strength and credibility, but in party politics the loss of a statewide officeholder is significant, regardless of how it comes.

The Corpus Christi Caller of August 26, contended that even if the Texas GOP couldn't hold the Senate seat, Tower's tenure had ensured the continuation of two-party politics in the state.

A *Lufkin News* editorial of August 24, tagged Tower as "Littlefoot."

Though short of physical stature, Tower has cast a large shadow across national politics. Littlefoot leaves behind a big pair of boots to fill.

Dave McNeely, who covered Tower throughout most of his tenure, observed in the August 28 edition of *The Austin American-Statesman* that

... respect for him in GOP congressional circles has grown steadily, especially over the last few years. It's partly because of his consistency, businesslike attitude and relative evenhandedness ... He has headed the Senate's Republican Policy Committee since 1973, and a commit-tee aide describes him as 'the only man in the Republican Party who can keep his colleagues under control.'

McNeely pointed out the demanding, tedious and unpleasant aspects of serving in a "year-round, almost seven-day-a-week job" filled with "four-teen-hour days." His supporters were certainly disappointed, McNeely surmised, "but from Tower's personal point of view, to go out undefeated, to go to a life in his sixties that's a bit more sedate and dignified than the turbulent Senate — why not?"

In a wide-ranging feature article, veteran editorial writer Ron Calhoun of the *Dallas Times Herald* took a careful and at points nostalgic look at the tenure of Tower.

[He] could have been reelected to another term next year, of that I'm reasonably certain ... Undoubtedly, Senator Tower has seen about all the territory that is worth seeing from the windows of a campaign plane, has heard all the flattery and condemnation that he can reasonably stand, and is weary of dousing all those campaign brush fires that inevitably flare at the wrong time. I am convinced he also was fed up with responding to all the special interests groups that make up Texas ...

Calhoun surmised that though Tower had strikes against him as a politician, in physical stature, and party affiliation, he possessed an equalizer.

... Tower has the best speaking voice I have heard in the Texas political arena, and that covers a lot of verbosity ... it was strong, clear and manly. His articulation inspired confidence and made Tower sound far more authoritative than he was in his early Senate days, and just as authoritative as he became in the latter part of his senatorial career. I'm going to miss Tower. Crossing verbal swords with him was a pleasure. No stuffed-shirt he, Tower had a great wit, was a good sport and was a fair amateur actor. I'll never forget appearing with him in those fun-filled Buddy Beck – Joe Barta productions here in Dallas of *Casablanca*, in which he played the Peter Lorre role; the Roaring Twenties party and celebration of the 50th anniversary of the Lindberg transAtlantic flight in which he played New York Mayor Jimmy Walker; the Gene Autry radio show takeoff in which he sang, *I'm Back in the Saddle Again*, and the memorable *Superman* comic strip takeoff in which he soared in the lead role and was photographed for the front page of the *New York Times* and *Time* magazine in his Superman outfit ... More than any other Republican, he was responsible for making Texas a healthy two-party state, and cracking the Democratic Solid South ... Now he wants to go back to teaching and close the circle a winner, knowing that he played a real-life role in keeping the nation the leader of the free world.

Calhoun pointed out that in historical perspective, Tower's tenure would make him the third longest in service among United States Senators from Texas. Morris Sheppard died in office in 1941, after serving more than twenty-eight years, and Tom Connally, one of the drafters of the United Nations charter, retired in 1953, after almost twenty-four years, only two months longer than Tower's tenure.

Tower, a quintessential Texas history buff who held the Senate seat in which Sam Houston had served, is one of the few Texans known to be able to whistle the difficult, obscure tune, *Will You Come To The Bower*, the only "marching song" played by Houston's army when it attacked

General Santa Anna at the decisive Battle of San Jacinto which spawned the Republic of Texas in 1836.

Tower's withdrawal created frenzied activity among Texas Republicans seeking a successor. Congressman Ron Paul of Lake Jackson announced his candidacy within an hour after Tower's statement, but party leaders temporized as several names were bandied about. Within forty eight hours, two prominent possibilities, Congressmen Bill Archer of Houston, and Tom Loeffler of Hunt, had issued statements declining candidacy and it was becoming obvious that Gramm had postured himself almost perfectly to make the race. Party leaders wanted him and he would satisfy their desires after receiving ample encouragement and publicity. On August 25, a front page photo of Gramm and a lead story in *The Dallas Morning News* propelled him onto center stage. This came along with the news that Paul Eggers, known to be close to Tower, favored Gramm, as did several members of the SREC. William Murchison, editorial page writer for *The Dallas Morning News*, wrote a prophetic ending to an article about Tower that appeared on August 30:

> The philosophical realignment is not all that John Tower has helped achieve during twenty-two years in the U.S. Senate, but it is among the things of which he can be proudest. How hard U.S. Senator Phil Gramm, that reform conservative Democrat, will have to work, come January '85, to keep up the pace!

On September 22, Gramm made it official with his announcement of candidacy at the state capitol. He bore down hard on the effects of economic change under the Reagan program.

> Our economic progress is not just reflected in abstract numbers. We have brought down the average mortgage payment for a new home in Texas by $191 a month. A Texas family earning $20,000 a year has $3,000 more buying power today than it would have had if the Carter inflation had continued ... We have dug out from under the economic rubble of a recession which started four months before any budget cut or tax cut went into effect and ignited a strong recovery which has created over a million and a half new jobs this year ... I will not, in this campaign, imitate the practice of those who seek to divide our state and nation into narrowly defined special interest groups whose votes can be bought by piling a heavier burden of taxes and inflation on the backs of our working people.

In the question and answer session, Gramm charged that the Democrats in Congress can outbid Republicans for special interest votes "because there is no bottom line and it isn't their money." Gramm was selling a

brand of what some would describe as populist conservatism, but by whatever tag the message might warrant, it would have broad acceptance at
the grass roots.

Rob Mosbacher, former aide to Senator Howard Baker and son of
a prominent Houston Republican fund-raiser, Bob Mosbacher, would enter
the race, but most observers considered Gramm to be the odds-on
favorite.

Tower was soon named to head the Reagan – Bush Texas Campaign,
a role he would relish as his last hurrah in the state's political arena,
but a move that would cause grumbling among longtime Reaganites
who held a grudge against Tower for the heresy he had committed by
supporting Ford in 1976. However, they were anxious to see Reagan
reelected and friction was held to a minimum. Since his own political
fortunes were no longer of concern, Tower had time and a campaign war
chest to use during the winter of 1983 to enhance the opportunity for
success of the ticket in 1984. He commissioned some spadework to be
done in the high impact Mexican-American counties of Bexar, El Paso,
and Nueces. There he expected Reagan – Bush to run strong, and qualified M-A candidates could strengthen the ticket. Local Republican leaders seemed to have taken close looks at what might be accomplished except in Bexar County where State Senate District Twenty-six became a
focal point. Incumbent Democrat Bob Vale, an M-A with an Anglo name,
had not drawn much attention from ART or the State GOP, largely because Clements had failed to carry that difficult district. It meanders from
heavily Democratic turf on the West Side of San Antonio out to the north-
ern edge of Bexar County where high growth areas tend to vote Republican.

Jim Lunz, former Bexar County GOP chairman, had a hunch that
the district hadn't been analyzed fully, that statistics being discussed only
reflected the surface. Lunz had honed his political skills by managing
winning campaigns for Congressman Tom Loeffler of Hunt, State Representative Gerald Geistweidt of Mason, and Judge Roy Barrera, Jr., who
was the top GOP vote-getter in Bexar County from 1982.

Winning a state senate seat in Bexar County would be a signal Republican breakthrough and Lunz didn't want to pass up an opportunity, uphill
though it might be. Working with the Tower Senate Club, he secured
an entirely different analysis done by Don MacIver, the political consultant
who had targetted state senate districts for ART during the highly productive 1980 program in which three incumbent Democrats were unseated.
MacIver isolated the vote of two successful countywide Republican candidates, Barrera and fellow district judge David Berchelmann, in the Vale

district. It was a particularly interesting study of ticket-splitting since Barrera — a Mexican-American Republican — had defeated an Anglo Democrat and Berchelmann — an Anglo Republican — had defeated a Mexican-American Democrat. The study revealed that Barrera carried the district with fifty-eight percent, Berchelmann by fifty-four.

Assuming a suitable candidate could be found, Lunz knew the race was not only winnable from an unusual standpoint of down-ballot ticket-splitting, but that in a Presidential election year, higher GOP Northside voter turnout was in prospect. Since Barrera had run so well in that district, Lunz asked him to consider making the race against Vale, a lackluster legislator who was vulnerable for having accepted considerable amounts of campaign funding from Clinton Manges. Barrera was interested, but found he didn't live in the district. Lunz then approached Ernesto Ancira, a prominent businessman, but he was unable to make the race. A Mexican-American candidate was preferable, but if a qualified candidate couldn't be found, an Anglo must make the race, Lunz reasoned, because he was convinced the race could be won. As the candidate filing deadline neared, Lunz discussed the situation with Cyndi Taylor Krier, a young San Antonio attorney and former key staff member for Tower, with whom Lunz served on the Bexar County GOP Candidate Recruitment Committee. She decided to make the race. She had substantial identity in the party from participation and from having represented Republican Alan Schoolcraft in his quest to be seated in the Texas House of Representatives, a position ultimately vindicated by the voters in a special election. It proved to be a fortunate situation for the GOP since Krier would attract unified support in Bexar County and from Tower and his "people" from all over the state. There hadn't been a Republican state senator from Bexar County in modern history nor were there any women serving in the Texas Senate since the retirement of Betty Andujar. Cyndi Krier had quite a challenge on her hands.

In the Republican Primary all eyes were on the United States Senate race to determine who would try to hold the seat Tower was leaving. Most Texas Republicans considered that to be "their seat," and they were taking dead aim to hold it. The leadership was obviously for Gramm and the only question seemed to be whether he would bring enough of the rank and file to win without a runoff. In addition to Congressman Ron Paul and Rob Mosbacher, who would be sufficiently funded to mount a major effort, Hank Grover, ever the candidate, had filed for the race. Gramm shrewdly ran close to Reagan with high-impact television spots and printed material displaying the admiration the President held for the former conservative Democrat who had tweaked Tip O'Neill in a way that really hurt. Gramm's campaign hit upon one of those powerful theme lines that enhance substantially the effectiveness of mass media advertising, *Common Sense ... Uncommon Courage.* That catchy language capsuled Gramm's recent political history in a memorable manner. In addition to the effective mass media, Gramm campaigned hard on a personal basis around the state, helping generate an extensive grass roots organization under the direction of Richard McBride, the campaign manager who was formerly a longtime operative for the Republican National Committee.

From his years of Congressional service and as a competitive candidate, Ron Paul had some grass roots support, but he was perceived by many as more of a Libertarian than a Republican, particularly relating to his isolationist foreign policy views. Mosbacher campaigned hard, attracting mostly younger people, but he was new in the Texas political arena and far behind Gramm in credibility and identification. Grover never lit a match in this one and finished a dismal fourth with less than three percent of the vote. Mosbacher was third with about eight percent and Paul garnered sixteen- and one-half. Gramm waltzed home with the nomination, piling up seventy-three percent from the 339,265 people who voted in the 1984 Republican Primary, a record turnout for a nonpresidential primary vote.

The GOP primary was also notable in that for the first time in his long tenure as a state senator, Ike Harris of Dallas received a serious challenge. Jeff Moseley of Carrollton, a former Gramm aide, took on Harris for allegedy having grown out of touch with his district. Moseley stirred up quite a bit of publicity, including a column in *The Dallas Times Herald* in which Ron Calhoun termed the contest "highly entertaining," because of the image contrast between Harris, "a certified fun-loving, bird hunting, good ole boy," versus Moseley, "a self-proclaimed born-again Christian" strongly opposed to horse race betting which Harris had championed for years. Harris didn't take the challenge lightly. With his aide, John Heal, he covered the district thoroughly en route to a convincing victory. Moseley's bid pointed up the reality that in Republican-packed districts,' such as Harris's, the danger to an incumbent is only in the primary. Such was the case two years previously when then-State Representative Bill Blythe of Houston challenged incumbent Senator Buster Brown of Lake Jackson, in a bitter primary battle won by Brown.

In the Democratic Primary for United States Senate, Krueger had been perceived as the frontrunner from having made the close race against Tower and having kept active politically in the interim. But Krueger was at his best when slashing away at a frontrunner as he had done in 1974 to Nelson Wolff and to John Tower in 1978. In 1984, he was caught in the middle with Doggett raking him over the coals for having been too conservative, supporting right-to-work and other liberal anathemas while Kent Hance, the Boll Weevil congressman from Lubbock, was an attractive, hard-hitting conservative who was solidifying support on the right. The result was that Krueger came in third, barely losing out of a runoff with Doggett and Hance, almost even with each other, running slightly ahead of Krueger. Old-line liberals suddenly found themselves in a political time warp. After all those years, they were confronted by a strong conservative, an echo of Shivers and Connally, who could reestablish conservative credibility in the Texas Democratic Party. Some had fought since Tower's first election in 1961 to undermine conservative Democrat strength with the goal of creating a lasting philosophical realignment in a strong two-party system.

Krueger's endorsement of Hance made the liberals' situation even more dicey in the runoff. A Hance nomination would mean a dramatic reversal of the trend, and the liberals pulled out all the stops behind the scenes, including the solicitation of help from a few veteran Republicans with the acumen and moxie to explain that a Hance nomination would seriously hurt Gramm's chances in November. How many votes may have turned on such esoteric political maneuvering is pure speculation, but the runoff was a cliffhanger which Doggett won by only about a thousand votes. With Doggett's nomination, liberal domination of Texas Democrats was reaffirmed and showcased. Gramm's posture firmly alongside President Reagan made Gramm's path to victory clear indeed.

In mid-April, the Reagan–Bush state headquarters had its formal opening under the leadership of Tower as chairman. His cochairman was Martha Weisend of Dallas, an SREC member who was also head of the Dallas County steering committee for Gramm. The headquarters was located in a two-story building near the corner of Congress Avenue and First Street in downtown Austin, a stone's throw from the Colorado River, also known as Town Lake. Executive director of the campaign was Linden Kettlewell, a savvy GOP organizational operative with extensive experience at state and national levels.

Activity picked up at the headquarters, but the adrenalin didn't flow until soon after the Democratic National Convention nominated Walter Mondale and Geraldine Ferraro in July. In the afterglow of that process, the Democratic ticket flared up in some polls to a position ahead of the yet to be nominated Reagan–Bush ticket. With his superb sense of timing, Reagan decided to make an immediate hard thrust instead of waiting for the August GOP national convention in Dallas. He and Bush came to Austin on July 25 for a hastily organized but highly successful rally at Auditorium Shores, a large open area adjacent to the south bank of Town Lake near the Hyatt Regency Hotel. With sprightly music and thousands of colorful balloons filling the air, some 12,000 supporters gathered to cheer Reagan and Bush. The President and Vice-President were bolstered on the stage by John Tower, Phil Gramm, Bill Clements, John Connally, and Allan Shivers, the distinguished former governor whose participation in the 1984 Reagan – Bush campaign would be his last hurrah. A few months later death would claim Shivers, whose prominent political activity spanned four decades.

Reagan sang to the choir with some strong notes, including his assertion that the Democratic ticket had moved *so far left they've left America*. Democrats, he said, gave Texas "the back of their hand" by not nominating Bentsen for vice president. Reagan scored more points by framing those on the Democratic ticket as big spenders who would raise taxes, and he hit on popular issues such as prayer in public schools and the need for a strong national defense. Perhaps most important was the timing, producing a colorful, successful rally that generated positive national news, blunting momentum the Mondale – Ferraro ticket had achieved.

Tower was elated, having the President choose the capital of Texas for such a major campaign event which he and others viewed as a kickoff that Tower's organization had helped make a success. It had been a hot rally politically and weatherwise at about ninety degrees with fifty-five percent humidity, causing at least sixty people to receive medical assistance, four of whom collapsed from heat exhaustion.

Free bus transportation had been provided from various points around the city and campaign observers on the buses reported to the state headquarters the most encouraging news of the day — most of those thousands of citizens using the buses were certainly not from the country club set about whom the Democrats railed, but from the middle class whose citizens would decide the election.

Apparently stung by the bold Reagan move, Mondale scheduled a rally in Austin for August 1, at which Ferraro would appear with him at the state capitol before an estimated crowd of 8,000 — or 4,000 less than the estimate for the Reagan – Bush rally. "The campaign for the future of America begins in Austin," Mondale declared, but as John C. Henry of *The Austin American-Statesman* pointed out, "the two Democrats called the Austin rally their formal campaign kickoff, a description they used earlier in the day at a similar rally in Jackson, Mississippi." In any event, the high-intensity rallies by both tickets in Austin early on underscored what every astute political analyst understood — Texas was viewed as a pivotal battleground.

The Republican National Convention in Dallas August 20 – 23 was notable not so much for what happened as for what did not happen. It went off without a major hitch, which was exactly what campaign planners had hoped and had worked for during long months of preparation. By GOP convention time, more problems had set in for the Democratic ticket, including those related to financial dealings by Ferraro's husband and the abortion issue in which Catholic Ferraro's pro-choice position was portrayed as against the basic teachings of her church. Polls were trending strongly toward Reagan – Bush, creating an atmosphere of optimism and caution, of *steady as you go* without taking chances or permitting brush fires from flaming into unfavorable hot "media event" situations.

Chief among those who made the convention a success was Fred Meyer, chairman of the Dallas County GOP and chairman of the Republican Host Committee for the convention. Working with Reagan – Bush campaign officials and those of the Republican National Committee, Meyer mixed the necessary funding and organizational matrix to bring about a smooth operation. Serving as chairman of the Arrangements Committee was Ernie Angelo, GOP national committeeman for Texas, and longtime Reagan campaign leader. Key fund-raisers included Trammell Crow, the real estate developer par excellence, chairman of the $3.9 million Convention Fund, raised from corporations and individuals; and Jim Francis, veteran political operative who had become an executive in Bright Industries which has controlling interest in the Dallas Cowboys. Martha Weisend was vice-chairman of Meyer's committee and Lynne Tweedell was chairman of that committee's volunteer brigade. Providing hospitality and entertainment for the delegates was a group known as the Dallas Welcoming Committee, headed by Dave Fox, prominent developer, and Linda Perryman, who served as executive director. About the only major problem for the delegates, particularly those from cooler climates, was the intense summer heat, but the convention hall was well-cooled as were most facilities where the varied convention-related activities took place.

With little concern about controversy during the convention, most of the news media people spent time with political leaders speculating about the stretch run of the campaigns about to unfold, and reflecting upon historical perspectives. In an interview with Dave McNeely that appeared in the *Austin American-Statesman* of August 26, Tower spoke of this being the ninth national convention that he had attended, serving as delegate in seven, including 1984. "What we're seeing nationally is sort of a party realignment that's going on," Tower said. "Traditional voting patterns are changing over the country. Some of the traditional

Republican areas in the Northeast are becoming more Democratic, and traditional Democratic areas in the Sun Belt and the West are becoming more Republican — which in my view is a good omen for Republicans because the demographic movement in this country is to the South and West." McNeely wrote that Tower's decision to bow out at the peak of his career had stunned Republicans, but he continued to believe he had made the right decision, and that his efforts on behalf of Reagan and Gramm would be successful. "I would expect both Reagan and Gramm to carry the state," Tower said, "provided our organization does its job in getting out its maximum potential vote. In 1982, (when Clements was defeated) the Democrats did a better job of getting their votes out than we did. We don't intend to see that repeated."

A key factor geared to that pledge was the voter registration drive. This was a two-tiered project covering urban Republican precincts with door-to-door contact, which also reached the high growth areas in which survey data indicated strong GOP potential. By the end of the registration period on October 6, Kettlewell estimated that some 773,000 new voters were registered in Texas. In Republican precincts there was a net gain of 140,000 above Democratic-oriented precincts. Such registration data was used by the Reagan – Bush and Gramm campaigns to provide an edge with contact and recontact by direct mail, much of that accomplished through a direct mail firm established by Karl Rove, the former assistant to then-Governor Clements.

For Reagan – Bush, Texas was divided into ten geographical regions, each having a chairman and two vice-chairmen, with the exception of South Texas where there were three vice-chairmen to cover the diverse areas of that region. There were county chairmen in 250 of the state's 254 counties, recruited by the regional leadership. To capitalize on population growth, there were county chairmen for voter registration only in fifty-five counties and "Victory Blitz" voter turnout county chairmen in sixty-eight counties. These various volunteer leaders directed thousands of volunteers involved in the crucial tasks of voter registration, phone contact, and ultimate turn-out-the-vote drives. There were fifty-two phone centers in the state covering high population centers, and home phoning was accomplished in 217 rural counties in which an estimated 300,000 calls were made.

Following the GOP national convention, Tower returned to Austin where he would live in the Driskill Hotel for the duration of the campaign. At the Reagan – Bush state headquarters the level of activity was steady and strong, from Wynell Edwards, the genial receptionist on the first floor, to the upstairs offices where the leaders executed the game plan. The vast headquarters was composed of cubicles where one person operated with a desk and phone to large offices in which the walls were covered by maps, charts and graphs. In addition, there were open areas with long tables where volunteers could congregate to lend their assistance. It all added up to form the nerve center for probably the most massive and effective organizational program ever implemented for a Republican campaign in Texas.

Tower, Weisend, and Kettlewell were the leaders and seemed to enjoy a productive working relationship in which each functioned to the best of his or her considerable ability. There were many new people involved and some of the veterans dating to the 1960s, such as Beryl Milburn. Key staff people included Karen Parfitt Hughes, a former television news reporter, who was press secretary for the campaign, and longtime Tower aide Bob Estrada, who was assisted in the Hispanic outreach program by José Martinez, whose experience with the Armed Services Committee made him ideal for contacting Mexican-American leaders in high-military impact areas.

Tower spent time recruiting top name conservative Democrats and was often out making speeches and holding news conferences. The implementation of the high-octane organizational program was in the hands of Martha Weisend, who had a sixth sense for dealing with the problems of overheated egos in times of stress and demanding workloads, and Linden Kettlewell, a tall attractive woman with a businesslike approach to the tedium of such activity.

The strategy was based on maximizing Republican turnout, melding with conservative Democrats and independents, plus garnering a substantial portion of the Hispanic vote.

After targetting the Mexican-American vote, Hispanic headquarters were opened in San Antonio, El Paso, Houston, and the Rio Grande Valley. The thrust was bolstered by bilingual television and radio commercials produced by Lionel Sosa who had produced broadcast material for Tower in 1978. Further, the State GOP had a strong M-A support program directed by Bob Bailon.

Numerous groups were organized, and hundreds of thousands of letters were sent to them with messages tailored to their interests. The campaign would distribute 890,000 bumper stickers; 495,000 buttons; 30,000 posters; four million brochures; 130,000 yard signs; 500,000 volunteer recruitment cards; and one million voter registration cards.

With that enormous amount of activity in progress, other GOP campaigns, particularly those of Gramm and targetted Congressional and legislative candidates, were sure to benefit. The only major problem came

from the first Reagan – Mondale debate in which it was thought that
Mondale gained a slight edge, a boost for his campaign that he needed
desperately. Tower, Weisend, and a few friends had watched the debate
in Tower's suite at the Driskill Hotel, with Tower scoring it even on
debating points. All were concerned about the perception that at times
Reagan appeared to falter or seemed to be ill-prepared. However, in the
aftermath of the debate, the widespread concern about any Reagan slip-
page seemed to spur the volunteers to work even harder to compensate
for whatever damage might have been sustained.

After Bush and Ferraro debated, in the midst of football season,
Tower used one of those sports-oriented one-liners he liked so well, to
make a point during a news conference, "There's no question as to who
has the better back-up quarterback." One-liners are an integral part of
Presidential campaigns. Writers strive to find that one clever, conclusive
line that will stick in peoples' minds longer than any masterful speech
or sharp television spot. Such was Reagan's quip about the difference
in the two campaigns:

> *They dream of an America in which every day is April 15th; we dream
> of an America in which every day is the Fourth of July.*

One of the early signs in the fall that the Democratic ticket was
in deep trouble in Texas came with the publication in the *San Antonio
Light* of an interview with Congressman Henry B. Gonzalez on September
14. For twenty years, Gonzalez had railed in San Antonio against Republicans, always predicting Democratic victories. Now he spoke gloomily
about the campaign in progress. "There might be room for miracles, but
I don't see it coming." Gonzalez said he feared for colleagues because
"there are no coattails to ride this election. There isn't even a petticoat."
When a Democratic national ticket is in trouble in San Antonio, it's
on its way to being clobbered in Houston and Dallas.

Not long thereafter, Tower was in Corpus Christi for the Republican State Convention at which he made his farewell address to a large
assembly of the party faithful. He praised Reagan and cautioned that
Mondale, if elected, would cost the state dearly in lost jobs and revenue
for defense projects. On a poignant note, he spoke directly to the troops,
many of whom had been in the trenches with him during those long
arduous campaigns in the past. "I will not miss the halls of Congress
as much as I will miss working for you in your public concerns and in
reflecting your views."

Tower took time in Corpus Christi to host a reception for a local
candidate for state representative, Ted Roberts, and to confer with some

of his top staff, including Will Ball, the popular AA from Washington, Molly Pryor, Bob Estrada, José Martinez, and Tom Kowalski from Austin. If there were any course corrections to be made, this was the time to consider them. But generally, reports from the field were favorable and Tower seemed to enjoy an almost serene mood at the convention. About the only sparks came from a contest for state vice-chairman between incumbent Diana Denman and challenger Lou Brown of Midland. Denman was reelected and relative harmony prevailed, though there was extended debate over the platform.

There had been some concern that Lloyd Bentsen and Mark White might be able to stem the Reagan – Bush tide in Texas. Bentsen, however, seemed more interested in fulfilling his duties as chairman of the Democratic Senatorial Campaign Committee than taking on the ticket supported by many of his own traditional backers in the business and industrial community. White, highly ambitious and stridently partisan, took a leadership position throughout as though he were determined to ingratiate himself with the National Democratic Party. That he may have done, but in the process he must have lost a substantial amount of support from those conservative Democrats who had put him in office but were not about to buy his fervent pitches for a clearly liberal ticket.

By mid-October it was obvious that only some catastrophe could derail the Reagan – Bush Campaign in Texas. It was hitting on all eight cylinders, roaring down a road to victory that a few Democratic activists began to fear might have more coattail effect than ever before. GOP Congressional candidates ran closely with Reagan and with Gramm, whose campaign appeared to be gaining momentum after a debate with Doggett. Carolyn Barta described Doggett in *The Dallas Morning News*, coming across "as pallid, and still a state senator." Gramm knew the economic issues so well that he often left Doggett with little to counter or rebut.

In the state senate race in San Antonio, Cyndi Taylor Krier had moved into a strong position, thanks to her upbeat, tireless campaigning and a strong organization directed by June Deason, the campaign manager and veteran GOP operative in Bexar County. Jim Lunz was finance chairman, providing the money to carry forth a well-rounded media program. The State GOP and ART were supporting Krier along with a bevy of candidates for state representative, many of whom looked marginal in October but were running in districts in which the Reagan – Bush ticket clearly had the momentum.

With all major components of the campaign functioning well, Tower found time to make speeches for Congressional candidates of whom Larry Combest of Lubbock was a favorite, and for Cyndi Taylor Krier, both of whom had served on his staff. The gerrymandering of 1981 had rendered few opportunities for state senate gains. Party leaders had started the year hoping just to hold the present number of six Congressional seats since Gramm's was a tough one to retain, and Combest was a new GOP candidate for a traditional conservative Democrat seat. With Reagan –Bush providing momentum at the top, darkhorses began to be perceived as serious challengers. Joe Barton of Ennis was running hard in his bid to succeed Gramm, and in the Panhandle, Beau Boulter, Amarillo attorney and former city commissioner (council member), was reportedly gaining on the entrenched incumbent Jack Hightower. Dick Armey of Denton, an educator-economist at North Texas State University, was making a spirited bid against incumbent Tom Vandergriff, the former mayor of Arlington, in the Twenty-sixth District. Longshot Mac Sweeney of Wharton was working hard in high growth areas of the Fourteenth District north of Austin. These would prove to be pivotal against incumbent Bill Patman, who apparently didn't realize he was in trouble until late in the campaign. Tom DeLay was expected to hold the seat vacated by Ron Paul without much trouble, but the idea of electing five Republicans who were making their first races for Congress against Democrats with longstanding campaign experience seemed farfetched indeed.

In the stretch run, Tower appeared confident of a resounding victory for Reagan – Bush. He found rare moments in which to relax and reflect upon a long political career winding down. On October 19, a cool autumn day in the capital city, he went to the Headliners Club for lunch with Ken Towery, whose anger of 1983 had subsided with the passing of a year, and another friend who had been active with him politically for many years. In the bar, with its panoramic view of the State Capitol and The University of Texas, there were some old friends and acquaintances who greeted him warmly and insisted he join them at the "Old Fitz" table where an informal group gathers daily for a drink and conversation before lunch. At the table were Dr. Joe Frantz, author and history professor at The University of Texas; Jimmy Banks and Dick Morehead, former capitol correspondents for *The Dallas Morning News*; Garth Jones and Ted Powers of the AP capitol bureau; Truman Roberts, former justice of the Texas Court of Criminal Appeals; William K. (Bill) Todd, publisher of three Central Texas newspapers; and Jack Warren, chairman of the Tower Senate Club, who tossed a semi-serious question at the senator soon after he sat down with a glass of wine. "Are you going to run for governor?" To which Tower replied, "I'll have to think about that for twenty years."

Later, during his lunch in a nearby room, Texas Supreme Court Justice Bill Kilgarlin, former Harris County Democratic chairman and state legislator, stopped by to pay his respects and chat for a while. It must have been gratifying to Tower to be treated with such respect since he was a lame duck almost at the end of his tenure.

For election night, the Reagan – Bush Campaign had a big bash set up in the Sheraton Crest Hotel with band and large screen television plus all the drinks and food one might desire. Like 1980, the early trend was there for Reagan – Bush as expected. This prompted a strong victory speech from Tower, who dutifully credited Weisend and Kettlewell for the superb organizational work they had directed. Soon thereafter Tower was informed that Cyndi Taylor Krier was winning by a landslide in Bexar County, running about sixty percent — equal to Reagan – Bush — and some major upsets were in the offing in Congressional and legislative races.

In an unprecedented development, GOP candidates were winning all the marginal Congressional races — Armey, Barton, Boulter, Combest, and Sweeney were on their way to significant victories. In the Texas House of Representatives, nineteen new Republicans were elected, representing a tremendous net gain of fifteen seats up to fifty-two, a figure representing potential veto power over the many two-thirds votes required in that 150-member body. New Republicans included Bill Blackwood of Mesquite; Ben Campbell of Denton; Bill Carter of Haltom City; Anne Cooper of San Marcos; Ron Givens of Lubbock; Kelly Godwin of Odessa; Chris Harris of Arlington; Jack Harris of Pearland; Sam Johnson of Plano; Bob Richardson of Austin. Also Randall Riley of Round Rock; Ted Roberts of Corpus Christi; Richard Smith of Bryan; John Smithee of Amarillo; Jim Tallas of Sugar Land; M. A. Taylor of Waco; Keith Valigura of Conroe; John Willy of Lake Jackson; and Gerald Yost of Longview.

ART and State GOP political operatives had pushed long and hard for the state representative races, particularly Kevin Moomaw, political director of the State GOP who guided thousands of dollars and modern technology into targetted races. The magnitude of the achievement can perhaps be put into context by viewing the fact that in the Austin – Travis County area, where liberal Democrats had ruled for years, three Republicans unseated Democrat incumbents.

Final voter turnout figures for Texas showed a heavy vote of 5,289,020 with the Reagan – Bush ticket scoring a landslide of almost sixty-four percent, and Gramm tallying a hefty fifty-nine percent. In the GOP targetted races for Congress and the Texas Legislature, that ticket strength was certainly there but heavy support for each campaign was necessary to chalk up all the wins. The crucial nature of candidate support by ART and the State GOP can be seen in historical perspective by comparing the 1984 election results to those of 1972. In that Nixon – Tower year, Nixon carried Texas by a landslide even greater than Reagan's in 1984, and Tower defeated his opponent by more than 300,000 votes, yet there were no substantial gains at the Congressional and legislative levels. The highly effective voter registration drive conducted by the Reagan – Bush Campaign resulted in more straight-ticket voting by Republicans in the high growth areas. A postelection study by Lance Tarrance contended a marked increase was recorded in straight-ticket voting in Texas and that the GOP received more straight-ticket votes than the Democratic Party in vote-rich Harris (Houston) and Dallas Counties where party chairmen Russ Mather and Fred Meyer respectively provided extensive organizational support for their candidates. The total result included Republicans being elected to most judicial positions they sought, a profound change from the one-party past when Texas Democrats almost totally controlled the judicial system. Through election of more Republicans and substantial numbers of incumbent Democrats changing party affiliation, the state's two most populous counties have moved from one-party domination by Democrats to Republican domination.

Perhaps the overriding consideration of the 1984 election was the apparent result that the Democratic Party had lost middle class America, and in Texas, once the heretofore presidential GOP voters had voted at the top of their ballots, they stayed with those other Republican candidates below with whom they could relate. Estimates of the Reagan – Bush vote among Hispanics varied widely, between twenty-seven percent and forty-five percent. Part of the problem here is that some estimates are based solely upon South and Southwest Texas plus barrio precincts elsewhere which do not reflect the true picture since Mexican-Americans amalgamated into Anglo precincts apparently voted fairly strongly for Reagan–Bush. Those who purport to know exactly what the M-A vote was for a statewide candidate can't be making accurate estimates for the amalgamated M-A vote unless they conduct thorough exit polls in Houston, Dallas and other urban centers in which middle class M-As reside. Such procedures have not been reported to date, but suffice to say that with a sixty-four percent majority in a state that was swept by Democrats two years previously, Reagan – Bush received substantial Mexican-American support. And most Republican leaders and operatives are committeed to pursuing greater M-A participation in the GOP.

In any event, gaining four Congressional seats, one in the state senate and fifteen in the Texas House added up to a banner year. Tower could be justly proud of this, especially since three of the record ten members of the Texas Congressional delegation — Loeffler, Combest, and Sweeney — had worked for him, and the only new state senator, Krier, had also been a member of his staff.

On Saturday, December 1, at the Wyndham Southpark Hotel in Austin, Tower made his final report to the SREC, recounting how the campaign was organized, operated and funded. It was a measured, modest report in which Tower gave most of the credit to his colleagues, and to the vast army of volunteers. Weisend, who had worked so effectively with Tower and Kettlewell to produce the tremendous results, spoke to her fellow SREC members in a calm, direct manner. "You can hear him think," she said of Tower, and "Texas is losing a giant."

When state GOP Chairman George Strake presented Tower with a plaque, tears welled in the senator's eyes as his final moments with the SREC were played out.

Tower soon joined a few friends and key staff members for an informal gathering in his suite to talk about future political developments in Texas. His eyes sparkled when he spoke of how things might transpire, although those in the room sensed that he would probably never again be a major factor in the Texas political arena.

Everyone in the room was proud to have worked with him over the years and were gratified to have shared his last hurrah. They knew that his legacy was the indelible mark in the history of two-party development in Texas.

Epilogue

Throughout Texas, the resounding 1984 victories scored by the Reagan–Bush ticket, plus those of Phil Gramm and other Republicans, had a more profound impact on Democrats than any previous general election in modern times.

Democratic stalwarts tried to slough off the debacle as principally the result of Reagan's personal popularity, but many astute politicians on their side wouldn't buy it. Instead of circling the wagons under the old banner as they had done in the past, incumbents and aspirants found the GOP more to their liking. The fundamental realignment, long a dream of Texas Republicans, had suddenly accelerated.

Foremost among those jumping ship was Kent Hance, the Lubbock conservative who had been elected to the state senate and Congress before making his spirited, but unsuccessful bid for the United States Senate nomination in 1984. Hance switched parties to pursue the GOP gubernatorial nomination of 1986.

Bill Clayton, the immediate past speaker of the Texas House, made it official when the West Texas conservative formally changed party affiliation after having endorsed the Reagan–Bush ticket in 1984.

Another prominent convert was Carole Rylander, popular former mayor of Austin, and member of the State Board of Insurance, who was appointed by the state's top Democrat, Governor Mark White.

Most local Democratic officials and state legislators crossing the line have been from the more populous areas, such as State Representative Charles Evans of Tarrant County, a close ally of Democrat Gib Lewis, speaker of the Texas House. There have been some notable exceptions, including State Representative Gary Thompson of Abilene, and Nueces County Sheriff James Hickey of Corpus Christi. When an incumbent Democratic sheriff in South Texas voluntarily becomes a Republican, there is indeed cause to take stock of what's transpiring.

Twenty years ago, following the disastrous 1964 election, there were

301

no Texas Republicans serving in Congress and only one in the entire 181-member Legislature. At the time of this writing, there are ten Texas Republicans serving in Congress and sixty-one in the Legislature, both all-time records. Of those sixty-one legislators, fifty-five are in the House, by any standard a formidable force among the 150-member body which elects its own presiding officer.

These trends and developments have formed a prevailing political wind that is sweeping across Texas, destined to provide a competitive two-party system.

Austin, Texas   *John R. Knaggs*
February 12, 1986

Acknowledgments

To a considerable degree, this book is the product of distilling ideas and information from about 2,200 pounds of political material gathered by myself and others over the past twenty-three years.

Special thanks to Marvin Collins of Corpus Christi, my former partner in a political consulting firm, and Jim Loyd of Austin, former survey research analyst in the Lance Tarrance polling company, for the large amount of material they contributed.

Patrick Conway of Austin, a onetime colleague at UPI, lent invaluable assistance by organizing and outlining much of the vast research material. Taber Ward of Austin, associated for many years with the Republican State Headquarters, was most helpful by providing information and analysis, as was Royal Masset of Austin, political director for the State GOP.

Many thanks to my wife, Helen, for the extensive assistance in coordinating the assimilation of research material, categorizing of subjects and processing of the manuscript.

Bob Ward of Austin, former editor of State GOP publications, contributed substantially by providing materials and pictures. Political photographers Jim Culberson of Houston and Charles Pantaze of Austin supplied all the pictures I chose from their files, for which I'm most grateful.

For pursuing supplementary research, thanks to Pamela Findlay of Austin, plus Drew Parma and Suzanne Taylor, students at The University of Texas at Austin, and my son, Ryan.

Valuable guidance for library research was provided by Jim Sanders and Sally Reynolds at the Legislative Reference Library in the state capitol. Jim Fish of the Texas Legislative Service supplied important information.

For sharing their recollections and perspectives, many thanks to those who worked closely with John Tower in Senate staff and/or campaign capacities during the span of this era — Jimmy Banks of Austin;

Jerry Friedheim of Washington, D.C.; Nola [Smith] Gee of Austin; Jim Leonard of Round Rock; Molly Pryor of Houston; and Ken Towery of Austin.

Insight was also provided from interviews with various present and past party leaders, campaign managers, and political operatives. Of particular help in this regard were Peter O'Donnell of Dallas, Nancy Palm of Houston, and Karl Rove of Austin.

In nailing down items of sports history used in a political context, assistance was provided by Lou Maysel, former sports editor of *The Austin American-Statesman*.

And thanks to those many staff people in various offices who lent a helping hand along the way.

INDEX